brief contents

v

The Well-Grounded Java Developer

Java Developer

VITAL TECHNIQUES OF JAVA 7 AND POLYGLOT PROGRAMMING

BENJAMIN J. EVANS
MARTIJN VERBURG

MANNING

SHELTER ISLAND

For online information and ordering of this and other Manning books, please visit
www.manning.com. The publisher offers discounts on this book when ordered in quantity.
For more information, please contact

Special Sales Department
Manning Publications Co.
20 Baldwin Road
PO Box 261
Shelter Island, NY 11964
Email: orders@manning.com

Manning Publications Co.   Development editors: Renae Gregoire, Karen G. Miller
20 Baldwin Road   Copyeditor: Andy Carroll
PO Box 261   Proofreader: Elizabeth Martin
Shelter Island, NY 11964   Typesetter: Dennis Dalinnik
                                     Cover designer: Marija Tudor

ISBN: 9781617290060
Printed in the United States of America
3 4 5 6 7 8 9 10 – MAL – 18 17 16 15 14 13

contents

foreword

"Kirk told me I could buy beer at the petrol station," was the first sentence I heard out of Ben Evans' mouth. He had come to Crete for an Open Spaces Java conference. I explained that I usually bought petrol at the petrol station, but that there was a shop around the corner that sold beer. Ben looked disappointed. I had lived on this Greek island for five years and had never thought of trying to buy beer at the local BP.

I felt a bit like this while reading this book. I consider myself a Java fundi. I have spent the past 15 years programming Java, writing hundreds of articles, speaking at conferences, and teaching advanced Java courses. And yet, when I read Ben and Martijn's book, I kept coming across ideas that I hadn't thought of. They start by explaining the development effort of changing certain parts of the Java ecosystem. Changing the internals of a library is relatively easy, and we might see some improved performance for certain input. `Arrays.sort()` is now using TimSort, instead of MergeSort. If you sort a partially ordered array, you might see a slight performance improvement without changing your code. Changing the class file format or adding a new VM feature requires a major effort. Ben knows. He sits on the JCP Executive Committee. This book is also about Java 7, so you'll learn all the new features, such as the syntactic sugar enhancements, switching on Strings, fork/join, and the Java NIO.2.

Concurrency? That's `Thread` and `synchronized`, right? If that's all you know about multithreading, it's time to upgrade your skills. As the authors point out, "the area of concurrency is undergoing a massive amount of research at present." There are daily discussions on the concurrency interest mailing list, and new ideas are emerging all the time. This book shows you how to think about divide-and-conquer and how to avoid some of the safety flaws.

When I saw the chapter on classloading, I thought they had gone a bit too far. Here were the tricks that my friends and I had used to create magical code, laid bare for all to learn! They explain how `javap` works, a little tool that can give you insight into the byte-code generated by the Java compiler. They also cover the new `invokedynamic` and explain how it differs from plain reflection.

One chapter that I particularly like is "Understanding performance tuning." This is the first book since Jack Shirazi's *Java Performance Tuning* that has captured the essence of how to make your system faster. I can summarize the chapter in three words: "Measure, don't guess." This is the essence of good performance tuning. It's impossible for a human to guess which code is slow. Instead of offering a single coding trick, this chapter explains performance from a hardware perspective. It also shows you *how* to measure the performance. An interesting little benchmark tool is their `CacheTester` class, which shows the cost of cache misses.

Part 3 of the book explains polyglot programming on the JVM. Java is so much more than a Java programming language. It's also a platform on which other languages can run. We've seen an explosion of different types of languages. Some are functional, some are declarative. Some are ports (Jython and JRuby), allowing other languages to run on the JVM. Languages can be dynamic (Groovy) or stable (Java and Scala). There are many reasons to use a non-Java language on the JVM. If you're starting a new project, look at what's available before deciding. You might save yourself a lot of boilerplate code.

Ben and Martijn show us three alternative languages: Groovy, Scala, and Clojure. In my opinion, these are the most viable languages at the moment. The authors describe the differences between these languages, how they compare to Java, and their special features. The chapter on each language is just enough to help you figure out which you should be using, without too much technical detail. Don't expect a reference manual to Groovy; do expect insight on which language is the right one for you.

Next, you'll gain insight into how to do test-driven development and continuous integration of your system. I found it amusing that the old faithful butler Hudson was so quickly replaced with Jenkins. In any case, these are essential tools for managing your project, along with tools like Checkstyle and FindBugs.

Studying this book will help you become a well-grounded Java developer. Not only that, it will give you tips on how to *stay* well-grounded. Java is constantly changing. We'll see lambdas and modularization in the next version. New languages are being designed; the concurrency constructs are being updated. Many of the things that you know are true now might not be true in the future. The lesson is, don't ever stop learning!

The other day I drove past the petrol station where Ben wanted to buy his beer. Like so many companies in depressed Greece, it had closed. I never did find out if they sold beer.

DR. HEINZ KABUTZ
THE JAVA SPECIALISTS' NEWSLETTER

preface

This book started life as a set of training notes written for new graduate intake in the Foreign Exchange IT department of Deutsche Bank. One of us (Ben), looking at the existing books on the market, found a lack of up-to-date material aimed at inexperienced Java developers. So he resolved to write that missing book.

With the encouragement of Deutsche's IT management team, Ben traveled to the Devoxx conference in Belgium to look for inspiration on additional topics. There, he met three IBM engineers (Rob Nicholson, Zoe Slattery, and Holly Cummins), who introduced him to the London Java Community (LJC—London's Java User Group).

The following Saturday was the annual Open Conference organized by the LJC—and it was at that conference that Ben met one of the leaders of the LJC, Martijn Verburg. By the end of the day—fueled by their mutual love of teaching, technical communities, and beer—they'd resolved to collaborate on the project and what would become *The Well-Grounded Java Developer* was born.

In this book, we hope that the theme of software development as a social activity rings out clearly. We believe that the technical aspects of the craft are important, but the more subtle concerns of communication and interaction between people are at least as important. It can be hard to explain these facets easily in a book, but that theme is present throughout.

Developers are sustained throughout their careers by their engagement with technology and the passion to keep learning. In this book, we hope that we've been able to highlight some of the topics that will ignite that passion. It's a sightseeing tour, rather than an encyclopedic study, but that's the intention—to get you started and then leave you to follow up on those topics that capture your imagination.

Over the course of the project's lifespan, the emphasis moved slightly away from being purely a bridging guide for graduates (it still largely achieves this goal) to becoming a guide for all Java developers wondering, "What do I need to know next? Where's my future heading? I want to care again!"

We take you from the new features of Java 7 through to best practices of modern software development and the future of the platform. Along the way, we show you some of the highlights that have had great relevance to us on our own journey as Java technologists. Concurrency, performance, bytecode, and classloading are the core techniques that fascinated us the most. We also talk about new, non-Java languages on the JVM (a.k.a. polyglot programming) because they will become more important to many developers in the years to come.

Above all, this is a journey that's forward-looking, and puts you and your interests front and center. We feel that becoming a well-grounded Java developer will help to keep you engaged and in control of your own development and will help you learn more about the changing world of Java and the ecosystem that surrounds it.

We hope that the distilled experience that you're holding in your hands is useful and interesting to you, and that reading it is thought-provoking and fun. Writing it certainly was!

acknowledgments

There's a cliché about it taking a village to raise a child, and in the case of this book, the phrase is entirely applicable. We could not have done this without our network of friends, partners, colleagues, peers, and even the occasional adversarial relationship. We have been exceptionally lucky in that most of our strongest critics can also be counted among our friends.

It's difficult to fit the names of the many people who helped us in this endeavor. Please visit http://www.java7developer.com and seek out the blog post announcing the printing of this book and the extra thank-yous. Those names deserve to be acknowledged.

If we've forgotten anyone, or our bookkeeping wasn't up to scratch, please accept our apologies! In no particular order, we'd like to thank the following folks for making this book possible.

THE LONDON JAVA COMMUNITY

The London Java Community (LJC) at www.meetup.com/londonjavacommunity is where we met and has become a huge part of our lives. We'd like to acknowledge the following people who helped review material: Peter Budo, Nick Harkin, Jodev Devassy, Craig Silk, N. Vanderwildt, Adam J. Markham, "Rozallin," Daniel Lemon, Frank Appiah, P. Franc, "Sebkom" Praveen, Dinuk Weerasinghe, Tim Murray Brown, Luis Murbina, Richard Doherty, Rashul Hussain, John Stevenson, Gemma Silvers, Kevin Wright, Amanda Waite, Joel Gluth, Richard Paul, Colin Vipurs, Antony Stubbs, Michael Joyce, Mark Hindess, Nuno, Jon Poulton, Adrian Smith, Ioannis Mavroukakis, Chris Reed, Martin Skurla, Sandro Mancuso, and Arul Dhesiaseelan.

We received some detailed help with non-Java languages from James Cook, Alex Anderson, Leonard Axelsson, Colin Howe, Bruce Durling, and Dr. Russel Winder. They deserve special thanks.

A special thank you also to the LJC JCP committee—Mike Barker, Trisha Gee, Jim Gough, Richard Warburton, Simon Maple, Somay Nakhal, and David Illsley.

Last, but not least, a thank-you to Barry Cranford, the founder of the LJC, who four years ago started with a few brave souls and a dream. Today, the LJC has approximately 2500 members and many other tech communities have sprung from it—a true cornerstone of the London tech scene.

WWW.CODERANCH.COM

We'd like to thank Maneesh Godbole, Ulf Ditmer, David O'Meara, Devaka Cooray, Greg Charles, Deepak Balu, Fred Rosenberger, Jesper De Jong, Wouter Oet, David O'Meara, Mark Spritzler, and Roel De Nijs for their detailed comments and valuable feedback.

MANNING PUBLICATIONS

Thanks to Marjan Bace at Manning for taking on two new authors with a crazy idea. We worked with a number of people over the course of the book. Many thanks for the hard work by Renae Gregoire, Karen G. Miller, Andy Carroll, Elizabeth Martin, Mary Piergies, Dennis Dalinnik, Janet Vail, and no doubt others behind the scenes that we've missed; we wouldn't have made it without you!

Thanks to Candace Gillhoolley for her marketing efforts and Christina Rudloff and Maureen Spencer for their ongoing support.

Thanks to John Ryan III who did a thorough final technical review of the manuscript during production, shortly before the book went to press.

Thanks to the following reviewers who read the manuscript at different stages of its development and provided valuable feedback to our editors and to us: Aziz Rahman, Bert Bates, Chad Davis, Cheryl Jerozal, Christopher Haupt, David Strong, Deepak Vohra, Federico Tomassetti, Franco Lombardo, Jeff Schmidt, Jeremy Anderson, John Griffin, Maciej Kreft, Patrick Steger, Paul Benedict, Rick Wagner, Robert Wenner, Rodney Bollinger, Santosh Shanbhag, Antti Koivisto, and Stephen Harrison.

SPECIAL THANKS

Thanks to Andy Burgess for the awesome www.java7developer.com website and to Dragos Dogaru, our incredible intern, who tried out the code samples as we went along.

Thanks to Matt Raible for his kind permission to reuse some material about how to choose your web framework in chapter 13.

Thanks to Alan Bateman, lead for Java 7's NIO.2; his feedback was invaluable in making this great new API available for the day-to-day Java developer.

Jeanne Boyarsky kindly served as our most excellent technical proofer and, true to her reputation, nothing fell past her eagle eyes. Thanks Jeanne!

Thanks to Martin Ling for a very detailed explanation of timing hardware, which was the primary motivation for the section in chapter 4.

Thanks to Jason Van Zyl for his kind permission to reuse some material from Sonatype's *Maven: The Complete Reference* for chapter 12.

Thanks to Kirk Pepperdine for his insight and comments on chapter 6, in addition to his friendship and his unique take on our industry.

Thanks to Dr. Heinz M. Kabutz for his great foreword and amazing hospitality in Crete, as well as the awesome *Java Specialists' Newsletter* (www.javaspecialists.eu/).

FROM BEN EVANS

So many people contributed in different ways that there's scarcely space to thank them all. Special thanks to these people:

To Bert Bates and others at Manning, for teaching me the difference between a manuscript and a book.

To Martijn, of course, for friendship, for keeping me writing during the tough times, and for so much more.

To my family, especially my grandfathers, John Hinton and John Evans, from whom I inherited so much of myself.

Lastly, to E-J (who is the reason otters occur so frequently in the book) and to Liz, who were both always understanding about "one more evening" being disrupted by writing. My love to you both.

FROM MARTIJN VERBURG

To my mum Janneke and my dad Nico, thanks for having the foresight to bring home a Commodore 64 when my sister and I were young. Although "Jumpman"[1] dominated computer time for the family, it was the programming manual that came with it that sparked my passion for all things tech. Dad also taught me that if you do the little things right, the large things that they make up tend to take care of themselves, a philosophy I still apply to my coding and work life today.

To my sister Kim, thanks for writing code with me in our preteen and teenage years! I'll never forget when that first (slow[2]) star field came into being onscreen; magic had truly happened! My brother-in-law Jos is an inspiration to us all (not just for being a space scientist, although, how cool is that!). My super-cute niece Gweneth features in this book; see if you can spot her!

Ben is simply one of the most amazing technologists I've run across in the industry. His level of technical ability is simply scary at times! It's been a privilege to write this book with him; I've certainly learned more about the JVM than I ever thought possible. Ben has also been a great leader for the LJC, and an entertaining cospeaker with me at conferences (apparently we even have something of a reputation as a comedy act now). It was good to write a book with a friend.

Finally, to my rocking wife Kerry, from putting up with having date nights canceled for the sake of yet another chapter to graciously delivering all of the graphics and screenshots for the book—as always you've simply been amazing. Would that everyone had the same sort of love and support I have from her.

---

[1] A really, really cool platform game; it was hysterical watching Mum move *with* the joystick :-).

[2] Let's just say that performance tuning wasn't my forte back then.

about this book

Welcome to *The Well-Grounded Java Developer.* This book is aimed at turning you into a Java developer for the modern age, reigniting your passion for both the language and platform. Along the way, you'll discover new Java 7 features, ensure that you're familiar with essential modern software techniques (such as dependency injection, test-driven development, and continuous integration), and start to explore the brave new world of non-Java languages on the JVM.

To begin, let's consider this description of the Java language provided by James Iry in a wonderful blog post "A Brief, Incomplete, and Mostly Wrong History of Programming Languages":

> 1996 – James Gosling invents Java. Java is a relatively verbose, garbage collected, class-based, statically typed, single dispatch, object-oriented language with single implementation inheritance and multiple interface inheritance. Sun loudly heralds Java's novelty.

While the point of Java's entry is mostly to set up a gag where C# is given the same write-up, this is not bad as descriptions of languages go. The full blog post contains a bunch of other gems—you can find it on the web at James' blog (http://james-iry .blogspot.com/). It's well worth a read in an idle moment.

This does present a very real question. Why are we still talking about a language that is now around 16 years old? Surely it's stable and not much new or interesting can be said about it?

If that were the case, this would be a short book. We are still talking about it, because one of Java's greatest strengths has been its ability to build on a few core design decisions, which have proved to be very successful in the marketplace:

- Automatic management of the runtime environment (for example, garbage collection, just-in-time compilation)
- Simple syntax and relatively few concepts in the core language
- Conservative approach to evolving the language
- Add functionality and complexity in libraries
- Broad, open ecosystem

These design decisions have kept innovation moving in the Java world—the simple core has kept the barrier to joining the developer community low, and the broad ecosystem has made it easy for newcomers to find pre-existing components that fit their needs.

These traits have kept the Java platform and language strong and vibrant—even if the language has had a historical tendency to change slowly. This trend has continued with Java 7. The language changes are evolutionary, not revolutionary. One major difference with earlier versions, however, is that Java 7 is the first version explicitly released with an eye to the next version. Java 7 contains the groundwork for major language changes in Java 8, due to Oracle's "Plan B" strategy for releases.

The other big shift in recent years has been the rise of non-Java languages on the JVM. This has led to cross-fertilization between Java and other JVM languages and there's now a large (and growing) number of projects running completely on the JVM that include Java as one of the languages that they use.

The emergence of the polyglot project, particularly involving languages such as Groovy, Scala, and Clojure, is a major factor in the current Java ecosystem, and is the topic of the final part of the book.

How to use this book

The material in this book is broadly designed to be read end-to-end, but we understand that some readers may want to dive straight into particular topics and have partly catered to that style of reading.

We strongly believe in hands-on learning and so we recommend that readers try out the sample code that comes with the book as they read through the text. The rest of this section deals with how you can approach the book if you are more of a standalone-chapter style of reader.

The Well-Grounded Java Developer is split into four parts:

- Developing with Java 7
- Vital techniques
- Polyglot programming on the JVM
- Crafting the polyglot project

Part 1 contains two chapters on Java 7. The book uses Java 7 syntax and semantics throughout, so chapter 1, "Introducing Java 7," should be considered *required* reading. Chapter 2, "New I/O," will be of specific interest to developers who work with files, filesystems, and network I/O.

Part 2 contains four chapters (3-6) covering the topics of dependency injection, modern concurrency, classfiles/byte code, and performance tuning.

Part 3 (chapters 7-10) covers polyglot programming on the JVM. Chapter 7 should be considered *required* reading as it sets the stage by discussing the categorization and use of alternative languages on the JVM. The following three language chapters move from a Java-like language (Groovy), through a hybrid OO-functional language (Scala), to a fully functional one (Clojure). Those languages can be read standalone although developers new to functional programming will probably want to read them in order.

Part 4 (the final four chapters) introduces new material as well as builds on topics that have been introduced earlier. Although the chapters can be read stand-alone, in some sections we assume that you've read the earlier chapters and/or already have familiarity with certain topics.

In short, chapter 1 is *required reading for the entire book*. Chapter 7 can be considered as *required reading for part 3*. The other chapters can be read in sequence or standalone, but there will be sections in later chapters that assume you've read earlier material.

Who should read this book

This book is firmly aimed at Java developers who wants to modernize their knowledge base in both the language and the platform. If you want to get up to speed with what Java 7 has to offer, this is the book for you.

If you are looking to brush up on your techniques and understanding of topics such as dependency injection, concurrency, and test-driven development, this book will give you a good grounding in those topics.

This is also a book for those developers who have acknowledged the polyglot programming trend and want to get started down that path. In particular, if you want to learn about functional programming, then our language chapters (especially Scala and Clojure) will be of great benefit to you.

Roadmap

In part 1 there are just two chapters. Chapter 1 introduces Java 7 with its wealth of small but productivity-enhancing features known collectively as Project Coin. Chapter 2 takes you through the new I/O APIs including an overhaul of the filesystem support, new asynchronous I/O capabilities, and more.

Part 2 contains four chapters on vital techniques. Chapter 3 takes you through a journey of how the industry arrived at dependency injection as a technique and goes on to show a standardized solution in Java with Guice 3. Chapter 4 covers how to deal with modern concurrency properly in Java, a topic that has once more come to the fore as the hardware industry firmly moves to multicore processors. Chapter 5 takes you into the classfiles and bytecode of the JVM, demystifying its secrets and enabling you to understand why Java works the way it does. Chapter 6 takes you through the initial steps in performance tuning your Java applications and understanding areas such as the garbage collector.

Part 3 is about polyglot programming on the JVM and consists of four chapters. Chapter 7 starts the polyglot story and gives you the context of why it's important and when it's appropriate to use another language. Chapter 8 is an introduction to Groovy, Java's dynamic friend. Groovy highlights how a syntactically similar yet dynamic language can provide great productivity boosts for a Java developer. Chapter 9 brings you into the hybrid functional/OO world of Scala. Scala is a language of great power and conciseness. Chapter 10 is for the Lisp fans out there. Clojure is widely lauded as "Lisp done right" and showcases the full power of a functional language on the JVM.

Part 4 takes learning from the first three parts and discusses polyglot techniques in several software development areas. Chapter 11 visits test-driven development and provides a methodology around dealing with mock objects as well as some practical tips. Chapter 12 introduces two widely used tools for your build pipeline (Maven 3) and continuous integration (Jenkins/Hudson) needs. Chapter 13 covers the topic of rapid web development and why Java has been traditionally weak in this area, and offers some new technologies to prototype with (Grails and Compojure). Chapter 14 wraps up and takes a look to the future, including the functional support arriving in Java 8.

Code conventions and downloads

The initial download and installation you'll need is Java 7. Simply follow the download and installation instructions for the binary you need for the OS you use. You can find binaries and instructions online at Oracle's website for Java SE: www.oracle.com/technetwork/java/javase/downloads/index.html.

For everything else, head to appendix A where the instructions for the installation and running of the source code can be found.

All source code in the book is in a `fixed-width font like this`, which sets it off from the surrounding text. In many listings, the code is annotated to point out the key concepts, and numbered bullets are sometimes used in the text to provide additional information about the code. We have tried to format the code so that it fits within the available page space in the book by adding line breaks and using indentation carefully. Sometimes, however, very long lines include line continuation markers.

Source code for all the working examples is available from www.manning.com/TheWell-GroundedJavaDeveloper. Code examples appear throughout the book. Longer listings appear under clear listing headers; shorter listings appear between lines of text.

Software requirements

Java 7 runs on just about every modern platform there is today. As long as you are running on one of the following operating systems you'll be able to run the source examples:

- MS Windows XP and above
- A recent version of *nix
- Mac OS X 10.6 and above

Most of you will want to try out the code samples in an IDE. Java 7 and the latest versions of Groovy, Scala, and Clojure are fairly well supported by the following versions of the main IDEs:

- Eclipse 3.7.1 and above
- NetBeans 7.0.1 and above
- IntelliJ 10.5.2 and above

We used NetBeans 7.1 and Eclipse 3.7.1 to create and run the examples.

Author Online

Purchase of *The Well-Grounded Java Developer* includes free access to a private web forum run by Manning Publications where you can make comments about the book, ask technical questions, and receive help from the authors and from other users. To access the forum and subscribe to it, point your web browser to www.manning.com/ TheWell-GroundedJavaDeveloper. This page provides information on how to get on the forum once you're registered, what kind of help is available, and the rules of conduct on the forum.

Manning's commitment to our readers is to provide a venue where a meaningful dialog between individual readers and between readers and the authors can take place. It's not a commitment to any specific amount of participation on the part of the authors, whose contribution to the forum remains voluntary (and unpaid). We suggest you try asking the authors some challenging questions lest their interest stray!

The Author Online forum and the archives of previous discussions will be accessible from the publisher's website as long as the book is in print.

about the authors

Ben Evans is an organizer for the LJC (London JUG) and a member of the Java Community Process Executive Committee, helping define standards for the Java ecosystem. He has lived through many years of "Interesting Times" in the tech industry and is CEO of a Java-based technology firm working mainly in the financial industry. Ben is a frequent public speaker on topics such as the Java platform, performance, and concurrency.

Martijn Verburg (CTO, jClarity) has over 10 years of experience as a technology professional and OSS mentor in environments from start-ups to large enterprises. He is the coleader of the London Java User Group (LJC), and leads the global effort of JUG members who contribute to JSRs (Adopt a JSR program) and the OpenJDK (Adopt OpenJDK program).

As a recognized expert on technical team optimization, his talks and presentations are in demand at major conferences (JavaOne, Devoxx, OSCON, FOSDEM, and so on) where he's known for challenging the industry status quo as the "Diabolical Developer."

about the cover illustration

The figure on the cover of *The Well-Grounded Java Developer* is captioned "A Posy Seller." The illustration is taken from a nineteenth-century edition of Sylvain Maréchal's four-volume compendium of regional dress customs published in France. Each illustration is finely drawn and colored by hand. The rich variety of Maréchal's collection reminds us vividly of how culturally apart the world's towns and regions were just 200 years ago. Isolated from each other, people spoke different dialects and languages. On the streets or in the countryside, it was easy to identify where they lived and what their trade or station in life was just by their dress.

Dress codes have changed since then and the diversity by region, so rich at the time, has faded away. It is now hard to tell apart the inhabitants of different continents, let alone different towns or regions. Perhaps we have traded cultural diversity for a more varied personal life—certainly for a more varied and fast-paced technological life.

At a time when it is hard to tell one computer book from another, Manning celebrates the inventiveness and initiative of the computer business with book covers based on the rich diversity of regional life of two centuries ago, brought back to life by Maréchal's pictures.

Part 1

Developing with Java 7

These first two chapters are about ramping up with Java 7. You'll ease in with an introductory chapter that covers some small syntax changes that will increase your productivity—all of which punch above their weight. This will set the stage for the larger topic in this part—a chapter on new I/O in Java.

The well-grounded Java developer needs to be aware of the latest language features available. Java 7 comes with several new features that will make your life as a working developer much easier. But it isn't enough simply to understand the syntax of these new changes. In order to write *efficient* and *safe* code *quickly,* you need an in-depth understanding of how and why the new features were implemented. The Java 7 language changes can be roughly split into two sets: Project Coin and NIO.2.

The first set is known as Project Coin, a group of small language-level changes that were designed to increase developer productivity without heavily impacting the underlying platform. These changes include:

- A try-with-resources construct (which automatically closes off resources)
- Strings in `switch`
- Enhanced numeric literals
- Multi-`catch` (declare multiple exceptions in a `catch` block)
- Diamond syntax (requiring less boilerplate when dealing with generics)

Each of these changes may seem small, but exploring the semantics behind the simple syntax changes also gives you extra insight into the split between Java the language and Java the platform.

The second set of changes is the new I/O (NIO.2) API, which completely overhauls Java's filesystem support as well as providing new powerful asynchronous capabilities. These changes include:

- A new `Path` construct in order to reference files and file-like entities
- A `Files` utility class that simplifies creating, copying, moving, and deleting files
- Built-in directory tree navigation
- Future and callback-based asynchronous I/O to deal with large I/O in the background

By the end of part 1, you'll be thinking and writing naturally in Java 7. This new knowledge is reinforced throughout the book, as Java 7 features are used in the later chapters as well.

Introducing Java 7

This chapter covers

- Java as a platform and a language
- Small yet powerful syntax changes
- The try-with-resources statement
- Exception-handling enhancements

Welcome to Java 7. Things around here are a little different than you may be used to. This is a really good thing—we have a lot to explore, now that the dust has settled and Java 7 has been unleashed. By the time you finish this book, you'll have taken your first steps into a larger world—a world of new features, of software craftsmanship, and of other languages on the Java Virtual Machine (JVM).

We're going to warm up with a gentle introduction to Java 7, but one that still acquaints you with powerful features. We'll start by explaining a distinction that is sometimes misunderstood—the duality between the *language* and the *platform*.

After that, we'll introduce Project Coin—a collection of small yet effective new features in Java 7. We'll show you what's involved in getting a change to the Java platform accepted, incorporated, and released. With that process covered, we'll move on to the six main new features that were introduced as part of Project Coin.

You'll learn new syntax, such as an improved way of handling exceptions (multi-catch) as well as try-with-resources, which helps you avoid bugs in code that deals with files or other resources. By the end of this chapter, you'll be writing Java in a new way and you'll be fully primed and ready for the big topics that lie ahead.

Let's get under way by discussing the language versus platform duality that lies at the heart of modern Java. This is a critically important point that we'll come back to again throughout the book, so it's an essential one to grasp.

1.1   *The language and the platform*

The critical concept we're kicking off with is the distinction between the Java language and the Java platform. Surprisingly, different authors sometimes give slightly different definitions of what constitutes the language and platform. This can lead to a lack of clarity and some confusion about the differences between the two and about which provides the programming features that application code uses.

Let's make that distinction clear right now, as it cuts to the heart of a lot of the topics in this book. Here are our definitions:

- *The Java language*—The Java language is the statically typed, object-oriented language that we lightly lampooned in the "About This Book" section. Hopefully, it's already very familiar to you. One very obvious point about the Java language is that it's human-readable (or it should be!).
- *The Java platform*—The platform is the software that provides a runtime environment. It's the JVM that links and executes your code as provided to it in the form of (not human-readable) class files. It doesn't directly interpret Java language source files, but instead requires them to be converted to class files first.

One of the big reasons for the success of Java as a software system is that it's a standard. This means that it has specifications that describe how it's supposed to work. Standardization allows different vendors and project groups to produce implementations that should all, in theory, work the same way. The specs don't make guarantees about how well different implementations will perform when handling the same task, but they can provide assurances about the correctness of the results.

There are a number of separate specs that govern the Java system—the most important are the Java Language Specification (JLS) and the JVM Specification (VMSpec). In Java 7, this separation is taken very seriously; in fact, the VMSpec no longer makes any reference whatsoever to the JLS. If you're thinking that this might be an indication of how seriously non-Java source languages are taken in Java 7, then well done, and stay tuned. We'll talk a lot more about the differences between these two specs later.

One obvious question, when you're faced with the described duality, is, "What's the link between them?" If they're now so separate in Java 7, how do they come together to make the familiar Java system?

The link between the language and platform is the shared definition of the class file format (the .class files). A serious study of the class file definition will reward you, and it's one of the ways a good Java programmer can start to become a great one. In figure 1.1 you can see the full process by which Java code is produced and used.

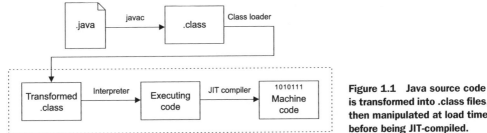

Figure 1.1 Java source code is transformed into .class files, then manipulated at load time before being JIT-compiled.

As you can see in the figure, Java code starts life as human-readable Java source, and it's then compiled by `javac` into a .class file. This is then loaded into a JVM. Note that it's very common for classes to be manipulated and altered during the loading process. Many of the most popular frameworks (especially those with "Enterprise" in their names) will transform classes as they're loaded.

Is Java a compiled or interpreted language?

The standard picture of Java is of a language that's compiled into .class files before being run on a JVM. If pressed, many developers can also explain that bytecode starts off by being interpreted by the JVM but will undergo just-in-time (JIT) compilation at some later point. Here, however, many people's understanding breaks down in a somewhat hazy conception of bytecode as basically being machine code for an imaginary or simplified CPU.

In fact, JVM bytecode is more like a halfway house between human-readable source and machine code. In the technical terms of compiler theory, bytecode is really a form of intermediate language (IL) rather than a true machine code. This means that the process of turning Java source into bytecode isn't really compilation in the sense that a C or C++ programmer would understand it, and javac isn't a compiler in the same sense as gcc is—it's really a class file generator for Java source. The real compiler in the Java ecosystem is the JIT compiler, as you can see in figure 1.1.

Some people describe the Java system as "dynamically compiled." This emphasizes that the compilation that matters is the JIT compilation at runtime, not the creation of the class file during the build process.

So, the real answer to, "Is Java compiled or interpreted?" is "Both."

With the distinction between language and platform hopefully now clearer, let's move on to talk about some of the visible changes in language syntax that have arrived with Java 7, starting with smaller syntax changes brought in with Project Coin.

1.2 *Small is beautiful—Project Coin*

Project Coin is an open source project that has been running as part of the Java 7 (and 8) effort since January 2009. In this section, we're going to explain how features get chosen and how the language evolution process works by using the small changes of Project Coin as a case study.

> ### Naming Project Coin
>
> The aim of Project Coin was to come up with small changes to the Java language. The name is a piece of wordplay—small change comes as coins, and "to coin a phrase" means to add a new expression to our language.
>
> These types of word games, whimsy, and the inevitable terrible puns are to be found everywhere in technical culture. You may just as well get used to them.

We think it's important to explain the "why" of language change as well as the "what." During the development of Java 7, there was a lot of interest around new language features, but the community didn't always understand how much work is required to get changes fully engineered and ready for prime time. We hope to shed a bit of light on this area, and hopefully dispel a few myths. But if you're not very interested in how Java evolves, feel free to skip ahead to section 1.3 and jump right into the language changes.

There is an effort curve involved in changing the Java language—some possible implementations require less engineering effort than others. In figure 1.2 we've tried to represent the different routes and show the relative effort required for each, in a complexity scale of increasing effort.

In general, it's better to take the route that requires the least effort. This means that if it's possible to implement a new feature as a library, you generally should. But not all features are easy, or even possible, to implement in a library or an IDE capability. Some features have to be implemented deeper inside the platform.

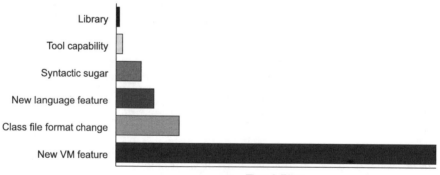

Figure 1.2   The relative effort involved in implementing new functionality in different ways

Here's how some (mostly Java 7) features fit into our complexity scale for new language features:

- *Syntactic sugar*—Underscores in numbers (Java 7)
- *Small new language feature*—try-with-resources (Java 7)
- *Class file format change*—Annotations (Java 5)
- *New JVM feature*—invokedynamic (Java 7)

Syntactic sugar

A phrase that's sometimes used to describe a language feature is "syntactic sugar." This means that the syntax form is redundant—it already exists in the language—but the syntactic sugar form is provided because it's easier for humans to work with.

As a rule of thumb, a feature referred to as syntactic sugar is removed from the compiler's representation of the program early on in the compilation process—it's said to have been "desugared" into the basic representation of the same feature.

This makes syntactic sugar changes to a language easier to implement because they usually involve a relatively small amount of work, and only involve changes to the compiler (javac in the case of Java).

Project Coin (and the rest of this chapter) is all about changes that are somewhere in the range from syntactic sugar to small new language features.

The initial period for suggestions for Project Coin changes ran on the coin-dev mailing list from February to March 2009 and saw almost 70 proposals submitted, representing a huge range of possible enhancements. The suggestions even included a joke proposal for adding multiline strings in the style of lolcat captions (superimposed captions on pictures of cats that are either funny or irritating, depending on your viewpoint—http://icanhascheezburger.com/).

The Project Coin proposals were judged under a fairly simple set of rules. Contributors needed to do three things:

- Submit a detailed proposal form describing their change (which should fundamentally be a Java language change, rather than a virtual machine change)
- Discuss their proposal openly on a mailing list and field constructive criticism from the other participants
- Be prepared to produce a prototype set of patches that could implement their change

Project Coin provides a good example of how the language and platform may evolve in the future, with changes discussed openly, early prototyping of features, and calls for public participation.

One question that might well be asked at this point is, "What constitutes a small change to the spec?" One of the changes we'll discuss in a minute adds a single word—"String"—to section 14.11 of the JLS. You can't really get much smaller than that as a change, and yet even this change touches several other aspects of the spec.

Java 7 is the first version developed in an open source manner

Java was not always an open source language, but following an announcement at the JavaOne conference in 2006, the source code for Java itself (minus a few bits that Sun didn't own the source for) was released under the GPLv2 license. This was around the time of the release of Java 6, so Java 7 is the first version of Java to be developed under an open source software (OSS) license. The primary focus for open source development of the Java platform is the OpenJDK project.

Mailing lists such as coin-dev, lambda-dev, and mlvm-dev have been major forums for discussing possible future features, allowing developers from the wider community to participate in the process of producing Java 7. In fact, we help lead the "Adopt OpenJDK" program to guide developers new to the OpenJDK, helping improve Java itself! See http://java.net/projects/jugs/pages/AdoptOpenJDK if you'd like to join us.

Any alteration produces consequences, and these have to be chased through the entire design of the language.

The full set of actions that that must be performed (or at least investigated) for *any* change is as follows:

- Update the JLS
- Implement a prototype in the source compiler
- Add library support essential for the change
- Write tests and examples
- Update documentation

In addition, if the change touches the VM or platform aspects:

- Update the VMSpec
- Implement the VM changes
- Add support in the class file and VM tools
- Consider the impact on reflection
- Consider the impact on serialization
- Think about any impacts on native code components, such as Java Native Interface (JNI).

This isn't a small amount of work, and that's after the impact of the change across the whole language spec has been considered!

An area of particular hairiness, when it comes to making changes, is the type system. That isn't because Java's type system is bad. Instead, languages with rich static type systems are likely to have a lot of possible interaction points between different bits of those type systems. Making changes to them is prone to creating unexpected surprises.

Project Coin took the very sensible route of suggesting to contributors that they mostly stay away from the type system when proposing changes. Given the amount of work that has gone into even the smallest of these small changes, this has proved a pragmatic approach.

With that bit of the background on Project Coin covered, it's time to start looking at the features chosen for inclusion.

1.3 *The changes in Project Coin*

Project Coin brought six main new features to Java 7. These are Strings in switch, new numeric literal forms, improved exception handling, try-with-resources, diamond syntax, and fixes for varargs warnings.

We're going to talk in some detail about these changes from Project Coin—we'll discuss the syntax and the meaning of the new features, and also try to explain the motivations behind the features whenever possible. We won't resort to the full formal details of the proposals, but all that material is available from the archives of the coin-dev mailing list, so if you're a budding language designer, you can read the full proposals and discussion there.

Without further ado, let's kick off with our very first new Java 7 feature—String values in a switch statement.

1.3.1 *Strings in switch*

The Java switch statement allows you to write an efficient multiple-branch statement without lots and lots of ugly nested ifs—like this:

```
public void printDay(int dayOfWeek) {
  switch (dayOfWeek) {
    case 0: System.out.println("Sunday"); break;
    case 1: System.out.println("Monday"); break;
    case 2: System.out.println("Tuesday"); break;
    case 3: System.out.println("Wednesday"); break;
    case 4: System.out.println("Thursday"); break;
    case 5: System.out.println("Friday"); break;
    case 6: System.out.println("Saturday"); break;
    default: System.err.println("Error!"); break;
  }
}
```

In Java 6 and before, the values for the cases could only be constants of type byte, char, short, int (or, technically, their reference-type equivalents Byte, Character, Short, Integer) or enum constants. With Java 7, the spec has been extended to allow for the String type to be used as well. They're constants after all.

```
public void printDay(String dayOfWeek) {
  switch (dayOfWeek) {
    case "Sunday": System.out.println("Dimanche"); break;
    case "Monday": System.out.println("Lundi"); break;
    case "Tuesday": System.out.println("Mardi"); break;
    case "Wednesday": System.out.println("Mercredi"); break;
    case "Thursday": System.out.println("Jeudi"); break;
    case "Friday": System.out.println("Vendredi"); break;
    case "Saturday": System.out.println("Samedi"); break;
    default: System.out.println("Error: '"+ dayOfWeek
      +"' is not a day of the week"); break;
  }
}
```

In all other respects, the switch statement remains the same. Like many Project Coin enhancements, this is really a very simple change to make life in Java 7 a little bit easier.

1.3.2 *Enhanced syntax for numeric literals*

There were several separate proposals around new syntax for the integral types. The following aspects were eventually chosen:

- Numeric constants (that is, one of the integer primitive types) may now be expressed as binary literals.
- Underscores may be used in integer constants to improve readability

Neither of these is, at first sight, particularly earth-shattering, but both have been minor annoyances to Java programmers.

These are both of special interest to the low-level programmer—the sort of person who works with raw network protocols, encryption, or other pursuits, where a certain amount of bit twiddling is involved. Let's begin with a look at binary literals.

BINARY LITERALS

Before Java 7, if you wanted to manipulate a binary value, you'd have had to either engage in awkward (and error-prone) base conversion or utilize parseX methods. For example, if you wanted to ensure that an int x represented the bit pattern for the decimal value 102 correctly, you'd write an expression like:

```
int x = Integer.parseInt("1100110", 2);
```

This is a lot of code just to ensure that x ends up with the correct bit pattern. There's worse to come though. Despite looking fine, there are a number of problems with this approach:

- It's really verbose.
- There is a performance hit for that method call.
- You'd have to know about the two-argument form of parseInt().
- You need to remember the details of how parseInt() behaves when it has two arguments.
- It makes life hard for the JIT compiler.
- It represents a compile-time constant as a runtime expression, which means the constant can't be used as a value in a switch statement.
- It will give you a RuntimeException (but no compile-time exception) if you have a typo in the binary value.

Fortunately, with the advent of Java 7, we can now write this:

```
int x = 0b1100110;
```

No one's saying that this is doing anything that couldn't be done before, but it has none of the problems we listed.

If you've got a reason to work with binary, you'll be glad to have this small feature. For example, when doing low-level handling of bytes, you can now have bit patterns as binary constants in switch statements.

Another small, yet useful, new feature for representing groups of bits or other long numeric representations is underscores in numbers.

UNDERSCORES IN NUMBERS

You've probably noticed that the human mind is radically different from a computer's CPU. One specific example of this is in the way that our minds handle numbers. Humans aren't, in general, very comfortable with long strings of numbers. That's one reason we invented hexadecimal—because our minds find it easier to deal with shorter strings that contain more information, rather than long strings containing not much information per character.

That is, we find 1c372ba3 easier to deal with than 00011100001101110010101110100011, even though a CPU would only ever see the second form. One way that we humans deal with long strings of numbers is to break them up. A U.S. phone number is usually represented like this: 404-555-0122.

> **NOTE** If you're like the (European) authors and have ever wondered why US phone numbers in films or books always start with 555, it's because the numbers 555-01xx are reserved for fictional use—precisely to prevent real people getting calls from people who take their Hollywood movies a little too seriously.

Other long strings of numbers have separators too:

- $100,000,000 (large sums of money)
- 08-92-96 (UK banking sort codes)

Unfortunately, both the comma (,) and hyphen (-) have too many possible meanings within the realm of handling numbers in programming, so we can't use either as a separator. Instead, the Project Coin proposal borrowed an idea from Ruby, and introduced the underscore (_) as a separator. Note that this is just a bit of easy-on-the-eyes compile-time syntax. The compiler strips out those underscores and stores the usual digits.

This means that you can write 100_000_000 and hopefully not confuse it with 10_000_000, whereas 100000000 is easily confused with 10000000. Let's look at a couple of examples, at least one of which should be familiar:

```
long anotherLong = 2_147_483_648L;
int bitPattern = 0b0001_1100__0011_0111__0010_1011__1010_0011;
```

Notice how much easier it is to read the value being assigned to anotherLong.

> **WARNING** In Java, it's still legal to use the lowercase *l* character to denote a long. For example 10101001. Make sure you always use an uppercase *L* so that maintainers don't get confused between the number *1* and the letter *l*: 1010100L is much clearer!

By now, you should be convinced of the benefit of these tweaks to the handling of integers, so let's move on to looking at Java 7's improved exception handling.

1.3.3   *Improved exception handling*

There are two parts to this improvement—multicatch and final rethrow. To see why they're a help, consider the following Java 6 code, which tries to find, open, and parse a config file and handle a number of different possible exceptions.

Listing 1.1   Handling several different exceptions in Java 6

```
public Configuration getConfig(String fileName) {
  Configuration cfg = null;
  try {
    String fileText = getFile(fileName);
    cfg = verifyConfig(parseConfig(fileText));
  } catch (FileNotFoundException fnfx) {
    System.err.println("Config file '" + fileName + "' is missing");
  } catch (IOException e) {
    System.err.println("Error while processing file '" + fileName + "'");
  } catch (ConfigurationException e) {
    System.err.println("Config file '" + fileName + "' is not consistent");
  } catch (ParseException e) {
    System.err.println("Config file '" + fileName + "' is malformed");
  }

  return cfg;
}
```

This method can encounter a number of different exceptional conditions:

- The config file may not exist.
- The config file may disappear while you're trying to read from it.
- The config file may be malformed syntactically.
- The config file may have invalid information in it.

These conditions fit into two distinct functional groups. Either the file is missing or bad in some way, or the file is present and correct but couldn't be retrieved properly (perhaps because of a hardware failure or network outage).

It would be nice to compress this down to just these two cases, and handle all the "file is missing or bad in some way" exceptions in one catch clause. Java 7 allows you to do this.

Listing 1.2   Handling several different exceptions in Java 7

```
public Configuration getConfig(String fileName) {
  Configuration cfg = null;
  try {
    String fileText = getFile(fileName);
    cfg = verifyConfig(parseConfig(fileText));
  } catch (FileNotFoundException|ParseException|ConfigurationException e) {
    System.err.println("Config file '" + fileName +
                       "' is missing or malformed");
  } catch (IOException iox) {
    System.err.println("Error while processing file '" + fileName + "'");
  }
```

```
    return cfg;
}
```

The exception e has a type that isn't precisely knowable at compile time. This means that it has to be handled in the catch block as the common supertype of the exceptions that it *could* be (which will often be Exception or Throwable, in practice).

An additional bit of new syntax helps with rethrowing exceptions. In many cases, developers may want to manipulate a thrown exception before rethrowing it. The problem is that in previous versions of Java you'll often see code like this:

```
try {
  doSomethingWhichMightThrowIOException();
  doSomethingElseWhichMightThrowSQLException();
} catch (Exception e) {
  ...
  throw e;
}
```

This forces you to declare the exception signature of this code as Exception—the real dynamic type of the exception has been swallowed.

Nevertheless, it's relatively easy to see that the exception can only be an IOException or a SQLException, and if you can see it, so can the compiler. This snippet changes a single word change to use the Java 7 syntax:

```
try {
  doSomethingWhichMightThrowIOException();
  doSomethingElseWhichMightThrowSQLException();
} catch (final Exception e) {
  ...
  throw e;
}
```

The appearance of the final keyword indicates that the type that's actually thrown is the runtime type of the exception that was encountered—in this example, that would be either IOException or SQLException. This is referred to as *final rethrow,* and it can protect against throwing an overly general type, which then has to be caught by a very general catch in a higher scope.

The final keyword is optional in the previous example, but in practice, we've found that it helps to use it while adjusting to the new semantics of catch and rethrow.

In addition to these general improvements in exception handling, the specific case of resource management has been improved in Java 7, so that's where we'll turn next.

1.3.4 *Try-with-resources (TWR)*

This change is easy to explain, but it has proved to have hidden subtleties, which made it much less easy to implement than originally hoped. The basic idea is to allow a resource (for example, a file or something a bit like one) to be scoped to a block in such a way that the resource is automatically closed when control exits the block.

This is an important change, for the simple reason that virtually no one gets manual resource closing 100 percent right. Until recently, even the reference how-tos from Sun were wrong. The proposal submitted to Project Coin for this change includes the astounding claim that two-thirds of the uses of close() in the JDK had bugs in them!

Fortunately, compilers can be made to produce exactly the sort of pedantic, boiler-plate code that humans so often get wrong, and that's the approach taken by this change.

This is a big help in writing error-free code. To see just how helpful, consider how you'd write a block of code that reads from a stream coming from a URL (url) and writes to a file (out) with Java 6. Here's one possible solution.

Listing 1.3 Java 6 syntax for resource management

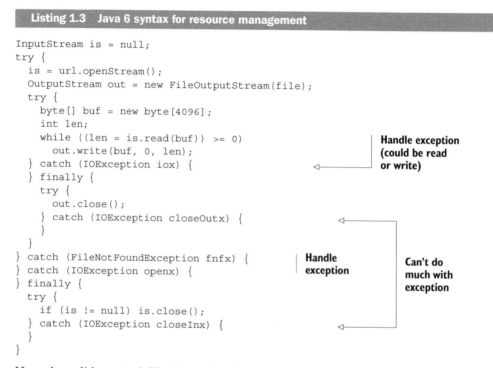

```
InputStream is = null;
try {
  is = url.openStream();
  OutputStream out = new FileOutputStream(file);
  try {
    byte[] buf = new byte[4096];
    int len;
    while ((len = is.read(buf)) >= 0)
      out.write(buf, 0, len);                   ←  Handle exception
  } catch (IOException iox) {                       (could be read
  } finally {                                       or write)
    try {
      out.close();
    } catch (IOException closeOutx) {      ←
    }
  }
} catch (FileNotFoundException fnfx) {    Handle        Can't do
} catch (IOException openx) {             exception     much with
} finally {                                             exception
  try {
    if (is != null) is.close();
  } catch (IOException closeInx) {        ←
  }
}
```

How close did you get? The key point here is that when handling external resources, Murphy's Law applies—anything can go wrong at any time:

- The InputStream can fail to open from the URL, to read from it, or to close properly.
- The File corresponding to the OutputStream can fail to open, to write to it, or to close properly.
- A problem can arise from some combination of more than one factor.

This last possibility is where a lot of the headaches come from—a combination of exceptions is very difficult to deal with well.

This is the main reason for preferring the new syntax—it's much less error-prone. The compiler isn't susceptible to the mistakes that every developer will make when trying to write this type of code manually.

Let's look at the Java 7 code for performing the same task as listing 1.3. As before, url is a URL object that points at the entity you want to download, and file is a File object where you want to save what you're downloading. Here's what this looks like in Java 7.

```
try (OutputStream out = new FileOutputStream(file);
     InputStream is = url.openStream() ) {
  byte[] buf = new byte[4096];
  int len;
  while ((len = is.read(buf)) > 0) {
    out.write(buf, 0, len);
  }
}
```

This basic form shows the new syntax for a block with automatic management—the try with the resource in round brackets. For C# programmers, this is probably a bit reminiscent of a using clause, and that's a good conceptual starting point when working with this new feature. The resources are used by the block, and they're automatically disposed of when you're done with them.

You still have to be careful with try-with-resources, as there are cases where a resource might still not be closed. For example, the following code would not close its FileInputStream properly if there was an error creating the ObjectInputStream from the file (someFile.bin).

```
try ( ObjectInputStream in = new ObjectInputStream(new
      FileInputStream("someFile.bin")) ) {
 ...
}
```

Let's assume that the file (someFile.bin) exists, but it might not be an ObjectInput file, so the file might not open correctly. Therefore, the ObjectInputStream wouldn't be constructed and the FileInputStream wouldn't be closed!

The correct way to ensure that try-with-resources always works for you is to split the resources into separate variables.

```
try ( FileInputStream fin = new FileInputStream("someFile.bin");
      ObjectInputStream in = new ObjectInputStream(fin) ) {
 ...
}
```

One other aspect of TWR is the appearance of enhanced stack traces and suppressed exceptions. Prior to Java 7, exception information could be swallowed when handling resources. This possibility also exists with TWR, so the stack traces have been enhanced to allow you to see the type information of exceptions that would otherwise be lost.

For example, consider this snippet, in which a null InputStream is returned from a method:

```
try(InputStream i = getNullStream()) {
  i.available();
}
```

This will give rise to an enhanced stack trace, in which the suppressed `NullPointer-Exception` (NPE for short) can be seen:

```
Exception in thread "main" java.lang.NullPointerException
    at wgjd.ch01.ScratchSuprExcep.run(ScratchSuprExcep.java:23)
    at wgjd.ch01.ScratchSuprExcep.main(ScratchSuprExcep.java:39)
    Suppressed: java.lang.NullPointerException
    at wgjd.ch01.ScratchSuprExcep.run(ScratchSuprExcep.java:24)
       1 more
```

TWR and AutoCloseable

Under the hood, the TWR feature is achieved by the introduction of a new interface, called `AutoCloseable`, which a class must implement in order to be able to appear as a resource in the new TWR `try` clause. Many of the Java 7 platform classes have been converted to implement `AutoCloseable` (and it has been made a superinterface of `Closeable`), but you should be aware that not every aspect of the platform has yet adopted this new technology. It's included as part of JDBC 4.1, though.

For your own code, you should definitely use TWR whenever you need to work with resources. It will help you avoid bugs in your exception handling.

We encourage you to use try-with-resources as soon as you're able, to eliminate unnecessary bugs from your codebase.

1.3.5 *Diamond syntax*

Java 7 also introduces a change that means less typing for you when dealing with generics. One of the problems with generics is that the definitions and setup of instances can be really verbose. Let's suppose that you have some users, whom you identify by `userid` (which is an integer), and each user has one or more lookup tables specific to that user. What would that look like in code?

```
Map<Integer, Map<String, String>> usersLists =
    new HashMap<Integer, Map<String, String>>();
```

That's quite a mouthful, and almost half of it is duplicated characters. Wouldn't it be better if you could write something like this,

```
Map<Integer, Map<String, String>> usersLists = new HashMap<>();
```

and have the compiler work out the type information on the right side? Thanks to the magic of Project Coin, you can. In Java 7, the shortened form for declarations like that is entirely legal. It's backwards compatible as well, so when you find yourself revisiting old code, you can cut the older, more verbose declaration and start using the new type-inferred syntax to save a few pixels.

We should point out that the compiler is using a new form of type inference for this feature. It's working out the correct type for the expression on the right side, and isn't just substituting in the text that defines the full type.

> **The "diamond syntax" name**
>
> This form is called "diamond syntax" because, well, the shortened type information looks like a diamond. The proper name in the proposal is "Improved Type Inference for Generic Instance Creation," which is a real mouthful and has ITIGIC as an acronym, which sounds stupid, so diamond syntax it is.

The new diamond syntax will certainly save your fingers from some typing. The last Project Coin feature we'll explore is the removal of a warning when you're using varargs.

1.3.6 *Simplified varargs method invocation*

This is one of the simplest changes of all—it moves a warning about type information for a very specific case where varargs combines with generics in a method signature.

Put another way, unless you're in the habit of writing code that takes as arguments a variable number of references of type T and does something to make a collection out of them, you can move on to the next section. On the other hand, if this bit of code looks like something you might write, you should read on:

```
public static <T> Collection<T> doSomething(T... entries) {
    ...
}
```

Still here? Good. So what's this all about?

As you probably know, a varargs method is one that takes a variable number of parameters (all of the same type) at the end of the argument list. What you may not know is how varargs is implemented; basically, all of the variable parameters at the end are put into an array (which the compiler automatically creates for you) and they're passed as a single parameter.

This is all well and good, but here we run into one of the admitted weaknesses of Java's generics—you aren't normally allowed to create an array of a known generic type. For example, this won't compile:

```
HashMap<String, String>[] arrayHm = new HashMap<>[2];
```

You can't make arrays of a specified generic type. Instead, you have to do this:

```
HashMap<String, String>[] warnHm = new HashMap[2];
```

This gives a warning that has to be ignored. Notice that you can define the type of warnHm to be an array of HashMap<String, String>—you just can't create any instances of that type, and instead have to hold your nose (or at least, suppress the warning) and force an instance of the raw type (which is array of HashMap) into warnHm.

These two features—varargs methods working on compiler-generated arrays, and arrays of known generic types not being an instantiable type—come together to cause a slight headache. Consider this bit of code:

```
HashMap<String, String> hm1 = new HashMap<>();
HashMap<String, String> hm2 = new HashMap<>();

Collection<HashMap<String, String>> coll = doSomething(hm1, hm2);
```

The compiler will attempt to create an array to contain `hm1` and `hm2`, but the type of the array should strictly be one of the forbidden array types. Faced with this dilemma, the compiler cheats and breaks its own rule about the forbidden array of generic type. It creates the array instance, but grumbles about it, producing a compiler warning that mutters darkly about "unchecked or unsafe operations."

From the point of view of the type system, this is fair enough. But the poor developer just wanted to use what seemed like a perfectly sensible API, and there are scary-sounding warnings for no adequately explained reason.

WHERE DID THE WARNING GO IN JAVA 7?

The new feature in Java 7 changes the emphasis of the warning. After all, there is a potential for violating type safety in these types of constructions, and *somebody* had better be informed about them. There's not much that the users of these types of APIs can really do, though. Either the code inside `doSomething()` is evil and violates type safety, or it doesn't. In any case, it's out of the API user's hands.

The person who should really be warned about this issue is the person who wrote `doSomething()`—the API producer, rather than the consumer. So that's where the warning goes—it's moved from where the API is used to where the API was defined.

The warning once was triggered when code that used the API was compiled. Instead, it's now triggered when an API that has the potential to trigger this kind of type safety violation is written. The compiler warns the coder implementing the API, and it's up to that developer to pay proper attention to the type system.

To make things easier for API developers, Java 7 also provides a new annotation type, `java.lang.SafeVarargs`. This can be applied to an API method (or constructor) that would otherwise produce a warning of the type discussed. By annotating the method with `@SafeVarargs`, the developer essentially asserts that the method doesn't perform any unsafe operations. In this case, the compiler will suppress the warning.

CHANGES TO THE TYPE SYSTEM

That's an awful lot of words to describe a very small change—moving a warning from one place to another is hardly a game-changing language feature, but it does serve to illustrate one very important point. Earlier in this chapter we mentioned that Project Coin encouraged contributors to mostly stay away from the type system when proposing changes. This example shows how much care is needed when figuring out how different features of the type system interact, and how that interaction will alter when a change to the language is implemented. This isn't even a particularly complex change—larger changes would be far, far more involved, with potentially dozens of subtle ramifications.

This final example illustrates how intricate the effect of small changes can be. Although they represent mostly small syntactic changes, they can have a positive impact on your code that is out of proportion with the size of the changes. Once you've started using them, you'll likely find that they offer real benefit to your programs.

1.4 Summary

Making changes to the language itself is hard. It's always easier to implement new features in a library (if you can—not everything can be implemented without a language change). The challenges involved can cause language designers to make smaller, and more conservative, changes than they might otherwise wish.

Now, it's time to move on to some of the bigger pieces that make up the release, starting with a look at how some of the core libraries have changed in Java 7. Our next stop is the I/O libraries, which have been considerably revamped. It will be helpful to have a grasp of how previous Java versions coped with I/O, because the Java 7 classes (sometimes called NIO.2) build upon the existing framework.

If you want to see some more examples of the TWR syntax in action, or want to learn about the new, high-performance asynchronous I/O classes, then the next chapter has all the answers.

New I/O 2

This chapter covers

- The new Java 7 I/O APIs (aka NIO.2)
- `Path`—the new foundation for file- and directory-based I/O
- The `Files` utility class and its various helper methods
- How to solve common I/O use cases
- An introduction to asynchronous I/O

One of the larger API changes in the Java language—a major update to the set of I/O APIs, called "more New I/O" or NIO.2 (aka JSR-203)—is the focus of this chapter. NIO.2 is a set of new classes and methods, that primarily live in the `java.nio` package.

- It's an out-and-out replacement of `java.io.File` for writing code that interacts with the filesystem.
- It contains new asynchronous classes that will allow you to perform file and network I/O operations in a background thread without manually configuring thread pools and other low-level concurrency constructs.
- It simplifies coding with sockets and channels by introducing a new `Network-Channel` construct.

20

Let's look at an example use case. Imagine your boss asked you to write a Java routine that went through all the directories on the production server and found all of the properties files that have been written with a variety of read/write and ownership permissions. With Java 6 (and below) this task is almost impossible for three reasons:

- There is no direct class or method support for navigating directory trees.
- There is no way of detecting and dealing with symbolic links.[1]
- It's not possible to read the attributes (such as readable, writable, or executable) of a file in one easy operation.

The new Java 7 NIO.2 API makes this programming task much more possible, with direct support for navigating a directory tree (`Files.walkFileTree()`, section 2.3.1), symbolic links (`Files.isSymbolicLink()`, listing 2.4) and simple one-line operations to read the file attributes (`Files.readAttributes()`, section 2.4.3).

In addition, your boss now wants you to read in those properties files without interrupting the flow of the main program. You know that one of the properties files is at least 1MB in size; reading this will likely interrupt the main flow of the program! Under Java 5/6, you'd likely have to use the classes in the `java.util.concurrent` package to create thread pools and worker queues and read this file in a separate background thread. As we'll discuss in chapter 4, modern concurrency in Java is still pretty difficult and the room for error is high. With Java 7 and the NIO.2 API, you can read the large file in the background without having to specify your own workers or queues by using the new `AsynchronousFileChannel` (section 2.5). Phew!

The new APIs won't make you a perfect cup of coffee (although that would be a nice feature), but they will be extremely useful because of major trends in our industry.

First, there is a trend to explore alternative means of data storage, especially in the area of nonrelational or large data sets. This means the use case for reading and writing large files (such as large report files from a microblogging service) is likely to come up in your immediate future. NIO.2 allows you to read and write large files in an asynchronous, efficient manner, taking advantage of underlying OS features.

A second trend is that of multicore CPUs, which open up the possibility for truly concurrent (and therefore faster) I/O. Concurrency isn't an easy domain to master,[2] and NIO.2 offers a large helping hand by presenting a simple abstraction for utilizing multithreaded file and socket access. Even if you don't use these features directly, they will have a large impact on your programming life as IDEs and application servers, and popular frameworks will utilize them heavily.

These are just some examples of how NIO.2 can help you. If NIO.2 sounds like it solves some of the problems you're facing as a developer, this chapter is for you! If not, you can always come back to the sections in this chapter that deal with Java I/O coding tasks.

---

[1] A symbolic link is a special type of file that points to another file or location on the file system—think of it as a shortcut.

[2] Chapter 4 explores the subtle complexities that concurrency can bring to your programming life.

This chapter will give you enough of a taste of Java 7's new I/O capabilities for you to start writing NIO.2-based code and confidently explore the new APIs. As an additional benefit, these APIs use some of the features we covered in chapter 1—proof that Java 7 does indeed eat its own dog food!

> **TIP** The combination of try-with-resources (from chapter 1) and the new APIs in NIO.2 make for very safe I/O programming, probably for the first time in Java!

We expect that you'll most likely be wanting to use the new file I/O capabilities, so we'll cover that in the greatest detail. You'll begin by learning about the new filesystem abstraction, Path, and its supporting classes. Building on top of Path, you'll work through common filesystem operations such as copying and moving files.

We'll also give you an introduction to asynchronous I/O and look at a filesystem-based example. Lastly we'll discuss the amalgamation of Socket and Channel functionality and what that means for developers of network applications. First, though, we'll look at how NIO.2 came about.

2.1 Java I/O—a history

To truly appreciate the design of the NIO.2 APIs (and to gain insight into how they're meant to be used), the well-grounded Java developer should understand the history of Java I/O. But we completely understand that you may want to get to the code! In that case, you should jump straight to section 2.2.

If you find some of the API usage particularly elegant or perhaps a little odd, this section will help you see NIO.2 from the API designer's mind. This is Java's third major I/O implementation, so let's look over the history of I/O support in Java to see how NIO.2 came about.

One of the reasons Java is so popular is its rich library support, which provides powerful and concise APIs to solve most of your programming needs. But experienced Java developers know that there are a few areas in which older versions of Java weren't quite up to scratch. One of the biggest headaches for developers has been Java's input/output (I/O) APIs.

2.1.1 Java 1.0 to 1.3

With the earliest versions of Java (1.0-1.3), there was a lack of comprehensive I/O support. Namely, developers faced the following problems when developing applications that required I/O support:

- There was no concept of buffers or channel abstractions for data, meaning lots of detailed low-level programming for developers.
- I/O operations would get blocked, limiting scalability.
- There was limited character set encoding support, leading to a plethora of hand-coded solutions to support certain types of hardware.
- There was no regular expression support, making data manipulation difficult.

Basically, Java lacked support for nonblocking I/O, so developers struggled to write scalable I/O solutions. We believe that this played a part in holding back Java from heavy use in server-side development until the release of Java 1.4.

2.1.2 Java 1.4 and NIO

In order to solve these problems, Java began to implement nonblocking I/O support, as well as other I/O features, to help developers deliver faster, more reliable I/O solutions. There have been two major advancements:

- The introduction of nonblocking I/O as part of Java 1.4
- An overhaul of nonblocking I/O as part of Java 7

Under the guise of JSR-51, nonblocking input/output (NIO) was added to Java when version 1.4 was released in 2002. The following broad feature set was added at that time, turning Java into an attractive language to use for server-side development:

- Buffer and channel abstraction layers for I/O operations
- The ability to encode and decode character sets
- An interface that can map files to data held in memory
- The capability to write nonblocking I/O
- A new regular expression library based on the popular Perl implementation

Perl—the king of regular expressions

The Perl programming language is the undisputed king of regular expression support. In fact, its design and implementation is so good that several programming languages (including Java) have pretty much copied Perl's syntax and semantics. If you're a curious language lover, visit http://www.perl.org/ to see what Perl is all about.

NIO was definitely a great step forward, but Java developers still faced hardship when programming I/O. In particular, the support for handling files and directories on a filesystem was still inadequate. The `java.io.File` class, at the time, had some annoying limitations:

- It did not deal with filenames consistently across all platforms.[3]
- It failed to have a unified model for file attributes (for example, modeling read/write access).
- It was difficult to traverse directories.
- It didn't allow you to use platform- or OS-specific features.[4]
- It didn't support nonblocking operations for filesystems.[5]

---

[3] This is an area that some critics of Java would say breaks the famous "Write once, run anywhere" slogan.
[4] Access to the symbolic linking mechanism on Linux/UNIX operating systems is the common request here.
[5] Nonblocking operations for network sockets did have support in Java 1.4.

2.1.3 *Introducing NIO.2*

JSR-203 (led by Alan Bateman) was formed to address the preceding limitations as well as to provide support for some of the new I/O paradigms in modern hardware and software. JSR-203 has become what we now know as the NIO.2 API in Java 7. It had three major goals, which are detailed in JSR-203, section 2.1 (http://jcp.org/en/jsr/detail?id=203):

1 A new filesystem interface that supports bulk access to file attributes, escape to filesystem-specific APIs, and a service-provider interface for pluggable filesystem implementations.

2 An API for asynchronous (as opposed to polled, nonblocking) I/O operations on both sockets and files.

3 The completion of the socket-channel functionality defined in JSR-51, including the addition of support for binding, option configuration, and multicast datagrams.

Let's start with the fundamentals of the new filesystem support with `Path` and friends.

2.2   *Path—a foundation of file-based I/O*

`Path` is one of the key classes you need to master for file-based I/O under NIO.2. A `Path` typically represents a location in the filesystem, such as C:\workspace\java7developer (a directory in the MS Windows filesystem) or /usr/bin/zip (the location of the zip utility in a *nix filesystem). If you gain a thorough understanding of how to create and manipulate paths, you'll be able to navigate any type of filesystem, including such filesystems as a zip archive.

Figure 2.1 (based on the layout of the source code for this book) provides a refresher on several filesystem concepts:

- A directory tree
- The root of a path
- An absolute path
- A relative path

We talk about absolute and relative paths because you need to think about where locations in the filesystem are in relation to where your application is running from. For example, your application might be running from the /java7developer/src/test directory and you have code that reads filenames from the /java7developer/src/main directory. To travel to /java7developer/src/main, you could use a relative path of ../main.

But what if your application was running from /java7developer/src/test/java/com/java7developer? Using the relative path of ../main would not take you to the directory you wanted to get to (it would take you to the nonexistent directory of /java7developer/src/test/java/com/main). Instead, you'd have to think about using an absolute path, such as /java7developer/src/main.

The converse case is also true; your application might consistently run from the same place (say from the target directory in figure 2.1). But the root of the directory

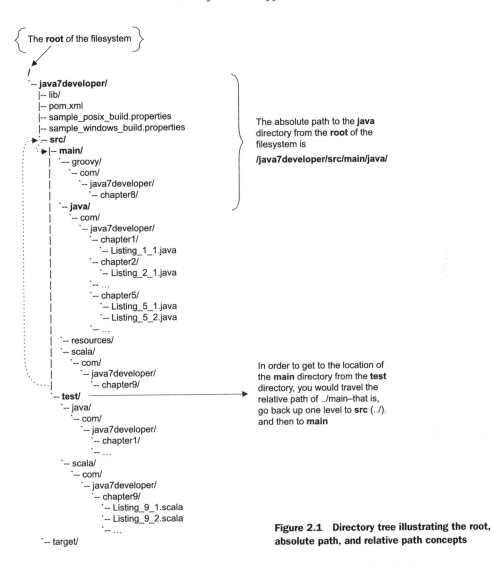

Figure 2.1 Directory tree illustrating the root, absolute path, and relative path concepts

tree might change (say from /java7developer to D:\workspace\j7d). In that case, you can't rely on an absolute path—you'll need to use relative paths to reliably move to the locations you need to get to.

A Path in NIO.2 is an abstract construct. You can create (and work with) a Path that isn't immediately bound to a corresponding physical location. Although this may seem counterintuitive, it makes a lot of sense for several use cases. For example, you might want to create a Path that represents the location of a new file that you're *about* to create. That file doesn't exist until you use the Files.createFile(Path target)[6] method. If you had tried to read the contents of that file represented by the Path *before*

---

[6] You'll meet this method in the Files section soon!

it was created, you'd get an IOException. The same logic applies if you were to specify a Path that didn't exist and tried to read from it using a method such as Files .readAllBytes(Path). In short, the JVM only binds a Path to the physical location at runtime.

> **WARNING**   Be careful when writing filesystem-specific code. Creating a Path of C:\workspace\java7developer, then trying to read from it, will only work for computers that have the C:\workspace\java7developer location on their filesystem. Always ensure that your logic and exception handling covers the case where your code might run on a different filesystem, or a filesystem that could have had its structure altered. One of the authors forgot this in the past, causing an entire series of hard disks to fail across his university CS department![7]

It's worth repeating that NIO.2 has a definite split between the concept of a location (represented by Path) and the manipulation of the physical filesystem (for example, copying a file), which is generally carried out by the Files helper class.

The Path class is described in further detail (along with some other classes you'll meet in this section) in table 2.1.

Table 2.1   Key foundation classes for learning file I/O

Class	Description
Path	The Path class includes methods that can be used to obtain information about the path, to access elements of the path, to convert the path to other forms, or to extract portions of a path. There are also methods for matching the path string and for removing redundancies in a path.
Paths	A utility class that provides helper methods to return a path, such as get(String first, String... more) and get(URI uri).
FileSystem	The class that interfaces with the filesystem, whether that be the default filesystem or an alternative filesystem retrieved by its uniform resource identifier (URI).
FileSystems	A utility class that provides various methods, such as one that returns the default filesystem, FileSystems.getDefault().

Remember that a Path doesn't have to represent a real file or directory. You can manipulate a Path to your heart's content, and use the Files functionality to check whether the file actually exists and to perform work on it.

> **TIP**   Path isn't limited to traditional filesystems. It can also cover filesystems such as a zip or jar filesystem.

Let's explore the Path class by performing a few simple tasks:

- Creating a Path
- Retrieving information about a Path

---

[7] We won't mention any names, but you're welcome to try to figure out this whodunit.

- Removing redundancies from a `Path`
- Converting a `Path`
- Joining two `Paths`, creating a `Path` between two `Paths`, and comparing two `Paths`

We'll begin by creating a `Path` to represent a location in a filesystem.

2.2.1 Creating a Path

Creating a `Path` is trivial. The quickest way to do so is to call the `Paths.get(String first, String... more)` method. The second variable isn't normally used, it's simply a way of joining additional strings to form the `Path` string.

> **TIP** You'll notice that in the NIO.2 APIs, the only checked exception thrown by the various methods in `Path` or `Paths` is an `IOException`. We think this aids the goal of simplicity, but it can obscure the underlying problem at times, and you may need to write extra exception handling if you want to deal with one of the explicit subclasses of `IOException`.

Let's use the `Paths.get(String first)` method to create an absolute `Path` for the useful file-compressing utility, zip, in the /usr/bin/ directory:

```
Path listing = Paths.get("/usr/bin/zip");
```

This `Paths.get("/usr/bin/zip")` call is equivalent to calling the following longer sequence:

```
Path listing = FileSystems.getDefault().getPath("/usr/bin/zip");
```

> **TIP** You can use a relative path when creating a `Path`. For example, your program might be running from the /opt directory, and to create a `Path` to /usr/bin/zip you might use ../usr/bin/zip. That takes you one directory up from /opt (which takes you to /) and then to /usr/bin/zip. It's easy to convert this relative path to an absolute path by calling the `toAbsolutePath()` method, like this: `listing.toAbsolutePath()`.

You can interrogate the `Path` for information, such as the parent of that `Path`, its filename (assuming one exists), and more.

2.2.2 Retrieving information from a Path

The `Path` class has a group of methods that return useful information about the path that you're dealing with. The following code listing creates a `Path` for the useful zip utility located in /usr/bin and prints useful information, including its root `Path`, and its parent `Path`. Assuming you're running an OS with the zip utility located in /usr/bin, you should expect to see the following output.

```
File Name [zip]
Number of Name Elements in the Path [3]
Parent Path [/usr/bin]
Root of Path [/]
Subpath from Root, 2 elements deep [usr/bin]
```

When you run this listing on your own machine, the results will depend on what OS you have and from where you're running the code listing.

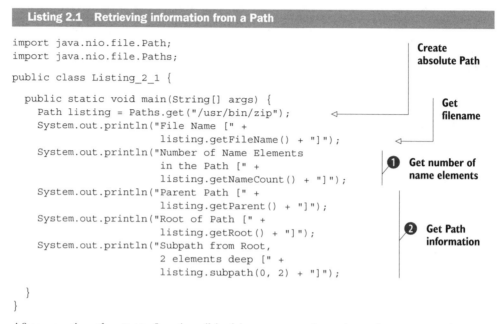

Listing 2.1   Retrieving information from a Path

```java
import java.nio.file.Path;
import java.nio.file.Paths;

public class Listing_2_1 {

  public static void main(String[] args) {
    Path listing = Paths.get("/usr/bin/zip");
    System.out.println("File Name [" +
                      listing.getFileName() + "]");
    System.out.println("Number of Name Elements
                      in the Path [" +
                      listing.getNameCount() + "]");
    System.out.println("Parent Path [" +
                      listing.getParent() + "]");
    System.out.println("Root of Path [" +
                      listing.getRoot() + "]");
    System.out.println("Subpath from Root,
                      2 elements deep [" +
                      listing.subpath(0, 2) + "]");

  }
}
```

Create absolute Path

Get filename

❶ Get number of name elements

❷ Get Path information

After creating the `Path` for /usr/bin/zip, you can investigate how many elements make up its `Path` (in this case, the number of directories) ❶. It's always useful to know where your `Path` is relative to its parent `Path` and the root. You can also pick out a sub-path by specifying starting and ending indexes. In this case, you're retrieving the subpath from root (0) to the second element in the `Path` (2) ❷.

Using these methods will be invaluable when you're first learning the NIO.2 file APIs because you can use them to log the results of manipulating paths.

2.2.3   *Removing redundancies*

When writing utility programs (such as a properties file analyzer) you might get passed a `Path` that can contain elements such as one or two periods:

- . represents this directory
- .. represents the parent directory

Let's assume your application is running from /java7developer/src/main/java/com/java7developer/chapter2/ (see figure 2.1). You're in the same directory as Listing_2_1.java, so if you were passed in a `Path` of ./Listing_2.1.java, the ./ part (which is effectively the directory you're running in) is irrelevant. In this case, the shorter `Path` of Listing_2_1.java would be sufficient.

Other types of redundancy can also occur when evaluating a `Path`, such as a symbolic link (which we'll cover in section 2.4.3). For example, suppose you're on a *nix OS and you're looking for information on a log file called log1.txt under a /usr/logs directory. But that /usr/logs directory is in fact a symbolic link to /application/logs, the *real* location of the log file. Because you want to know the real location, you'll want to remove the redundant symbolic information.

All of these types of redundancy can result in a `Path` not leading to the file location you think it's pointing to.

With Java 7, there are a couple of helper methods you can use to clarify what your `Path` really is. First, you can remove redundant information from a `Path` by using its `normalize()` method. The following snippet would return the `Path` of Listing_2_1.java, stripping out the redundant notation that indicates it's in the same directory (the ./ part).

```
Path normalizedPath = Paths.get("./Listing_2_1.java").normalize();
```

There is also a powerful `toRealPath()` method that combines the functionality of the `toAbsolutePath()` and `normalize()` methods and detects and follows symbolic links.

Let's go back to the example where you're on a *nix OS and you have a log file called log1.txt under a /usr/logs directory, which is in fact a symbolic link to /application/logs. By using `toRealPath()`, you'd get the *real* `Path` of /application/logs/log1.txt.

```
Path realPath = Paths.get("/usr/logs/log1.txt").toRealPath();
```

The last feature of the `Path` API that we'll cover is manipulating multiple `Paths` in order to compare them, find the `Path` between them, and more.

2.2.4 Converting Paths

Utility programs are the most common use case for converting paths. For example, you might be asked to compare where files are in relation to each other so that you know that the structure of your source code directory tree meets the coding standards. Or you could be passed a variety of `Path` arguments from the shell script executing your program, and you need to turn those into a sensible `Path`. In NIO.2 you can easily join `Paths`, create a `Path` between two other `Paths`, and compare `Paths` against each other.

The following snippet demonstrates joining two `Paths`, uat and conf/application.properties, via the `resolve` method in order to represent the full `Path` of /uat/conf/application.properties.

```
Path prefix = Paths.get("/uat/");
Path completePath = prefix.resolve("conf/application.properties");
```

To retrieve the `Path` between two other `Paths`, you use the `relativize(Path)` method. The following code snippet calculates the `Path` to the configuration directory from the logging directory.

```
String logging = args[0];
String configuration = args[1];
Path logDir = Paths.get(logging);
Path confDir = Paths.get(configuration);
Path pathToConfDir = logDir.relativize(confDir);
```

As you'd expect, you can use startsWith(Path prefix) and endsWith(Path suffix) as well as the full equals(Path path) equality comparison to compare paths.

Now that you're comfortable using the Path class, what about all of that existing pre-Java 7 code that you have? The NIO.2 team has thought about this backward compatibility issue and added a couple of new API features to ensure interoperability between the new Path-based I/O and previous versions of Java.

2.2.5   *NIO.2 Path and Java's existing File class*

The classes in the new filesystem API can be used as a complete replacement for the old java.io.File-based API. But it won't be uncommon for you to have to interact with large amounts of legacy code that uses the older java.io.File-based I/O. Java 7 introduces two new methods:

- A new toPath() method on the existing java.io.File class, which immediately converts an existing File to the newer Path construct.
- A toFile() method on the Path class, which immediately converts an existing Path into a File.

The following code snippet quickly demonstrates this capability.

```
File file = new File("../Listing_2_1.java");
Path listing = file.toPath();
listing.toAbsolutePath();
file = listing.toFile();
```

That completes our exploration of the Path class. Next up, we'll visit Java 7's support for dealing with directories, and directory trees in particular.

2.3   *Dealing with directories and directory trees*

As you'll likely have surmised from reading section 2.2 on paths, a directory is just a Path with special attributes. A compelling new feature in Java 7 is the ability to navigate directories. The addition of the new java.nio.file.DirectoryStream<T> interface and its implementing classes allow you to perform the following broad functions:

- Iterate over entries in a directory; for example, to find files in a directory
- Filter entries in a directory using glob expressions (such as *Foobar*) and MIME-based content detection (such as text/xml files)
- Perform recursive move, copy, and delete operations via the walkFileTree method

In this section, we'll cover the two most common use cases: finding files in a single directory and then performing that same task over a directory tree. Let's begin with the simplest case—finding arbitrary files in a directory.

2.3.1   *Finding files in a directory*

First, we'll cover a simple example of using a pattern-matching filter to list all .properties files in the java7developer project directory. Take a look at the following listing.

Listing 2.2 Listing properties files in a directory

```
Path dir = Paths.get("C:\\workspace\\java7developer");     ← ➊  Set starting path

try(DirectoryStream<Path> stream
        = Files.newDirectoryStream(dir, "*.properties")) {  ←
    for (Path entry: stream)                                     Declare filtering
    {                                                        ➋  stream
        System.out.println(entry.getFileName());
    }                                                            List each
}                                                            ➌  .properties
catch (IOException e)                                            file and print
{
    System.out.println(e.getMessage());
}
```

You start by declaring the familiar `Paths.get(String)` call ➊. The key part comes with the call to Files.newDirectoryStream(Path directory, String patternMatch) ➋, which returns a `DirectoryStream` filtered by files ending in .properties. Finally, you print each entry ➌.

The pattern matching that's used is called a *glob pattern match*, which is similar to, but has some differences from, the sorts of Perl-like regular expression pattern matching you're used to. See appendix B for complete details on how you can apply glob pattern matching.

Listing 2.2 shows the power of the new API when dealing with a single directory. But what if you need to recursively filter across multiple directories?

2.3.2 *Walking the directory tree*

Java 7 introduces support for navigating a full directory tree. This means you can easily search for files in a directory tree (searching through subfolders) and perform actions on them as you wish. You may want to have a utility class that deletes all of the .class files under the /opt/workspace/java directory on your development box as a cleanup step for your build.

Walking the directory tree is a new feature in Java 7, and you'll need to know a number of interfaces and implementation details in order to use it correctly. The key method to use for walking the directory tree is

```
Files.walkFileTree(Path startingDir, FileVisitor<? super Path> visitor);
```

Providing the `startingDir` is easy enough, but in order to provide an implementation of the `FileVisitor` interface (the tricky-looking `FileVisitor<? super Path> visitor` parameter) it gets a bit trickier, because the `FileVisitor` interface forces you to implement at least the following five methods (where `T` is typically `Path`):

- `FileVisitResult preVisitDirectory(T dir)`
- `FileVisitResult preVisitDirectoryFailed(T dir, IOException exc)`
- `FileVisitResult visitFile(T file, BasicFileAttributes attrs)`
- `FileVisitResult visitFileFailed(T file, IOException exc)`
- `FileVisitResult postVisitDirectory(T dir, IOException exc)`

Looks like a good deal of work, right? Luckily, the Java 7 API designers have supplied a default implementation, the SimpleFileVisitor<T> class.

We'll extend and alter the behavior of listing 2.2, which listed the .properties files in the C:\workspace\java7developer directory. The following listing lists .java source files from all of the directories that sit both in and underneath C:\workspace\java7developer\src. This listing demonstrates the use of the Files.walkFileTree method with the default SimpleFileVisitor implementation, enhanced with a specific implementation of the visitFile method.

Listing 2.3 Listing Java source code in subdirectories

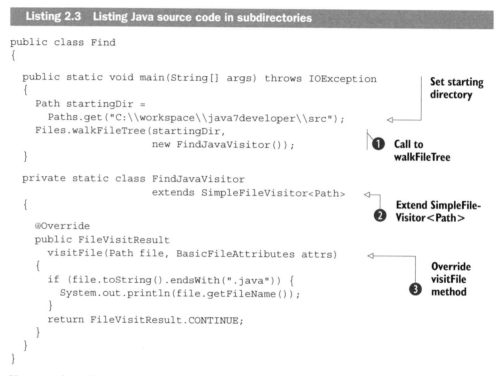

```
public class Find
{
    public static void main(String[] args) throws IOException    ⎫ Set starting
    {                                                             ⎭ directory
        Path startingDir =
            Paths.get("C:\\workspace\\java7developer\\src");  ◄──┘
        Files.walkFileTree(startingDir,
                    new FindJavaVisitor());        ❶ Call to
    }                                                 walkFileTree

    private static class FindJavaVisitor
                    extends SimpleFileVisitor<Path>  ◄──┐ Extend SimpleFile-
    {                                                ❷ Visitor<Path>
        @Override
        public FileVisitResult
            visitFile(Path file, BasicFileAttributes attrs)  ◄──┐
        {                                                           Override
            if (file.toString().endsWith(".java")) {             ❸ visitFile
                System.out.println(file.getFileName());             method
            }
            return FileVisitResult.CONTINUE;
        }
    }
}
```

You start by calling the Files.walkFileTree method ❶. The key point to take in here is that you're passing in FindJavaVisitor, which extends the default SimpleFileVisitor implementation ❷. You want SimpleFileVisitor to do most of the work for you, traversing the directories, and so on. The only code you have to write is when you override the visitFile(Path, BasicFileAttributes) method ❸, in which we you write simple Java to see if a file ends with .java and to echo it to stdout if it does.[8]

Other use cases could be to recursively move, copy, delete, or otherwise modify files. In most cases, you'll only need to extend SimpleFileVisitor, but the flexibility exists in the API if you want to implement your own complete FileVisitor.

---

[8] You'll learn about BasicFileAttributes in section 2.4, so just file that one away for now.

NOTE The `walkFileTree` method doesn't automatically follow symbolic links, making operations like recursion safer. If you do need to follow symbolic links, you'll need to detect that attribute (as discussed in section 2.4.3) and act on it accordingly.

Now that you're comfortable with paths and directory trees, it's time to move on from the manipulation of locations to performing operations on the actual filesystem itself, using the new `Files` class and friends.

2.4 *Filesystem I/O with NIO.2*

Support for performing operations on the filesystem, such as moving files, changing file attributes, and working with file contents, has been improved under NIO.2. The main class that provides this support is the `Files` class.

`Files` is described in further detail in table 2.2, along with one other important class you'll meet in this section (`WatchService`).

Table 2.2 Key foundation classes for working with files

Class	Description
Files	The major utility class that contains all of the methods you need to easily copy, move, delete, or otherwise manipulate files.
WatchService	The core class used to keep an eye on files, directories, and whether or not they have changed.

In this section, you'll learn about performing tasks with files and the filesystem:

- Creating and deleting files
- Moving, copying, renaming, and deleting files
- Reading and writing file attributes
- Reading from files and writing to them
- Dealing with symbolic links
- Using the `WatchService` for file change notification
- Using `SeekableByteChannel`, an enhanced byte channel where you can specify position and size

The scale of these changes may seem daunting, but the API is well designed with lots of helper methods that hide the layers of abstraction and allow you to work with filesystems quickly and easily.

WARNING Although the NIO.2 APIs offer much improved support for atomic operations, it still pays to code defensively when dealing with a filesystem. Even when an operation is midflight, it's all too easy for a network share to fail, a cup of coffee to be spilled on a server, or (in the case of an infamous incident by one of the authors) the `shutdown now` command to be executed on the wrong UNIX box. The API does throw `RuntimeException` from some of its methods, but some exceptional cases can be mitigated by helper methods such as `Files.exists(Path)`.

A great way to learn any new API is to read and write code in it. Let's move on to some real-world use cases, starting with the basic creation and deletion of files.

2.4.1   *Creating and deleting files*

By using the simple helper methods in the `Files` class, you can create files and delete them easily as well. Of course, creating and deleting isn't always as simple as the default case, so let's work through a few of the extra options, such as setting the read/write/execute security permissions on a newly created file.

> **TIP**   If you're running the code snippets in this section, replace the actual paths with ones that match your filesystem!

The following code snippet shows basic file creation, using the `Files.create-File(Path target)` method. Assuming your OS has a directory at D:\\Backup, then a file MyStuff.txt will be created there.

```
Path target = Paths.get("D:\\Backup\\MyStuff.txt");
Path file = Files.createFile(target);
```

More often than not, you'll want to specify some `FileAttributes` on that file for security purposes as well to define whether the file is being created for the purpose of reading, writing, executing, or some combination of the three. As this is filesystem-dependent, you need to utilize a filesystem-specific file permissions class.

An example of setting read/write permissions for the owner, users in the owners group, and all users in a POSIX filesystem[9] is as follows. Basically this means allowing all users to read from and write to the D:\\Backup\\MyStuff.txt file that's about to be created.

```
Path target = Paths.get("D:\\Backup\\MyStuff.txt");
Set<PosixFilePermission> perms =
    PosixFilePermissions.fromString("rw-rw-rw-");
FileAttribute<Set<PosixFilePermission>> attr =
    PosixFilePermissions.asFileAttribute(perms);
Files.createFile(target, attr);
```

The `java.nio.file.attribute` package contains a list of provided `*FilePermission` classes. File attribute support is also covered in further detail in section 2.4.3.

> **WARNING**   When creating files with specific permissions, be aware of any umask restrictions or restrictive permissions that the parent directory of that file is enforcing. For example, you may find that even though you specify `rw-rw-rw` for your new file, it's actually created as `rw-r--r--` due to directory masking.

---

[9]   Portable Operating System Interface (for UNIX)—A base standard that many OSs support.

Deleting a file is a bit simpler and is performed by the `Files.delete(Path)` method. The following snippet deletes the file at D:\\Backup\\MyStuff.txt that you just created. Of course, the user that your Java process is running under will need to have permission to do this!

```
Path target = Paths.get("D:\\Backup\\MyStuff.txt");
Files.delete(target);
```

Next up, you'll learn to copy and move files in a filesystem.

2.4.2 *Copying and moving files*

By using the simple helper methods in the `Files` class, you can perform your copy and move operations with ease.

The following code snippet showcases a basic copy, using the `Files.copy(Path source, Path target)` method.

```
Path source = Paths.get("C:\\My Documents\\Stuff.txt");
Path target = Paths.get("D:\\Backup\\MyStuff.txt");
Files.copy(source, target);
```

More often than not, you'll want to specify options with the copy operation. The next example uses an overwrite (replace existing) option.

```
import static java.nio.file.StandardCopyOption.*;

Path source = Paths.get("C:\\My Documents\\Stuff.txt");
Path target = Paths.get("D:\\Backup\\MyStuff.txt");
Files.copy(source, target, REPLACE_EXISTING);
```

Other copy options include `COPY_ATTRIBUTES` (copies over the file attributes) and `ATOMIC_MOVE` (ensures that both sides of a move operation succeed or the operation gets rolled back).

The move operation is very similar to the copy operation and is executed using the atomic `Files.move(Path source, Path target)` method. Again, you typically want copy options to go with that move, so you can use the `Files.move(Path source, Path target, CopyOptions...)` method (note the use of varargs).

In this case, we want to keep the attributes of the source file when we move it, as well as overwrite the target file (if it exists).

```
import static java.nio.file.StandardCopyOption.*;

Path source = Paths.get("C:\\My Documents\\Stuff.txt");
Path target = Paths.get("D:\\Backup\\MyStuff.txt");

Files.move(source, target, REPLACE_EXISTING, COPY_ATTRIBUTES);
```

Now that you can create, delete, copy, and move files, it's time to take a closer look at Java 7's support for file attributes.

2.4.3   *File attributes*

File attributes control *what* can be done to a file by *whom*. The classic *what* permissions include whether you can do one or more of reading from, writing to, or executing a file. The classic *whom* permissions include owner, group, and all.

This section will start by covering the group of basic file attributes, such as when a file was last accessed, whether it's a directory or a symbolic link, and so on. The second part of this section will cover file attribute support for specific filesystems, which is tricky because different filesystems have their own set of attributes and their own interpretation of what those attributes mean.

Let's start with the basic file attribute support.

BASIC FILE ATTRIBUTE SUPPORT

Although there aren't many file attributes that are truly universal, there is a group that most filesystems support. The `BasicFileAttributes` interface defines this common set, but you actually use the `Files` utility class to answer various questions about a file, such as the following:

- What was the last modified time?
- What is its size?
- Is it a symbolic link?
- Is it a directory?

Listing 2.4 demonstrates the methods on the `Files` class for gathering these basic file attributes. The listing prints information about /usr/bin/zip and you should see output similar to the following:

```
/usr/bin/zip
2011-07-20T16:50:18Z
351872
false
false
{lastModifiedTime=2011-07-20T16:50:18Z,
fileKey=(dev=e000002,ino=30871217), isDirectory=false,
lastAccessTime=2011-06-13T23:31:11Z, isOther=false,
isSymbolicLink=false, isRegularFile=true,
creationTime=2011-07-20T16:50:18Z, size=351872}
```

Note that all of the attributes are shown with the call to `Files.readAttributes(Path path, Stringattributes, LinkOption... options)`.

Listing 2.4   Universal file attributes

```
try
{
  Path zip = Paths.get("/usr/bin/zip");                              Get Path
  System.out.println(Files.getLastModifiedTime(zip));
  System.out.println(Files.size(zip));
  System.out.println(Files.isSymbolicLink(zip));                     Print
  System.out.println(Files.isDirectory(zip));                        attributes
```

```
    System.out.println(Files.readAttributes(zip, "*"));
}
catch (IOException ex)
{
    System.out.println("Exception [" + ex.getMessage() + "]");
}
```

Perform
bulk read

There is further common file attribute information that can be gathered from methods on the `Files` class. This includes such information about the owner of the file, whether it's a symbolic link, and more. See the Javadoc for the `Files` class for a full listing of these helper methods.

Java 7 also provides support for viewing and manipulating file attributes across specific filesystems.

SPECIFIC FILE ATTRIBUTE SUPPORT

You've already seen some of Java 7's support with the `FileAttribute` interface and the `PosixFilePermissions` class when you created a file in section 2.4.1. In order to support filesystem-specific file attributes, Java 7 allows filesystem providers to implement the `FileAttributeView` and `BasicFileAttributes` interfaces.

> **WARNING**   We've said this before, but it's worth repeating. Be careful when writing filesystem-specific code. Always ensure that your logic and exception handling covers the case where your code might run on a different filesystem.

Let's look at an example where you want to use Java 7 to ensure that the correct file permissions have been set on a particular file. Figure 2.2 shows a directory listing for the home directory of the user Admin. Note the special .profile hidden file, which has the write permission set for the Admin user (but not anyone else), yet allows all others to read that file.

In the following code listing, you're going to enforce that the file permissions on the .profile file are set correctly, in accordance with figure 2.2. The user (Admin) wishes to allow all users to have permission to read that file, but only Admin can write to it. By using the specific POSIX `PosixFilePermission` and `PosixFileAttributes` classes, you can ensure that the permissions (rw-r–r–) are correct.

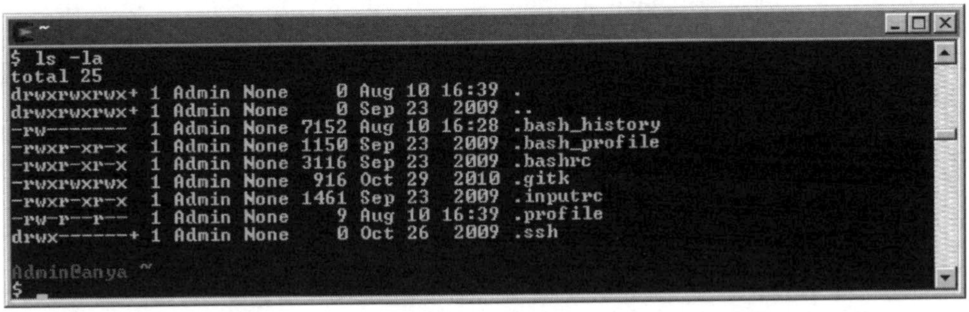

Figure 2.2   Directory listing for the home directory of the Admin user, showing the .profile permissions

Listing 2.5   File attribute support in Java 7

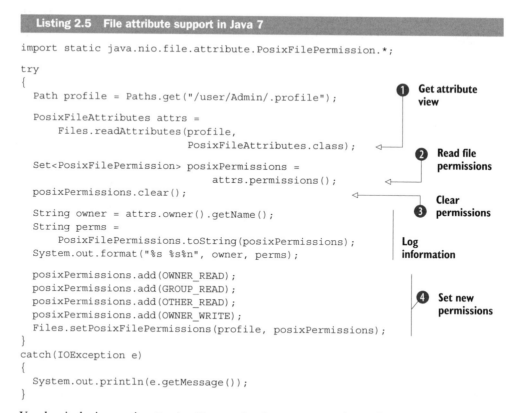

```
import static java.nio.file.attribute.PosixFilePermission.*;

try
{
  Path profile = Paths.get("/user/Admin/.profile");          ❶ Get attribute
                                                                view
  PosixFileAttributes attrs =
      Files.readAttributes(profile,
                           PosixFileAttributes.class);       ❷ Read file
  Set<PosixFilePermission> posixPermissions =                  permissions
                           attrs.permissions();
  posixPermissions.clear();
                                                             ❸ Clear
  String owner = attrs.owner().getName();                      permissions
  String perms =
      PosixFilePermissions.toString(posixPermissions);       Log
  System.out.format("%s %s%n", owner, perms);                information

  posixPermissions.add(OWNER_READ);
  posixPermissions.add(GROUP_READ);
  posixPermissions.add(OTHER_READ);                          ❹ Set new
  posixPermissions.add(OWNER_WRITE);                           permissions
  Files.setPosixFilePermissions(profile, posixPermissions);
}
catch(IOException e)
{
  System.out.println(e.getMessage());
}
```

You begin by importing `PosixFilePermission` constants (as well as other imports not shown), then get the `Path` for the .profile file. The `Files` class has a helpful utility method that allows you to read the filesystem-specific attributes, which in this case is `PosixFileAttributes` ❶. You can then gain access to the `PosixFilePermission` ❷. After clearing the existing permissions ❸, you then add the new permissions to the file, again via a helpful `Files` utility method ❹.

You may have noticed that the `PosixFilePermission` is an `enum` and therefore doesn't implement the `FileAttributeView` interface. So why is there no `PosixFile-AttributeView` implementation being used? Well, actually there is! But the `Files` helper class is hiding this abstraction from you by allowing you to read the file attributes directly (via the `readAttributes` method) and to set the permissions directly (via the `setPosixFilePermissions` method).

Apart from basic attributes, Java 7 also has an extensible system for supporting special OS features. Unfortunately, we can't cover every special case in this chapter, but we'll take you through one example of this extendible system—Java 7's symbolic link support.

SYMBOLIC LINKS

A symbolic link can be thought of as a pointer to another file or directory, and in most cases they're treated transparently. For example, changing directory to a symbolic link will put you in the directory that the symbolic link is pointing to. But when you're writing software, such as a backup utility or deployment script, you need to be able to make sensible decisions about whether you should follow (or not) a symbolic link, and NIO.2 allows for this.

Let's reuse an example from section 2.2.3. You're on a *nix OS, and you're looking for information about a log file called log1.txt under the /usr/logs directory. But that /usr/logs directory is in fact a symbolic link (a pointer) to the /application/logs directory, which is the *real* location of the log file.

Symbolic links are utilized in a host of operating systems, including (but not limited to) UNIX, Linux, Windows 7, and Mac OS X. Java 7's support for symbolic links follows the semantics of the UNIX operating system implementation.

The following listing checks to see if the Path for a Java installation in /opt/platform is a symbolic link before trying to read its basic file attributes; we want to read the attributes for the *real* file location.

Listing 2.6 Exploring symbolic links

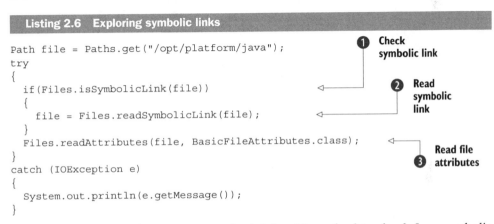

```
Path file = Paths.get("/opt/platform/java");     ❶ Check
try                                                 symbolic link
{
  if(Files.isSymbolicLink(file))                  ❷ Read
  {                                                   symbolic
    file = Files.readSymbolicLink(file);            link
  }
  Files.readAttributes(file, BasicFileAttributes.class);   ❸ Read file
}                                                     attributes
catch (IOException e)
{
  System.out.println(e.getMessage());
}
```

The Files class provides an isSymbolicLink(Path) method to check for a symbolic link ❶. It has a helper method to return the real Path that's the target of the symbolic link ❷, so you can then read the correct file attributes ❸.

By default, symbolic links are followed in the NIO.2 API. In order to not follow a symbolic link, you need to apply LinkOption.NOFOLLOW_LINKS. This can be applied with several method calls. If you wanted to read the basic file attributes of the symbolic link itself, you'd call

```
Files.readAttributes(target,
                BasicFileAttributes.class,
                LinkOption.NOFOLLOW_LINKS);
```

Symbolic links are the most popular example of specific filesystem support in Java 7, and the API design allows for future filesystem-specific features to be added (such as that super-secret quantum filesystem you've been working on).

Now that you've had practice at manipulating files, you're ready to tackle manipulating their contents.

2.4.4 *Reading and writing data quickly*

One of the goals for Java 7 is to provide as many helper methods as possible for reading from files, as well as for writing to them. Of course, these new methods use Path locations, but interoperability with the old stream-based classes in the java.io package is also taken care of. The net result is that you can perform tasks like reading all lines from a file or reading all bytes from a file with a single method invocation.

This section will take you through the process of opening files (with the options that go with that) and through a group of small examples that cover common read/write use cases. Let's begin with the different ways in which you can open a file for processing.

OPENING FILES

Java 7 allows you to directly open files for processing with buffered readers and writers or (for compatibility with older Java I/O code) input and output streams. The following snippet demonstrates how you'd open a file (using the Files.newBufferedReader method) for reading lines in Java 7.

```
Path logFile = Paths.get("/tmp/app.log");
try (BufferedReader reader =
           Files.newBufferedReader(logFile, StandardCharsets.UTF_8)) {
  String line;
  while ((line = reader.readLine()) != null) {
    ...
  }
}
```

Opening a file for writing is just as easy.

```
Path logFile = Paths.get("/tmp/app.log");

try (BufferedWriter writer =
    Files.newBufferedWrite(logFile, StandardCharsets.UTF_8,
                          StandardOpenOption.WRITE)) {
  writer.write("Hello World!");
  ..
}
```

Note the use of the StandardOpenOption.WRITE, which is one of several varargs Open-Option options you can add. This ensures that the file has the correct permissions for writing to. Other commonly used open options include READ and APPEND.

Interoperability with InputStream and OutputStream are provided through special Files.newInputStream(Path, OpenOption...) and Files.newOutputStream(Path, OpenOption...) methods. This nicely bridges the gap between the old I/O based around the java.io package and the new world of file I/O based around the java.nio package.

> **TIP** Don't forget that when you're dealing with a String, you should always know its character encoding. Forgetting to set the character encoding (via the StandardCharsets class, for example, new String(byte[], StandardCharsets.UTF_8)) can lead to unexpected character encoding issues further down the line.

The previous code snippets show fairly typical code for reading from and writing to files that you'd use with Java 6 and older versions today. This is still fairly laborious low-level code, and Java 7 gives you some nice higher-level abstractions that avoid a lot of unnecessary boilerplate code.

SIMPLIFYING READING AND WRITING

The `Files` helper class has a couple of helpful methods that perform the common tasks of reading all of the lines in a file and reading all of the bytes in a file. This means you no longer have to write the boilerplate code of having a `while` loop read byte arrays of data into a buffer. The following snippet shows you how to call the helper methods.

```
Path logFile = Paths.get("/tmp/app.log");
List<String> lines = Files.readAllLines(logFile, StandardCharsets.UTF_8);
byte[] bytes = Files.readAllBytes(logFile);
```

For certain software applications, the question of knowing when to read and when to write comes up, especially with regards to properties files or logs. This is where the new file change notification system can come in handy.

2.4.5 *File change notification*

Java 7 enables you to monitor a file or directory for changes through the `java.nio.file.WatchService` class. This class uses client threads to keep an eye on registered files or directories for changes, and will return an event when a change is detected. This sort of event notification can be useful for security monitoring, refreshing data from a properties file, and many other use cases. It's ideal for replacing the (comparatively poorly performing) polling mechanisms that some applications use today.

In the following listing, the `WatchService` is used to detect any changes to the home directory of the user karianna and to print out that modification event to the console. As with many continuously polling loop designs, it's always worth including a lightweight shutdown mechanism.

Listing 2.7 Using the `WatchService`

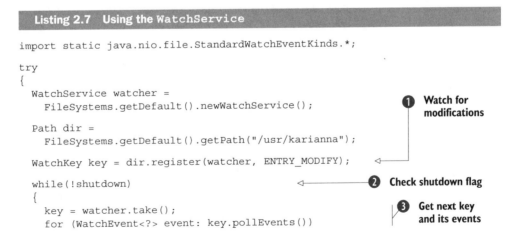

```
import static java.nio.file.StandardWatchEventKinds.*;

try
{
  WatchService watcher =
    FileSystems.getDefault().newWatchService();          ❶ Watch for
                                                             modifications
  Path dir =
    FileSystems.getDefault().getPath("/usr/karianna");

  WatchKey key = dir.register(watcher, ENTRY_MODIFY);

  while(!shutdown)                                        ❷ Check shutdown flag
  {
    key = watcher.take();                                 ❸ Get next key
    for (WatchEvent<?> event: key.pollEvents())             and its events
```

```
      {
        if (event.kind() == ENTRY_MODIFY)                     ◁─────────┐  Check for
        {                                                               ❹  modification
          System.out.println("Home dir changed!");
        }
      }
      key.reset();                                            ◁───────── ❺ Reset watch key
    }
}
catch (IOException | InterruptedException e)
{
  System.out.println(e.getMessage());
}
```

After getting the default `WatchService`, you register a modification watch on the kar-ianna home directory ❶. Then, in an endless loop (until the `shutdown` flag is changed) ❷, the `take()` method on the `WatchService` waits until a `WatchKey` is available. As soon as a `WatchKey` is made available, the code polls that `WatchKey` for Watch-Events ❸. If a `WatchEvent` is found of Kind `ENTRY_MODIFY` ❹, you communicate that fact to the outside world. Lastly, you reset the key ❺ so it's ready for the next event.

There are other kinds of events you can monitor, such as `ENTRY_CREATE`, `ENTRY_DELETE`, and `OVERFLOW` (which can indicate that an event may have been lost or discarded).

Next up, we'll move on to a very important new abstraction API for reading and writing data—the asynchronous I/O—enabling `SeekableByteChannel`.

2.4.6   *SeekableByteChannel*

Java 7 introduces a `SeekableByteChannel` interface, which is designed to be extended by implementations that give developers the ability to change the position and the size of the byte channel. For example, you could have an application server with multiple threads that accesses a byte channel attached to a large log file in order to parse the log for a particular error code.

The `java.nio.channels.SeekableByteChannel` interface has one implementing class in the JDK, `java.nio.channels.FileChannel`. This class gives you the ability to hold the current position of where you are when reading from, or writing to, a file. For example, you might want to write code that reads the last 1000 characters of a log file, or write some price data into a particular place inside a text file.

The following snippet shows how you can use the new seekable aspects of the `FileChannel` to read the last 1000 characters from a log file.

```
Path logFile = Paths.get("c:\\temp.log");
ByteBuffer buffer = ByteBuffer.allocate(1024);
FileChannel channel = FileChannel.open(logFile, StandardOpenOption.READ);
channel.read(buffer, channel.size() - 1000);
```

The new seekable capability of the `FileChannel` class should mean that developers can be far more flexible in dealing with file contents. We expect to see some interesting open source projects come out of this for parallel access to large files, and, with extensions to the interface, perhaps continuous streams of network data as well.

The next major change in the NIO.2 API is the introduction of asynchronous I/O, which gives you the ability to use multiple underlying threads when reading and writing files, sockets, and channels.

2.5 Asynchronous I/O operations

Another major new feature of NIO.2 is asynchronous capabilities for both socket- and file-based I/O. Asynchronous I/O is simply a type of I/O processing that allows other activity to take place before the reading and writing has finished. In practical terms, it allows you to take advantage of the latest hardware and software advances, such as multicore CPUs and OS socket- and file-handling support. Asynchronous I/O is a vital performance and scalability feature for any language that wishes to remain relevant on the server side and in the systems programming space. We believe that this will be one of the major factors in extending Java's lifespan as an important server-side language.

Consider the simple use case of writing 100 GB of data to a filesystem or network socket. With previous versions of Java, you'd have to manually write multithreaded code (using `java.util.concurrent` constructs) in order to write to multiple areas of that file or socket at the same time. Nor was it easily possible to read from more than one part of a file at a time. Again, unless you had some clever manual code, your main thread was blocked when utilizing I/O, which meant having to wait for potentially long I/O operations to complete before you could continue with your main work.

> **TIP** If you haven't worked with NIO channels in a while, this is probably a good time to refresh your knowledge before continuing with this section. There is a lack of modern titles in this area, so even though it's slightly out of date, we recommend *Java NIO* by Ron Hitchens (O'Reilly, 2002) as a good place to start.

Java 7 has three new asynchronous channels that you can work with:

- `AsynchronousFileChannel`—For file I/O
- `AsynchronousSocketChannel`—For socket I/O, supports timeouts
- `AsynchronousServerSocketChannel`—For asynchronous sockets accepting connections

There are two main paradigms (styles) for utilizing the new asynchronous I/O APIs: the *Future* paradigm and the *Callback* paradigm. Interestingly, these new asynchronous APIs use some of the modern concurrency techniques discussed in chapter 4, so you're really getting a bit of a sneak preview!

We'll begin with the Future style of asynchronous file access. Hopefully it's a concurrency technique you've used before, but if not, don't worry. The following section covers it in enough detail for a developer new to this topic to understand it.

2.5.1 *Future style*

Future style is a term used by those who designed the NIO.2 APIs—it indicates the use of the `java.util.concurrent.Future` interface. You'll typically want a Future style of asynchronous processing if you want your main thread of control to initiate the I/O and then poll for the results of that I/O.

The Future style uses the existing `java.util.concurrent` technique of declaring a `Future` that will hold the result of your asynchronous operation. Crucially, this means that your current thread isn't halted by the potentially slow operation of performing I/O. Instead, a separate thread initiates the I/O operation and returns a result when it's done. In the meantime, your main thread can continue to perform other tasks as needed. Once those other tasks are completed, your main thread will then wait until the I/O operation is completed before continuing. Figure 2.3 illustrates this process being used to read a large file. (Listing 2.8 shows the code used in such a situation.)

Typically you'll use the `Future get()` method (with or without a timeout parameter) to retrieve the result when that asynchronous I/O activity has completed. Let's say that you want to read 100,000 bytes from a file on disk (a relatively slow operation) as part of some overall activity. With previous versions of Java, you had to wait until the read had completed (unless you implemented a thread pool and worker threads using `java.util.concurrent` building blocks, which is a nontrivial task). With Java 7 you can continue to perform useful work in your main thread, as the following listing demonstrates.

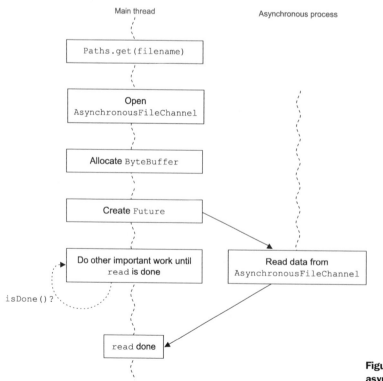

Figure 2.3   Future style asynchronous read

Listing 2.8 Asynchronous I/O—Future style

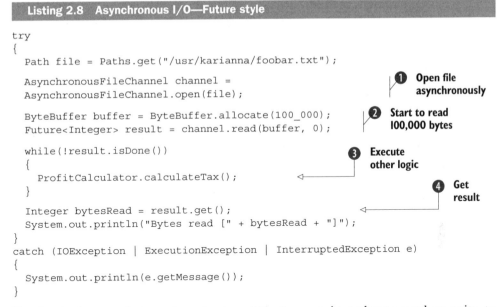

```
try
{
  Path file = Paths.get("/usr/karianna/foobar.txt");

  AsynchronousFileChannel channel =
  AsynchronousFileChannel.open(file);

  ByteBuffer buffer = ByteBuffer.allocate(100_000);
  Future<Integer> result = channel.read(buffer, 0);

  while(!result.isDone())
  {
    ProfitCalculator.calculateTax();
  }

  Integer bytesRead = result.get();
  System.out.println("Bytes read [" + bytesRead + "]");
}
catch (IOException | ExecutionException | InterruptedException e)
{
  System.out.println(e.getMessage());
}
```

❶ Open file asynchronously

❷ Start to read 100,000 bytes

❸ Execute other logic

❹ Get result

You begin by opening an `AsynchronousFileChannel` in order to read or write to foobar.txt with a background thread ❶. The next step is for the I/O to proceed concurrently with the thread that initiated it. This concurrent I/O process is used automatically, because you're using an `AsynchronousFileChannel`, utilizing a `Future` to hold the result of that read ❷. While the read is happening, your main thread continues to perform useful work (such as calculating tax) ❸. Finally, when the useful work is complete, you check the result of the read ❹.

It's important to notice that we artificially made sure the result would be finished (by using `isDone()`). Normally the result would either be finished (and your main thread would continue), or it would wait until the background I/O is complete.

You may be wondering how this works behind the scenes. In short, the API/JVM provides thread pools and channel groups to perform this work. Alternatively, you can supply and configure your own. The details take some explaining, but they're well covered in the official documentation, so we'll use the text directly from the Javadoc for `AsynchronousFileChannel`:

> An `AsynchronousFileChannel` is associated with a thread pool to which tasks are submitted to handle I/O events and dispatch to completion handlers (that consume the results of I/O operations on the channel). The completion handler for an I/O operation initiated on a channel is guaranteed to be invoked by one of the threads in the thread pool.

> When an `AsynchronousFileChannel` is created without specifying a thread pool then the channel is associated with a system-dependent and default thread pool (that may be shared with other channels). The default thread pool is configured by the system properties defined by the `AsynchronousChannelGroup` class.

There is also an alternative technique known as *Callback*. Some developers find the Callback style more comfortable to use, because it's similar to event handling techniques they have seen before in Swing, messaging, and other Java APIs.

2.5.2   *Callback style*

In contrast to the Future style, the Callback style uses a technique similar to event handlers that you may be familiar with from Swing UI programming. The basic idea is that the main thread will send a scout (the `CompletionHandler`) to the separate thread performing the I/O operation. This scout will get the result of the I/O operation, which triggers its own `completed` or `failed` method (which you override) and returns back to the main thread.

This style is typically used when you want to immediately act upon the success or failure of an asynchronous event. For example, if you were reading financial data that was mandatory for a profit-calculating business process, and that read failed, you'd immediately want to execute rollback or exception handling.

More formally, the `java.nio.channels.CompletionHandler<V, A>` interface (where `V` is the result type and `A` is the attached object you're getting the result from) is invoked when the asynchronous I/O activity has completed. Its `completed(V, A)` and `failed(V, A)` methods must then be implemented so that your program knows how to behave when the asynchronous I/O operation has completed successfully or failed for some reason. Figure 2.4 illustrates this process. (Listing 2.9 shows code that implements this.)

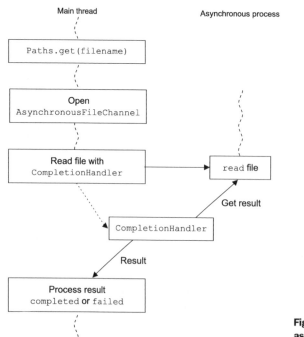

Figure 2.4   Callback style asynchronous read

In the following example, you once more read 100,000 bytes from foobar.txt, using `CompletionHandler<Integer, ByteBuffer>` to declare your success or failure.

Listing 2.9 Asynchronous I/O—Callback style

```
try
{
  Path file = Paths.get("/usr/karianna/foobar.txt");
  AsynchronousFileChannel channel =                         Open
    AsynchronousFileChannel.open(file);                     asynchronous file

  ByteBuffer buffer = ByteBuffer.allocate(100_000);

  channel.read(buffer, 0, buffer,                           Read from
    new CompletionHandler<Integer, ByteBuffer>()            channel
  {
    public void completed(Integer result,
                          ByteBuffer attachment)            Complete reading
    {                                                       callback
      System.out.println("Bytes read [" + result + "]");
    }

    public void failed(Throwable exception, ByteBuffer attachment)
    {
      System.out.println(exception.getMessage());
    }
  });
}
catch (IOException e)
{
  System.out.println(e.getMessage());
}
```

The two code listings in this section were file-based, but the Future and Callback styles of asynchronous access can also be applied to `AsynchronousServerSocketChannel` and `AsynchronousSocketChannel`. This allows developers writing applications that deal with network sockets, such as voice over IP, to write better-performing clients and servers.

Next up is a series of small changes that unify sockets and channels, enabling you to have a single point of contact in the API to manage your socket and channel interaction.

2.6 *Tidying up Socket-Channel functionality*

Software applications need greater access to networks than ever before. It seems that before too long, even your most common household item will be networked in some way (if it isn't already!). With older versions of Java, the programming constructs of a `Socket` and a `Channel` were not married up very well—it was awkward to fit the two together. Java 7 makes life a little easier for developers working with channels and sockets by introducing the concept of a `NetworkChannel`, which binds a `Socket` and a `Channel` together.

Writing low-level networking code is a reasonably specialized area. If you're not already working in this area, this section is definitely optional reading! But if you do work in this area, this section will give you a brief overview of the new features.

We'll begin by refreshing your memory of what roles channels and sockets play in Java with their definitions from the Javadoc:

> `java.nio.channels` package
>
> Defines channels, which represent connections to entities that are capable of performing I/O operations, such as files and sockets; defines selectors, for multiplexed, non-blocking I/O operations.

> `java.net.Socket` class
>
> This class implements client sockets (also called just "sockets"). A socket is an endpoint for communication between two machines.

In older versions of Java, you'd indeed try to tie a channel to an implementation of `Socket` in order to perform some sort of I/O operation, such as writing data to a TCP port. But there were gaps between tying up a `Channel` and a `Socket`:

- In older versions of Java, you had to mix channel and socket APIs in order to manipulate socket options and to perform binds on sockets.
- In older versions of Java, you couldn't make use of platform-specific socket behavior.

Let's explore two areas of this "tidying up" effort with the new interface, `Network-Channel`, and its subinterface, the `MulticastChannel`.

2.6.1   *NetworkChannel*

The new `java.nio.channels.NetworkChannel` interface represents a mapping of a channel to a network socket. It defines a group of useful methods, such as methods to see what socket options are available and to set new socket options on that channel. The following listing highlights those utility methods by echoing out the supported options of the internet socket address at port 3080, setting an IP Terms of Service, and identifying the `SO_KEEPALIVE` option on that socket channel.

Listing 2.10 `NetworkChannel` options

```
SelectorProvider provider = SelectorProvider.provider();
try
{
  NetworkChannel socketChannel =
                      provider.openSocketChannel();        Bind
  SocketAddress address = new InetSocketAddress(3080);     NetworkChannel
  socketChannel = socketChannel.bind(address);             to port 3080

  Set<SocketOption<?>> socketOptions =                      Check socket
    socketChannel.supportedOptions();                       options
  System.out.println(socketOptions.toString());

  socketChannel.setOption(StandardSocketOptions.IP_TOS,    Set ToS
                      3);                                   socket option
  Boolean keepAlive =
```

```
        socketChannel.getOption(StandardSocketOptions.SO_KEEPALIVE);
  ..
  ..
}
catch (IOException e)
{
    System.out.println(e.getMessage());
}
```

Get SO_KEEPALIVE option

An extra addition enabled by this new `NetworkChannel` functionality is multicast operations.

2.6.2 MulticastChannel

The ability to multicast is a common use case for peer-to-peer networking applications, such as BitTorrent. With previous versions of Java, you could cobble together a multicast implementation, but Java didn't have a nice abstraction in its API set. Java 7 introduces the new `MulticastChannel` interface to address this.

The term *multicast* refers to one-to-many communications over a network, often with reference to the Internet Protocol (IP). The basic premise is that you send one packet out

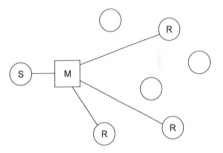

Figure 2.5　Multicast example

to a multicast group address and have the network replicate that packet as often as needed for all receivers who have registered with that multicast group to get a copy. Figure 2.5 illustrates this behavior.

In order to support the new `NetworkChannels` joining multicast groups, there is a new `java.nio.channels.MulticastChannel` interface with a default implementing class called `DatagramChannel`. This means you can easily send to and receive from multicast groups.

In the following hypothetical example, you send and receive system status messages to and from a multicast group by joining that group at the IP address of 180.90.4.12.

Listing 2.11　`NetworkChannel` options

```
try
{
  NetworkInterface networkInterface =
  NetworkInterface.getByName("net1");

  DatagramChannel dc =
  DatagramChannel.open(StandardProtocolFamily.INET);

  dc.setOption(StandardSocketOptions.SO_REUSEADDR,
              true);
  dc.bind(new InetSocketAddress(8080));
  dc.setOption(StandardSocketOptions.IP_MULTICAST_IF,
              networkInterface);
```

Select network interface

Open DatagramChannel

Set channel to multicast

```
    InetAddress group =
                InetAddress.getByName("180.90.4.12");
    MembershipKey key = dc.join(group, networkInterface);
}
catch (IOException e)
{
    System.out.println(e.getMessage());
}
```

Join multicast group

That completes our initial investigation of the new NIO.2 APIs; we hope you've enjoyed the whirlwind tour!

2.7   *Summary*

Hardware and software I/O is advancing rapidly, and Java 7 is well-placed to take maximum advantage of the new capabilities with the new APIs introduced as part of NIO.2. The new libraries in Java 7 allow you to manipulate locations (Path) and perform operations on the filesystem, such as manipulating files, directories, symbolic links, and more. In particular, navigating through filesystems with full support for platform-specific behavior is now a breeze, and large directory structures can now be dealt with.

NIO.2 has been focused on giving you one-stop methods for performing tasks that would normally have taken large amounts of code to solve. In particular, the new Files utility class is full of helper methods that make writing file I/O code a good deal faster and simpler than the old java.io.File based I/O.

Asynchronous I/O is a powerful new feature for dealing with large files without drastically reducing performance. It's also useful for applications that have heavy traffic on their network sockets and channels.

NIO.2 also eats Java 7's own dog food, with features from Project Coin (chapter 1) retrofitted to it. This makes dealing with I/O much safer in Java 7 than previously, as well as allowing you to write less verbose code.

Now it's time to step up a gear and challenge the brain muscles with a look at some advanced modern Java in part 2 of this book, including dependency injection, modern concurrency, and tuning a Java-based software system. We suggest you grab a coffee in your favorite Duke mug,[10] and jump in when you're ready!

---

[10] We mentioned it earlier, but didn't explain: Duke is Java's mascot! http://kenai.com/projects/duke/pages/Home

Part 2

Vital techniques

This part of the book (chapters 3 to 6) is all about exploring vital programming knowledge and techniques with Java.

We'll start with a chapter on Dependency Injection, a common technique used to decouple code and increase testability and comprehension. As well as explaining the basics of Dependency Injection, we'll also cover how it evolved and discuss how a best practice turned into a design pattern and from there into a framework (and even a Java standard).

Next, we'll get to grips with the multicore CPU revolution occurring in hardware. The well-grounded Java developer needs to be aware of Java's concurrency capabilities, and how to use them to get the most out of modern processors. Despite Java having strong support for concurrent programming since 2006 (Java 5), it's an area that has been poorly understood and underutilized, so we'll dedicate a chapter to this material.

You'll learn about the Java Memory Model and how threading and concurrency is implemented in that model. Once you have some theory under your belt, we'll guide you through the features of the `java.util.concurrent` package (and beyond) to start building your practical grounding in Java concurrency.

Next, we'll turn to classloading. Many Java developers don't have a good understanding of how the JVM actually loads, links, and verifies classes. This leads to frustration and wasted time when an "incorrect" version of some class is executed due to some sort of classloader conflict.

We'll also cover Java 7's `MethodHandle`, `MethodType`, and `invokedynamic`, giving developers who write code using Reflection a faster and safer way of performing the same tasks.

Being able to dive into the internals of a Java class file and the bytecode it contains is a powerful debugging skill. We'll show you how to use `javap` to navigate and understand the meaning of bytecode.

Performance tuning is often seen as an art, as opposed to a science, and tracking down and fixing performance issues often takes development teams extraordinary time and effort. In chapter 6, the final chapter in this part, we'll teach you that you should measure, not guess, and that "tuning by folklore" is wrong. We'll show you a scientific approach that quickly gets you to the heart of your performance issues.

In particular, we focus on garbage collection (GC) and the just-in-time (JIT) compiler, two major parts of the JVM that affect performance. Among other performance knowledge, you'll learn how to read GC logs and use the free Java VisualVM (jvisualvm) tool to analyze memory usage.

By the end of part 2, you'll no longer be a developer who only thinks of the source code sitting in your IDE. You'll know how Java and the JVM work under the hood, and you'll be able to take full advantage of what is arguably the most powerful general-purpose VM the planet has to offer.

Dependency Injection 3

This chapter covers

- Inversion of Control (IoC) and Dependency Injection (DI)
- Why DI is an important technique to master
- How JSR-330 united DI for Java
- Common JSR-330 annotations such as `@Inject`
- Guice 3, the reference implementation (RI) for JSR-330

Dependency Injection (a form of Inversion of Control) is an important programming paradigm that has become part of mainstream Java development since about 2004. In short, DI is a technique in which your object gets its dependencies given to it, as opposed to having to construct them itself. There are many benefits to using DI—it makes your codebase loosely coupled, easier to test, and easier to read.

This chapter begins by cementing your knowledge of DI theory and the benefits that it brings to your codebase. Even if you already work with an IoC/DI framework, there's material in this chapter that will give you a deeper understanding of what DI is truly about. This is especially important if (like many of us) you started working with DI frameworks before you had a real chance to fully explore the reasoning behind them.

You'll learn about JSR-330, the official standard for DI in Java, which will give you the behind-the-scenes understanding of the standard set of DI annotations for Java. Following on from that, we'll introduce the Guice 3 framework, which is the reference implementation (RI) for JSR-330 and is also considered by many to be a nice, light-weight approach for DI in Java.

Let's begin with some of the theory and reasoning behind this popular paradigm and why you'll want to master it.

3.1 Inject some knowledge—understanding IoC and DI

So why do you need to know about Inversion of Control (IoC), Dependency Injection (DI), and their underlying principles? There are many possible answers to this question and, indeed, if you were to ask this question at the popular programmers .stackexchange.com Q&A site, you'd get lots of different answers!

You could simply start using the various DI frameworks and learn from examples on the internet, but much like the area of object-relational mapping (ORM) frameworks (such as Hibernate), you'll become a much stronger developer by understanding what goes on under the hood.

We'll begin this section by covering some of the theory behind the two core terms (IoC and DI) and discussing the benefits of using this paradigm. To make the concepts a little more concrete, you'll then be shown the transition of a `HollywoodService` from a version that finds its own dependencies to a version that has its dependencies injected.

Let's begin with IoC, a term that often (incorrectly) gets interchanged with DI.

3.1.1 Inversion of Control

When you use a non-IoC programming paradigm, the flow of the program logic is usually controlled by a central piece of functionality. Assuming a fairly decent design, this central functionality then calls methods on reusable objects that perform specific functions.

Using IoC, this "central control" design principle is inverted. The caller's code deals with the program's execution order, but the program logic is encapsulated by the called subroutines.

Also known as the *Hollywood Principle*, IoC boils down to the idea that there is another piece of code that has the initial thread of control and will therefore call your code, rather than your code calling it.

> **The Hollywood Principle: "Don't call us, we'll call you"**
> Hollywood agents always call you, as opposed to your calling them! Some of you may have experienced this principle when contacting agents in Hollywood with your "Heroic Java programmer who saves the world" proposal for next summer's blockbuster.

Another way to look at IoC is to think about how the UI for Zork (http://en.wikipedia .org/wiki/Zork), an early text-based video game, would be controlled in its text-based versus a GUI-based version.

With the text-based version, the UI would simply have a blank prompt, waiting for the user to provide input. The user would then enter an action such as "go east" or "run from Grue," and the main application logic then invokes the correct event handler to process the action and return the result. The important point here is that the application logic has control over which event handler to invoke.

With the GUI version of the same game, IoC comes into play. The GUI framework has control over which event handler will be executed; it's no longer the role of the application logic to do so. When the user clicks on an action, such as "go east," the event handler is invoked directly and the application logic can focus on processing the action.

The main control of the program has been *inverted*, moving control away from the application logic to the GUI framework itself.

There are several implementations of IoC, including the Factory patterns, Service Locator pattern, and, of course, Dependency Injection, a term popularized by Martin Fowler in his "Inversion of Control Containers and the Dependency Injection pattern" article.[1]

3.1.2 Dependency Injection

DI is a particular form of IoC, whereby the process of finding your dependencies is outside the direct control of your currently executing code. You can write your own DI mechanism, but most developers use a third-party DI framework with a built-in IoC container, such as Guice.

> **NOTE** An IoC container can be seen as a runtime execution environment. Example containers for Java DI include Guice, Spring, and PicoContainer.

IoC containers can provide useful services, like ensuring that a reusable dependency is configured as a singleton. Some of these services will be explored in section 3.3 when we introduce Guice.

> **TIP** Dependencies can be injected into objects by many means. You can use specialized DI frameworks to do this, but they certainly aren't obligatory! Instantiating and passing objects (dependencies) explicitly to your object can be just as good as injection by a framework.[2]

Like many programming paradigms, it's important to understand *why* DI is used. We've summarized what we consider its major benefits in table 3.1.

---

[1] You can find the article by searching for Dependency Injection at Martin Fowler's site: http:// martinfowler.com/.

[2] Thanks to Thiago Arrais (http://stackoverflow.com/users/17801/thiago-arrais) for this tip!

Table 3.1 Benefits of DI

Benefit	Description	Example
Loose coupling	Your code is no longer tightly bound to creating the dependencies it needs. Combined with the technique of coding to interfaces, it can also mean that your code is no longer tightly bound to specific implementations of a dependency.	Instead of your `HollywoodService` object needing to create its own `SpreadsheetAgentFinder`, it can have it passed in to it. If you're coding to interfaces, this means that the `HollywoodService` can have any type of `AgentFinder` passed to it.
Testability	As an extension to loose coupling, there's a special use case worth mentioning. For the purposes of testing, you can inject a *test double*[3] as a dependency.	You can inject a stub ticket pricing service that always returns the same price, as opposed to using the 'real' pricing service, which is external and not always available.
Greater cohesion	Your code is more focused on performing its task as opposed to dealing with loading and configuring dependencies. A side benefit to this is increased readability.	Your DAO object is focused on executing queries and not on looking up JDBC driver details.
Reusable components	As an extension to loose coupling, your code can be utilized by a wider range of users who can provide their own specific implementations.	An enterprising software developer could sell you a LinkedIn agent finder.
Lighter code	Your code no longer needs to pass dependencies between layers. Dependencies can instead be injected directly at the point they're required.	Instead of passing down the JDBC driver details from a service class, you can directly inject the driver at the DAO where it's really needed.

We find that transforming code into dependency injected code is the best way to really grasp the theory, so let's move on to that next.

3.1.3 *Transitioning to DI*

This section will highlight how code can be transitioned from using no IoC, to using a Factory (or Service Locator) style implementation, to using DI. A key technique behind much of this is coding to interfaces, a practice which allows for potential substitution of objects at runtime.

> **NOTE** This section is aimed toward solidifying your understanding of DI. Some boilerplate code has therefore been deliberately left out.

Let's say that you've inherited a small project that will return all friendly agents in Hollywood—the ones who deal with Java developers. The following listing has an

---

[3] Chapter 11 covers Test Doubles in detail

AgentFinder interface with two implementations, a SpreadsheetAgentFinder and WebServiceAgentFinder.

Listing 3.1 AgentFinder interface and its implementing classes

```
public interface AgentFinder
{
  public List<Agent> findAllAgents();
}

public class SpreadsheetAgentFinder implements AgentFinder
{
  @Override
  public List<Agent> findAllAgents(){ ... }          ◁──┐
}                                                        │ Lots of
public class WebServiceAgentFinder implements AgentFinder│ implementation
{                                                        │
  @Override                                              │
  public List<Agent> findAllAgents(){ ... }          ◁──┘
}
```

In order to use the agent finders, the project has a default HollywoodService class that gets a list of agents from a SpreadsheetAgentFinder, filters them on friendliness, and returns that friendly list as shown in the following code listing.

Listing 3.2 HollywoodService, with hard-coded AgentFinder

```
public class HollywoodService                    ❶ Use Spreadsheet-
{                                                   AgentFinder

  public static List<Agent> getFriendlyAgents()
  {
    AgentFinder finder = new SpreadsheetAgentFinder();  ◁──┐ Call interface
    List<Agent> agents = finder.findAllAgents();        ◁──┘ method
    List<Agent> friendlyAgents =
        filterAgents(agents, "Java Developers");
    return friendlyAgents;                          ◁────── Return friendly
  }                                                          agents

  public static List<Agent> filterAgents(List<Agent> agents,
      String agentType)
  {
    List<Agent> filteredAgents = new ArrayList<>();
    for (Agent agent:agents) {
      if (agent.getType().equals("Java Developers")) {
        filteredAgents.add(agent);
      }
    }
    return filteredAgents;
  }
}
```

Look back over the HollywoodService in the listing and notice how the code is locked in to using the SpreadsheetAgentFinder implementation of the AgentFinder ❶.

This type of implementation lock-in was a problem for many Java developers. And as with many common problems, patterns evolved to resolve the problem. To begin with, many developers used variations on the Factory and Service Locator patterns, all of which were a type of IoC.

HOLLYWOOD SERVICE WITH FACTORY AND/OR SERVICE LOCATOR PATTERNS

One of (or a combination of) the Abstract Factory, Factory Method, or Service Locator patterns was commonly used to resolve the issue of being locked in to one dependency.

> **NOTE**   The Factory Method and Abstract Factory patterns are discussed in *Design Patterns: Elements of Reusable Object-Oriented Software*, by Erich Gamma, Richard Helm, Ralph Johnson, and John Vlissides (Addison-Wesley Professional, 1994). The Service Locator pattern is discussed in *Core J2EE Patterns: Best Practices and Design Strategies*, second edition, by Deepak Alur, John Crupi, and Dan Malks (Prentice Hall, 2003).

The following code listing is a version of the `HollywoodService` class utilizing an `AgentFinderFactory` in order to dynamically pick which `AgentFinder` to use.

Listing 3.3   `HollywoodService`, with factory lookup for `AgentFinder`

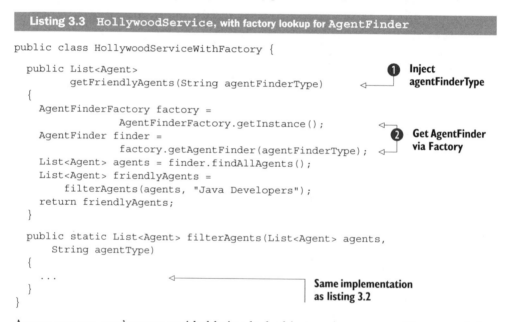

```
public class HollywoodServiceWithFactory {

  public List<Agent>
        getFriendlyAgents(String agentFinderType)          ❶ Inject
  {                                                           agentFinderType
    AgentFinderFactory factory =
               AgentFinderFactory.getInstance();
    AgentFinder finder =                                    ❷ Get AgentFinder
               factory.getAgentFinder(agentFinderType);       via Factory
    List<Agent> agents = finder.findAllAgents();
    List<Agent> friendlyAgents =
        filterAgents(agents, "Java Developers");
    return friendlyAgents;
  }

  public static List<Agent> filterAgents(List<Agent> agents,
      String agentType)
  {
    ...                                                     Same implementation
  }                                                         as listing 3.2
}
```

As you can see, you've now avoided being locked in to using one specific `AgentFinder` implementation. You inject the `agentFinderType` ❶, then ask the `AgentFinderFactory` to get an `AgentFinder` based on that type ❷.

This is getting pretty close to DI, but you still have two issues:

- The code is injecting a lookup reference (`agentFinderType`) as opposed to the real implementation of the `AgentFinder` object.
- The `getFriendlyAgents` method still contains code to find its dependency, which ideally isn't its core concern.

As developers moved toward writing cleaner code, the technique of DI became more widely used, often replacing Factory and Service Locator pattern implementations.

HOLLYWOODSERVICE WITH DI

You can probably already guess what your next logical refactoring will be! The next step is to directly supply the `getFriendlyAgents` method with the `AgentFinder` it needs. The following listing demonstrates this.

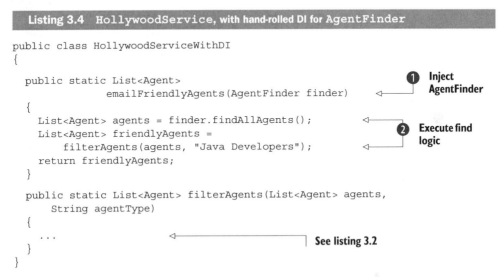

Listing 3.4 `HollywoodService`, with hand-rolled DI for `AgentFinder`

```
public class HollywoodServiceWithDI
{

  public static List<Agent>                                ❶ Inject
              emailFriendlyAgents(AgentFinder finder)         AgentFinder
  {
    List<Agent> agents = finder.findAllAgents();           ❷ Execute find
    List<Agent> friendlyAgents =                             logic
        filterAgents(agents, "Java Developers");
    return friendlyAgents;
  }

  public static List<Agent> filterAgents(List<Agent> agents,
      String agentType)
  {
    ...                                    See listing 3.2
  }
}
```

Now you effectively have a hand-coded DI solution—the `AgentFinder` is injected into the `getFriendlyAgents` method ❶. You can already see how clean the `getFriendly-Agents` method has become, focusing purely on the business logic ❷.

But there is still a major headache remaining for a developer hand-rolling their own DI in this manner. The issue of how to configure which implementation of `AgentFinder` you want to use still remains—the work that the `AgentFinderFactory` was performing has to be done *somewhere*.

That's where a DI framework with an IoC container can really help out. As a basic analogy, the DI framework is a runtime wrapper around your code, injecting the dependencies that you need, when you need them.

DI frameworks have the advantage that they can do this at just about any point in the code where you need a dependency. The framework is able to do this because it has an IoC container that holds the dependencies ready for your code to use at runtime.

Let's look at what the `HollywoodService` might look like when using a standard JSR-330 annotation that any of the compliant frameworks can use.

HOLLYWOODSERVICE WITH JSR-330 DI

Let's look at a final code example where we want a framework to perform the DI for us. In this case, the DI framework injects the dependency directly into the `getFriendly-Agents` method using the standard JSR-330 `@Inject` annotation, as the following listing demonstrates.

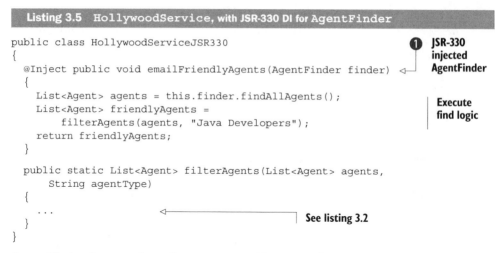

Listing 3.5 `HollywoodService`, with **JSR-330 DI** for `AgentFinder`

```
public class HollywoodServiceJSR330
{
  @Inject public void emailFriendlyAgents(AgentFinder finder)
  {
    List<Agent> agents = this.finder.findAllAgents();
    List<Agent> friendlyAgents =
        filterAgents(agents, "Java Developers");
    return friendlyAgents;
  }

  public static List<Agent> filterAgents(List<Agent> agents,
      String agentType)
  {
    ...
  }
}
```

❶ JSR-330
injected
AgentFinder

**Execute
find logic**

See listing 3.2

A specific implementation of `AgentFinder` (for example, `WebServiceAgentFinder`) is now injected at runtime by the DI framework that supports the JSR-330 `@Inject` annotation **❶**.

> **TIP** Although JSR-330 annotations allow you to inject dependencies for a method, it's typically only done for constructors or setters. This convention is discussed further in the next section.

Let's look back at the some of the benefits of DI again, with reference to the `Hollywood-ServiceJSR330` class in listing 3.5:

- Loose coupling—The `HollywoodService` is no longer dependent on a specific type of `AgentFinder` to perform its work.
- Testability—To test the `HollywoodService` class, you could inject a basic Java class (such as `POJOAgentFinder`) that returns a fixed number of agents (this is known as a stub class in test-driven development terminology). This is perfect for unit testing, as you won't need a web service, spreadsheet, or other third-party implementation.
- Greater cohesion—Your code is no longer dealing with factories and their associated lookups; it executes only the business logic.
- Reusable components—Imagine how easy it would be for another developer using your API to now inject whichever specific implementation of `AgentFinder` they need, such as a `JDBCAgentFinder`.
- Lighter code—The code in the `HollywoodServiceJSR330` class has been reduced significantly from its `HollywoodService` beginnings.

Using DI has become an increasingly standard practice for the well-grounded Java developer, and several popular containers provide excellent DI capabilities. But in the not too distant past, the various DI frameworks all had differing standards for how you should configure your code to take advantage of their IoC containers. Even if the various frameworks had followed a similar configuration style (for example, XML or Java annotations) there was still the question of what the common annotations or configuration would be.

The new standardized approach to DI for Java (JSR-330) solves this issue. It also nicely sums up the core capabilities that most Java-based DI frameworks implement. We'll therefore explore this standardized approach in some depth, as it gives a nice solid grounding on the under-the-hood workings of a DI framework, such as Guice.

3.2 Standardized DI in Java

Since 2004 there have been several widely used IoC containers for the purposes of DI (Guice, Spring, and PicoContainer to name a few). Up until recently, all of the implementations have had different approaches to configuring DI for your code, which made it difficult for developers to swap between frameworks.

A resolution of sorts came about in May 2009 when two leading members of the DI community, Bob Lee (from Guice) and Rod Johnson (from SpringSource) announced that they had come together to work on a standard set of interface annotations.[4] Subsequently JSR-330 (`javax.inject`) was raised to provide standardized DI for Java SE with effectively 100 percent support from all major players in that space.

> ### What about Enterprise Java?
> Enterprise Java is already getting its own DI in JEE 6 (a.k.a. CDI), covered under JSR-299 ("Contexts and Dependency Injection for the Java EE platform"). You can find out more by searching for JSR-299 at http://jcp.org/. In short, JSR-299 builds on top of JSR-330 in order to provide standardized configuration for enterprise scenarios.

With the addition of `javax.inject` into Java (Java SE versions 5, 6, and 7 are supported), it's now possible to use standardized DI and move between DI frameworks as required. For example, you can run your code within the Guice framework as a lightweight solution for your DI needs, and then perhaps move to the Spring framework in order to use its richer set of features.

> **WARNING** In practice, this isn't as easy as it sounds. As soon as your code utilizes a feature that's only supported by a particular DI framework, you are locked in to that framework. The `javax.inject` package provides a subset of common DI functionality, but you may need to use more advanced DI features than that. As you can imagine, there was quite a bit of debate as to what should be part of the common standard and what should not. The situation isn't perfect, but at least there is now a way to avoid framework lock-in.

---

[4] Bob Lee, "Announcing @javax.inject.Inject" (8 May 2009). www.theserverside.com/news/thread.tss?thread_id=54499.

To understand how the latest DI frameworks utilize the new standard, you need to investigate the `javax.inject` package. A key thing to remember is that the `javax.inject` package simply provides an interface and several annotation types that the various DI frameworks implement. You wouldn't typically implement these yourself unless you're creating your own JSR-330 compatible IoC container for Java. (And if you are, then hats off to you!)

> ### Why should I care how this stuff works?
> The well-grounded Java developer doesn't simply use libraries and frameworks without understanding at least the basics of how they work under the hood. In the DI space, a lack of understanding can lead to incorrectly configured dependencies, dependencies mysteriously falling out of scope, dependencies being shared when they shouldn't be, step debugging mysteriously dying, and a whole host of other insidious problems.

The Javadoc for `javax.inject` does an excellent job of explaining the purpose of this package, so we'll quote it verbatim:

> Package javax.inject[5]
>
> This package specifies a means for obtaining objects in such a way as to maximize reusability, testability and maintainability compared to traditional approaches such as constructors, factories, and service locators (e.g., JNDI). This process, known as dependency injection, is beneficial to most nontrivial applications.

The `javax.inject` package consists of five annotation types (`@Inject`, `@Qualifier`, `@Named`, `@Scope`, and `@Singleton`) and a single `Provider<T>` interface. These are explained over the next few sections, starting with the `@Inject` annotation.

3.2.1 The @Inject annotation

The `@Inject` annotation can be used with three class member types to indicate where you'd like a dependency to be injected. The class member types that can be injected, in the order that they're processed at runtime are:

1 Constructors
2 Methods
3 Fields

You can annotate a constructor with `@Inject` and expect its parameters to be provided at runtime by your configured IoC container. For example, the `Header` and `Content` objects are injected into the `MurmurMessage` when the constructor is invoked.

```
@Inject public MurmurMessage(Header header, Content content)
{
```

---

[5] "Package javax.inject," Javadoc, http://atinject.googlecode.com/svn/trunk/javadoc/javax/inject/package-summary.html.

```
    this.header = header;
    this.content = content;
}
```

The specification allows for zero or more parameters to be injected for constructors, so injecting a zero-parameter constructor is still valid.

> **WARNING** As per the specification, there can only be one constructor in a class with an `@Inject` annotation. This makes sense, as the JRE would not be able to decide which injected constructor took precedence.

You can annotate a method with `@Inject` and, like a constructor, expect its zero or more parameters to be injected at runtime. There are some restrictions in that injected methods can't be declared `abstract` and can't declare type parameters of their own.[6] The following short code sample demonstrates the use of `@Inject` with a setter method, a common technique when using DI to set optional fields.

```
@Inject public void setContent(Content content)
{
    this.content = content;
}
```

This technique of method parameter injection is especially powerful when it comes to providing service methods with the resources they need to do their jobs. For example, you could pass a data access object (DAO) argument to a finder service method that was tasked to retrieve some data.

> **TIP** It has become a default best practice to use constructor injection for setting mandatory dependencies for a class and to use setter injection for non-mandatory dependencies, such as fields that already have sensible defaults.

It's also possible to inject fields (as long as they aren't `final`), but the practice isn't common, because it makes unit testing more difficult. The syntax again is quite simple.

```
public class MurmurMessenger
{
    @Inject private MurmurMessage murmurMessage;
    ...
}
```

You can read further about the `@Inject` annotation in the Javadoc,[7] where you can discover some nuances about what types of values can be injected and how circular dependencies are dealt with.

You should now be comfortable with the `@Inject` annotation, so it's time to look at how you can qualify (further identify) those injected objects for use in your code.

---

[6] By this, we mean you can't use the "Generic Methods" trick as discussed in *The Java Tutorials* on Oracle's website: http://download.oracle.com/javase/tutorial/extra/generics/methods.html.

[7] "Annotation Type Inject," Javadoc, http://atinject.googlecode.com/svn/trunk/javadoc/javax/inject/Inject.html.

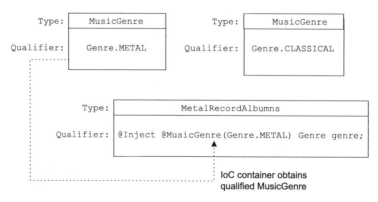

Figure 3.1 A `@Qualifier` annotation used to differentiate between two beans of the same `MusicGenre` type

3.2.2 *The @Qualifier annotation*

The `@Qualifier` annotation defines the contract for implementing frameworks that can be used to qualify (identify) the objects you wish to inject into your code. For example, if you had two objects of the same type configured in your IoC container, you'd want to be able to distinguish between those two objects when it came to injecting them into your code. The visual representation in figure 3.1 helps explain this concept.

When you use an implementation provided by one of the frameworks, you should be aware that there are rules around creating an implementation of the `@Qualifier` annotation:

- It must be annotated with the `@Qualifier` and `@Retention(RUNTIME)` annotations. This ensures that the qualifier is retained at runtime.
- It should typically be `@Documented` so that the implementation is added as part of the public Javadoc for that API.
- It can have attributes.
- It may have restricted usage if annotated with `@Target`; for example, it might restrict usage to fields as opposed to the default of fields *and* method parameters.

To bring the preceding list into perspective, here's a brief hypothetical example of a `@Qualifier` implementation that an IoC container might provide for you. A music library framework might provide a `@MusicGenre` qualifier, which can be used by developers when they create a `MetalRecordAlbums` class. The qualifier ensures that the injected `Genre` is of the right type.

```
@Documented
@Retention(RUNTIME)
@Qualifier
public @interface MusicGenre
{
   Genre genre() default Genre.TRANCE;
```

```
    public enum GENRE { CLASSICAL, METAL, ROCK, TRANCE }
}

public class MetalRecordAlbumns
{
    @Inject @MusicGenre(GENRE.METAL) Genre genre;

}
```

It's unlikely that you'll be creating your own @Qualifier annotations, but it's important to have a basic understanding of how the various IoC container implementations work.

One type of @Qualifier that the specification defines for all IoC containers to implement is the @Named annotation interface.

3.2.3 *The @Named annotation*

The @Named annotation interface is a specific @Qualifier that provides a contract for implementers to qualify injected objects by their names. When you combine the @Inject annotation with the qualifying @Named annotation, that specifically named object of the correct type will be injected.

In the following example, the MurmurMessage that's named "murmur" as well as one named "broadcast" will be injected.

```
public class MurmurMessenger
{
    @Inject @Named("murmur") private MurmurMessage murmurMessage;
    @Inject @Named("broadcast") private MurmurMessage broadcastMessage;
    ...
}
```

Although there are other qualifiers that could be seen as common, it was decided that only the @Named qualifier would be implemented by all of the DI frameworks as part of JSR-330.

Another area that the various backers of the original specification came to agreement on was having a standardized interface to deal with what scopes the injected objects can live in.

3.2.4 *The @Scope annotation*

The @Scope annotation defines a contract that can be used to define how the injector (that is, the IoC container) reuses instances of the injected object. The specification defines a few default behaviors:

- When no implementation of the @Scope annotation interface is declared, the injector should create an instance of the object to inject but only use that instance once for injection purposes.
- If an implementation of the @Scope annotation interface is declared, the lifespan of that injected object is defined by the implementation of that scope.
- If an injected object can be used by multiple threads in an implementation of @Scope, that injected object needs to be thread-safe. For more details on threads and thread safety, see chapter 4.

- The IoC container should generate an exception if there is more than one `@Scope` annotation declared in the same class or if it discovers a `@Scope` annotation that it doesn't support.

Those default behaviors give the DI frameworks some boundaries to work within when managing the lifecycles of their injected objects. Several IOC containers do support their own `@Scope` implementations, especially in the web frontend space (at least until JSR-299 is universally adopted in that area). Only the `@Singleton` annotation was deemed to be a common `@Scope` implementation for JSR-330, and it's therefore also defined as a specific annotation in the specification.

3.2.5   *The @Singleton annotation*

The `@Singleton` annotation interface is a widely used annotation in DI frameworks. More often than not, you're wanting to inject a value object that doesn't change, and a singleton is an efficient solution.

> **The Singleton pattern**
>
> A Singleton is simply a design pattern that enforces that the instantiation of a class occurs once and once only. For more details, see *Design Patterns: Elements of Reusable Object-Oriented Software*, by Erich Gamma, Richard Helm, Ralph Johnson, and John Vlissides (Addison-Wesley Professional, 1994), p. 127. Do take care with the Singleton pattern, it can be an antipattern in some cases!

Most DI frameworks treat `@Singleton` as a hidden default. For example, if you don't declare a scope, then by default the framework assumes you want to use a singleton. If you do declare it explicitly, you can do so in the following manner.

```
public MurmurMessage
{
   @Inject @Singleton MessageHeader defaultHeader;
}
```

In this example, the assumption is that the `defaultHeader` never changes (it's effectively static data) and can therefore be injected as a singleton.

Last, we'll cover the most flexible option for when one of the standard annotations isn't enough.

3.2.6   *The Provider<T> interface*

To give you extra control over the object being injected into your code by the DI framework, you can ask the DI framework to inject an implementation of the `Provider<T>` interface for that object (`T`) instead. This gives you the following benefits in controlling that injected object:

- You can retrieve multiple instances of that object.
- You can defer the retrieval of the object to when it's needed (lazy loading) or even not at all.

- You can break circular dependencies.
- You can define the scope, allowing you to look up objects in a smaller scope than the entire loaded application.

The interface contains only one method, `T get()`, which is expected to provide a fully constructed, injected instance of the object (`T`). For example, you can inject an implementation of the `Provider<T>` interface (`Provider<Message>`) into the `Murmur-Message` constructor. This will get different `Message` objects based on arbitrary criteria, as the following listing demonstrates.

> **Listing 3.6   Use of the `Provider<T>` interface**

```
import com.google.inject.Inject;
import com.google.inject.Provider;

class MurmurMessage
{
  @Inject MurmurMessage (Provider<Message> messageProvider)
  {
    Message msg1 = messageProvider.get();
    if (someGlobalCondition)
    {
      Message copyOfMsg1 = messageProvider.get();
    }
    ...
  }
}
```

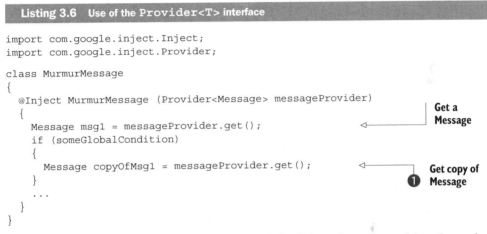

Get a
Message

Get copy of
1 Message

Notice how you can grab further instances of the injected `Message` object from the `Provider<Message>`, as opposed to just the single instance if you had injected a `Message` directly. In this case you're using a second copy of that injected `Message` object, only loading it in when you need it **1**.

Now that we've covered the theory and a few small examples of the new `javax.inject` package, it's time to put all of that knowledge into practice by using a full-fledged DI framework, Guice.

3.3   *Guice 3—the reference implementation for DI in Java*

Guice (pronounced "Juice"), led by Bob Lee, has been around since 2006 and is hosted at http://code.google.com/p/google-guice/. There you can find out about its motivations, read the documentation, and download the binary JAR files you'll need to run the examples.

It's in a DI framework like Guice that you actually configure your dependencies, how they will bind, and what scope they will bind to when your code uses the `@Inject` annotation (and its JSR-330 friends).

Guice 3 is the full RI for JSR-330, and we'll be using that version throughout this section. Guice is more than a simple DI framework, but for the purposes of this section we'll be focusing primarily on its DI capabilities and showcase examples in which you can use JSR-330 standard annotations with Guice to write your DI code.

3.3.1   *Getting started with Guice*

You've now got an understanding of the various JSR-330 annotations you can use in your code via Guice! Guice enables you to build a collection of Java objects (including their dependencies) that you want to inject. In Guice terminology, in order to have an *injector* build this *object graph* you need to create *modules* that declare a collection of *bindings* that define the specific implementations you want to inject. Sound complicated? Don't worry, it's actually quite simple once you see the concepts laid out in code.

> **TIP**   *Object graph, binding, module,* and *injector* are common terms used in the Guice world, so it's a good idea to get comfortable with that terminology if you're going to be building Guice-based applications.

In this section, we'll revisit the `HollywoodService` example. We'll start by creating a configuration class (*module*) that will hold the bindings. This is effectively the external configuration of the dependencies that the Guice framework is going to manage for you.

Where to get your Guice

Download the latest version of Guice 3 from http://code.google.com/p/google-guice/downloads/list; its corresponding documentation set can be found at http://code.google.com/p/google-guice/wiki/Motivation?tm=6.

To get full IoC container and DI support, you'll need to download the Guice zip file and unzip the contents into a location of your choice. In order to utilize Guice in your Java code, you'll need to ensure that the JAR files are included in your classpath.

For the purposes of the following code samples in this book, the Guice 3 JARs will also automatically come down as part of the Maven build.

Let's begin by creating an `AgentFinderModule` of bindings. This `AgentFinderModule` class needs to `extend AbstractModule`, and the bindings are declared in the overridden `configure()` method. In this particular case, you'll bind the `WebServiceAgent-Finder` class as the object to inject when the `HollywoodServiceGuice` asks to `@Inject` an `AgentFinder`. We're going to follow the convention of constructor injection here, as the following listing demonstrates.

Listing 3.7   `HollywoodService`, with Guice DI for `AgentFinder`

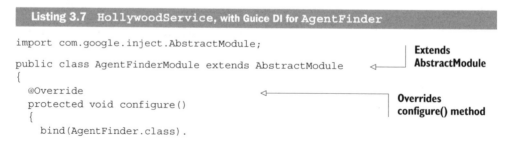

```
import com.google.inject.AbstractModule;

public class AgentFinderModule extends AbstractModule        ◁──┐  Extends
{                                                                 AbstractModule
  @Override
  protected void configure()                        ◁──────────┐  Overrides
  {                                                              configure() method
    bind(AgentFinder.class).
```

```
                  to(WebServiceAgentFinder.class);
  }
}
public class HollywoodServiceGuice
{
  private AgentFinder finder = null;

  @Inject
  public HollywoodServiceGuice(AgentFinder finder)
  {
    this.finder = finder;
  }

  public List<Agent> getFriendlyAgents()
  {
    List<Agent> agents = finder.findAllAgents();
    List<Agent> friendlyAgents = filterAgents(agents, "Java Developers");
    return friendlyAgents;
  }

  public List<Agent> filterAgents(List<Agent> agents, String agentType)
  {
    ...
  }
}
```

❶ Binds implementation to inject

Same implementation as listing 3.2

The heart of the binding occurs when you use Guice's bind method, passing it the class you want to bind (AgentFinder), then using the to method to declare which implementation will be injected ❶.

Now that you have your *binding* declared in your *module,* you can get the *injector* to build an *object graph.* We'll look at how to do that both in a standalone Java application and in a web application.

BUILDING A GUICE OBJECT GRAPH—STANDALONE JAVA

In a standard Java application, you can build the Guice object graph via the public static void main(String[] args) method. The following code listing shows how this is done.

Listing 3.8   HollywoodServiceClient—building the object graph with Guice

```
import com.google.inject.Guice;
import com.google.inject.Injector;
import java.util.List;

public class HollywoodServiceClient
{
  public static void main(String[] args)
  {
    Injector injector =
        Guice.createInjector(new AgentFinderModule());

    HollywoodServiceGuice hollywoodService =
        injector.getInstance(HollywoodServiceGuice.class);
```

```
        List<Agent> agents = hollywoodService.getFriendlyAgents();
        ...
    }
}
```

For web applications, it's a little different.

BUILDING A GUICE OBJECT GRAPH—WEB APPLICATION

In web applications, you add the guice-servlet.jar file to your web application and add the following snippet to your web.xml file.

```
<filter>
  <filter-name>guiceFilter</filter-name>
  <filter-class>com.google.inject.servlet.GuiceFilter</filter-class>
</filter>
<filter-mapping>
  <filter-name>guiceFilter</filter-name>
  <url-pattern>/*</url-pattern>
</filter-mapping>
```

It's fairly standard practice to then extend the ServletContextListener to use a Guice ServletModule (synonymous with AbstractModule in listing 3.7).

```
public class MyGuiceServletConfig extends GuiceServletContextListener {
  @Override
  protected Injector getInjector() {
    return Guice.createInjector(new ServletModule());
  }
}
```

As a last step, add the following to web.xml so the servlet container triggers this class when the app is deployed:

```
<listener>
  <listener-class>com.java7developer.MyGuiceServletConfig</listener-class>
</listener>
```

By creating HollywoodServiceGuice from the injector, you have a fully configured class that you can immediately call the getFriendlyAgents method on.

Pretty simple, right? Well yes, but it does get a little bit more complicated because you might want to have more complex bindings than the simple WebServiceAgent-Finder binding to the AgentFinder, as shown in listing 3.7.

3.3.2 *Sailor's knots—the various bindings of Guice*

Guice offers a multitude of bindings. The official documentation lists the following types:

- Linked bindings
- Binding annotations
- Instance bindings
- @Provides methods
- Provider bindings
- Untargeted bindings

- Built-in bindings
- Just-in-time bindings

We don't want to repeat the documentation verbatim, so we'll cover the most commonly used ones—linked bindings, binding annotations, as well as @Provides and Provider<T> bindings.

LINKED BINDINGS

Linked bindings are the simplest form of binding and are the same type of binding you used when configuring the AgentFinderModule in listing 3.6. This type of binding simply indicates to the injector that it should inject the implementing or extending class (yes, you can inject direct subclasses) at runtime.

```
@Override
protected void configure()
{
  bind(AgentFinder.class).to(WebServiceAgentFinder.class);
}
```

You've already seen that binding in action, so let's look at the next most common type of binding, the binding annotation.

BINDING ANNOTATIONS

Binding annotations are used to combine the type of class you want to inject with an additional identifier in order to identify exactly which object to inject. You can write your own binding annotations (see the Guice documentation online), but we'll highlight the use of the JSR-330 standard @Named binding that comes built into Guice.

In this case, you still have the familiar @Inject annotation, but you supplement that with the @Named annotation to pull in a particularly named AgentFinder. You configure this @Named type of binding in your AgentModule by using the annotatedWith method as shown in the following listing.

Listing 3.9 HollywoodService, using @Named

```
public class HollywoodService
{
  private AgentFinder finder = null;

  @Inject
  public HollywoodService(@Named("primary") AgentFinder finder)   ◁─┐
  {
    this.finder = finder;                                            │  Use
  }                                                                  │  @Named
}                                                                    │  annotation
public class AgentFinderModule extends AbstractModule
{
  @Override
  protected void configure()
  {
    bind(AgentFinder.class)
```

```
                .annotatedWith(Names.named("primary"))
                .to(WebServiceAgentFinder.class);
        }
}
```

Bind with named
parameter

Now that you've learned to configure your named dependencies, you can move on to the next type of binding—one that allows you to pass in a full-fledged dependency via the @Provides annotation and the Provider<T> interface.

@PROVIDES AND PROVIDER<T>—PROVIDING FULL INSTANTIATED OBJECTS

You can use the @Provides annotation as well as, or instead of, using binding in the configure() method if you want to return a full instantiated object. For example, you might want to inject a very specific MS Excel spreadsheet implementation of the SpreadsheetAgentFinder.

The injector will look at the return type of all of the methods with a @Provides annotation in order to determine which object to inject. For example, the Hollywood-Service will use the AgentFinder provided by the provideAgentFinder method with the @Provides annotation, as shown in the following code listing.

Listing 3.10   `AgentFinderModule`, using `@Provides`

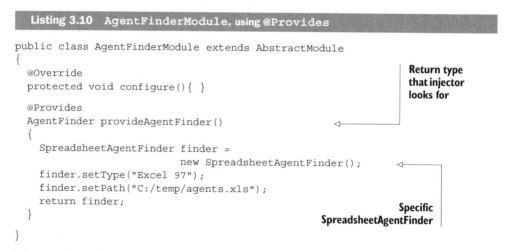

```
public class AgentFinderModule extends AbstractModule
{
  @Override
  protected void configure(){ }

  @Provides
  AgentFinder provideAgentFinder()
  {
    SpreadsheetAgentFinder finder =
                        new SpreadsheetAgentFinder();
    finder.setType("Excel 97");
    finder.setPath("C:/temp/agents.xls");
    return finder;
  }
}
```

Return type
that injector
looks for

Specific
SpreadsheetAgentFinder

The number of @Provides methods can grow to be rather large, so you may want to split them out into their own classes (as opposed to cluttering up your *module* classes). Guice supports the JSR-330 Provider<T> interface for this purpose; if you remember back to the JSR-330 section, you'll recall the T get() method. This method is invoked when the AgentFinderModule class configures the binding of the AgentFinderProvider via the toProvider method. The following code listing demonstrates this binding.

Listing 3.11   `AgentFinderModule`, using the `Provider<T>` interface

```
public class AgentFinderProvider implements Provider<AgentFinder>
{
  @Override
  public AgentFinder get()
  {
```

Use T get()
method

```
        SpreadsheetAgentFinder finder = new SpreadsheetAgentFinder();
        finder.setType("Excel 97");
        finder.setPath("C:/temp/agents.xls");
        return finder;
    }
}

public class AgentFinderModule extends AbstractModule
{
    @Override
    protected void configure()
    {
        bind(AgentFinder.class)
            .toProvider(AgentFinderProvider.class);
    }
}
```

<- ──────┘ **Bind provider**

That wraps up the last of our binding examples. You should now be able to use Guice to bind your dependencies ready for use by your code. But we haven't yet covered what scope these dependencies live in—understanding scope is important, because if objects end up living in the wrong scope, they'll live longer and take up more memory than necessary.

3.3.3 *Scoping your injected objects with Guice*

Guice provides several levels of scope for objects that you wish to inject. The narrowest scope is @RequestScope, followed by @SessionScope, and the familiar JSR-330 @Singleton scope, which is, in fact, an application-level scope.

The scope for your dependencies can be applied to your code in a number of ways:

- On the class that you're going to inject
- As part of the binding sequence (for example, bind().to().in())
- As an extra annotation to the @Provides contract

The preceding list is a little abstract, so we'll look at what they mean in the context of some small code examples, starting with scoping the class that you want to inject.

SCOPING THE CLASS THAT YOU WANT TO INJECT

Let's say you only ever want to have one instance of the SpreadsheetAgentFinder that you'll use across your entire application. For this, you can set the @Singleton scope on the class declaration, like so:

```
@Singleton
public class SpreadsheetAgentFinder
{
    ...
}
```

An added bonus of using this method is that it indicates to a developer how thread-safe the class should be. As SpreadsheetAgentFinder in theory can be injected at multiple times, the @Singleton scope indicates that you need to make sure that the class is thread-safe (see more on thread safety in chapter 4).

If you prefer to have all of your scoping information declared when you bind the dependency, you can do so.

USING THE BIND() SEQUENCE FOR SCOPING

Some developers may be more comfortable with having all of their rules related to an injected object in one place. Remember how you used a binding in listing 3.9 that had the primary AgentFinder bound? Adding the scope to this binding works in a similar manner—you simply add .in(<Scope>.class) as an extra method call on the bind sequence.

In the following code snippet, you enhance listing 3.9 by adding the extra in(Session.class) to the sequence, making the injected primary AgentFinder object available in a session scope.

```java
public class AgentFinderModule extends AbstractModule
{
  @Override
  protected void configure()
  {
    bind(AgentFinder.class)
      .annotatedWith(Names.named("primary"))
      .to(WebServiceAgentFinder.class)
      .in(Session.class);
  }
}
```

There is one final approach to scoping objects that you're injecting: joining up with the @Provides annotation.

SCOPING A @PROVIDES OBJECT PROVIDER

You can add a scope alongside a @Provides annotation in order to define the scope of the objects provided by that method. For example, if you look back to listing 3.9, you can add the extra @Request annotation in order to bind the resulting Spreadsheet-AgentFinder instances to a request scope.

```java
@Provides @Request
AgentFinder provideAgentFinder()
{
  SpreadsheetAgentFinder finder = new SpreadsheetAgentFinder();
  finder.setType("Excel 97");
  finder.setPath("C:/temp/agents.xls");
  return finder;
}
```

Guice also provides specific scopes based on web applications (servlet request scope, for example), and you can also write custom scopes for your needs.

Now you've got a good basic understanding of how Guice works with JSR-330 annotations in order to implement DI in your codebase. There are also non-JSR-330 features that you can explore further, such as Guice's aspect-oriented programming (AOP) support, which can be useful for implementing the cross cutting concerns of security and logging. For that, you'll need to refer to Guice's online documentation and code samples.

Choose your scope carefully!

One key decision that the well-grounded Java developer always takes into consideration is the scope of the objects that they're dealing with. Stateless objects that are relatively cheap to create don't need to worry about having their scope set. The JVM will have no trouble creating and destroying these as needed. (Chapter 6 covers the JVM and performance in more detail.)

On the other hand, stateful objects always need to be scoped! You should think about whether you want the lifespan of that object to be for the entire application, the current session, or the current request. As a second step, you should always think about the thread safety of that object. (Chapter 4 covers this in further detail.)

3.4 Summary

IoC can be a difficult concept to get your head around. But by exploring the concepts of Factory and Service Locator patterns, you can see how a basic IoC implementation works. The Factory pattern can be seen as an intermediate step toward understanding DI and the benefits it can bring your codebase. Even if you're struggling with the DI paradigm, it's worth sticking with it, because it enables you to write loosely coupled code that's easy to test and clearer to read.

JSR-330 isn't only an important standard that unifies common DI functionality, it also provides behind-the-scenes rules and limitations that you should be aware of. By studying the standard set of DI annotations, you can gain a much greater appreciation for how the various DI frameworks implement the specification, and therefore how you can use them most effectively.

Guice is the reference implementation for JSR-330 and it's also a popular, lightweight way to start using DI in your code. Indeed, for many applications, using Guice and the JSR-330 compatible set of annotations is probably enough for most of your DI needs.

If you've been reading this book from the start, we think you deserve a break! Go and inject some nonreading activity into your day and come back refreshed for a topic that every well-grounded Java developer needs to master, that of concurrency.

Modern concurrency

This chapter covers

- Concurrency theory
- Block-structured concurrency
- The java.util.concurrent libraries
- Lightweight concurrency with the fork/join framework
- The Java Memory Model (JMM)

In this chapter, we'll begin with basic concepts and a whistle-stop tour of block-structured concurrency. This was the only game in town prior to Java 5, and it's still worth understanding. Next, we'll cover what every working developer should know about java.util.concurrent and how to use the basic concurrency building blocks it provides.

We'll conclude with a look at the new fork/join framework, so that by the end of the chapter, you'll be ready to start applying these new concurrency techniques in your own code. You'll also have enough theory to fully grasp the different views of concurrency that we'll discuss in later parts of the book, when we meet non-Java languages.

This chapter isn't intended to be a complete statement of everything you'll ever need to know about concurrency—it's enough to get you started and give you an

But I already know about Thread!

It's one of the most common (and potentially deadly) mistakes a developer can make—to assume that an acquaintance with `Thread`, `Runnable`, and the language-level basic primitives of Java's concurrency mechanism is enough to be a competent developer of concurrent code. In fact, the subject of concurrency is a very large one, and good multithreaded development is difficult and continues to cause problems for even the best developers with years of experience under their belts.

One other point you should be aware of is that the area of concurrency is undergoing a massive amount of active research at present—research that will certainly have an impact on Java and the other languages you'll use over the course of your career. If we were to pick one fundamental area of computing that's likely to change radically in terms of industry practice over the next five years, it would be concurrency.

appreciation of what you'll need to learn more about, and to stop you being dangerous when writing concurrent code. But you'll need to know more than we can cover here if you're going to be a truly first-rate developer of multithreaded code. There are a number of excellent books about nothing but Java concurrency—two of the best are *Concurrent Programming in Java*, second edition, by Doug Lea (Prentice Hall, 1999), and *Java Concurrency in Practice* by Brian Goetz and others (Addison-Wesley Professional, 2006).

The aim of this chapter is to make you aware of the underlying platform mechanisms that explain why Java's concurrency works the way it does. We'll also cover enough general concurrency theory to give you the vocabulary to understand the issues involved, and to teach you about both the necessity and the difficulty involved in getting concurrency right. In fact, that's where we're going to start.

4.1 Concurrency theory—a primer

To make sense of Java's approach to concurrent programming, we're going to start off by talking about theory. First, we'll discuss the fundamentals of the Java threading model.

After that, we'll discuss the impact that "design forces" have in the design and implementation of systems. We'll talk about the two most important of these forces, *safety* and *liveness*, and mention some of the others. After that we'll turn to why the forces are often in conflict, and look at some reasons for overhead in concurrent systems.

We'll conclude this section by looking at an example of a multithreaded system, and illustrate how `java.util.concurrent` is a very natural way to write code.

4.1.1 Explaining Java's threading model

Java's threading model is based on two fundamental concepts:

- Shared, visible-by-default mutable state
- Preemptive thread scheduling

Let's consider some of the most important aspects of these ideas:

- Objects can be easily shared between all threads within a process.
- Objects can be changed ("mutated") by any threads that have a reference to them.
- The thread scheduler can swap threads on and off cores at any time, more or less.
- Methods must be able to be swapped out while they're running (otherwise a method with an infinite loop would steal the CPU forever).

   This, however, runs the risk of an unpredictable thread swap leaving a method "half-done" and an object in an inconsistent state. There is also the risk of changes made in one thread not being visible in other threads when they need to be. To mitigate these risks, we come to the last point.
- Objects can be *locked* to protect vulnerable data.

Java's thread- and lock-based concurrency is very low-level, and often hard to work with. To cope with this, a set of concurrency libraries, known as `java.util.concurrent`, was introduced in Java 5. This provided a set of tools for writing concurrent code that many programmers find easier to use than the classic block-structured concurrency primitives.

> **Lessons learned**
>
> Java was the first mainstream programming language to have built-in support for multithreaded programming. This represented a huge step forward at the time, but now, 15 years later, we've learned a lot more about how to write concurrent code.
>
> It turns out that some of Java's initial design decisions are quite difficult for most programmers to work with. This is unfortunate, because the increasing trend in hardware is toward processors with many cores, and the only good way to take advantage of those cores is with concurrent code. We'll discuss some of the difficulties of concurrent code in this chapter. The subject of modern processors naturally requiring concurrent programming is covered in some detail in chapter 6 where we discuss performance.

As developers become more experienced with writing concurrent code, they find themselves running up against recurring concerns that are important to their systems. We call these concerns "design forces." They're high-level forces that exist (and often conflict) in the design of practical concurrent OO systems.

We're going to spend a little bit of time looking at some of the most important of these forces in the next couple of sections.

4.1.2 Design concepts

The most important design forces were catalogued by Doug Lea as he was doing his landmark work producing `java.util.concurrent`:

- Safety (also known as *concurrent type safety*)
- Liveness
- Performance
- Reusability

Let's look at each of these forces now.

SAFETY AND CONCURRENT TYPE SAFETY

Safety is about ensuring that object instances remain self-consistent regardless of any other operations that may be happening at the same time. If a system of objects has this property, it's said to be *concurrently type-safe*.

As you might guess from the name, one way to think about concurrency is in terms of an extension to the regular concepts of object modeling and type safety. In nonconcurrent code, you want to ensure that regardless of what public methods you call on an object, it's in a well-defined and consistent state at the end of the method. The usual way to do this is to keep all of an object's state private and expose a public API of methods that only alter the object's state in a self-consistent way.

Concurrent type safety is the same basic concept as type safety for an object, but applied to the much more complex world in which other threads are potentially operating on the same objects on different CPU cores at the same time.

> **Staying safe**
>
> One strategy for safety is to never return from a non-private method in an inconsistent state, and to never call any non-private method (and certainly not a method on any other object) while in an inconsistent state. If this is combined with a way of protecting the object (such as a synchronization lock or critical section) while it's inconsistent, the system can be guaranteed to be safe.

LIVENESS

A live system is one in which every attempted activity eventually either progresses or fails.

The key word in the definition is *eventually*—there is a distinction between a transient failure to progress (which isn't that bad in isolation, even if it's not ideal) and a permanent failure. Transient failures could be caused by a number of underlying problems, such as:

- Locking or waiting to acquire a lock
- Waiting for input (such as network I/O)
- Temporary failure of a resource
- Not enough CPU time available to run the thread

Permanent failures could be due to a number of causes. These are some of the most common:

- Deadlock
- Unrecoverable resource problem (such as if the NFS goes away)
- Missed signal

We'll discuss locking and several of these other problems later in the chapter, although you may already be familiar with some or all of them.

PERFORMANCE

The performance of a system can be quantified in a number of different ways. In chapter 6, we'll talk about performance analysis and techniques for tuning, and we'll introduce a number of other metrics you should know about. For now, think of performance as being a measure of how much work a system can do with a given amount of resources.

REUSABILITY

Reusability forms a fourth design force, because it isn't really covered by any of the other considerations. A concurrent system that has been designed for easy reuse is sometimes very desirable, although this isn't always easy to implement. One approach is to use a reusable toolbox (like `java.util.concurrent`) and build non-reusable application code on top of it.

4.1.3   *How and why do the forces conflict?*

The design forces are often in opposition to each other, and this tension can be viewed as a central reason why designing good concurrent systems is difficult.

- Safety stands in opposition to liveness—safety is about ensuring that bad things don't happen, whereas liveness requires progress to be made.
- Reusable systems tend to expose their internals, which can cause problems with safety.
- A naïvely written safe system will typically not be very performant, as it usually resorts to the heavy use of locking to provide safety guarantees.

The balance that you should ultimately try to achieve is for the code to be flexible enough to be useful for a wide range of problems, closed enough to be safe, and still reasonably live and performant. This is quite a tall order, but, fortunately, there are some practical techniques to help with this. Here are some of the most common in rough order of usefulness:

- Restrict the external communication of each subsystem as much as possible. Data hiding is a powerful tool for aiding with safety.
- Make the internal structure of each subsystem as deterministic as possible. For example, design in static knowledge of the threads and objects in each subsystem, even if the subsystems will interact in a concurrent, nondeterministic way.

- Apply policy approaches that client apps must adhere to. This technique is powerful, but relies on user apps cooperating, and it can be hard to debug if a badly behaved app disobeys the rules.

- Document the required behavior. This is the weakest of the alternatives, but it's sometimes necessary if the code is to be deployed in a very general context.

The developer should be aware of each of these possible safety mechanisms and should use the strongest possible technique, while being aware that there are circumstances in which only the weaker mechanisms are possible.

4.1.4 Sources of overhead

There are many aspects of a concurrent system that can contribute to the inherent overhead:

- Locks and monitors
- Number of context switches
- Number of threads
- Scheduling
- Locality of memory
- Algorithm design

This should form the basis of a checklist in your mind. When developing concurrent code, you should ensure that you have thought about everything on this list, before considering the code "done."

Algorithm design

This is an area in which developers can really distinguish themselves—learning about algorithm design will make you a better programmer in any language. Two of the best books are *Introduction to Algorithms* by Thomas H. Corman et al. (MIT, 2009)—don't be deceived by the title, this is a serious work—and *The Algorithm Design Manual*, second edition, by Steven Skiena (Springer-Verlag, 2008). For both single-threaded and concurrent algorithms, these are excellent choices for further reading.

We'll mention many of these sources of overhead in this chapter (and in chapter 6, about performance).

4.1.5 A transaction processor example

To round off this rather theoretical section, let's apply some of this theory to the design of an example concurrent application. We'll see how we might approach it using a high-level view of the classes from `java.util.concurrent`.

Consider a basic transaction processing system. A simple and standard way to construct such an application is to have different phases of the application correspond to different parts of the business process. Each phase is then represented by a thread pool that takes in work items one by one, does an amount of processing on each item, and hands off the item to the next thread pool. In general, it's good design to have each thread pool concentrate on processing that is pertinent to one specific functional area. You can see an example application in figure 4.1.

If you design applications like this, you can improve throughput because you can have several work items in flight at once. One work item can be in processing in the Credit Check phase at the same time as another is in Stock Check. Depending on the details of the application, there can even be multiple different orders in Stock Check at the same time.

Designs of this type are very well-suited to being implemented using the classes found in `java.util.concurrent`. The package contains thread pools for execution (and a nice set of factory methods in the `Executors` class to create them) and queues for handing work off between pools. There are also concurrent data structures (for building shared caches and other use cases) and many other useful low-level tools.

But, you might ask, what would we have done before the advent of Java 5, when we didn't have these classes available? In many cases, application groups would come up with their own concurrent programming libraries—they'd end up building components similar in aims to the ones found in `java.util.concurrent`. But many of these bespoke components would have design problems, and subtle (or not-so-subtle) concurrency bugs. If `java.util.concurrent` didn't exist, application developers would end up reinventing much of it for themselves (probably in a buggy, badly tested form).

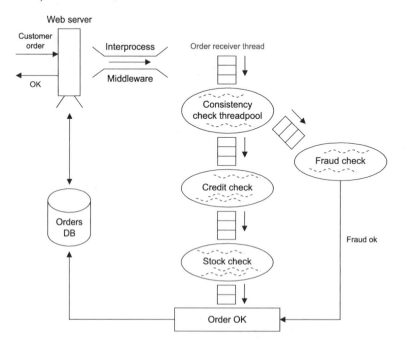

Figure 4.1   An example multithreaded application

With this example in mind, let's turn to our next subject—a review of Java's "classic" concurrency and a close look at why programming with it can be difficult.

4.2 *Block-structured concurrency (pre-Java 5)*

Much of this chapter is taken up with discussing alternatives to the block-synchronization-based approach to concurrency. But to get the most out of the discussion of the alternatives, it's important to have a firm grasp of what's good and bad about the classic view of concurrency.

To that end, we'll discuss the original, quite low-level way of tackling multithreaded programming using Java's concurrency keywords—synchronized, volatile, and so on. This discussion will take place in the context of the design forces and with an eye to what will come in the next sections.

Following on from that, we'll briefly consider the lifecycle of a thread, and then discuss common techniques (and pitfalls) of concurrent code, such as fully synchronized objects, deadlocks, the volatile keyword, and immutability.

Let's get started with a review of synchronization.

4.2.1 *Synchronization and locks*

As you already know, the synchronized keyword can be applied either to a block or to a method. It indicates that before entering the block or method, a thread must acquire the appropriate lock. For a method, that means acquiring the lock belonging to the object instance (or the lock belonging to the Class object for static synchronized methods). For a block, the programmer should indicate which object's lock is to be acquired.

Only one thread can be progressing through any of an object's synchronized blocks or methods at once; if other threads try to enter, they're suspended by the JVM. This is true regardless of whether the other thread is trying to enter either the same or a different synchronized block on the same object. In concurrency theory, this type of construct is referred to as a *critical section.*

> **NOTE** Have you ever wondered why the Java keyword used for a critical section is synchronized? Why not "critical" or "locked"? What is it that's being *synchronized?* We'll return to this in section 4.2.5, but if you don't know or have never thought about it, you may want to take a couple of minutes to ponder it before continuing.

We're really focusing on some of the newer concurrency techniques in this chapter. But as we're talking about synchronization, let's look at some basic facts about synchronization and locks in Java. Hopefully you already have most (or all) of these at your fingertips:

- Only objects—not primitives—can be locked.
- Locking an array of objects doesn't lock the individual objects.
- A synchronized method can be thought of as equivalent to a synchronized (this) { ... } block that covers the entire method (but note that they're represented differently in bytecode).

- A `static synchronized` method locks the `Class` object, because there's no instance object to lock.
- If you need to lock a class object, consider carefully whether you need to do so explicitly, or by using `getClass()`, because the behavior of the two approaches will be different in a subclass.
- Synchronization in an inner class is independent of the outer class (to see why this is so, remember how inner classes are implemented).
- `synchronized` doesn't form part of the method signature, so it can't appear on a method declaration in an interface.
- Unsynchronized methods don't look at or care about the state of any locks, and they can progress while synchronized methods are running.
- Java's locks are reentrant. That means a thread holding a lock that encounters a synchronization point for the same lock (such as a synchronized method calling another synchronized method in the same class) will be allowed to continue.

WARNING   Non-reentrant locking schemes exist in other languages (and can be synthesized in Java—see the Javadoc for `ReentrantLock` in `java.util.concurrent.locks` if you want the gory details) but they're generally painful to deal with, and they're best avoided unless you really know what you're doing.

That's enough review of Java's synchronization. Now let's move on to discuss the states that a thread moves through during its lifecycle.

4.2.2   *The state model for a thread*

In figure 4.2, you can see how a thread lifecycle progresses—from creation to running, to possibly being suspended, before running again (or blocking on a resource), and eventually completing.

A thread is initially created in the Ready state. The scheduler will then find a core for it to run upon, and some small amount of waiting time may be involved if the machine is heavily loaded. From there, the thread will usually consume its time allocation and be placed back into the Ready state to await further processor time slices. This is the action of the forcible thread scheduling that we mentioned in section 4.1.1.

As well as the standard action by the scheduler, the thread itself can indicate that it isn't able to make use of the core at this time. This can be because the program code indicates that the thread should pause before continuing (via `Thread.sleep()`) or because the thread must wait until notified (usually that some external condition has been met). Under these circumstances, the thread is removed from the core and releases all its locks. It can only run again by being woken up (after sleeping for the right length of time, or because it has received the appropriate signal) and placed back in the Ready state.

The thread can be blocked because it's waiting on I/O or to acquire a lock held by another thread. In this case, the thread isn't swapped off the core but is kept busy, waiting for the lock or data to become available. If this happens, the thread will continue to execute until the end of its timeslice.

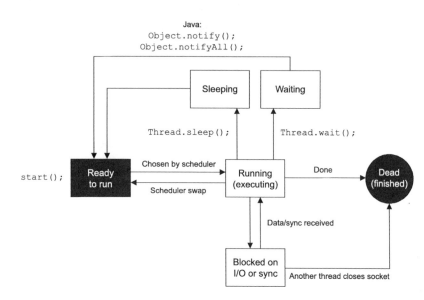

Figure 4.2   The state model of a Java thread

Let's move on to talk about one well-known way to solve the synchronization problem. This is the idea of fully synchronized objects.

4.2.3   *Fully synchronized objects*

Earlier in this chapter, we introduced the concept of concurrent type safety and mentioned one strategy for achieving this (in the "Staying Safe" sidebar). Let's look at a more complete description of this strategy, which is usually called *fully synchronized objects*. If all of the following rules are obeyed, the class is known to be thread-safe and will also be live.

A fully synchronized class is a class that meets all of these conditions:

- All fields are always initialized to a consistent state in every constructor.
- There are no public fields.
- Object instances are guaranteed to be consistent after returning from any non-private method (assuming the state was consistent when the method was called).
- All methods provably terminate in bounded time.
- All methods are synchronized.
- There is no calling of another instance's methods while in an inconsistent state.
- There is no calling of any non-private method while in an inconsistent state.

Listing 4.1 shows an example of such a class from the backend of an imaginary distributed microblogging tool. The `ExampleTimingNode` class will receive updates by having its `propagateUpdate()` method called and can also be queried to see if it has received a specific update. This situation provides a classic conflict between a read and a write operation, so synchronization is used to prevent inconsistency.

Listing 4.1   A fully synchronized class

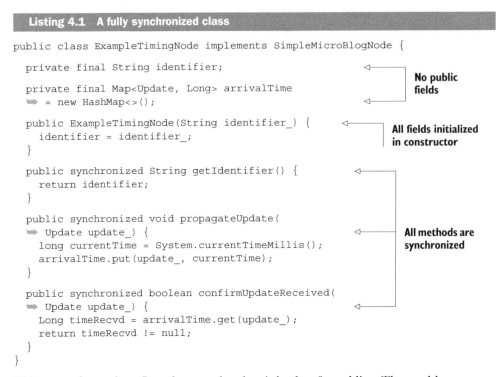

```
public class ExampleTimingNode implements SimpleMicroBlogNode {

  private final String identifier;                          ◄         No public
                                                                      fields
  private final Map<Update, Long> arrivalTime
  ➡ = new HashMap<>();                                      ◄

  public ExampleTimingNode(String identifier_) {            ◄         All fields initialized
    identifier = identifier_;                                         in constructor
  }

  public synchronized String getIdentifier() {              ◄
    return identifier;
  }

  public synchronized void propagateUpdate(
  ➡ Update update_) {                                       ◄         All methods are
    long currentTime = System.currentTimeMillis();                    synchronized
    arrivalTime.put(update_, currentTime);
  }

  public synchronized boolean confirmUpdateReceived(
  ➡ Update update_) {                                       ◄
    Long timeRecvd = arrivalTime.get(update_);
    return timeRecvd != null;
  }
}
```

This seems fantastic at first glance—the class is both safe and live. The problem comes with performance—just because something is safe and live doesn't mean it's necessarily going to be very quick. You have to use synchronized to coordinate all the accesses (both get and put) to the arrivalTime map, and that locking is ultimately going to slow you down. This is a central problem of this way of handling concurrency.

> **Code fragility**
>
> In addition to the performance problems, the code in listing 4.1 is quite fragile. You can see that you never touch arrivalTime outside of a synchronized method (and in fact there's only get and put access), but this is only possible because of the small amount of code in play. In real, larger systems, this would not be possible due to the amount of code. It's very easy for bugs to creep into larger codebases that use this approach, which is another reason that the Java community began to look for more robust approaches.

4.2.4   *Deadlocks*

Another classic problem of concurrency (and not just Java's take on it) is the *deadlock*. Consider listing 4.2, which is a slightly extended form of the last example. In this version, as well as recording the time of the last update, each node that receives an update informs another node of that receipt.

This is a naïve attempt to build a multithreaded update handling system. It's designed to demonstrate deadlocking—you shouldn't use this as the basis for real code.

Listing 4.2 A deadlocking example

```java
public class MicroBlogNode implements SimpleMicroBlogNode {
  private final String ident;

  public MicroBlogNode(String ident_) {
    ident = ident_;
  }

  public String getIdent() {
    return ident;
  }

  public synchronized void propagateUpdate(Update upd_, MicroBlogNode
    backup_) {
    System.out.println(ident +": recvd: "+ upd_.getUpdateText()
      +" ; backup: "+backup_.getIdent());
    backup_.confirmUpdate(this, upd_);
  }

  public synchronized void confirmUpdate(MicroBlogNode other_, Update
    update_) {
    System.out.println(ident +": recvd confirm: "+
      update_.getUpdateText() +" from "+other_.getIdent()k);
  }
}
```

```java
final MicroBlogNode local =                            │ Keyword final
  new MicroBlogNode("localhost:8888");          ◁──────┘ is required
final MicroBlogNode other = new MicroBlogNode("localhost:8988");
final Update first = getUpdate("1");
final Update second = getUpdate("2");

new Thread(new Runnable() {                            │ First update
  public void run() {                                  │ sent to first
    local.propagateUpdate(first, other);      ◁────────┘ thread
  }
}).start();

new Thread(new Runnable() {                            │ Second update
  public void run() {                                  │ sent to other
    other.propagateUpdate(second, local);     ◁────────┘ thread
  }
}).start();
```

At first glance, this code looks sensible. You have two updates being sent to separate threads, each of which has to be confirmed on backup threads. This doesn't seem too outlandish a design—if one thread has a failure, there is another thread that can potentially carry on.

If you run the code, you'll normally see an example of a deadlock—both threads will report receiving the update, but neither will confirm receiving the update for which they're the backup thread. The reason for this is that each thread requires the

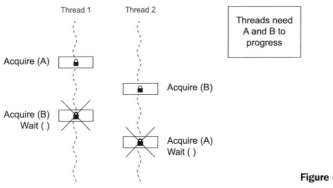

Figure 4.3   Deadlocked threads

other to release the lock it holds before the confirmation method can progress. This is illustrated in figure 4.3.

To deal with deadlocks, one technique is to always acquire locks in the same order in every thread. In the preceding example, the first thread to start acquires them in the order A, B, whereas the second thread acquires them in the order B, A. If both threads had insisted on acquiring in order A, B, the deadlock would have been avoided, because the second thread would have been blocked from running at all until the first had completed and released its locks.

In terms of the fully synchronized object approach, this deadlock is prevented because the code violates the consistent state rule. When a message arrives, the receiving node calls another object while the message is still being processed—the state isn't consistent when it makes this call.

Next, we'll return to a puzzle we posed earlier: why the Java keyword for a critical section is `synchronized`. This will lead us into a discussion of immutability and then the `volatile` keyword.

4.2.5   *Why synchronized?*

One of the biggest changes in concurrent programming in recent years has been in the realm of hardware. It wasn't that many years ago that a working programmer could go for years on end without encountering a system that had more than one or at most two processing cores. It was thus possible to think of concurrent programming as being about the timesharing of the CPU—threads swapping on and off a single core.

Today, anything larger than a mobile phone has multiple cores, so the mental model should be different too, encompassing multiple threads all running on different cores at the same physical moment (and potentially operating on shared data). You can see this in figure 4.4. For efficiency, each thread that is running simultaneously may have its own cached copy of data being operated on. With this picture in mind, let's turn to the question of the choice of keyword used to denote a locked section or method.

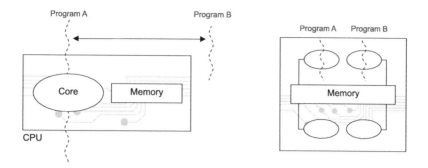

Figure 4.4 Old and new ways of thinking about concurrency and threads

We asked earlier, what is it that's being synchronized in the code in listing 4.1? The answer is: *The memory representation in different threads of the object being locked is what is being synchronized.* That is, after the synchronized block (or method) has completed, any and all changes that were made to the object being locked are flushed back to main memory before the lock is released, as illustrated in figure 4.5.

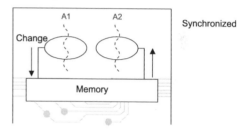

Figure 4.5 A change to an object propagates between threads via main memory

In addition, when a synchronized block is entered, then after the lock has been acquired, any changes to the locked object are read in *from* main memory, so the thread with the lock is synchronized to main memory's view of the object before the code in the locked section begins to execute.

4.2.6 *The volatile keyword*

Java has had the volatile keyword since the dawn of time (Java 1.0), and it's used as a simple way to deal with the synchronization of object fields, including primitives. The following rules govern a volatile field:

- The value seen by a thread is always reread from main memory before use.
- Any value written by a thread is always flushed through to main memory before the instruction completes.

This can be thought of as acting like a tiny little synchronized block around the operation. It allows the programmer to write simplified code, but at the cost of the extra flushes on every access. Notice also that the volatile variable doesn't introduce any locks, so you can't deadlock by using volatile variables.

One slightly more subtle consequence of volatile variables is that for true thread-safety, a volatile variable should only be used to model a variable where writes to the variable don't depend on the current state (the read state) of the variable. For cases where the current state matters, you must always introduce a lock to be completely safe.

4.2.7   *Immutability*

One technique that can be of great value is the use of immutable objects. These are objects that either have no state, or that have only final fields (which must therefore be populated in the constructors of the objects). These are always safe and live, because their state can't be mutated, so they can never be in an inconsistent state.

One problem is that any values that are required to initialize a particular object must be passed into the constructor. This can lead to unwieldy constructor calls, with many parameters. Alternatively, many coders use a FactoryMethod instead. This can be as simple as using a static method on the class, instead of a constructor, to produce new objects. The constructors are usually made protected or private, so that the static FactoryMethods are the only way of instantiating.

This still has the problem of potentially needing many parameters to be passed in to the FactoryMethod. This isn't always very convenient, especially when you may need to accumulate state from several sources before creating a new immutable object.

To solve this, you can use the Builder pattern. This is a combination of two constructs: a static inner class that implements a generic builder interface, and a private constructor for the immutable class itself.

The static inner class is the builder for the immutable class, and it provides the only way that a developer can get hold of new instances of the immutable type. One very common implementation is for the Builder class to have exactly the same fields as the immutable class, but to allow mutation of the fields.

This listing shows how you might use this to model a microblogging update (again, building on the earlier listings in this chapter).

Listing 4.3   Immutable objects and builders

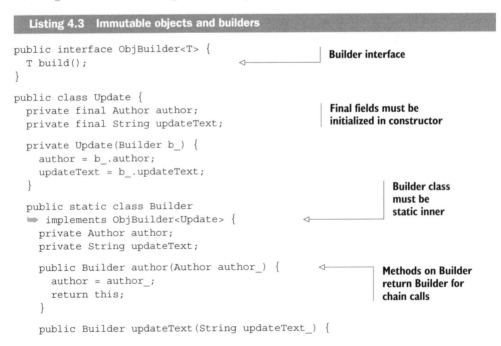

```
public interface ObjBuilder<T> {          ←————————  Builder interface
  T build();
}

public class Update {
  private final Author author;            Final fields must be
  private final String updateText;        initialized in constructor

  private Update(Builder b_) {
    author = b_.author;
    updateText = b_.updateText;
  }                                                    Builder class
                                                       must be
  public static class Builder                          static inner
➥    implements ObjBuilder<Update> {      ←————————
    private Author author;
    private String updateText;

    public Builder author(Author author_) {  ←————    Methods on Builder
      author = author_;                              return Builder for
      return this;                                   chain calls
    }

    public Builder updateText(String updateText_) {
```

```
      updateText = updateText_;
      return this;
    }
    public Update build() {
      return new Update(this);
    }
  }
}
```

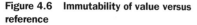

hashCode() and equals() methods omitted

With this code, you could then create a new Update object like this:

```
Update.Builder ub = new Update.Builder();
Update u = ub.author(myAuthor).updateText("Hello").build();
```

This is a very common pattern and one that has wide applicability. In fact, we've already made use of the properties of immutable objects in listings 4.1 and 4.2.

One last point about immutable objects—the final keyword only applies to the object directly pointed to. As you can see in figure 4.6, the reference to the main object can't be assigned to point at object 3, but within the object, the reference to 1 can be swung to point at object 2. Another way of saying this is that a final reference can point at an object that has nonfinal fields.

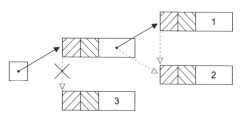

Figure 4.6   Immutability of value versus reference

Immutability is a very powerful technique, and you should use it whenever feasible. Sometimes it's just not possible to develop efficiently with only immutable objects, because every change to an object's state requires a new object to be spun up. So we're left with the necessity of dealing with mutable objects.

We'll now turn to one of the biggest topics in this chapter—a tour of the more modern and conceptually simple concurrency APIs presented in java.util.concurrent. We'll look at how you can start to use them in your own code.

4.3   *Building blocks for modern concurrent applications*

With the advent of Java 5, a new way of thinking about concurrency in Java emerged. This was spearheaded by the package java.util.concurrent, which contained a rich new toolbox for working with multithreaded code. This toolbox has been enhanced with subsequent versions of Java, but the classes and packages that were introduced with Java 5 still work the same way and they're still very valuable to the working developer.

We're going to take a whirlwind tour through some of the headline classes in java.util.concurrent and related packages, such as the atomic and locks packages. We'll get you started using the classes and look at examples of use cases for them. You should also read the Javadoc for them and try to build up your familiarity with the packages as a whole—they make programming concurrent classes much easier.

> ### Migrating code
>
> If you have existing multithreaded code that is still based on the older (pre-Java 5) approaches, you should refactor it to use `java.util.concurrent`. In our experience, your code will be improved if you make a conscious effort to port it to the newer APIs—the greater clarity and reliability will be well worth the effort expended to migrate in almost all cases.

Consider this discussion a starter toolkit for concurrent code, not a full workshop. To get the most out of `java.util.concurrent`, you'll need to read more than we can present here.

4.3.1   *Atomic classes—java.util.concurrent.atomic*

The package `java.util.concurrent.atomic` contains several classes that have names starting with `Atomic`. They're essentially providing the same semantics as a `volatile`, but wrapped in a class API that includes atomic (meaning all-or-nothing) methods for suitable operations. This can be a very simple way for a developer to avoid race conditions on shared data.

The implementations are written to take advantage of modern processor features, so they can be nonblocking (lock-free) if suitable support is available from the hardware and OS, which it should be for most modern systems. A common use is to implement sequence numbers, using the atomic `getAndIncrement()` method on the `AtomicInteger` or `AtomicLong`.

To be a sequence number, the class should have a `nextId()` method that will return a number guaranteed to be unique (and strictly increasing) each time it's called. This is very similar to the database concept of a sequence number (hence the name of the variable).

Let's look at a bit of code that replicates sequence numbers:

```
private final AtomicLong sequenceNumber = new AtomicLong(0);

public long nextId() {
  return sequenceNumber.getAndIncrement();
}
```

> **CAUTION** Atomic classes don't inherit from the similarly named classes, so `AtomicBoolean` can't be used in place of a `Boolean`, and `AtomicInteger` isn't an `Integer` (but it does extend `Number`).

Next, we'll examine how `java.util.concurrent` models the core of the synchronization model—the `Lock` interface.

4.3.2 Locks—java.util.concurrent.locks

The block-structured approach to synchronization is based around a simple notion of what a lock is. This approach has a number of shortcomings:

- There is only one type of lock.
- It applies equally to all synchronized operations on the locked object.
- The lock is acquired at the start of the synchronized block or method.
- The lock is released at the end of the block or method.
- The lock is either acquired or the thread blocks—no other outcomes are possible.

If we were going to reengineer the support for locks, there are several things we could potentially change for the better:

- Add different types of locks (such as reader and writer locks).
- Not restrict locks to blocks (allow a lock in one method and unlock in another).
- If a thread cannot acquire a lock (for example, if another thread has the lock), allow the thread to back out or carry on or do something else—a `try-Lock()` method.
- Allow a thread to attempt to acquire a lock and give up after a certain amount of time.

The key to realizing all of these possibilities is the `Lock` interface in `java.util.concurrent.locks`. This ships with a couple of implementations:

- `ReentrantLock`—This is essentially the equivalent of the familiar lock used in Java synchronized blocks, but it's slightly more flexible.
- `ReentrantReadWriteLock`—This can provide better performance in cases where there are many readers but few writers.

The `Lock` interface can be used to completely replicate any functionality that is offered by block-structured concurrency. Here is the deadlock example rewritten to use the `ReentrantLock`.

Listing 4.4   Rewriting deadlock example to use `ReentrantLock`

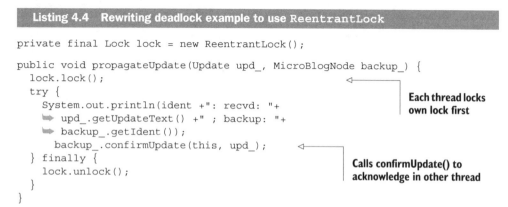

```
private final Lock lock = new ReentrantLock();

public void propagateUpdate(Update upd_, MicroBlogNode backup_) {
  lock.lock();                                          ◁─────────┐  Each thread locks
  try {                                                           │  own lock first
    System.out.println(ident +": recvd: "+
  ➥ upd_.getUpdateText() +" ; backup: "+
  ➥ backup_.getIdent());
    backup_.confirmUpdate(this, upd_);                  ◁─┐
  } finally {                                             │
    lock.unlock();                                        │  Calls confirmUpdate() to
  }                                                       │  acknowledge in other thread
}
```

```
public void confirmUpdate(MicroBlogNode other_, Update upd_) {
  lock.lock();
  try{
    System.out.println(iden +": recvd confirm: "+
    ➥ upd_.getUpdateText() +" from "+ other_.getIdentifier());
  } finally {
    lock.unlock();
  }
}
```

Attempts to lock other thread ❶

The attempt ❶ to lock the other thread will generally fail, because it's already locked (as per figure 4.3). That's how the deadlock arises.

> ## Using try ... finally with lock
>
> The pattern of `lock()` with a `try ... finally` block, where the lock is released is a good addition to your toolbox. It works very well if you're replicating a situation that is similar to one where you'd have used block-structured concurrency. On the other hand, if you need to pass around the `Lock` objects (such as by returning it from a method), you can't use this pattern.
>
> Using `Lock` objects can be considerably more powerful than a block-structured approach, but it is still sometimes hard to use them to design a robust locking strategy.

There are a number of strategies for dealing with deadlocks, but there's one in particular that doesn't work that you should be aware of. Consider the version of the `propagateUpdate()` method shown in the next listing (and imagine that the same change has been made to the `confirmUpdate()` code). In this example, we've replaced the unconditional lock with `tryLock()` with a timeout. This is an attempt to remove the deadlock by giving other threads a chance to get at the lock.

Listing 4.5   A flawed attempt to fix deadlock

```
public void propagateUpdate(Update upd_, MicroBlogNode backup_) {
  boolean acquired = false;

  while (!acquired) {
    try {
      int wait = (int)(Math.random() * 10);
      acquired = lock.tryLock(wait, TimeUnit.MILLISECONDS);
      if (acquired) {
        System.out.println(ident +": recvd: "+
        ➥ upd_.getUpdateText() +" ; backup: "+backup_.getIdent());
        backup_.confirmUpdate(this, update_);
      } else {
        Thread.sleep(wait);
      }
    } catch (InterruptedException e) {
    } finally {
```

Try and lock, with random timeout

Confirm on other thread

```
    if (acquired) lock.unlock();
  }
}
}
```
Only unlock if locked

If you run the code in listing 4.5, you'll see that it seems to resolve the deadlock, but only sometimes. You'll see the "received confirm of update" text, but only some of the time.

In fact, the deadlock hasn't really been resolved, because if the initial lock is obtained (in `propagateUpdate()`) the thread calls `confirmUpdate()` and never releases the first lock until completion. If both threads manage to acquire their first lock before either can call `confirmUpdate()`, the threads will still be deadlocked.

The real solution is to ensure that if the attempt to get the second lock fails, the thread should release the lock it's holding and wait briefly, as shown in the next listing. This gives the other threads a chance to get a complete set of the locks needed to progress.

Listing 4.6 Fixing deadlock

```
public void propagateUpdate(Update upd_, MicroBlogNode backup_) {
  boolean acquired = false;
  boolean done = false;

  while (!done) {
    int wait = (int)(Math.random() * 10);
    try {
      acquired = lock.tryLock(wait, TimeUnit.MILLISECONDS);
      if (acquired) {
        System.out.println(ident +": recvd: "+
        ➥ upd_.getUpdateText() +" ; backup: "+backup_.getIdent());
        done = backupNode_.tryConfirmUpdate(this, update_);    ⟵┐
      }
    } catch (InterruptedException e) {
    } finally {
      if (acquired) lock.unlock();
    }
    if (!done) try {
      Thread.sleep(wait);
    } catch (InterruptedException e) { }    ⟵
  }
}

public boolean tryConfirmUpdate(MicroBlogNode other_, Update upd_) {
  boolean acquired = false;
  try {
    int wait = (int)(Math.random() * 10);
    acquired = lock.tryLock(wait, TimeUnit.MILLISECONDS);

    if (acquired) {
      long elapsed = System.currentTimeMillis() - startTime;
      System.out.println(ident +": recvd confirm: "+
      ➥ upd_.getUpdateText() +" from "+other_.getIdent()
      ➥ +" - took "+ elapsed +" millis");
```

Examine return from tryConfirm-Update()

If not done, release lock and wait

```
        return true;
      }
    } catch (InterruptedException e) {
    } finally {
      if (acquired) lock.unlock();
    }

    return false;
  }
```

In this version, you examine the return code of tryConfirmUpdate(). If it returns false, the original lock will be released. The thread will pause briefly, allowing the other thread to potentially acquire its lock.

Run this code a few times, and you should see that both threads are basically always able to progress—you've eliminated the deadlock. You may like to experiment with some different forms of the preceding versions of the deadlock code—the original, the flawed solution, and the corrected form. By playing with the code, you can get a better understanding of what is happening with the locks, and you can begin to build your intuition about how to avoid deadlock issues.

Why does the flawed attempt seem to work sometimes?

You've seen that the deadlock still exists, so what is it that causes the code in the flawed solution to sometimes succeed? The extra complexity in the code is the culprit. It affects the JVM's thread scheduler and makes it less easy to predict. This means that it will sometimes schedule the threads so that one of them (usually the first thread) is able to get into confirmUpdate() and acquire the second lock before the second thread can run. This is also possible in the original code, but much less likely.

We've only scratched the surface of the possibilities of Lock—there are a number of ways of producing more complex lock-like structures. One such concept, the latch, is our next topic.

4.3.3   *CountDownLatch*

The CountDownLatch is a simple synchronization pattern that allows for multiple threads to all agree on a minimum amount of preparation that must be done before any thread can pass a synchronization barrier.

This is achieved by providing an int value (the count) when constructing a new instance of CountDownLatch. After that point, two methods are used to control the latch: countDown() and await(). The former reduces the count by 1, and the latter causes the calling thread to wait until the count reaches 0 (it does nothing if the count is already 0 or less). This simple mechanism allows the minimum preparation pattern to be easily deployed.

In the following listing, a group of processing threads within a single process want to know that at least half of them have been properly initialized (assume that initialization of a processing thread takes a certain amount of time) before the system as a whole starts sending updates to any of them.

Listing 4.7 Using latches to help with initialization

```
public static class ProcessingThread extends Thread {
  private final String ident;
  private final CountDownLatch latch;

  public ProcessingThread(String ident_, CountDownLatch cdl_) {
    ident = ident_;
    latch = cdl_;
  }
  public String getIdentifier() {
    return identifier;
  }                                                          initialize
  public void initialize() {        ←───────────────        node
    latch.countDown();
  }
  public void run() {
    initialize();
  }
}

final int quorum = 1 + (int)(MAX_THREADS / 2);
final CountDownLatch cdl = new CountDownLatch(quorum);

final Set<ProcessingThread> nodes = new HashSet<>();
try {
  for (int i=0; i<MAX_THREADS; i++) {
    ProcessingThread local = new ProcessingThread("localhost:"+
    ➥ (9000 + i), cdl);
    nodes.add(local);
    local.start();                                Begin sending—
  }                                               quorum reached
  cdl.await();                      ←─────────────
} catch (InterruptedException e) {
} finally {
}
```

In the code, you set up a latch with a quorum value. Once that many threads are initialized, you can start processing. Each thread will cause a countDown() once it has finished initialization, so the main thread need only wait until the quorum level has been reached before starting (and sending updates, although we omitted that part of the code).

The next class we'll discuss is one of the most useful classes in the multithreaded developer's toolkit: the ConcurrentHashMap from java.util.concurrent.

4.3.4 *ConcurrentHashMap*

The ConcurrentHashMap class provides a concurrent version of the standard HashMap. This is an improvement on the synchronizedMap() functionality provided in the Collections class, because those methods return collections that have more locking than is strictly necessary.

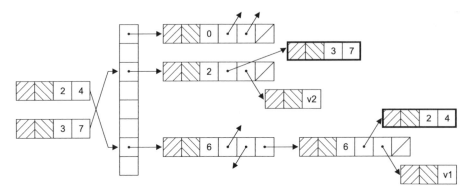

Figure 4.7   The classic view of a `HashMap`

As you can see from figure 4.7, the classic `HashMap` uses a function (the hash function) to determine which "bucket" it will store the key/value pair in. This is where the "hash" part of the class's name comes from. This suggests a rather straightforward multithreaded generalization—instead of needing to lock the whole structure when making a change, it's only necessary to lock the bucket that's being altered.

TIP A well-written implementation of a concurrent `HashMap` will be essentially lock-free on reads, and for writes will only lock the bucket being modified. Java basically achieves this, but there are some additional low-level details that most developers won't need to worry about too much.

The `ConcurrentHashMap` class also implements the `ConcurrentMap` interface, which contains some new methods to provide truly atomic functionality:

- `putIfAbsent()`—Adds the key/value pair to the HashMap if the key isn't already present.
- `remove()`—Atomically removes the key/value pair only if the key is present and the value is equal to the current state.
- `replace()`—The API provides two different forms of this method for atomic replacement in the HashMap.

As an example, you can replace the `synchronized` methods in listing 4.1 with regular, unsynchronized access if you alter the `HashMap` called `arrivalTime` to be a `Concurrent-HashMap` as well. Notice the lack of locks in the following listing—there is no explicit synchronization at all.

Listing 4.8   Using `ConcurrentHashMap`

```
public class ExampleMicroBlogTimingNode implements SimpleMicroBlogNode {
    ...
private final Map<Update, Long> arrivalTime =
➥ new ConcurrentHashMap <>();
    ...
public void propagateUpdate(Update upd_) {
    arrivalTime.putIfAbsent(upd_, System.currentTimeMillis());
```

```
  }
  public boolean confirmUpdateReceived(Update upd_) {
    return arrivalTime.get(upd_) != null;
  }
}
```

The `ConcurrentHashMap` is one of the most useful classes in `java.util.concurrent`. It provides additional multithreaded safety and higher performance, and it has no serious drawbacks in normal usage. The counterpart to it for `List` is the `CopyOnWrite-ArrayList`, which we'll discuss next.

4.3.5 *CopyOnWriteArrayList*

As the name suggests, the `CopyOnWrite-ArrayList` class is a replacement for the standard `ArrayList` class. `CopyOn-WriteArrayList` has been made thread-safe by the addition of copy-on-write semantics, which means that any operations that mutate the list will create a new copy of the array backing the list (as shown in figure 4.8). This also means that any iterators formed don't have to worry about any modifications that they didn't expect.

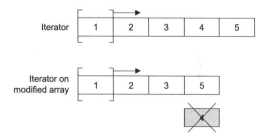

Figure 4.8   Copy-on-write array

This approach to shared data is ideal when a quick, consistent snapshot of data (which may occasionally be different between readers) is more important than perfect synchronization (and the attendant performance hit). This is often seen in non-mission-critical data.

Let's look at an example of copy-on-write in action. Consider a timeline of microblogging updates. This is a classic example of data that isn't 100 percent mission-critical and where a performant, self-consistent snapshot for each reader is preferred over total global consistency. This listing shows a holder class that represents an individual user's view of their timeline. (Then we'll use that class in listing 4.10 to show exactly how the copy-on-write behavior works.)

Listing 4.9   Copy-on-write example

```
public class MicroBlogTimeline {
  private final CopyOnWriteArrayList<Update> updates;
  private final ReentrantLock lock;
  private final String name;
  private Iterator<Update> it;                    ◁─────┐ Constructor
                                                        │ omitted
  public void addUpdate(Update update_) {
    updates.add(update_);
  }                                                   ┌──── Set up
  public void prep() {                           ◁────┘     Iterator
    it = updates.iterator();
  }
```

```
  public void printTimeline() {
    lock.lock();                                          ←──────────────  Need to
    try {                                                                  lock here
      if (it != null) {
        System.out.print(name+ ": ");
        while (it.hasNext()) {
          Update s = it.next();
          System.out.print(s+ ", ");
        }
        System.out.println();
      }
    } finally {
      lock.unlock();
    }
  }
}
```

This class is specifically designed to illustrate the behavior of an Iterator under copy-on-write semantics. You need to introduce locking in the print method to prevent the output being jumbled between the two threads, and to allow you to see the separate state of the two threads.

You can call the MicroBlogTimeline class from the code shown here.

Listing 4.10   Exposing copy-on-write behavior

```
final CountDownLatch firstLatch = new CountDownLatch(1);            ❶ Set up
final CountDownLatch secondLatch = new CountDownLatch(1);             initial
final Update.Builder ub = new Update.Builder();                      state

final List<Update> l = new CopyOnWriteArrayList<>();               ←──────┐
l.add(ub.author(new Author("Ben")).updateText("I like pie").build());
l.add(ub.author(new Author("Charles")).updateText(
➥ "I like ham on rye").build());

ReentrantLock lock = new ReentrantLock();
final MicroBlogTimeline tl1 = new MicroBlogTimeline("TL1", l, lock);
final MicroBlogTimeline tl22 = new MicroBlogTimeline("TL2", l, lock);

Thread t1 = new Thread() {
  public void run() {
    l.add(ub.author(new Author("Jeffrey")).updateText(
    ➥ "I like a lot of things").build());
    tl1.prep();
    firstLatch.countDown();
    try { secondLatch.await(); }
    ➥ catch (InterruptedException e) {  }                          ←──────┐
    tl1.printTimeline();                                                   │
  }                                                                        │  Enforce strict
};                                                                         │  event ordering
                                                                           │  with latches
Thread t2 = new Thread(){
  public void run(){
    try {
      firstLatch.await();                                          ←──────┘
      l.add(ub.author(new Author("Gavin")).updateText(
      ➥ "I like otters").build());
```

```
        tl2.prep();
        secondLatch.countDown();
    } catch (InterruptedException e) { }
    tl2.printTimeline();
}
};
t1.start();
t2.start();
```

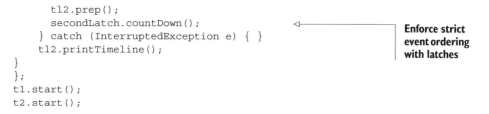

Enforce strict
event ordering
with latches

There is a lot of scaffolding in the listing—unfortunately this is difficult to avoid. There are quite a few things to notice about this code:

- CountDownLatch is used to maintain close control over what is happening between the two threads.
- If the CopyOnWriteArrayList was replaced with an ordinary List (❶), the result would be a ConcurrentModificationException.
- This is also an example of a Lock object being shared between two threads to control access to a shared resource (in this case, STDOUT). This code would be much messier if expressed in the block-structured view.

The output of this code will look like this:

```
TL2: Update [author=Author [name=Ben], updateText=I like pie, createTime=0],
     Update [author=Author [name=Charles], updateText=I like ham on rye,
     createTime=0], Update [author=Author [name=Jeffrey], updateText=I like a
     lot of things, createTime=0], Update [author=Author [name=Gavin],
     updateText=I like otters, createTime=0],

TL1: Update [author=Author [name=Ben], updateText=I like pie, createTime=0],
     Update [author=Author [name=Charles], updateText=I like ham on rye,
     createTime=0], Update [author=Author [name=Jeffrey], updateText=I like a
     lot of things, createTime=0],
```

As you can see, the second output line (tagged as TL1) is missing the final update (the one that mentions otters), despite the fact that the latching meant that mbex1 was accessed after the list had been modified. This demonstrates that the Iterator contained in mbex1 was copied by mbex2, and that the addition of the final update was invisible to mbex1. This is the copy-on-write property that we want these objects to display.

Performance of CopyOnWriteArrayList

The use of the CopyOnWriteArrayList class does require a bit more thought than using ConcurrentHashMap, which really is a drop-in concurrent replacement for HashMap. This is because of performance issues—the copy-on-write property means that if the list is altered while a read or a traversal is taking place, the entire array must be copied.

This means that if changes to the list are common, compared to read accesses, this approach won't necessarily yield high performance. But as we'll say repeatedly in chapter 6, the only way to reliably get well-performing code is to test, retest, and measure the results.

The next major common building block of concurrent code in `java.util.concurrent` is the Queue. This is used to hand off work elements between threads, and it can be used as the basis for many flexible and reliable multithreaded designs.

4.3.6   *Queues*

The queue is a wonderful abstraction (and no, we're not just saying that because we live in London, the world capital of queuing). The queue provides a simple and reliable way to distribute processing resources to work units (or to assign work units to processing resources, depending on how you want to look at it).

There are a number of patterns in multithreaded Java programming that rely heavily on the thread-safe implementations of Queue, so it's important that you fully understand it. The basic Queue interface is in `java.util`, because it can be an important pattern even in single-threaded programming, but we'll focus on the multithreaded use cases and assume that you have already encountered queues in basic use cases.

One very common use case, and the one we'll focus on, is the use of a queue to transfer work units between threads. This pattern is often ideally suited for the simplest concurrent extension of Queue—the BlockingQueue.

BLOCKINGQUEUES

The BlockingQueue is a queue that has two additional special properties:

- When trying to put() to the queue, it will cause the putting thread to wait for space to become available if the queue is full.
- When trying to take() from the queue, it will cause the taking thread to block if the queue is empty.

These two properties are very useful because if one thread (or pool of threads) is outstripping the ability of the other to keep up, the faster thread is forced to wait, thus regulating the overall system. This is illustrated in figure 4.9.

> **Two implementations of BlockingQueue**
>
> Java ships with two basic implementations of the BlockingQueue interface: the LinkedBlockingQueue and the ArrayBlockingQueue. They offer slightly different properties; for example, the array implementation is very efficient when an exact bound is known for the size of the queue, whereas the linked implementation may be slightly faster under some circumstances.

USING WORKUNIT

The Queue interfaces are all generic—they're Queue<E>, BlockingQueue<E>, and so on. Although it may seem strange, it's sometimes wise to exploit this and introduce an artificial container class to wrap the items of work.

For example, if you have a class called MyAwesomeClass that represents the units of work that you want to process in a multithreaded way, then rather than having this,

```
BlockingQueue<MyAwesomeClass>
```

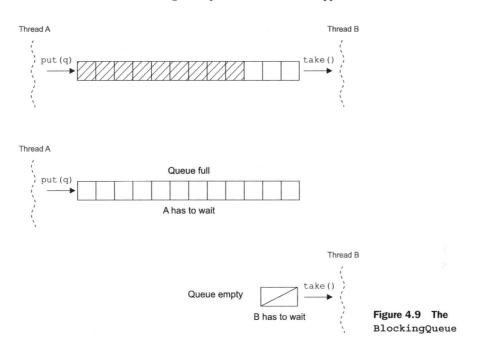

Figure 4.9 The `BlockingQueue`

it can be better to have this,

```
BlockingQueue<WorkUnit<MyAwesomeClass>>
```

where `WorkUnit` (or `QueueObject`, or whatever you want to call the container class) is a packaging interface or class that may look something like this:

```
public class WorkUnit<T> {
  private final T workUnit;

  public T getWork(){ return workUnit; }

  public WorkUnit(T workUnit_) {
    workUnit = workUnit_;
  }
}
```

The reason for doing this is that this level of indirection provides a place to add additional metadata without compromising the conceptual integrity of the contained type (`MyAwesomeClass` in this example).

This is surprisingly useful. Use cases where additional metadata is helpful are abundant. Here are a few examples:

- Testing (such as showing the change history for an object)
- Performance indicators (such as time of arrival or quality of service)
- Runtime system information (such as how this instance of `MyAwesomeClass` has been routed)

It can be much harder to add in this indirection after the fact. If you find that more metadata is required in certain circumstances, it can be a major refactoring job to add in what would have been a simple change in the WorkUnit class.

A BLOCKINGQUEUE EXAMPLE

Let's see the BlockingQueue in action in a simple example—pets waiting to be seen by a veterinarian. This example represents a collection of pets that may be seen at a vet's surgery.

Listing 4.11   Modeling pets in Java

```java
public abstract class Pet {
  protected final String name;

  public Pet(String name) {
    this.name = name;
  }
  public abstract void examine();
}

public class Cat extends Pet {
  public Cat(String name) {
    super(name);
  }
  public void examine(){
    System.out.println("Meow!");
  }
}

public class Dog extends Pet
  public Dog(String name) {
    super(name);
  }
  public void examine(){
    System.out.println("Woof!");
  }
}

public class Appointment<T> {
  private final T toBeSeen;

  public T getPatient(){ return toBeSeen; }

  public Appointment(T incoming) {
    toBeSeen = incoming;
  }
}
```

From this simple model, you can see that we can model the veterinarian's queue as LinkedBlockingQueue<Appointment<Pet>>, with the Appointment class taking the role of WorkUnit.

The veterinarian object is constructed with a queue (where appointments will be placed, by an object modeling a receptionist) and a pause time, which is the amount of downtime the veterinarian has between appointments.

We can model the veterinarian as shown in the next listing. As the thread runs, it repeatedly calls `seePatient()` in an infinite loop. Of course, in the real world, this would be unrealistic, because the veterinarian would probably want to go home for evenings and weekends, rather than hanging around the office waiting for sick animals to show up.

Listing 4.12 Modeling a veterinarian

```
public class Veterinarian extends Thread {
  protected final BlockingQueue<Appointment<Pet>> appts;
  protected String text = "";
  protected final int restTime;
  private boolean shutdown = false;

  public Veterinarian(BlockingQueue<Appointment<Pet>> lbq, int pause) {
    appts = lbq;
    restTime = pause;
  }

  public synchronized void shutdown(){
    shutdown = true;
  }

  @Override
  public void run(){
    while (!shutdown) {
      seePatient();
      try {
        Thread.sleep(restTime);
      } catch (InterruptedException e) {
        shutdown = true;
      }
    }
  }

  public void seePatient() {
    try {
      Appointment<Pet> ap = appts.take();          Blocking
      Pet patient = ap.getPatient();                take
      patient.examine();
    } catch (InterruptedException e) {
      shutdown = true;
    }
  }
}
```

Inside the `seePatient()` method, the thread will dequeue appointments and examine the pets corresponding to each in turn, and will block if there are no appointments currently waiting on the queue.

FINE-GRAINED CONTROL OF BLOCKINGQUEUE
In addition to the simple `take()` and `offer()` API, `BlockingQueue` offers another way to interact with the queue that provides even more control, at the cost of a bit of extra complexity. This is the possibility of putting or taking with a timeout, to allow

the thread encountering issues to back out from its interaction with the queue and do something else instead.

In practice, this option isn't often used, but it can be a useful technique on occasion, so we'll demonstrate it for completeness. You can see it in the following example from our microblogging scenario.

Listing 4.13 `BlockingQueue` behavior example

```java
public abstract class MicroBlogExampleThread extends Thread {
  protected final BlockingQueue<Update> updates;
  protected String text = "";
  protected final int pauseTime;
  private boolean shutdown = false;

  public MicroBlogExampleThread(BlockingQueue<Update> lbq_, int pause_) {
    updates = lbq_;
    pauseTime = pause_;
  }

  public synchronized void shutdown(){          ◁───────┐
    shutdown = true;
  }

  @Override
  public void run(){
    while (!shutdown) {                          ◁────   Allow clean thread-
      doAction();                                        shutdown
      try {
        Thread.sleep(pauseTime);
      } catch (InterruptedException e) {
        shutdown = true;                         ◁───────┘
      }
    }
  }
  public abstract void doAction();               ◁──────┐  Force subclass to
}                                                       └  implement action

final Update.Builder ub = new Update.Builder();
final BlockingQueue<Update> lbq = new LinkedBlockingQueue<>(100);

MicroBlogExampleThread t1 = new MicroBlogExampleThread(lbq, 10) {
  public void doAction(){
    text = text + "X";
    Update u = ub.author(new Author("Tallulah")).updateText(text).build();
    boolean handed = false;
    try {
      handed = updates.offer(u, 100, TimeUnit.MILLISECONDS);
    } catch (InterruptedException e) {
    }
    if (!handed) System.out.println(
    ➥ "Unable to hand off Update to Queue due to timeout");
  }
};

MicroBlogExampleThread t2 = new MicroBlogExampleThread(lbq, 1000) {
  public void doAction(){
    Update u = null;
```

```
      try {
        u = updates.take();
      } catch (InterruptedException e) {
        return;
      }
    }
  }
};
t1.start();
t2.start();
```

Running this example as is shows how the queue will quickly fill, meaning that the offering thread is outpacing the taking thread. Within a very short time, the message "Unable to hand off Update to Queue due to timeout" will start to appear.

This represents one extreme of the "connected thread pool" model—when the upstream thread pool is running quicker than the downstream one. This can be problematic, introducing such issues as an overflowing LinkedBlockingQueue. Alternatively, if there are more consumers than producers, the queue can empty. Fortunately Java 7 has a new twist on the BlockingQueue that can help—the TransferQueue.

TRANSFERQUEUES—NEW IN JAVA 7

Java 7 introduced the TransferQueue. This is essentially a BlockingQueue with an additional operation—transfer(). This operation will immediately transfer a work item to a receiver thread if one is waiting. Otherwise it will block until there is a thread available to take the item. This can be thought of as the "recorded delivery" option— the thread that was processing the item won't begin processing another item until it has handed off the current item. This allows the system to regulate the speed at which the upstream thread pool takes on new work.

It would also be possible to regulate this by using a blocking queue of bounded size, but the TransferQueue has a more flexible interface. In addition, your code may show a performance benefit by replacing a BlockingQueue with a TransferQueue. This is because the TransferQueue implementation has been written to take into account modern compiler and processor features and can operate with great efficiency. As with all discussions of performance, however, you must measure and prove benefits and not simply assume them. You should also be aware that Java 7 ships with only one implementation of TransferQueue—the linked version.

In the next code example, we'll look at how easy it is to drop in a TransferQueue as a replacement for a BlockingQueue. Just these simple changes to listing 4.13 will upgrade it to a TransferQueue implementation, as you can see here.

Listing 4.14 Replacing a `BlockingQueue` with a `TransferQueue`

```
public abstract class MicroBlogExampleThread extends Thread {
  protected final TransferQueue<Update> updates;
  ...

public MicroBlogExampleThread(TransferQueue<Update> lbq_, int pause_) {
    updates = lbq_;
    pauseTime = pause_;
  }
```

```
    ...
    }
final TransferQueue<Update> lbq = new LinkedTransferQueue<Update>(100);

MicroBlogExampleThread t1 = new MicroBlogExampleThread(lbq, 10) {
  public void doAction(){
    ...
try {
      handed = updates.tryTransfer(u, 100, TimeUnit.MILLISECONDS);
    } catch (InterruptedException e) {
    }
    ...
    }
};
```

This concludes our tour of the main building blocks that provide the raw materials for developing solid multithreaded applications. The next step is to combine them with the engines that drive concurrent code—the executor frameworks. These allow tasks to be scheduled and controlled, which lets you assemble efficient concurrent flows for handling work items and to build large multithreaded applications.

4.4   *Controlling execution*

We've spent some time in this chapter discussing work as abstract units. There's a subtlety to this, however. The part that we haven't mentioned so far is that these units are smaller than a Thread—they provide a way of running the computations contained in the work unit without having to spin up a new thread for each unit. This is often a much more efficient way of working with multithreaded code because it means that the Thread startup cost doesn't need to be paid for each unit. Instead, the threads that are actually executing the code are reused; after they finish processing one task, they will carry on with a new unit.

For the cost of a bit of extra complexity, you can access such abstractions as thread pools, worker and manager patterns and executors—some of the most versatile patterns in the developer's vocabulary. The classes and interfaces we'll focus on most closely are those that model tasks (Callable, Future, and FutureTask) and the executor classes, in particular ScheduledThreadPoolExecutor.

4.4.1   *Modeling tasks*

Our ultimate goal is to have tasks (or work units) that can be scheduled without spinning up a new thread for each one. Ultimately, this means that they have to be modeled as code that can be called (usually by an executor), rather than directly as a runnable thread.

We'll look at three different ways of modeling tasks—the Callable and Future interfaces and the FutureTask class.

CALLABLE INTERFACE
The Callable interface represents a very common abstraction. It represents a piece of code that can be called and that returns a result. Despite being a straightforward

idea, this is actually a subtle and powerful concept that can lead to some extremely useful patterns.

One typical use of a `Callable` is the anonymous implementation. The last line of this snippet sets s to be the value of `out.toString()`:

```
final MyObject out = getSampleObject();

Callable<String> cb = new Callable<String>() {
  public String call() throws Exception {
    return out.toString();
  }
};
String s = cb.call();
```

Think of an anonymous implementation of `Callable` as being a deferred invocation of the single abstract method, `call()`, which the implementation must provide.

Callable is an example of what is sometimes called a SAM type (short for "single abstract method")—this is the closest that Java 7 gets to having functions as first-class types. We'll talk more about the concept of functions as values or first-class types in later chapters, when we encounter them in non-Java languages.

FUTURE INTERFACE

The `Future` interface is used to represent an asynchronous task, in the sense of a future result from a task that may not have finished yet. We met these briefly in chapter 2 when we talked about NIO.2 and asynchronous I/O.

These are the primary methods on a `Future`:

- `get()`—This gets the result. If the result isn't yet available, `get()` will block until it is. There's also a version that takes a timeout, which won't block forever.
- `cancel()`—This allows the computation to be canceled before completion.
- `isDone()`—This allows the caller to determine whether the computation has finished.

The next snippet shows a sample use of a `Future` in a prime number finder:

```
Future<Long> fut = getNthPrime(1_000_000_000);

Long result = null;
while (result == null) {
  try {
    result = fut.get(60, TimeUnit.SECONDS);
  } catch (TimeoutException tox) { }
  System.out.println("Still not found the billionth prime!");
}
System.out.println("Found it: "+ result.longValue());
```

In this snippet, you should imagine that `getNthPrime()` returns a `Future` that is executing on some background thread (or even on multiple threads)—perhaps on one of the executor frameworks we'll discuss in the next subsection. Even on modern hardware, this calculation may be running for a long time—you may need the Future's `cancel()` method after all.

FUTURETASK CLASS

The FutureTask class is a commonly used implementation of the Future interface, which also implements Runnable. As you'll see, this means that a FutureTask can be fed to executors, which is a crucial point. The interface is basically those of Future and Runnable combined: get(), cancel(), isDone(), isCancelled(), and run(), although this last method would be called by the executor, rather than directly.

Two convenience constructors for FutureTask are also provided: one that takes a Callable and one that takes a Runnable. The connections between these classes suggest a very flexible approach to tasks, allowing a job to be written as a Callable, then wrapped into a FutureTask that can then be scheduled (and cancelled if necessary) on an executor, due to the Runnable nature of FutureTask.

4.4.2   *ScheduledThreadPoolExecutor*

The ScheduledThreadPoolExecutor (STPE) is the backbone of the thread pool classes—it's versatile and as a result is quite common. The STPE takes in work in the form of tasks and schedules them on a pool of threads.

- The thread pools can be of a predefined size or adaptive.
- Tasks can be scheduled to execute periodically or just once.
- STPE extends the ThreadPoolExecutor class (which is similar, but lacks the periodic scheduling capabilities).

One of the most common patterns for medium- to large-scale multithreaded applications is of STPE thread pools of executing threads connected by the java.util.concurrent utility classes that we've already met (such as ConcurrentHashMap, CopyOnWrite-ArrayList, BlockingQueue).

STPE is only one of a number of related executors that can be obtained very easily by using factory methods available on the Executors class in java.util.concurrent. These factory methods are largely convenience methods; they allow the developer to access a typical configuration easily, while exposing the full available interface if required.

The next listing shows an example of periodic read. This is a common usage of newScheduledThreadPool(): the msgReader object is scheduled to poll() the queue, get the work item from the WorkUnit object on the queue, and then print it.

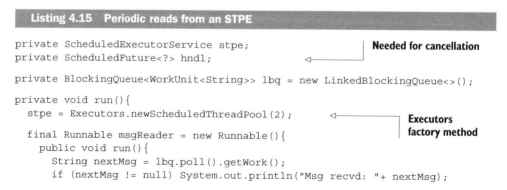

Listing 4.15 Periodic reads from an STPE

```
private ScheduledExecutorService stpe;                              Needed for cancellation
private ScheduledFuture<?> hndl;

private BlockingQueue<WorkUnit<String>> lbq = new LinkedBlockingQueue<>();

private void run(){
    stpe = Executors.newScheduledThreadPool(2);                     Executors
                                                                    factory method
    final Runnable msgReader = new Runnable(){
        public void run(){
            String nextMsg = lbq.poll().getWork();
            if (nextMsg != null) System.out.println("Msg recvd: "+ nextMsg);
```

```
    }
  };
  hndl = stpe.scheduleAtFixedRate(msgReader, 10, 10,
  ➥ TimeUnit.MILLISECONDS);
}
public void cancel() {
  final ScheduledFuture<?> myHndl = hndl;

  stpe.schedule(new Runnable() {                              Needed for
    public void run() { myHndl.cancel(true); }      ◁————————   cancellation
  }, 10, TimeUnit.MILLISECONDS);
}
```

In the example, an STPE wakes up a thread every 10 milliseconds and has it attempt to poll() from a queue. If the read returns null (because the queue is currently empty), nothing else happens and the thread goes back to sleep. If a work unit was received, the thread prints out the contents of the work unit.

Problems representing invocation with callable

There are a number of problems with the simple forms of Callable, FutureTask, and their relatives—notably that the type system gets in the way.

To see this, consider the case of trying to account for all possible signatures that an unknown method could have. Callable only provides a model of methods that take zero arguments. You'd need many different variations of Callable to account for all the possibilities.

In Java, you can work around this by being prescriptive about what method signatures exist in the systems you model. But as you'll see in part 3 of the book, dynamic languages don't share this static view of the world. This mismatch between type systems is a major theme to which we'll return. For now, just note that Callable, while useful, is a little too restrictive to build a general framework for modeling execution.

We'll now turn to one of the highlights of Java 7—the fork/join framework for lightweight concurrency. This new framework allows a wide range of concurrent problems to be handled even more efficiently than the executors we've seen in this section can do (which is no mean feat).

4.5   *The fork/join framework*

As we'll discuss in chapter 6, processor speeds (or, more properly, transistor counts on CPUs) have increased hugely in recent years. This has had the side effect that waiting for I/O is now a very common situation. This suggests that we could make better use of the processing capabilities inside our computers. The fork/join framework is an attempt to do just that—a way that also provides the biggest new additions to the concurrency arena in Java 7.

Fork/join is all about automatic scheduling of tasks on a thread pool that is invisible to the user. In order to do this, the tasks must be able to be broken up, in a way that the user specifies. In many applications, fork/join has a notion of "small" and "large" tasks that is very natural for the framework.

Let's take a quick look at some of the headline facts and fundamentals related to fork/join.

- The fork/join framework introduces a new kind of executor service, called a ForkJoinPool.
- The ForkJoinPool service handles a unit of concurrency (the ForkJoinTask) that is "smaller" than a Thread.
- The ForkJoinTask is an abstraction that can be scheduled in a more lightweight manner by the ForkJoinPool.
- Fork/join usually makes use of two kinds of tasks (although they're both represented as instances of ForkJoinTask):
  - "Small" tasks are those that can be performed straightaway without consuming too much processor time.
  - "Large" tasks are those that need to be split up (possibly more than once) before they can be directly performed.
- The framework provides basic methods to support the splitting up of large tasks, and it has automatic scheduling and rescheduling.

One key feature of the framework is that it's expected that these lightweight tasks may well spawn other instances of ForkJoinTask, which will be scheduled by the same thread pool that executed their parent. This pattern is sometimes called *divide and conquer.*

We'll start with a simple example of using the fork/join framework, then briefly touch on the feature called "work-stealing," and finally discuss the features of problems that are well suited to parallel-processing techniques. The best way to get started with fork/join is with an example.

4.5.1   *A simple fork/join example*

As a simple example of what the fork/join framework can do, consider the following case: we have an array of updates to the microblogging service that may have arrived at different times, and we want to sort them by their arrival times, in order to generate timelines for the users, like the one you generated in listing 4.9.

To achieve this, we'll use a multithreaded sort, which is a variant of MergeSort. Listing 4.16 uses a specialized subclass of ForkJoinTask—the RecursiveAction. This is simpler than the general ForkJoinTask because it's explicit about not having any overall result (the updates will be reordered in place), and it emphasizes the recursive nature of the tasks.

The MicroBlogUpdateSorter class provides a way of ordering a list of updates using the compareTo() method on Update objects. The compute() method (which you have to implement because it's abstract in the RecursiveAction superclass) basically orders an array of microblog updates by the time of creation of an update.

Listing 4.16 Sorting with a RecursiveAction

```
public class MicroBlogUpdateSorter extends RecursiveAction {
  private static final int SMALL_ENOUGH = 32;
  private final Update[] updates;
  private final int start, end;
  private final Update[] result;

  public MicroBlogUpdateSorter(Update[] updates_) {
    this(updates_, 0, updates_.length);
  }

  public MicroBlogUpdateSorter(Update[] upds_,
      int startPos_, int endPos_) {
    start = startPos_;
    end = endPos_;
    updates = upds_;
    result = new Update[updates.length];
  }

  private void merge(MicroBlogUpdateSorter left_,
      MicroBlogUpdateSorter right_) {
    int i = 0;
    int lCt = 0;
    int rCt = 0;
    while (lCt < left_.size() && rCt < right_.size()) {
      result[i++] = (left_.result[lCt].compareTo(right_.result[rCt]) < 0)
        ? left_.result[lCt++]
        : right_.result[rCt++];
    }
    while (lCt < left_.size()) result[i++] = left_.result[lCt++];
    while (rCt < right_.size()) result[i++] = right_.result[rCt++];
  }

  public int size() {
    return end - start;
  }

  public Update[] getResult() {
    return result;
  }

  @Override
  protected void compute() {
    if (size() < SMALL_ENOUGH) {
      System.arraycopy(updates, start, result, 0, size());
      Arrays.sort(result, 0, size());
    } else {
      int mid = size() / 2;
      MicroBlogUpdateSorter left = new MicroBlogUpdateSorter(
          updates, start, start + mid);
      MicroBlogUpdateSorter right = new MicroBlogUpdateSorter(
          updates, start + mid, end);
      invokeAll(left, right);
      merge(left, right)
    }
  }
}
```

32 or fewer sorted serially — (annotation pointing to `SMALL_ENOUGH = 32`)

RecursiveAction method — (annotation pointing to `protected void compute()`)

To use the sorter, you can drive it with some code like that shown next, which will generate some updates (that consist of a string of *X*s) and shuffle them, before passing them to the sorter. The output is the reordered updates.

Listing 4.17   Using the recursive sorter

```
List<Update> lu = new ArrayList<Update>();
String text = "";
final Update.Builder ub = new Update.Builder();
final Author a = new Author("Tallulah");

for (int i=0; i<256; i++) {
  text = text + "X";
  long now = System.currentTimeMillis();
  lu.add(ub.author(a).updateText(text).createTime(now).build());
  try {
    Thread.sleep(1);
  } catch (InterruptedException e) {                         Pass zero-sized
  }                                                          array, save
}                                                            allocation
Collections.shuffle(lu);
Update[] updates = lu.toArray(new Update[0]);        ◁────────┘

MicroBlogUpdateSorter sorter = new MicroBlogUpdateSorter(updates);
ForkJoinPool pool = new ForkJoinPool(4);
pool.invoke(sorter);

for (Update u: sorter.getResult()) {
  System.out.println(u);
}
```

TimSort

With the arrival of Java 7, the default sort algorithm for arrays has changed. Previously it had been a form of QuickSort, but with Java 7 it has become "TimSort"—a version of MergeSort that has been hybridized with an insertion sort. TimSort was originally developed for Python by Tim Peters, and it has been the default sort in Python since version 2.3 (2002).

Want to see evidence of TimSort's presence in Java 7? Just pass a null array of Update objects into listing 4.16. The comparisons inside the array sorting routine Arrays.sort() will fail with a null pointer exception, and you'll see the TimSort classes in the stack trace.

4.5.2   *ForkJoinTask and work stealing*

ForkJoinTask is the superclass of RecursiveAction. It's a generic class in the return type of an action (so RecursiveAction extends ForkJoinTask<Void>). This makes ForkJoinTask very suitable for map-reduce approaches that return a result from boiling down a dataset.

    ForkJoinTasks are scheduled on a ForkJoinPool, which is a new type of executor service designed specifically for these lightweight tasks. The service maintains a list of tasks for each thread, and if one task finishes, the service can reassign tasks from a fully loaded thread to an idle one.

The reason for this "work-stealing" algorithm is that without it, there could be scheduling problems related to the two sizes of tasks. In general, the two sizes of tasks will take very different lengths of time to run. For example, one thread may have a run queue consisting only of small tasks, whereas another may have only large tasks. If the small tasks run five times faster than large tasks, the thread with only small tasks may well find itself idle before the large-task thread finishes.

Work-stealing has been implemented precisely to work around this problem and allow all the pool threads to be utilized throughout the lifecycle of the fork/join job. It's completely automatic and you don't need to do anything specific to get the benefits of work-stealing. It's another example of the runtime environment doing more to help developers manage concurrency, rather than making it a manual task.

4.5.3 *Parallelizing problems*

The promise of fork/join is tantalizing, but in practice, not every problem is easily reduced to as simple a form as the multithreaded `MergeSort` in section 4.5.1.

These are some examples of problems well suited to the fork/join approach:

- Simulating the motion of large numbers of simple objects (such as particle effects)
- Log file analysis
- Data operations where a quantity is calculated from inputs (such as map-reduce operations)

Another way of looking at this is to say that a good problem for fork/join is one that can be broken up as in figure 4.10.

One practical way of determining whether a problem is likely to reduce well is to apply this checklist to the problem and its subtasks:

- Can the problem's subtasks work without explicit cooperation or synchronization between the subtasks?
- Do the subtasks calculate some value from their data without altering it (are they what a functional programmer would call "pure" functions)?
- Is divide-and-conquer natural for the subtasks? Is one outcome of a subtask the creation of more subtasks (which could be finer-grained than the task that spawned them)?

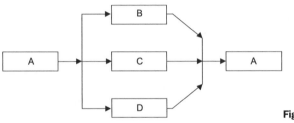

Figure 4.10 Fork and join

If the answer to the preceding questions is "Yes!" or "Mostly, but with edge cases," your problem may well be amenable to a fork/join approach. If, on the other hand, the answer to those questions is "Maybe" or "Not Really," you may well find that fork/join performs poorly, and a different synchronization approach may pay off better.

> **NOTE**   The preceding checklist could be a useful way of testing to see if a problem (such as one of the kind often seen in Hadoop and NoSQL databases) could be well handled by fork/join.

Designing good multithreaded algorithms is hard, and fork/join doesn't work in every circumstance. It's very useful within its own domain of applicability, but in the end, you have to decide whether your problem fits within the framework, and if not, you must be prepared to develop your own solution, building on the superb toolbox of `java.util.concurrent`.

In the next section, we'll discuss the often-misunderstood details of the Java Memory Model (JMM). Many Java programmers are aware of the JMM and have been coding to their own understanding of it without ever being formally introduced to it. If that sounds like you, this new understanding will build upon your informal awareness and place it onto firm foundations. The JMM is quite an advanced topic, so you can skip it if you're in a hurry to get on to the next chapter.

4.6   *The Java Memory Model (JMM)*

The JMM is described in section 17.4 of the Java Language Specification (JLS). This is quite a formal part of the spec, and it describes the JMM in terms of synchronization actions and the mathematical construct known as a *partial order*. This is great from the point of view of language theorists and implementers of the Java spec (compiler and VM makers), but it's worse for application developers who need to understand the details of how their multithreaded code will execute.

Rather than repeat the formal details, we'll list the most important rules here in terms of a couple of basic concepts: the *Synchronizes-With* and *Happens-Before* relationships between blocks of code.

- *Happens-Before*—This relationship indicates that one block of code fully completes before the other can start.
- *Synchronizes-With*—This means that an action will synchronize its view of an object with main memory before continuing.

If you've studied formal approaches to OO programming, you may have heard the expressions *Has-A* and *Is-A* used to describe the building blocks of object orientation. Some developers find it useful to think of *Happens-Before* and *Synchronizes-With* as basic conceptual building blocks for understanding Java concurrency. This is by analogy with *Has-A* and *Is-A*, but there is no direct technical connection between the two sets of concepts.

In figure 4.11 you can see an example of a volatile write that Synchronizes-With a later read access (for the `println`).

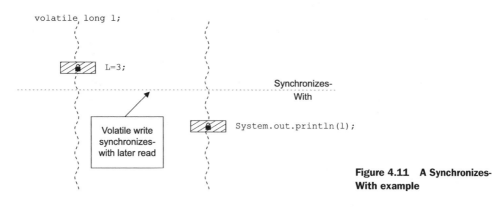

Figure 4.11   A Synchronizes-With example

The JMM has these main rules:

- An unlock operation on a monitor *Synchronizes-With* later lock operations.
- A write to a volatile variable *Synchronizes-With* later reads of the variable.
- If an action A *Synchronizes-With* action B, then A *Happens-Before* B.
- If A comes before B in program order, within a thread, then A *Happens-Before* B.

The general statement of the first two rules is that "releases happen before acquires." In other words, the locks that a thread holds when writing are released before the locks can be acquired by other operations (including reads).

There are additional rules, which are really about sensible behavior:

- The completion of a constructor *Happens-Before* the finalizer for that object starts to run (an object has to be fully constructed before it can be finalized).
- An action that starts a thread *Synchronizes-With* the first action of the new thread.
- `Thread.join()` *Synchronizes-With* the last (and all other) actions in the thread being joined.
- If X *Happens-Before* Y and Y *Happens-Before* Z then X *Happens-Before* Z (transitivity).

These simple rules define the whole of the platform's view of how memory and synchronization works. Figure 4.12 illustrates the transitivity rule.

NOTE   In practice, these rules are the minimum guarantees made by the JMM. Real JVMs may behave much better in practice than these guarantees suggest. This can be quite a pitfall for the developer because it's easy for the false sense of safety given by the behavior of a particular JVM to turn out to be just a quirk hiding an underlying concurrency bug.

From these minimum guarantees, it's easy to see why immutability is an important concept in concurrent Java programming. If objects can't be changed, there are no issues related to ensuring that changes are visible to all threads.

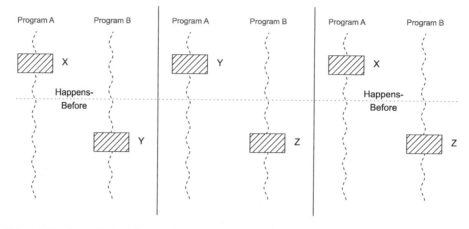

Figure 4.12 Transitivity of Happens-Before

4.7 *Summary*

Concurrency is one of the most important features of the Java platform, and a good developer will increasingly need a solid understanding of it. We've reviewed the underpinnings of Java's concurrency and the design forces that occur in multi-threaded systems. We've discussed the Java Memory Model and low-level details of how the platform implements concurrency.

More important to the modern Java developer, we've addressed the classes in `java.util.concurrent`, which should be your preferred toolkit for all new multi-threaded Java code. We've updated you with details of some of the brand new classes in Java 7, such as `LinkedTransferQueue` and the fork/join framework.

We hope we've prepared the ground for you to begin using the classes of `java.util.concurrent` in your own code. This is the single most important takeaway from this chapter. Although we've looked at some great theory, the most important part is the practical examples. Even if you just start with `ConcurrentHashMap` and the `Atomic` classes, you'll be using well-tested classes that can immediately provide real benefit to your code.

It's time to move on to the next big topic that will help you stand out as a Java developer. In the next chapter, you'll gain a firm grounding in another fundamental area of the platform—classloading and bytecode. This topic is at the heart of many of the platform's security and performance features, and it underpins many of the advanced techniques in the ecosystem. This makes it an ideal subject of study for the developer who wishes to gain an edge.

Class files and bytecode

This chapter covers

- Classloading
- Method handles
- The anatomy of class files
- JVM bytecode and why it matters
- The new `invokedynamic` opcode

One tried-and-trusted way to become a more well-grounded Java developer is to improve your understanding of how the platform works. Getting to grips with core features such as classloading and the nature of JVM bytecode can greatly help with this goal.

Imagine you have an application that makes heavy use of Dependency Injection (DI) techniques such as Spring, and it develops problems starting up and fails with a cryptic error message. If the problem is more than a simple configuration error, you may need to understand how the DI framework is implemented to track down the problem. This means understanding classloading.

Or suppose that a vendor you're dealing with goes out of business—you're left with a final drop of compiled code, no source code, and patchy documentation. How can you explore the compiled code and see what it contains?

All but the simplest applications can fail with a `ClassNotFoundException` or `NoClassDefFoundError`, but many developers don't know what these are, what the difference is between them, or why they occur.

This chapter focuses on the aspects of the platform that underlie these development concerns. We'll also discuss some more advanced features—they're intended for the enthusiasts and can be skipped if you're in a hurry.

We'll get started with an overview of classloading—the process by which the VM locates and activates a new type for use in a running program. Central to that discussion are the `Class` objects that represent types in the VM. Next, we'll look at the new Method Handles API and compare it to existing Java 6 techniques, such as reflection.

After that, we'll discuss tools for examining and dissecting class files. We'll use `javap`, which ships with the Oracle JDK, as our reference tool. Following this class file anatomy lesson, we'll turn to bytecode. We'll cover the major families of JVM opcodes and look at how the runtime operates at a low level.

Armed with a working knowledge of bytecode, we'll dive into the new `invoke-dynamic` opcode, introduced in Java 7 to help non-Java languages get the most out of the JVM as a platform.

Let's get started by discussing classloading—the process by which new classes are incorporated into a running JVM process.

5.1   *Classloading and class objects*

A .class file defines a type for the JVM, complete with fields, methods, inheritance information, annotations, and other metadata. The class file format is well-described by the standards, and any language that wants to run on the JVM must adhere to it.

The class is the smallest unit of program code that the platform can load. In order to get a new class into the current execution state of the JVM, a number of steps must be performed. First, a class file must be loaded and linked, and then it must be extensively verified. After this, a new `Class` object representing the type will be available to the running system, and new instances can be created.

In this section, we'll cover all of these steps and provide an introduction to classloaders, which are the classes that control this entire process. Let's get started by looking at loading and linking.

5.1.1   *Overview—loading and linking*

The purpose of the JVM is to consume class files and execute the bytecode they contain. To do so, the JVM must retrieve the contents of the class file as a data stream of bytes, convert it to a useable form, and add it to the running state. This two-step process is referred to as *loading and linking* (but linking breaks down into a number of subphases).

LOADING

The first step is to take the data stream of bytes that constitute the class file and to thaw out this frozen representation of the class. This process starts with a byte array (often read in from a filesystem) and produces a `Class` object that corresponds to the class you're loading. During this process, some basic checks are performed on the class, but at the end of the loading process, the `Class` object isn't fully fledged, and the class isn't yet usable.

LINKING

After loading, the class must be linked. This step breaks down into three subphases—verification, preparation, and resolution. Verification confirms that the class file conforms to expectations and won't cause runtime errors or other problems for the running system. After this, the class is prepared, and all other types referenced in the class file will be located to ensure that this class is ready to run.

This relationship between the phases of linking can be seen in figure 5.1.

5.1.2 Verification

Verification can be quite a complex process, consisting of several stages.

First is a basic integrity check. This is really part of loading and ensures that the class file is sufficiently well-formed to attempt to link.

Then comes a pass that checks that the symbolic information contained in the constant pool (discussed in detail in section 5.3.3) is self-consistent and obeys the basic behavior rules for constants. Other static checks that don't involve looking at the code (such as checking that `final` methods aren't overridden) are also performed at this time.

After this comes the most complex part of verification—checking the bytecode of methods. This involves ensuring that the bytecode is well-behaved and doesn't try to circumvent the VM's environmental controls. The following are some of the main checks that are performed:

- Check that all methods respect access control keywords
- Check that methods are called with the right number of parameters of the correct static types
- Make sure that the bytecode doesn't try to manipulate the stack in evil ways
- Ensure that variables are properly initialized before they're used
- Check that variables are only assigned suitably typed values

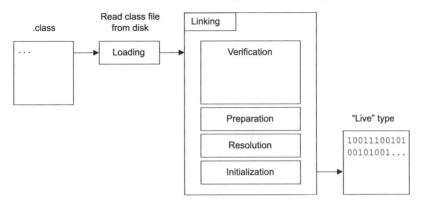

Figure 5.1 Loading and linking (with subphases of linking)

These checks are done for performance reasons—they enable the skipping of runtime checks, thus making the interpreted code run faster. They also simplify the compilation of bytecode into machine code at runtime (this is just-in-time compilation, which we'll cover in section 6.6).

PREPARATION

Preparing the class involves allocating memory and getting static variables in the class ready to be initialized, but it doesn't initialize variables or execute any VM bytecode.

RESOLUTION

Resolution causes the VM to check that every type referred to by the new class file is known to the runtime. If the types aren't known, they may also need to be loaded. This can kick off the classloading process again for any new types that have now been seen.

Once all additional types that need to be loaded have been located and resolved, the VM can initialize the class it was originally asked to load. In this final phase, any static variables can be initialized and any static initialization blocks run—you're now running bytecode from the newly loaded class. When this completes, the class is fully loaded and ready to go.

5.1.3   *Class objects*

The end result of the linking and loading process is a `Class` object, which represents the newly loaded and linked type. It's now fully functional in the VM, although for performance reasons some aspects of the `Class` object are only initialized on demand. Your code can now go ahead and use the new type and create new instances. In addition, the `Class` object of a type provides a number of useful methods, such as `getSuper-Class()`, which returns the `Class` object corresponding to the supertype.

Class objects can be used with the Reflection API for indirect access to methods, fields, constructors, and so forth. A `Class` object has references to `Method` and `Field` objects that correspond to the members of the class. These objects can be used in the Reflection API to provide indirect access to the capabilities of the class. You can see the high-level structure of this in figure 5.2.

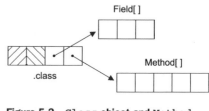

Figure 5.2 **Class** object and **Method** references

So far, we haven't discussed exactly which part of the runtime is responsible for locating and linking the byte stream that will become the newly loaded class. This is handled by classloaders—subclasses of the abstract class `ClassLoader`, and they're our next subject.

5.1.4   *Classloaders*

The platform ships with a number of typical classloaders, which are used to do different jobs during the startup and normal operation of the platform:

- *Primordial (or bootstrap) classloader*—This is instantiated very early in the process of starting up the VM, and is usually implemented as native code. It's often best to think of it as being a part of the VM itself. It's typically used to get the basic system JARs—basically `rt.jar`—loaded and it does no verification.
- *Extension classloader*—This is used to load installation-wide standard extensions. This often includes security extensions.
- *Application (or system) classloader*—This is the most widely used classloader. It's the one that will load the application classes and do the majority of the work in most SE environments.
- *Custom classloader*—In more complex environments, such as EE or the more sophisticated SE frameworks, there will often be a number of additional (a.k.a. custom) classloaders. Some teams even write classloaders that are specific to their individual applications.

In addition to their core role, classloaders are also often used to load resources (files that aren't classes, such as images or config files) from JAR files or other locations on the classpath.

Example—an instrumenting classloader

One simple example of a classloader that transforms as it loads is the one used in the EMMA testing coverage tool. EMMA is available from http://emma.sourceforge.net/.

EMMA's classloader alters the bytecode of classes as they're loaded to add extra instrumentation information. When test cases are run against the transformed code, EMMA records which methods and code branches are actually tested by the test cases. From this, the developer can see how thorough the unit tests for a class are. We'll have more to say about testing and coverage in chapters 11 and 12.

It's also quite common to encounter frameworks and other code that makes use of specialized (or even user-defined) classloaders with additional properties. These will frequently transform the bytecode as it's being loaded, as we alluded to in chapter 1.

In figure 5.3, you can see the inheritance hierarchy of classloaders, and how the different loaders relate to each other.

Let's take a look at an example of a specialized classloader and look at how classloading can be used to implement DI.

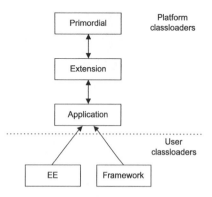

Figure 5.3 Classloader hierarchy

5.1.5 *Example—classloaders in Dependency Injection*

The core idea of DI is twofold:

- Units of functionality within a system have dependencies and configuration information upon which they rely for proper functioning.
- The dependencies are usually difficult or clumsy to express within the context of the objects themselves.

The picture that should be in your head is of classes that contain behavior, and configuration and dependencies that are external to the objects. This latter part is what is usually referred to as the *runtime wiring* of the objects.

In chapter 3, we met the Guice framework as an example of DI. In this subsection, we'll discuss how a framework could make use of classloaders to implement DI. However, the approach we'll discuss in this example is quite different from Guice. In fact, it's like a simplified version of the Spring framework.

Let's look at how we'd start an application under our imaginary DI framework:

```
java -cp <CLASSPATH> org.framework.DIMain /path/to/config.xml
```

The CLASSPATH must contain the JAR files for the DI framework, and for any classes that are referred to in the config.xml file (along with any dependencies that they have).

Let's adapt an example we've already met before to this style. The service shown in listing 3.7 is easy to adapt—and the result is shown in listing 5.1.

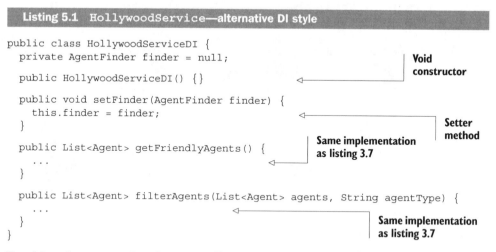

Listing 5.1 HollywoodService—alternative DI style

```java
public class HollywoodServiceDI {
  private AgentFinder finder = null;

  public HollywoodServiceDI() {}                    // Void constructor

  public void setFinder(AgentFinder finder) {       // Setter method
    this.finder = finder;
  }

  public List<Agent> getFriendlyAgents() {          // Same implementation as listing 3.7
    ...
  }

  public List<Agent> filterAgents(List<Agent> agents, String agentType) {
    ...                                             // Same implementation as listing 3.7
  }
}
```

For this to be managed under DI, you'll need a config file too, like this:

```xml
<beans>
  <bean id="agentFinder" class="wgjd.ch03.WebServiceAgentFinder"
    ... />

  <bean id="hwService" class="wgjd.ch05.HollywoodServiceDI"
      p:finder-ref="agentFinder"/>
</beans>
```

In this approach, the DI framework will use the config file to determine which objects to construct. This example will need the hwService and agentFinder beans, and the framework will call the void constructor for each bean, followed by the setter methods (for example, setFinder() for the AgentFinder dependency of HollywoodServiceDI).

This means that classloading occurs in two separate phases. The first phase (which is handled by the application classloader) loads the class DIMain and any classes that it refers to. Then DIMain starts to run and receives the location of the config file as a parameter to main().

At this point, the framework is up and running in the JVM, but the user classes specified in config.xml haven't yet been touched. In fact, until DIMain examines the config file, the framework has no way of knowing what the classes to be loaded are.

To bring up the application configuration specified in config.xml, a second phase of classloading is required. This uses a custom classloader. First, the config.xml file is checked for consistency and to make sure it's error-free. Then, if all is well, the custom classloader tries to load the types from the CLASSPATH. If any of these fail, the whole process is aborted.

If this succeeds, the DI framework can proceed to instantiate the required objects and call the appropriate setter methods on the created instances. If all of this completes OK, the application context is up and can begin to run.

We've briefly touched on a Spring-like approach to DI, which makes heavy use of classloading. Many other areas of the Java technology space are big users of classloaders and related techniques. These are some of the best-known examples:

- Plugin architectures
- Frameworks (whether vendor or homegrown)
- Class file retrieval from unusual locations (not filesystems or URLs)
- Java EE
- Any circumstance where new, unknown code may need to be added after the JVM process has already started running

This concludes our discussion of classloading, so let's move on to the next section where we'll talk about a new Java 7 API that addresses some of the same needs as reflection.

5.2 Using method handles

If you aren't familiar with the Java Reflection API (Class, Method, Field, and friends), you may want to just skim (or even skip) this section. On the other hand, if your code-bases include a lot of reflective code, you'll definitely want to read this, as it explains a new Java 7 way to achieve the same ends, with much cleaner code.

Java 7 introduces a new API for invoking methods indirectly. The key to this is the java.lang.invoke package, a.k.a. method handles. It can be thought of as a more modern approach to reflection, but without the verbosity, overhead, and rough edges that the Reflection API sometimes displays.

> ## Replacing reflective code
>
> Reflection has a lot of boilerplate code. If you've written more than a few lines of reflective code, you'll remember all the times that you have to refer to the types of the arguments of introspected methods as `Class[]`, all the packaging-up method arguments as `Object[]`, the having to catch nasty exceptions if you get it wrong, and the lack of intuition that comes from looking at reflective code.
>
> These are all very good reasons to reduce the boilerplate and improve the feel of your code by migrating your code to method handles.

Method handles were produced as part of the project to bring `invokedynamic` (which we'll discuss in section 5.5) to the JVM. But they have applications in framework and regular user code that go far beyond the `invokedynamic` use cases. We'll start by introducing the basic technology of method handles; then we'll look at an extended example that compares them to the existing alternatives and summarizes the differences.

5.2.1   *MethodHandle*

What is a `MethodHandle`? The official answer is that it's a typed reference to a method (or field, constructor, and so on) that is directly executable. Another way of saying this is that a method handle is an object that represents the ability to call a method safely.

Let's get a method handle to a two-argument method (which we may not even know the name of), and then let's call our handle on the object `obj`, passing `arg0` and `arg1` as arguments:

```
MethodHandle mh = getTwoArgMH();

MyType ret;
try {
  ret = mh.invokeExact(obj, arg0, arg1);
} catch (Throwable e) {
    e.printStackTrace();
}
```

This capability is a bit like reflection and a bit like the `Callable` interface, which you met in section 4.4. In fact, `Callable` is an earlier attempt to model the ability to call a method. The problem with `Callable` is that it can only model methods that take no arguments. In order to cope with a realistic set of different combinations of parameters and call possibilities, we'd need to make other interfaces, with specific combinations of parameters.

This is done in a lot of Java 6 code but very quickly leads to a huge proliferation of interfaces, which can cause problems for the developer (such as running out of Perm-Gen memory to store classes in—see chapter 6). By contrast, method handles can model any method signature, without needing to produce a vast number of small classes. This is achieved by means of the new `MethodType` class.

5.2.2 *MethodType*

A `MethodType` is an immutable object that represents the type signature of a method. Every method handle has a `MethodType` instance that includes the return type and the argument types. But it doesn't include the name of the method or the "receiver type"—the type that an instance method is called on.

To get new `MethodType` instances, you can use factory methods in the `MethodType` class. Here are a few examples:

```
MethodType mtToString = MethodType.methodType(String.class);
MethodType mtSetter = MethodType.methodType(void.class, Object.class);
MethodType mtStringComparator = MethodType.methodType(int.class,
String.class, String.class);
```

These are the `MethodType` instances that represent the type signatures of `toString()`, a setter method (for a member of type `Object`) and the `compareTo()` method defined by a `Comparator<String>`. The general instance follows the same pattern, with the return type passed in first, followed by the types of the arguments (all as `Class` objects), like this:

```
MethodType.methodType(RetType.class, Arg0Type.class, Arg1Type.class, ...);
```

As you can see, different method signatures can now be represented as normal instance objects, without your needing to define a new type for each signature that was required. This also gives you a simple way to ensure as much type safety as possible. If you want to know whether a candidate method handle can be called with a certain set of arguments, you can examine the `MethodType` belonging to the handle.

Now that you've seen how `MethodType` objects solve the interface-proliferation problem, let's see how we can get new method handles that point at methods from our types.

5.2.3 *Looking up method handles*

The next listing shows how to get a method handle that points at the `toString()` method on the current class. Notice that `mtToString` exactly matches the signature of `toString()`—it has a return type of `String` and takes no arguments. This means that the corresponding `MethodType` instance is `MethodType.methodType(String.class)`.

Listing 5.2 Looking up a method handle

```
public MethodHandle getToStringMH() {
    MethodHandle mh;
    MethodType mt = MethodType.methodType(String.class);          Obtain lookup
    MethodHandles.Lookup lk = MethodHandles.lookup();    ◁──────  context

    try {
        mh = lk.findVirtual(getClass(), "toString", mt);     ◁──┐  Look up
    } catch (NoSuchMethodException | IllegalAccessException mhx) {  handle
        throw (AssertionError)new AssertionError().initCause(mhx);  from
    }                                                              context
```

```
    return mh;
  }
```

The way to obtain a new method handle is to use a lookup object, like lk in listing 5.2. This is an object that can provide a method handle on any method that's visible from the execution context where the lookup was created.

To get a method handle from a lookup object, you need to provide the class that holds the method you want, the name of the method, and a MethodType corresponding to the signature you want.

> **NOTE** You can use a lookup context to get handles on methods belonging to any type, including system types. Of course, if you get handles from a class that you have no connection with, the lookup context will only be able to see or obtain handles to public methods. This means that method handles are always safe to use under security managers—there's no equivalent of the reflection setAccessible() hack.

Now that you have a method handle, the natural thing to do with it is to execute it. The Method Handles API provides two main ways to do this: the invokeExact() and invoke() methods. The invokeExact() method requires the types of arguments to exactly match what the underlying method expects. The invoke() method will perform some transformations to try to get the types to match if they're not quite right (for example, boxing or unboxing as required).

In the next subsection, we'll show a longer example of how method handles can be used to replace older techniques, such as reflection and small proxy classes.

5.2.4 *Example—reflection vs. proxies vs. MethodHandles*

If you've spent any time dealing with a codebase that contains a lot of reflection, you're probably all too familiar with some of the pain that comes from reflective code. In this subsection, we want to show you how method handles can be used to replace a lot of reflective boilerplate, and hopefully make your coding life a little easier.

Listing 5.3 shows an example adapted from an earlier chapter. The ThreadPool-Manager is responsible for scheduling new jobs onto a thread pool, and is lightly adapted from listing 4.15. It also provides the capability to cancel a running job, but this method is private.

To show the differences between method handles and other techniques, we've provided three different ways to access the private cancel() method from outside the class—the methods shown in bold in the listing. We also show two Java 6 style techniques—reflection and a proxy class, and compare them to a new MethodHandle-based approach. We're using a queue-reading task called QueueReaderTask (which implements Runnable). You'll find an implementation of QueueReaderTask in the source code which accompanies this chapter.

Listing 5.3   Providing access three ways

```java
public class ThreadPoolManager {

  private final ScheduledExecutorService stpe =
Executors.newScheduledThreadPool(2);
  private final BlockingQueue<WorkUnit<String>> lbq;

  public ThreadPoolManager(BlockingQueue<WorkUnit<String>> lbq_) {
    lbq = lbq_;
  }

  public ScheduledFuture<?> run(QueueReaderTask msgReader) {
    msgReader.setQueue(lbq);
    return stpe.scheduleAtFixedRate(msgReader, 10, 10,
TimeUnit.MILLISECONDS);
  }

  private void cancel(final ScheduledFuture<?> hndl) {          ◁──┐   Private method
    stpe.schedule(new Runnable() {                                  │   to access
      public void run() { hndl.cancel(true); }
    }, 10, TimeUnit.MILLISECONDS);
  }

  public Method makeReflective() {
    Method meth = null;

    try {
      Class<?>[] argTypes = new Class[] { ScheduledFuture.class };
      meth = ThreadPoolManager.class.getDeclaredMethod("cancel",
argTypes);
      meth.setAccessible(true);                                 ◁──┐   Required
    } catch (IllegalArgumentException | NoSuchMethodException       │   to access
| SecurityException e) {                                           │   private
      e.printStackTrace();                                         │   method
    }

    return meth;
  }

  public static class CancelProxy {
    private CancelProxy() { }

    public void invoke(ThreadPoolManager mae_, ScheduledFuture<?> hndl_) {
      mae_.cancel(hndl_);
    }
  }

  public CancelProxy makeProxy() {
    return new CancelProxy();                                          MethodType
  }                                                                    creation

  public MethodHandle makeMh() {
    MethodHandle mh;
    MethodType desc = MethodType.methodType(void.class,
ScheduledFuture.class);                                        ◁──┐   MethodHandle
                                                                   │   lookup
    try {
      mh = MethodHandles.lookup()
.findVirtual(ThreadPoolManager.class, "cancel", desc);        ◁──┘
```

```
      } catch (NoSuchMethodException | IllegalAccessException e) {
        throw (AssertionError)new AssertionError().initCause(e);
      }

      return mh;
    }
}
```

This class provides the capabilities to access the private `cancel()` method. In practice, only one of these capabilities would usually be provided—we're only showing all three in order to discuss the distinctions between them.

To see how to use the capabilities, look at this listing:

Listing 5.4   Using access capabilities

```
private void cancelUsingReflection(ScheduledFuture<?> hndl) {
  Method meth = manager.makeReflective();

  try {
    System.out.println("With Reflection");
    meth.invoke(hndl);
  } catch (IllegalAccessException | IllegalArgumentException
| InvocationTargetException e) {
    e.printStackTrace();
  }
}

private void cancelUsingProxy(ScheduledFuture<?> hndl) {
  CancelProxy proxy = manager.makeProxy();

  System.out.println("With Proxy");
  proxy.invoke(manager, hndl);              ◄──────  Proxy
}                                                     invocation
                                                      is statically
                                                      typed

private void cancelUsingMH(ScheduledFuture<?> hndl) {
  MethodHandle mh = manager.makeMh();
                                                      Signature
  try {                                               must match
    System.out.println("With Method Handle");   ◄──  exactly
    mh.invokeExact(manager, hndl);
  } catch (Throwable e) {                       ◄──
    e.printStackTrace();                              Must catch
  }                                                   Throwable
}

BlockingQueue<WorkUnit<String>> lbq = new LinkedBlockingQueue<>();
manager = new ThreadPoolManager(lbq);

final QueueReaderTask msgReader = new QueueReaderTask(100) {
  @Override
  public void doAction(String msg_) {
    if (msg_ != null) System.out.println("Msg recvd: "+ msg_);  ◄──  Use hndl
  }                                                                   to cancel
};                                                                    task later
hndl = manager.run(msgReader);                ◄──────
```

The `cancelUsing` methods all take a `ScheduledFuture` as a parameter, so you can use the preceding code to experiment with the different methods of cancellation. In practice, as a user of an API, you should not need to care how it's implemented.

In the next subsection, we'll discuss why an API or framework developer would want to use method handles over the alternatives.

5.2.5 Why choose MethodHandles?

In the last subsection, we looked at an example of how to use method handles in situations that could have used reflection or proxies in Java 6. This leaves the question—why should we use method handles instead of the older approaches?

In table 5.1 you can see that the main advantage of reflection is familiarity. Proxies may be easier to understand for simple use cases, but we believe method handles represent the best of both worlds. We strongly recommend their use in all new applications.

Table 5.1 Comparing Java's indirect method access technologies

Feature	Reflection	Proxy	Method handle
Access control	Must use `setAccesible()`. Can be disallowed by an active security manager.	Inner classes can access restricted methods.	Full access to all methods allowed from suitable context. No issue with security managers.
Type discipline	None. Ugly exception on mismatch.	Static. Can be too strict. May need a lot of PermGen for all proxies.	Type-safe at runtime. Doesn't consume PermGen.
Performance	Slow compared to alternatives.	As fast as any other method call.	Aiming to be as fast as other method calls.

One additional feature that method handles provide is the ability to determine the current class from a static context. If you've ever written logging code (such as for log4j) that looked like this,

```
Logger lgr = LoggerFactory.getLogger(MyClass.class);
```

you know that this code is fragile. If it's refactored to move into a superclass or subclass, the explicit class name would cause problems. With Java 7, however, you can write this:

```
Logger lgr = LoggerFactory.getLogger(MethodHandles.lookup().lookupClass());
```

In this code, the `lookupClass()` expression can be thought of as an equivalent to `getClass()`, which can be used in a static context. This is particularly useful in situations such as dealing with logging frameworks, which typically have a logger per user class.

With the new technology of method handles in your toolbox of techniques, let's move on to examine some of the low-level details of class files and the tools needed to make sense of them.

5.3   *Examining class files*

Class files are binary blobs, so they aren't easy to work with directly. But there are many circumstances in which you'll find that investigating a class file is necessary.

Imagine that your application needs additional methods to be made public to allow better runtime monitoring (such as via JMX). The recompile and redeploy seems to complete fine, but when the management API is checked, the methods aren't there. Additional rebuild and redeploy steps have no effect.

To debug the deployment issue, you may need to check that `javac` has produced the class file that you think it has. Or you may need to investigate a class that you don't have source for and where you suspect the documentation is incorrect.

For these and similar tasks, you must make use of tools to examine the contents of class files. Fortunately, the standard Oracle JVM ships with a tool called `javap`, very handy for peeking inside and disassembling class files.

We'll start off by introducing `javap` and some of the basic switches it provides to examine aspects of class files. Then we'll discuss some of the representations for method names and types that the JVM uses internally. We'll move on to take a look at the constant pool—the JVMs "box of useful things"—which plays an important role in understanding how bytecode works.

5.3.1   *Introducing javap*

`javap` can be used for numerous useful tasks, from seeing what methods a class declares to printing the bytecode. Let's examine the simplest form of `javap` usage, as applied to a version of the microblogging `Update` class we discussed in chapter 4.

```
$ javap wgjd/ch04/Update.class
Compiled from "Update.java"
public class wgjd.ch04.Update extends java.lang.Object {
  public wgjd.ch04.Author getAuthor();
  public java.lang.String getUpdateText();
  public int hashCode();
  public boolean equals(java.lang.Object);
  public java.lang.String toString();
  wgjd.ch04.Update(wgjd.ch04.Update$Builder, wgjd.ch04.Update);
}
```

By default, `javap` shows the `public`, `protected`, and default (that is, package-protected) visibility methods. The `-p` switch will also show the `private` methods and fields.

5.3.2   *Internal form for method signatures*

The JVM uses a slightly different form for method signatures internally than the human-readable form displayed by `javap`. As we delve deeper into the JVM, you'll see these internal names more frequently. If you're keen to keep going, you can jump ahead, but remember that this section's here—you may need to refer to it from later sections and chapters.

In the compact form, type names are compressed. For example, int is represented by I. These compact forms are sometimes referred to as *type descriptors*. A complete list is provided in table 5.2.

Table 5.2 Type descriptors

Descriptor	Type
B	byte
C	char (a 16-bit Unicode character)
D	double
F	float
I	int
J	long
L<type name>;	Reference type (such as Ljava/lang/String; for a string)
S	short
Z	boolean
[	array-of

In some cases, the type descriptor can be longer than the type name that appears in source code (for example, Ljava/lang/Object; is longer than Object, but the type descriptors are fully qualified so they can be directly resolved.

javap provides a helpful switch, -s, which will output the type descriptors of signatures for you, so you don't have to work them out using the table. You can use a slightly more advanced invocation of javap to show the signatures for some of the methods we looked at earlier:

```
$ javap -s wgjd/ch04/Update.class
Compiled from "Update.java"
public class wgjd.ch04.Update extends java.lang.Object {
  public wgjd.ch04.Author getAuthor();
    Signature: ()Lwgjd/ch04/Author;

  public java.lang.String getUpdateText();
    Signature: ()Ljava/lang/String;

  public int compareTo(wgjd.ch04.Update);
    Signature: (Lwgjd/ch04/Update;)I

  public int hashCode();
    Signature: ()I

  ...
}
```

As you can see, each type in a method signature is represented by a type descriptor.

In the next section, you'll see another use of type descriptors. This is in a very important part of the class file—the constant pool.

5.3.3   *The constant pool*

The constant pool is an area that provides handy shortcuts to other (constant) elements of the class file. If you've studied languages like C or Perl, which make explicit use of symbol tables, you can think of the constant pool as being a JVM equivalent. But unlike some other languages, Java doesn't give full access to the information contained in the constant pool.

Let's use a very simple example to demonstrate the constant pool, so we don't swamp ourselves with detail. The next listing shows a simple "playpen" or "scratchpad" class. This provides a way to quickly test out a Java syntax feature or library, by writing a small amount of code in run().

Listing 5.5   Sample playpen class

```
package wgjd.ch04;

public class ScratchImpl {
  private static ScratchImpl inst = null;

  private ScratchImpl() {
  }

  private void run() {
  }

  public static void main(String[] args) {
    inst = new ScratchImpl();
    inst.run();
  }
}
```

To see the information in the constant pool, you can use javap -v. This prints a lot of additional information—much more than just the constant pool—but let's focus on the constant pool entries for the playpen.

Here's the constant pool:

```
#1  = Class         #2          //  wgjd/ch04/ScratchImpl
#2  = Utf8          wgjd/ch04/ScratchImpl
#3  = Class         #4          //  java/lang/Object
#4  = Utf8          java/lang/Object
#5  = Utf8          inst
#6  = Utf8          Lwgjd/ch04/ScratchImpl;
#7  = Utf8          <clinit>
#8  = Utf8          ()V
#9  = Utf8          Code
#10 = Fieldref      #1.#11
➥ // wgjd/ch04/ScratchImpl.inst:Lwgjd/ch04/ScratchImpl;
#11 = NameAndType   #5:#6       //  instance:Lwgjd/ch04/ScratchImpl;
#12 = Utf8          LineNumberTable
```

```
#13 = Utf8           LocalVariableTable
#14 = Utf8           <init>
#15 = Methodref      #3.#16     //   java/lang/Object."<init>":()V
#16 = NameAndType    #14:#8     //   "<init>":()V
#17 = Utf8           this
#18 = Utf8           run
#19 = Utf8           ([Ljava/lang/String;)V
#20 = Methodref      #1.#21     //   wgjd/ch04/ScratchImpl.run:()V
#21 = NameAndType    #18:#8     //   run:()V
#22 = Utf8           args
#23 = Utf8           [Ljava/lang/String;
#24 = Utf8           main
#25 = Methodref      #1.#16     //   wgjd/ch04/ScratchImpl."<init>":()V
#26 = Methodref      #1.#27
➥ //   wgjd/ch04/ScratchImpl.run:([Ljava/lang/String;)V
#27 = NameAndType    #18:#19    //   run:([Ljava/lang/String;)V
#28 = Utf8           SourceFile
#29 = Utf8           ScratchImpl.java
```

As you can see, constant pool entries are typed. They also refer to each other, so, for example, an entry of type Class will refer to an entry of type Utf8. A Utf8 entry means a string, so the Utf8 entry that a Class entry points out will be the name of the class.

Table 5.3 shows the set of possibilities for entries in the constant pool. Entries from the constant pool are sometimes discussed with a CONSTANT_ prefix, such as CONSTANT_Class.

Table 5.3 Constant pool entries

Name	Description
Class	A class constant. Points at the name of the class (as a Utf8 entry).
Fieldref	Defines a field. Points at the Class and NameAndType of this field.
Methodref	Defines a method. Points at the Class and NameAndType of this field.
InterfaceMethodref	Defines an interface method. Points at the Class and NameAndType of this field.
String	A string constant. Points at the Utf8 entry that holds the characters.
Integer	An integer constant (4 bytes).
Float	A floating-point constant (4 bytes).
Long	A long constant (8 bytes).
Double	A double-precision floating-point constant (8 bytes).
NameAndType	Describes a name and type pair. The type points at the Utf8 that holds the type descriptor for the type.
Utf8	A stream of bytes representing Utf8-encoded characters.

Table 5.3 Constant pool entries *(continued)*

Name	Description
InvokeDynamic	(New in Java 7) See section 5.5.
MethodHandle	(New in Java 7) Describes a MethodHandle constant.
MethodType	(New in Java 7) Describes a MethodType constant.

Using this table, you can look at an example constant resolution from the constant pool of the playpen. Consider the Fieldref at entry #10.

To resolve a field, you need a name, a type, and a class where it resides: #10 has the value #1.#11, which means constant #11 from class #1. It's easy to check that #1 is indeed a constant of type Class, and #11 is a NameAndType. #1 refers to the ScratchImpl class itself, and #11 is #5:#6—a variable called inst of type ScratchImpl. So, overall, #10 refers to the static variable inst in the ScratchImpl class itself (which you might have been able to guess from the output in listing 5.6).

In the verification step of classloading, there's a step to check that the static information in the class file is consistent. The preceding example shows the kind of integrity check that the runtime will perform when loading a new class.

We've discussed some of the basic anatomy of a class file. Let's move on to the next topic, where we'll delve into the world of bytecode. Understanding how source code is turned into bytecode will help you gain a better understanding of how your code will run. In turn, this will lead to more insights into the platform's capabilities when we reach chapter 6 and beyond.

5.4 *Bytecode*

Bytecode has been a somewhat behind-the-scenes player in our discussion so far. Let's start bringing it into full view by reviewing what we've already learned about it:

- Bytecode is an intermediate representation of a program—halfway between human readable source and machine code.
- Bytecode is produced by javac from Java source code files.
- Some high-level language features have been compiled away and don't appear in bytecode. For example, Java's looping constructs (for, while, and the like) are gone, turned into bytecode branch instructions.
- Each opcode is represented by a single byte (hence the name *bytecode*).
- Bytecode is an abstract representation, not "machine code for an imaginary CPU."
- Bytecode can be further compiled to machine code, usually "just in time."

When explaining bytecode, there can be a slight chicken-and-egg problem. In order to fully understand what's going on, you need to understand both bytecode and the runtime environment that it executes in.

This is a rather circular dependency, so to solve it, we'll start by diving in and looking at a relatively simple example. Even if you don't get everything that's in this example on the first pass, you can come back to it after you've read more about bytecode in the following sections.

After the example, we'll provide some context about the runtime environment, and then catalogue the JVM's opcodes, including bytecodes for arithmetic, invocation, shortcut forms, and more. At the end, we'll round off with another example, based on string concatenation. Let's get started by looking at how you can examine bytecode from a .class file.

5.4.1 *Example—disassembling a class*

Using `javap` with the `-c` switch, you can disassemble classes. In our example, we'll use the playpen/scratchpad class we met in listing 5.5. The main focus will be to examine the bytecode contained within methods. We'll also use the `-p` switch so we can see bytecode that's contained within private methods.

Let's work section by section—there's a lot of information in each part of `javap`'s output, and it's easy to become overwhelmed. First, the header. There's nothing terribly unexpected or exciting in here:

```
$ javap -c -p wgjd/ch04/ScratchImpl.class
Compiled from "ScratchImpl.java"
public class wgjd.ch04.ScratchImpl extends java.lang.Object {
  private static wgjd.ch04.ScratchImpl inst;
```

Next is the static block. This is where variable initialization is placed, so this represents initializing `inst` to `null`. Looks like `putstatic` might be a bytecode to put a value in a static field.

```
static {};
  Code:
     0: aconst_null
     1: putstatic      #10    // Field inst:Lwgjd/ch04/ScratchImpl;
     4: return
```

The numbers in the preceding code represent the offset into the bytecode stream since the start of the method. So byte 1 is the `putstatic` opcode, and bytes 2 and 3 represent a 16-bit index into the constant pool. In this case, the 16-bit index is the value `10`, which means that the value (in this case `null`) will be stored in the field indicated by constant pool entry #10. Byte 4 from the start of the bytecode stream is the return opcode—the end of the block of code.

Next up is the constructor.

```
private wgjd.ch04.ScratchImpl();
  Code:
     0: aload_0
     1: invokespecial #15    // Method java/lang/Object."<init>":()V
     4: return
```

Remember that in Java, the void constructor will always implicitly call the superclass constructor. Here you can see this in the bytecode—it's the `invokespecial` instruction. In general, any method call will be turned into one of the VM's invoke instructions.

There's no code in the run() method, as this is just an empty scratchpad class:

```
private void run();
  Code:
     0: return
```

In the main method, you initialize inst and do a bit of object creation. This demonstrates some very common basic bytecode patterns that you can learn to recognize:

```
public static void main(java.lang.String[]);
  Code:
     0: new           #1     // class wgjd/ch04/ScratchImpl
     3: dup
     4: invokespecial #21    // Method "<init>":()V
```

This pattern of three bytecode instructions—new, dup, and invokespecial of an <init>—always represents the creation of a new instance.

The new opcode only allocates memory for a new instance. The dup opcode duplicates the element that's on top of the stack. To fully create the object, you need to call the body of the constructor. The <init> method contains the code for the constructor, so you call that code block with invokespecial. Let's look at the remaining bytecodes for the main method:

```
     7: putstatic     #10    // Field inst:Lwgjd/ch04/ScratchImpl;
    10: getstatic     #10    // Field inst:Lwgjd/ch04/ScratchImpl;
    13: invokespecial #22    // Method run:()V
    16: return
}
```

Instruction 7 saves the singleton instance that has been created. Instruction 10 puts it back on top of the stack, so that instruction 13 can call a method on it. Note that 13 is an invokespecial because the method that's being called—run()—is private. Private methods can't be overridden, so you don't want Java's standard virtual lookup to be applied. Most method calls will be turned into invokevirtual instructions.

NOTE In general, the bytecode produced by javac is quite a simple representation—it isn't highly optimized. The overall strategy is that JIT compilers do a lot of optimizing, so it helps if they have a relatively plain and simple starting point. The expression, "Bytecode should be dumb," describes the general feeling of VM implementers toward the bytecode produced from source languages.

Let's move on to discuss the runtime environment that bytecode needs. After that, we'll introduce the tables that we'll use to describe the major families of bytecode instructions—load/store, arithmetic, execution control, method invocation, and platform operations. Then we'll discuss possible shortcut forms of opcodes, before moving on to another example.

5.4.2 *The runtime environment*

Understanding the operation of the stack machine that the JVM uses is critical to understanding bytecode.

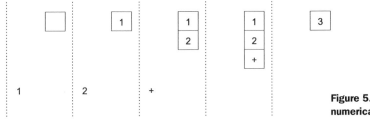

Figure 5.4 Using a stack for numerical calculations

One of the most obvious ways that the JVM doesn't look like a hardware CPU (such as an x64 or ARM chip) is that the JVM doesn't have processor registers, and instead uses a stack for all calculations and operations. This is sometimes called the operand (or evaluation) stack. Figure 5.4 shows how the operand stack might be used to perform an addition operation on two ints.

As we discussed earlier in this chapter, when a class is linked into the running environment, its bytecode will be checked, and a lot of that verification boils down to analyzing the pattern of types on the stack.

> **NOTE** Manipulations of the values on the stack will only work if the values on the stack have the correct types. Undefined or bad things could happen if, for example, we pushed a reference to an object onto the stack and then tried to treat it as an int and do arithmetic on it. The verification phase of classloading performs extensive checks to ensure that methods in newly loaded classes don't try to abuse the stack. This prevents a malformed (or deliberately evil) class from ever being accepted by the system and causing problems.

As a method runs, it needs an area of memory to use as an evaluation stack, for computing new values. In addition, every running thread needs a call stack that records which methods are currently in flight (the stack that would be reported by a stack trace). These two stacks will interact in some cases. Consider this bit of code:

```
return 3 + petRecords.getNumberOfPets("Ben");
```

To evaluate this, you put 3 on the operand stack. Then you need to call a method to calculate how many pets Ben has. To do this, you push the receiver object (the one you're calling the method on—petRecords in this example) onto the evaluation stack, followed by any arguments you want to pass in.

Then the getNumberOfPets() method will be called using an invoke opcode, which will cause control to transfer to the called method, and the just-entered method to appear in the call stack. But as you enter the new method, you need to start using a different operand stack, so that the values already on the caller's operand stack can't possibly affect results calculated in the called method.

As getNumberOfPets() completes, the return value is placed onto the operand stack of the caller, as part of the process whereby getNumberOfPets() is removed from the call stack. Then the addition operation can take the two values and add them.

Let's now turn to examining bytecode. This is a large subject, with lots of special cases, so we're going to present an overview of the main features rather than a complete treatment.

5.4.3 Introduction to opcodes

JVM bytecode consists of a sequence of operation codes (opcodes), possibly with some arguments following each instruction. Opcodes expect to find the stack in a given state, and transform the stack, so that the arguments are removed and results placed there instead.

Each opcode is denoted by a single-byte value, so there are at most 255 possible opcodes. Currently, only around 200 are used. This is too many for us to list exhaustively, but fortunately most opcodes fit into one of a number of families. We'll discuss each family in turn, to help you get a feel for them. There are a number of operations that don't fit cleanly into any of the families, but they tend to be encountered less often.

> **NOTE** The JVM isn't a purely object-oriented runtime environment—it has knowledge of primitive types. This shows up in some of the opcode families— some of the basic opcode types (such as store and add) are required to have a number of variations that differ depending on the primitive type they're acting upon.

The opcode tables have four columns:

- *Name*—This is a general name for the type of opcode. In many cases there will be several related opcodes that do similar things.
- *Args*—The arguments that the opcode takes. Arguments that start with i are bytes that are used as a lookup index in the constant pool or local variable table. If there are more of them, they're joined together, so that i1, i2 means "make a 16-bit index out of these two bytes." If an arg is shown in brackets, it means that not all forms of the opcode will use it.
- *Stack layout*—This shows the state of the stack before and after the opcode has executed. Elements in brackets indicate that not all forms of the opcode use them, or that the elements are optional (such as for invocation opcodes).
- *Description*—What the opcode does.

Let's look at an example of a row from table 5.4, by examining the entry for the `getfield` opcode. This is used to read a value from a field of an object.

```
getfield   i1, i2   [obj] → [val]      Gets the field at the constant pool index specified
                                        from the object on top of the stack.
```

The first column gives the name of the opcode—`getfield`. The next column says that there are two arguments that follow the opcode in the bytecode stream. These arguments are put together to make a 16-bit value that is looked up in the constant pool to see which field is wanted (remember that constant pool indexes are always 16-bit).

The stack layout column shows you that after the index has been looked up in the constant pool of the class of the object on top of the stack, the object is removed and is replaced by the value of that field for the object that was on top of the stack.

This pattern of removing object instances as part of the operation is just a way to make bytecode compact, without lots of tedious cleanup and remembering to remove object instances that you're finished with.

5.4.4 Load and store opcodes

The family of load and store opcodes is concerned with loading values onto the stack, or retrieving them. Table 5.4 shows the main operations in the load/store family.

Table 5.4 Load and store opcodes

Name	Args	Stack layout	Description
load	(i1)	[] → [val]	Loads a value (primitive or reference) from a local variable onto the stack. Has shortcut forms and type-specific variants.
ldc	i1	[] → [val]	Loads a constant from the pool onto the stack. Has type-specific and wide variants.
store	(i1)	[val] → []	Stores a value (primitive or reference) in a local variable, removing it from the stack in the process. Has shortcut forms and type-specific variants.
dup		[val] → [val, val]	Duplicates the value on top of the stack. Has variant forms.
getfield	i1, i2	[obj] → [val]	Gets the field at the constant pool index specified from the object on top of the stack.
putfield	i1, i2	[obj, val] → []	Puts the value into the object's field at the specified constant pool index.

As we noted earlier, there are a number of different forms of the load and store instructions. For example, there is a `dload` opcode to load a double onto the stack from a local variable, and an `astore` opcode to pop an object reference off the stack and into a local variable.

5.4.5 Arithmetic opcodes

These opcodes perform arithmetic on the stack. They take arguments from the top of the stack and perform the required calculation on them. The arguments (which are always primitive types) must always match exactly, but the platform provides a wealth of opcodes to cast one primitive type to another. Table 5.5 shows the basic arithmetic operations.

The cast opcodes have very short names, such as `i2d` for an `int` to `double` cast. In particular, the word *cast* doesn't appear in the names, which is why it's in parentheses in the table.

Table 5.5   Arithmetic opcodes

Name	Args	Stack layout	Description
add		[val1, val2] → [res]	Adds two values (which must be of the same primitive type) from the top of the stack and stores the result on the stack. Has shortcut forms and type-specific variants.
sub		[val1, val2] → [res]	Subtracts two values (of the same primitive type) from top of the stack. Has shortcut forms and type-specific variants.
div		[val1, val2] → [res]	Divides two values (of the same primitive type) from top of the stack. Has shortcut forms and type-specific variants.
mul		[val1, val2] → [res]	Multiplies two values (of the same primitive type) from top of the stack. Has shortcut forms and type-specific variants.
(cast)		[value] → [res]	Casts a value from one primitive type to another. Has forms corresponding to each possible cast.

5.4.6   *Execution control opcodes*

As mentioned earlier, the control constructs of high-level languages aren't present in JVM bytecode. Instead, flow control is handled by a small number of primitives, which are shown in table 5.6.

Table 5.6   Execution control opcodes

Name	Args	Stack layout	Description
if	b1, b2	[val1, val2] → [] or [val1] → []	If the specific condition matches, jump to the specified branch offset.
goto	b1, b2	[] → []	Unconditionally jump to the branch offset. Has wide form.
jsr	b1, b2	[] → [ret]	Jump to a local subroutine, and place the return address (the offset of the next opcode) on the stack. Has wide form.
ret	index	[] → []	Return to the offset specified in the local variable at index.
tableswitch	{depends}	[index] → []	Used to implement switch.
lookupswitch	{depends}	[key] → []	Used to implement switch.

Like the index bytes used to look up constants, the b1, b2 args are used to construct a bytecode location within this method to jump to. The jsr instructions are used to access small self-contained regions of bytecode that can be outside the main flow (it could be at offsets past the end of the main bytecode of the method). This can be useful in certain circumstances, such as in exception-handling blocks.

The wide forms of the `goto` and `jsr` instructions take 4 bytes of arguments, and construct an offset, which can be larger than 64 KB. This isn't often needed.

5.4.7 Invocation opcodes

The invocation opcodes comprise four opcodes for handling general method calling, plus the special `invokedynamic` opcode, new with Java 7, which we'll discuss in more detail in section 5.5. The five method invocation opcodes are shown in table 5.7.

Table 5.7 Invocation opcodes

Name	Args	Stack layout	Description
invokestatic	i1, i2	[(val1, ...)] → []	Calls a static method.
invokevirtual	i1, i2	[obj, (val1, ...)] → []	Calls a "regular" instance method.
invokeinterface	i1, i2, count, 0	[obj, (val1, ...)] → []	Calls an interface method.
invokespecial	i1, i2	[obj, (val1, ...)] → []	Calls a "special" instance method.
invokedynamic	i1, i2, 0, 0	[val1, ...] → []	Dynamic invocation; see section 5.5.

There are a couple of wrinkles to notice with the invocation opcodes. First off is that `invokeinterface` has extra parameters. These are present for historical and backward compatibility reasons and aren't used these days. The two extra zeros on `invokedynamic` are present for forward-compatibility reasons.

The other important point is the distinction between a regular and a special instance method call. A regular call is virtual. This means that the exact method to be called is looked up at runtime using the standard Java rules of method overriding. Special calls don't take overrides into account. This is important for two cases—`private` methods and calls to a superclass method. In both cases, you don't want the override rules to be triggered, so you need a different invocation opcode to allow for this case.

5.4.8 Platform operation opcodes

The platform operation family of opcodes includes the `new` opcode, for allocating new object instances, and the thread-related opcodes, such as `monitorenter` and `monitorexit`. The details of this family can be seen in table 5.8.

The platform opcodes are used to control certain aspects of object lifecycle, such as creating new objects and locking them. It's important to notice that the `new` opcode only allocates storage. The high-level conception of object construction also includes running the code inside the constructor.

Table 5.8   Platform opcodes

Name	Args	Stack layout	Description
new	i1, i2	[] → [obj]	Allocates memory for a new object, of the type specified by the constant at the specified index.
monitorenter		[obj] → []	Locks an object.
monitorexit		[obj] → []	Unlocks an object.

At the bytecode level, the constructor is turned into a method with a special name—<init>. This can't be called from user Java code, but can be called by bytecode. This leads to a distinctive bytecode pattern that directly corresponds to object creation—a new followed by a dup followed by an invokespecial to call the <init> method.

5.4.9   *Shortcut opcode forms*

Many of the opcodes have shortcut forms to save a few bytes here and there. The general pattern is that certain local variables will be accessed much more frequently than others, so it makes sense to have a special opcode that means "do the general operation directly on the local variable," rather than having to specify the local variable as an argument. This gives rise to opcodes such as aload_0 and dstore_2 within the load/store family.

Let's put some of this theory to the test, and do another example.

5.4.10   *Example—string concatenation*

Let's add content to the playpen class to demonstrate slightly more advanced bytecode—code that touches on most of the major bytecode families we've already met.

Remember that in Java, String is immutable. So what happens when you concatenate two strings together with the + operator? You have to create a new String object, but there's more going on here than might be apparent at first.

Consider the playpen with the run() method adjusted as shown:

```java
private void run(String[] args) {
  String str = "foo";
  if (args.length > 0) str = args[0];
  System.out.println("this is my string: " + str);
}
```

The bytecode corresponding to this relatively simple method is as follows:

```
$ javap -c -p wgjd/ch04/ScratchImpl.class
Compiled from "ScratchImpl.java"

  private void run(java.lang.String[]);
    Code:
      0: ldc           #17                 // String foo
      2: astore_2
      3: aload_1
```

```
 4: arraylength
 5: ifle          12 #A
```

If the size of the array you're passed is less than or equal to 0, jump forward to instruction 12.

```
 8: aload_1
 9: iconst_0
10: aaload
11: astore_2
12: getstatic     #19
```
➡ `// Field java/lang/System.out:Ljava/io/PrintStream;`

The preceding line shows how the bytecode represents an access to System.out.

```
15: new           #25                   // class java/lang/StringBuilder
18: dup
19: ldc           #27                   // String this is my string:
21: invokespecial #29
```
➡ `// Method java/lang/StringBuilder."<init>":(Ljava/lang/String;)V`
```
24: aload_2
25: invokevirtual #32
```
➡ `// Method java/lang/StringBuilder.append`
➡ `(Ljava/lang/String;)Ljava/lang/StringBuilder;`
```
28: invokevirtual #36
```
➡ `// Method java/lang/StringBuilder.toString:()Ljava/lang/String;`

These instructions show the creation of the concatenated string you want to output. In particular, instructions 15–23 show object creation (new, dup, invokespecial), but this case includes an ldc (load constant) after the dup. This bytecode pattern indicates that you're calling a nonvoid constructor—StringBuilder(String) in this case.

This result may at first be a little surprising. You're just concatenating some strings, and all of a sudden the bytecode is telling you that underneath you're really creating additional StringBuilder objects, and calling append(), then toString() on them. The reason behind this is that Java's strings are immutable. You can't modify the string object by concatenating it, so instead you have to make a new object. The String-Builder is just a convenient way to do this.

Finally, let's call the method to print out the result:

```
31: invokevirtual #40
```
➡ `// Method java/io/PrintStream.println:(Ljava/lang/String;)V`
```
34: return
```

Finally, with the output string assembled, you can call the println() method. This is being called on System.out because the top two elements of the stack at this point are [System.out, <output string>]—just as you'd expect from table 5.7, which defines the stack layout for a valid invokevirtual.

To become a truly well-grounded Java developer, you should run javap against some of your own classes and learn to recognize common bytecode patterns. For now, with this brief introduction to bytecode under our belts, let's move on to tackle our next subject. This is one of the major new features of Java 7—invokedynamic.

5.5   *Invokedynamic*

This section deals with one of the most technically sophisticated new features of Java 7. But despite being enormously powerful, it isn't a feature that will necessarily be used directly by every working developer, because it involves a very advanced use case. This feature is for frameworks developers and non-Java languages at present.

This means that if you're not interested in knowing how the platform works under the hood, or the details of the new bytecode, feel free to skip ahead to the summary section or the next chapter.

If you're still here, good. We can get on with explaining how unusual the appearance of `invokedynamic` is. Java 7 introduces a brand new bytecode—a development that has not previously occurred in the Java world. The new opcode is `invokedynamic`, and it's a new type of invocation instruction, so it's used for making method calls. It's used to indicate to the VM that it must defer figuring out which method to call. That is, the VM doesn't need to work all the details out at compile or link time as it usually does.

Instead, the details of what method is needed should be decided at runtime. This is done by calling a helper method that makes the decision of which method ought to be called.

> ### javac won't emit invokedynamic
>
> There is no direct Java language support for `invokedynamic` in Java 7—no Java expression will be directly compiled into an `invokedynamic` bytecode by `javac`. Java 8 is expected to add more language constructs (such as default methods) that will make use of the dynamic capabilities.
>
> Instead, `invokedynamic` is an improvement that is squarely targeted at non-Java languages. The bytecode has been added for dynamic languages to make use of when targeting the Java 7 VM (but some clever Java frameworks have found ways to make it work for them too).

In this section, we'll cover the details of how `invokedynamic` works, and look at a detailed example of decompiling a call site that makes use of the new bytecode. Note that it isn't necessary to fully understand this in order to use languages and frameworks that leverage `invokedynamic`.

5.5.1   *How invokedynamic works*

To support `invokedynamic`, several new entries have been added to the constant pool definitions. These provide necessary support to `invokedynamic` that can't be provided within the constraints of Java 6 technology.

The index provided to an `invokedynamic` instruction must point at a constant of type `CONSTANT_InvokeDynamic`. It has two 16-bit indices (that is, 4 bytes) attached to it. The first index is into a table of methods that will determine what to call. These are called bootstrap methods (sometimes BSMs), and they have to be static and have a certain argument signature. The second index is to a `CONSTANT_NameAndType`.

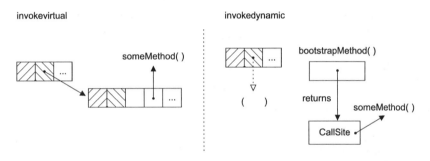

Figure 5.5   Virtual vs. dynamic dispatch

From this, you can see that a CONSTANT_InvokeDynamic is like an ordinary CONSTANT_MethodRef, except that instead of specifying which class's constant pool to look up the method in, an invokedynamic call uses a bootstrap method to provide an answer.

Bootstrap methods take in information about the call site, and link the dynamic call, by returning an instance of CallSite. This call site holds a MethodHandle, which is the effect of calling the call site.

An invokedynamic instruction starts off without a target method—it's said to be unlinked. The first time that the call is executed, the bootstrap method for the site is called. The bootstrap method returns a CallSite, which is then linked to the invokedynamic instruction. This can be seen in figure 5.5.

With the CallSite linked, the actual method call can then be made—it's to the MethodHandle being held by the CallSite. This setup means that invokedynamic calls can potentially be optimized by the JIT compiler in a similar way to invokevirtual calls. We'll talk more about these optimizations in the next chapter.

It's also worth noting that some CallSite objects can be relinked (made to point at different target methods over their lifetime). Some dynamic languages will make quite heavy use of this feature.

In the next subsection, we'll look at a simple example of how an invokedynamic call is represented in bytecode.

5.5.2   *Example—disassembling an invokedynamic call*

As we noted previously, Java 7 doesn't have syntax support for invokedynamic. Instead, you have to use a bytecode manipulation library to produce a .class file with the dynamic call instruction in it. One good choice for this is the ASM library (http://asm.ow2.org/)—this is an industrial strength library used in a wide range of well-known Java frameworks.

Using this library, we can construct a representation of a class that includes an invokedynamic instruction, then convert it to a byte stream. This can either be written out to disk or handed to a classloader for insertion into the running VM.

One simple example is to have ASM produce a class that has just a single static method containing a single invokedynamic instruction. This method can then be called from normal Java code—it's wrapping (or hiding) the dynamic nature of the real call. Remi Forax and the ASM team provided a simple tool to produce test classes that do exactly this, as part of the development of invokedynamic, and ASM was one of the first tools to fully support the new bytecode.

As an example, let's look at the bytecode for such a wrapper method:

```
public static java.math.BigDecimal invokedynamic();
  Code:
     0: invokedynamic #22,  0
➡ // InvokeDynamic #0:_:()Ljava/math/BigDecimal;
     5: areturn
```

So far, there's not much to see—most of the complexity is happening in the constant pool. So let's look at those entries that relate to the dynamic call:

```
BootstrapMethods:
  0: #17 invokestatic test/invdyn/DynamicIndyMakerMain.bsm:
➡ (Ljava/lang/invoke/MethodHandles$Lookup;Ljava/lang/String;
➡ Ljava/lang/invoke/MethodType;Ljava/lang/Object;)
➡ Ljava/lang/invoke/CallSite;
    Method arguments:
       #19 1234567890.1234567890
#10 = Utf8                 ()Ljava/math/BigDecimal;
#18 = Utf8                 1234567890.1234567890
#19 = String               #18    //   1234567890.1234567890
#20 = Utf8                 _
#21 = NameAndType          #20:#10   //   _:()Ljava/math/BigDecimal;
#22 = InvokeDynamic        #0:#21    //   #0:_:()Ljava/math/BigDecimal;
```

This does take a bit of looking at to fully decode. Let's step through it:

- The invokedynamic opcode points at entry #22. This refers to the bootstrap method #0 and the NameAndType #21.
- The BSM at #0 is an ordinary static method bsm() on a class called Dynamic-IndyMakerMain. It has the correct signature for a BSM.
- The entry at #21 gives the name of this particular dynamic linkage site, "_", and the return type, BigDecimal (which is stored at #10).
- Entry #19 is a static argument that is passed into the bootstrap method.

As you can see, there is quite a lot of machinery required to ensure type safety. There are still plenty of ways this can go wrong at runtime, but this mechanism goes a long way to providing safety while still remaining flexible.

NOTE   There is an additional level of indirection, or flexibility, available, in that the BootstrapMethods table points at method handles, rather than methods directly. We've omitted this in the preceding discussion, as it can obscure what's happening and doesn't really help when trying to understand how the mechanism works.

This marks the end of our discussion of invokedynamic and the inner workings of bytecode and classloading.

5.6 *Summary*

In this chapter, we've taken a quick first look into bytecode and classloading. We've dissected the class file format and taken a brief tour through the runtime environment that the JVM provides. By learning more about the internals of the platform, you'll become a better developer.

These are some of the things that we hope you've learned from this chapter:

- The class file format and classloading are central to the operation of the JVM. They're essential for any language that wants to run on the VM.
- The various phases of classloading enable both security and performance features at runtime.
- Method handles are a major new API with Java 7—an alternative to reflection.
- JVM bytecode is organized into families with related functionality.
- Java 7 introduces invokedynamic—a new way of calling methods.

It's time to move on to the next big topic that will help you stand out as a well-grounded Java developer. By reading the next chapter, you'll get a firm grounding in the often-misunderstood subject of performance analysis. You'll learn how to measure and tune for performance and how to get the most out of some of the powerful technology at the heart of the JVM, such as the JIT compiler, which turns bytecode into super-fast machine code.

Understanding
performance tuning

Poor performance kills applications—it's bad for your customers and your application's reputation. Unless you have a totally captive market, your customers will vote with their feet—they'll already be out of the door, heading to a competitor. To stop poor performance harming your project, you need to understand performance analysis and how to make it work for you.

Performance analysis and tuning is a huge subject, and there are too many treatments out there that focus on the wrong things. So we're going to start by telling you the big secret of performance tuning.

Here it is—the single biggest secret of performance tuning: *You have to measure. You can't tune properly without measuring.*

And here's why: The human brain is pretty much always wrong when it comes to guessing what the slow parts of systems are. Everyone's is. Yours, mine, James

Gosling's—we're all subject to our subconscious biases and tend to see patterns that may not be there.

In fact, the answer to the question, "Which part of my Java code needs optimizing?" is quite often, "None of it."

Consider a typical (if rather conservative) ecommerce web application, providing services to a pool of registered customers. It has an SQL database, Apache web servers fronting Java application servers, and a fairly standard network configuration connecting all this up. Very often, the non-Java parts of the system (database, filesystem, network) are the real bottleneck, but without measurement, the Java developer would never know that. Instead of finding and fixing the real problem, the developer may will waste time on micro-optimization of code aspects that aren't really contributing to the issue.

The kind of fundamental questions that you want to be able to answer are these:

- If you have a sales drive and suddenly have 10 times as many customers, will the system have enough memory to cope?
- What is the average response time your customers see from your application?
- How does that compare to your competitors?

To do performance tuning, you have to get out of the realm of guessing about what's making the system slow. You have to start knowing, and the only way to know for sure is to measure.

You also need to understand what performance tuning isn't. It isn't

- A collection of tips and tricks
- Secret sauce
- Fairy dust that you sprinkle on at the end of a project

Be especially careful of the "tips and tricks" approaches. The truth is that the JVM is a very sophisticated and highly tuned environment, and without proper context, most of these tips are useless (and may actually be harmful). They also go out of date very quickly as the JVM gets smarter and smarter at optimizing code.

Performance analysis is really a type of experimental science. You can think of your code as a type of science experiment that has inputs and produces "outputs"—performance metrics that indicate how efficiently the system is performing the work asked of it. The job of the performance engineer is to study these outputs and look for patterns. This makes performance tuning a branch of applied statistics, rather than a collection of old wives' tales and applied folklore.

This chapter is here to help you get started—it's an introduction to the practice of Java performance tuning. But this is a big subject, and we only have space to give you a primer on some essential theory and some signposts. We'll try to answer the most fundamental questions:

- Why does performance matter?
- Why is performance analysis hard?

- What aspects of the JVM make it potentially complex to tune?
- How should performance tuning be thought about and approached?
- What are the most common underlying causes of slowness?

We'll also give you an introduction to the two subsystems in the JVM that are the most important when it comes to performance-related matters:

- The garbage collection subsystem
- The JIT compiler

This should be enough to get you started and help you apply this (admittedly somewhat theory-heavy) knowledge to the real problems you face in your code.

Let's get going by taking a quick look at some fundamental vocabulary that will enable you to express and frame your performance problems and goals.

6.1   *Performance terminology—some basic definitions*

To get the most out of our discussions in this chapter, we need to formalize some notions of performance that you may be aware of. We'll begin by defining some of the most important terms in the performance engineer's lexicon:

- Latency
- Throughput
- Utilization
- Efficiency
- Capacity
- Scalability
- Degradation

A number of these terms are discussed by Doug Lea in the context of multithreaded code, but we're considering a much wider context here. When we speak of performance, we could mean anything from a single multithreaded process all the way up to an entire clustered server platform.

6.1.1   *Latency*

Latency is the end-to-end time taken to process a single work-unit at a given workload. Quite often latency is quoted just for "normal" workloads, but an often-useful performance measure is the graph showing latency as a function of increasing workload.

The graph in figure 6.1 shows a sudden, nonlinear degradation of a performance metric (for example latency) as the workload increases. This is usually called a performance elbow.

6.1.2   *Throughput*

Throughput is the number of units of work that a system can perform in some time period with given resources. One commonly quoted number is transactions per second

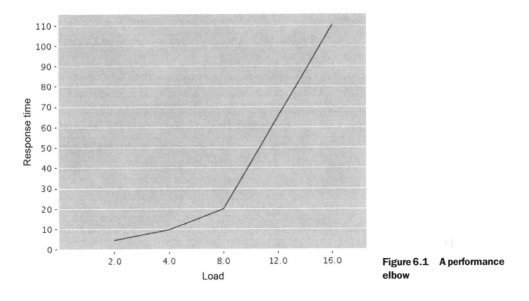

Figure 6.1 **A performance elbow**

on some reference platform (for example, a specific brand of server with specified hardware, OS, and software stack).

6.1.3 Utilization

Utilization represents the percentage of available resources that are being used to handle work units, instead of housekeeping tasks (or just being idle). People will commonly quote a server as being 10 percent utilized—this refers to the percentage of CPU processing work units during normal processing time. Note that there can be a very large difference between the utilization levels of different resources, such as CPU and memory.

6.1.4 Efficiency

The *efficiency* of a system is equal to the throughput divided by the resources used. A system that requires more resources to produce the same throughput is less efficient.

For example, consider comparing two clustering solutions. If solution A requires twice as many servers as solution B for the same throughput, it's half as efficient.

Remember that resources can also be considered in cost terms—if solution X costs twice as much (or requires twice as many staff to run the production environment) as solution Y, it's only half as efficient.

6.1.5 Capacity

Capacity is the number of work units (such as transactions) that can be in flight through the system at any time. That is, it's the amount of simultaneous processing available at specified latency or throughput.

6.1.6   Scalability

As resources are added to a system, the throughput (or latency) will change. This change in throughput or latency is the *scalability* of the system.

If solution A doubles its throughput when the available servers in a pool are doubled, it's scaling in a perfectly linear fashion. Perfect linear scaling is very, very difficult to achieve under most circumstances.

You should also note that the scalability of a system is dependent on a number of factors, and it isn't constant. A system can scale close to linearly up until some point and then begin to degrade badly. That's a different kind of performance elbow.

6.1.7   Degradation

If you add more work units, or clients for network systems, without adding more resources, you'll typically see a change in the observed latency or throughput. This change is the *degradation* of the system under additional load.

Positive and negative degradation

The degradation will, under normal circumstances, be negative. That is, adding work units to a system will cause a negative effect on performance (such as causing the latency of processing to increase). But there are circumstances under which degradation could be positive.

For example, if the additional load causes some part of the system to cross a threshold and switch to a high-performance mode, this can cause the system to work more efficiently and reduce processing times even though there is actually more work to be done. The JVM is a very dynamic runtime system, and there are several parts of it that could contribute to this sort of effect.

The preceding terms are the most frequently used indicators of performance. There are others that are occasionally important, but these are the basic system statistics that will normally be used to guide performance tuning. In the next section, we'll lay out an approach that is grounded in close attention to these numbers and that is as quantitative as possible.

6.2   A pragmatic approach to performance analysis

Many developers, when they approach the task of performance analysis, don't start with a clear picture of what they want to achieve by doing the analysis. A vague sense that the code "ought to run faster" is often all that developers or managers have when the work begins.

But this is completely backward. In order to do really effective performance tuning, there are key areas that you should have think about before beginning any kind of technical work. You should know the following things:

- What observable aspects of your code you're measuring
- How to measure those observables

- What the goals for the observables are
- How you'll recognize when you're done with performance tuning
- What the maximum acceptable cost is (in terms of developer time invested and additional complexity in the code) for the performance tuning
- What not to sacrifice as you optimize

Most importantly, as we'll say many times in this chapter, you *have* to measure. Without measurement of at least one observable, you aren't doing performance analysis.

It's also very common when you start measuring your code, to discover that time isn't being spent where you think it is. A missing database index, or contended filesystem locks can be the root of a lot of performance problems. When thinking about optimizing your code, you should always remember that it's very possible that the code isn't the issue. In order to quantify where the problem is, the first thing you need to know is what you're measuring.

6.2.1 *Know what you're measuring*

In performance tuning, you always have to be measuring something. If you aren't measuring an observable, you're not doing performance tuning. Sitting and staring at your code, hoping that a faster way to solve the problem will strike you, isn't performance analysis.

> **TIP** To be a good performance engineer, you should understand terms such as mean, median, mode, variance, percentile, standard deviation, sample size, and normal distribution. If you aren't familiar with these concepts, you should start with a quick web search and do further reading if needed.

When undertaking performance analysis, it's important to know exactly which of the observables we described in the last section are important to you. You should always tie your measurements, objectives, and conclusions to one or more of the basic observables we introduced.

Here are some typical observables that are good targets for performance tuning:

- Average time taken for method `handleRequest()` to run (after warmup)
- The 90th percentile of the system's end-to-end latency with 10 concurrent clients
- The degradation of the response time as you increase from 1 to 1,000 concurrent users

All of these represent quantities that the engineer might want to measure, and potentially tune. In order to obtain accurate and useful numbers, a basic knowledge of statistics is essential.

Knowing what you're measuring and having confidence that your numbers are accurate is the first step. But vague or open-ended objectives don't often produce good results, and performance tuning is no exception.

6.2.2   *Know how to take measurements*

There are only two ways to determine precisely how long a method or other piece of code takes to run:

- Measure it directly, by inserting measurement code into the source class
- Transform the class that is to be measured at class loading time

Most simple, direct performance measuring techniques will rely on one (or both) of these techniques.

We should also mention the JVM Tool Interface (JVMTI), which can be used to create very sophisticated profilers, but it has drawbacks. It requires the performance engineer to write native code, and the profiling numbers it produces are essentially statistical averages, rather than direct measurements.

DIRECT MEASUREMENT

Direct measurement is the easiest technique to understand, but it's also intrusive. In its simplest form, it looks like this:

```
long t0 = System.currentTimeMillis();
methodToBeMeasured();
long t1 = System.currentTimeMillis();
long elapsed = t1 - t0;
System.out.println("methodToBeMeasured took "+ elapsed +" millis");
```

This will produce an output line that should give a millisecond-accurate view of how long `methodToBeMeasured()` took to run. The inconvenient part is that code like this has to be added throughout the codebase, and as the number of measurements grows, it becomes difficult to avoid being swamped with data.

There are other problems too—what happens if `methodToBeMeasured()` takes under a millisecond to run? As we'll see later in this chapter, there are also cold-start effects to worry about—later runs of the method may well be quicker than earlier runs.

AUTOMATIC INSTRUMENTATION VIA CLASSLOADING

In chapters 1 and 5 we discussed how classes are assembled into an executing program. One of the key steps that is often overlooked is the transformation of bytecode as it's loaded. This is incredibly powerful, and it lies at the heart of many modern techniques in the Java platform. One simple example of it is automatic instrumentation of methods.

In this approach, `methodToBeMeasured()` is loaded by a special classloader that adds in bytecode at the start and end of the method to record the times at which the method was entered and exited. These timings are typically written to a shared data structure, which is accessed by other threads. These threads act on the data, typically either writing output to log files or contacting a network-based server that processes the raw data.

This technique lies at the heart of many high-end performance monitoring tools (such as OpTier CoreFirst) but at time of writing, there seems to be no actively maintained open source tool that fills the same niche.

> **NOTE** As we'll discuss later, Java methods start off interpreted, then switch to compiled mode. For true performance numbers, you have to discard the

timings generated when in interpreted mode, as they can badly skew the results. Later we'll discuss in more detail how you can know when a method has switched to compiled mode.

Using one or both of these techniques will allow you to produce numbers for how quickly a given method executes. The next question is, what do you want the numbers to look like when you've finished tuning?

6.2.3 *Know what your performance goals are*

Nothing focuses the mind like a clear target, so just as important as knowing what to measure is knowing and communicating the end goal of tuning. In most cases, this should be a simple and precisely stated goal:

- Reduce 90th percentile end-end latency by 20 percent at 10 concurrent users
- Reduce mean latency of `handleRequest()` by 40 percent and variance by 25 percent

In more complex cases, the goal may be to reach several related performance targets at once. You should be aware that the more separate observables that you measure and try to tune, the more complex the performance exercise can become. Optimizing for one performance goal can negatively impact on another.

Sometimes it's necessary to do some initial analysis, such as determining what the important methods are, before setting goals, such as making them run faster. This is fine, but after the initial exploration it's almost always better to stop and state your goals before trying to achieve them. Too often developers will plow on with the analysis without stopping to elucidate their goals.

6.2.4 *Know when to stop optimizing*

In theory, knowing when it's time to stop optimizing is easy—you're done when you've achieved your goals. In practice, however, it's easy to get sucked into performance tuning. If things go well, the temptation to keep pushing and do even better can be very strong. Alternatively, if you're struggling to reach your goal, it's hard to keep from trying out different strategies in an attempt to hit the target.

Knowing when to stop involves having an awareness of your goals, but also a sense of what they're worth. Getting 90 percent of the way to a performance goal can often be enough, and the engineer's time may well be spent better elsewhere.

Another important consideration is how much effort is being spent on rarely used code paths. Optimizing code that accounts for 1 percent or less of the program's runtime is almost always a waste of time, yet a surprising number of developers will engage in this behavior.

Here's a set of very simple guidelines for knowing what to optimize. You may need to adapt these for your particular circumstances, but they work well for a wide range of situations:

- Optimize what matters, not what is easy to optimize.
- Hit the most important (usually the most often called) methods first.

- Take low-hanging fruit as you come across it, but be aware of how often the code that it represents is called.

At the end, do another round of measurement. If you haven't hit your performance goals, take stock. Look and see how close you are to hitting those goals, and whether the gains you've made have had the desired impact on overall performance.

6.2.5   *Know the cost of higher performance*

All performance tweaks have a price tag attached.

- There's the time taken to do the analysis and develop an improvement (and it's worth remembering that the cost of developer time is almost always the greatest expense on any software project).
- There's the additional technical complexity that the fix will probably have introduced. (There are performance improvements that also simplify the code, but they're not the majority of cases.)
- Additional threads may have been introduced to perform auxiliary tasks to allow the main processing threads to go faster, and these threads may have unforeseen effects on the overall system at higher loads.

Whatever the price tag, pay attention to it and try identify it before you finish a round of optimization.

It often helps to have some idea of what the maximum acceptable cost for higher performance is. This can be set as a time constraint on the developers doing the tuning, or as numbers of additional classes or lines of code. For example, a developer could decide that no more than a week should be spent optimizing, or that the optimized classes should not grow by more than 100 percent (double their original size).

6.2.6   *Know the danger of premature optimization*

One of the most famous quotes on optimization is from Donald Knuth:

> Programmers waste enormous amounts of time thinking about, or worrying about, the speed of noncritical parts of their programs, and these attempts at efficiency actually have a strong negative impact ... premature optimization is the root of all evil.[1]

This statement has been widely debated in the community, and in many cases only the second part is remembered. This is unfortunate for several reasons:

- In the first part of the quote, Knuth is reminding us implicitly of the need to measure, without which we can't determine the critical parts of programs.
- We need to remember yet again that it might not be the code that's causing the latency—it could be something else in the environment.

---

[1] Donald E. Knuth, "Structured Programming with go to Statements," *Computing Surveys*, 6, no. 4 (Dec. 1974). http://pplab.snu.ac.kr/courses/adv_pl05/papers/p261-knuth.pdf.

- In the full quote, it's easy to see that Knuth is talking about optimization that forms a conscious, concerted effort.
- The shorter form of the quote leads to the quote being used as a fairly pat excuse for poor design or execution choices.

Some optimizations are really a part of good style:

- Don't allocate an object you don't need to.
- Remove a debug log message if you'll never need it.

In the following snippet, we've added a check to see if the logging object will do anything with a debug log message. This kind of check is called a loggability guard. If the logging subsystem isn't set up for debug logs, this code will never construct the log message, saving the cost of the call to `currentTimeMillis()` and the construction of the `StringBuilder` object used for the log message.

```
if (log.isDebugEnabled()) log.debug("Useless log at: "+
System.currentTimeMillis());
```

But if the debug log message is truly useless, we can save a couple of processor cycles (the cost of the loggability guard) by removing the code altogether.

One aspect of performance tuning is to write good, well-performing code in the first place. Gaining a better awareness of the platform and how it behaves under the hood (for example, understanding the implicit object allocations that come from the concatenation of two strings) and thinking about aspects of performance as you go, leads to better code.

We now have some basic vocabulary we can use to frame our performance problems and goals, and an outline approach for how to tackle problems. But we still haven't explained why this is a software engineer's problem, and where this need came from. To understand this, we need to delve briefly into the world of hardware.

6.3 *What went wrong? Why we have to care*

For a few halcyon years in the middle of last decade, it seemed as though performance was not really a concern. Clock speeds were going up and up, and it seemed that all software engineers had to do was to wait a few months, and the improved CPU speeds would give an uptick to even badly written code.

How, then, did things go so wrong? Why are clock speeds not improving that much anymore? More worryingly, why does a computer with a 3 GHz chip not seem much faster than one with a 2 GHz chip? Where has this trend for software engineers across the industry to be concerned about performance come from?

In this section, we'll talk about the forces driving this trend, and why even the purest of software developers needs to care a bit about hardware. We'll set the stage for the topics in the rest of the chapter, and give you the concepts you'll need to really understand JIT compilation and some of our in-depth examples.

You may have heard the term "Moore's Law" bandied about. Many developers are aware that it has something to do with the rate at which computers get faster but are vague on the details. Let's get under way by explaining exactly what it means and what the consequences are of it possibly coming to an end in the near future.

6.3.1   *Moore's Law—historic and future performance trends*

Moore's Law is named for Gordon Moore, one of the founders of Intel. Here is one of the most common formulations of his law: *The maximum number of transistors on a chip which is economic to produce roughly doubles every two years.*

The law, which is really an observation about trends in computer processors (CPUs), is based on a paper he wrote in 1965, in which he originally forecast for 10 years—that is, up until 1975. That it has lasted so well (and is forecast to remain valid up until about 2015) is truly remarkable.

In figure 6.2 we've plotted a number of real CPUs from the Intel x86 family—all the way from 1980 through to the i7 in 2010. The graph shows the transistor counts of the chips against their release dates.

This is a log-linear graph, so each increment on the *y* axis is 10 times the previous one. As you can see, the line is essentially straight, and takes about six or seven years to cross each vertical level. This demonstrates Moore's Law, because taking six or seven years to increase tenfold is the same as roughly doubling every two years.

Keep in mind that the *y* axis on the graph is a log scale—this means that a mainstream Intel chip produced in 2005 had around 100 million transistors. This is *100 times* as many as a chip produced in 1990.

It's important to notice that Moore's Law specifically talks about transistor counts. This is the basic point that must be understood in order to grasp why Moore's Law alone isn't enough for the software engineer to continue to obtain a free lunch from the hardware engineers.

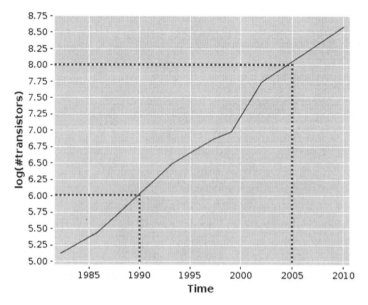

Figure 6.2   Log-linear plot of transistor count over time

NOTE Transistor counts aren't the same thing as clock speed, and even the still-common idea that a higher clock speed means better performance is a gross oversimplification.

Moore's Law has been a good guide to the past, and it should remain accurate for a while longer (estimates vary, but until at least 2015 seems reasonable). But Moore's Law is formulated in terms of transistor counts, and these are increasingly not a good guide to the performance that developers should expect from their code. Reality, as we'll see, is more complicated.

The truth is that real-world performance depends on a number of factors, all of which are important. If we had to pick just one, however, it would be how fast data relevant to the instructions can be located. This is such an important concept to performance that we should take an in-depth look at it.

6.3.2 *Understanding the memory latency hierarchy*

Computer processors require data to work on. If the data to process isn't available, then it doesn't matter how fast the CPU cycles—it just has to wait, performing no-operation (NOP) and basically stalling until the data is available.

This means that two of the most fundamental questions when addressing latency are, "Where is the nearest copy of the data that the CPU core needs to work on?" and "How long will it take to get to where the core can use it?" These are the main possibilities:

- *Registers*—This is a memory location that's on the CPU and ready for immediate use. This is the part of memory that instructions operate on directly.
- *Main memory*—This is usually DRAM. The access time for this is around 50 ns (but see later on for details about how processor caches are used to avoid this latency).
- *Solid-state drive (SSD)*—It takes 0.1 ms or less to access these disks, but they're less expensive compared to traditional hard disks.
- *Hard disk*—It takes around 5 ms to access the disk and load the required data into main memory.

Moore's Law has described an exponential increase in transistor count, and this has benefited memory as well—memory access speed has also increased exponentially. But the exponents for these two have not been the same. Memory speed has improved more slowly than CPUs have added transistors, which means there's a risk that the processing cores will fall idle due to not having the relevant data on hand to process.

To solve this problem, caches have been introduced between the registers and main memory. These are small amounts of faster memory (SRAM, rather than DRAM). This faster memory costs a lot more than DRAM, both in terms of money and transistor budget, which is why computers don't simply use SRAM for their entire memory.

Caches are referred to as L1 and L2 (some machines also have L3), with the numbers indicating how close to the CPU the cache is (and closer caches will be faster). We'll talk more about caches in section 6.6 (on JIT compilation), and show an example of how important the L1 cache effects are to running code. Figure 6.3 shows just

Figure 6.3   Relative
access times for
registers, processor
caches, and main
memory

how much faster L1 and L2 cache are than main memory. Later on, we'll have an example of just how much these speed differences affect the performance of running code.

As well as adding caches, another technique that was used extensively in the 1990s and early 2000s was to add increasingly complex processor features to try to work around the latency of memory. Sophisticated hardware techniques, such as instruction-level parallelism (ILP) and chip multithreading (CMT), were used to try to keep the CPU operating on data, even in the face of the widening gap between CPU capability and memory latency.

These techniques came to consume a large percentage of the transistor budget of the CPU, and the impact they had on real performance was subject to diminishing returns. This trend led to the viewpoint that the future of CPU design is chips with multiple (or many) cores.

This means the future of performance is intimately tied to concurrency—one of the main ways that a system can be made more performant overall is by having more cores. That way, even if one core is waiting for data, the other cores may still be able to progress. This connection is so important that we're going to say it again:

- The future of CPU is multicore
- This ties performance and concurrency together as concerns

These hardware concerns aren't specific to Java programmers, but there are some additional complexities that the managed nature of the JVM brings in. Let's take a look at these in the next section.

6.3.3   *Why is Java performance tuning hard?*

Tuning for performance on the JVM (or indeed, any other managed runtime) is inherently more difficult than for code that runs unmanaged. This is because C/C++ programmers have to do almost everything for themselves. The OS supplies only minimal services, such as rudimentary thread scheduling.

In a managed system, the entire point is to allow the runtime to take some control of the environment, so that the developer doesn't have to cope with every detail. This makes programmers much more productive overall, but it does mean that some control has to be given up. The only alternative is to give up all the advantages that a managed runtime brings, which is almost always a much higher cost than the additional effort required to performance tune.

Some of the most important aspects of the platform that contribute to making tuning hard are

- Thread scheduling
- Garbage collection (GC)
- Just-in-time (JIT) compilation

These aspects can interact in subtle ways. For example, the compilation subsystem uses timers to decide which methods to compile. This means that the set of methods that are candidates for compilation can be affected by concerns such as scheduling and GC. The methods that get compiled could be different from run to run.

As you've seen throughout this section, accurate measurement is key to the decision-making processes of performance analysis. An understanding of the details of (and limitations of) how time is handled in the Java platform is therefore very useful if you want to get serious about performance tuning.

6.4 A question of time—from the hardware up

Have you ever wondered where time is stored and handled inside a computer? Hardware is ultimately responsible for keeping track of time, but the picture isn't as simple as you might hope!

For performance tuning, you need a good understanding of the details of how time works. To get there, we'll start with the underlying hardware, then talk about how Java integrates with these subsystems, and introduce some of the complexities of the nanoTime() method.

6.4.1 Hardware clocks

There can be as many as four different hardware time sources in an average x64-based machine these days: RTC, 8254, TSC, and possibly HPET.

The real-time clock (RTC) is basically the same electronics you'd find in a cheap digital watch (quartz crystal based) and it's kept powered by the motherboard battery when the system is powered off. That's where the system time is initially set from at startup, although many machines will use Network Time Protocol (NTP) to synchronize to a time server on the network during the OS boot-up sequence.

> **Everything old was new once**
> The name *Real-Time Clock* is rather unfortunate—it was indeed considered real time in the 1980s when it was introduced, but it's now nowhere near accurate enough for serious applications. This is often the fate of innovations that are named for being "new" or "fast," such as the Pont Neuf ("New Bridge") in Paris. It was built in 1607 and is now the oldest still-standing bridge in the city.

The 8254 is a programmable timer chip that's been kicking around since the dawn of time. The clock source for this is a 119.318 kHz crystal, which is one-third of the NTSC color subcarrier frequency, for reasons that go back to the CGA graphics system. This is what once was used for feeding regular ticks (for timeslicing) to OS schedulers, but that's done from elsewhere (or isn't required) now.

This brings us to the most widely used modern counter—Time Stamp Counter (TSC). This is basically a CPU counter that tracks how many cycles the CPU has run. At first glance this seems ideal as a clock. But this counter is per-CPU and can potentially be affected by power saving and other factors at runtime. This means that different CPUs can drift away from each other and from wall-clock time.

Finally, there are High Precision Event Timers (HPETs). These started appearing in more recent years in order to stop people tearing their hair out trying to get better timing from the older clock hardware. HPET uses at least a 10 MHz timer, so it should be accurate to at least 1 µs—but it's not yet available on all hardware, and it's not yet supported by all operating systems.

If all of this seems like a bit of a mess, that's because, well, it is. Fortunately the Java platform provides facilities to make sense of this confusion—it hides the dependency on the hardware and OS support available within a specific machine configuration. As we'll see, however, the attempts to hide the dependency aren't entirely successful.

6.4.2 The trouble with nanoTime()

Java has two main methods for accessing the time: `System.currentTimeMillis()` and `System.nanoTime()`, the latter of which is used to measure times at better than millisecond accuracy. Table 6.1 summarizes the main differences between them.

Table 6.1 Comparing Java's built-in time access methods

`currentTimeMillis`	`nanoTime`
Resolution in milliseconds	Quoted in nanoseconds
Closely corresponds to wall-clock time under almost all circumstances	May drift away from wall-clock time

If the description of `nanoTime()` in table 6.1 sounds a bit like it might be some kind of countervalue, that's good, because on most OSs these days, it will be sourced from the CPU counterclock—TSC.

The output of `nanoTime()` is relative to a certain fixed time. This means it must be used to record a duration—by subtracting the result of one call to `nanoTime()` from an earlier one. This snippet, from a case study later in the chapter, shows exactly this:

```
long t0 = System.nanoTime();
doLoop1();
long t1 = System.nanoTime();
...
long el = t1 - t0;
```

The time `el` is the time in nanoseconds that elapsed while `doLoop1()` was executing.

To make proper use of these basic methods in performance tuning, it's necessary to understand something about the behavior of nanoTime(). The following listing outputs the maximum observed drift between the millisecond timer and the nano timer (which will usually be provided by TSC).

Listing 6.1 Timer drift

```
private static void runWithSpin(String[] args) {
  long nowNanos = 0, startNanos = 0;
  long startMillis = System.currentTimeMillis();
  long nowMillis = startMillis;

  while (startMillis == nowMillis) {                    ⟵   Align startNanos at
    startNanos = System.nanoTime();                          milisecond boundary
    nowMillis = System.currentTimeMillis();
  }

  startMillis = nowMillis;
  double maxDrift = 0;
  long lastMillis;

  while (true) {
    lastMillis = nowMillis;
    while (nowMillis - lastMillis < 1000) {
      nowNanos = System.nanoTime();
      nowMillis = System.currentTimeMillis();
    }

    long durationMillis = nowMillis - startMillis;
    double driftNanos = 1000000 *
(((double)(nowNanos - startNanos)) / 1000000 - durationMillis);
    if (Math.abs(driftNanos) > maxDrift) {
      System.out.println("Now - Start = "+ durationMillis
+" driftNanos = "+ driftNanos);
      maxDrift = Math.abs(driftNanos);
    }
  }
}
```

This prints the maximum observed drift, and it turns out to behave in a highly OS-specific manner. Here's an example on Linux:

```
Now - Start = 1000 driftNanos = 14.99999996212864
Now - Start = 3000 driftNanos = -86.99999989403295
Now - Start = 8000 driftNanos = -89.00000011635711
Now - Start = 50000 driftNanos = -92.00000204145908
Now - Start = 67000 driftNanos = -96.0000033956021
Now - Start = 113000 driftNanos = -98.00000407267362
Now - Start = 136000 driftNanos = -98.99999713525176
Now - Start = 150000 driftNanos = -101.0000123642385
Now - Start = 497000 driftNanos = -2035.000012256205            Notice the
Now - Start = 1006000 driftNanos = 20149.99999664724            big jump
Now - Start = 1219000 driftNanos = 44614.00001309812
```

And here's the result with an older Solaris installation on the same hardware:

```
Now - Start = 1000 driftNanos = 65961.0000000157
Now - Start = 2000 driftNanos = 130928.0000000399
Now - Start = 3000 driftNanos = 197020.9999999497
Now - Start = 4000 driftNanos = 261826.99999981196
Now - Start = 5000 driftNanos = 328105.9999999343
Now - Start = 6000 driftNanos = 393130.99999981205
Now - Start = 7000 driftNanos = 458913.9999998224
Now - Start = 8000 driftNanos = 524811.9999996561
Now - Start = 9000 driftNanos = 590093.9999992261
Now - Start = 10000 driftNanos = 656146.9999996916
Now - Start = 11000 driftNanos = 721020.0000008626
Now - Start = 12000 driftNanos = 786994.0000000497
```

Smooth
progression

Notice how Solaris has a steadily increasing maximum value, whereas Linux seems to be OK for longer periods and then has large jumps. The example code has been quite carefully chosen to avoid creating any additional threads, or even objects, to minimize the intervention of the platform (for example, no object creation means no GC), but even here, we see the influence of the JVM.

The large jumps in the Linux timings turn out to be due to discrepancies between the TSC counters held on different CPUs. The JVM will periodically suspend the running Java thread and migrate it to running on a different core. This can cause the differences between the CPU counters to become visible to application code.

This means that nanoTime() can become basically untrustworthy over long periods of time. It's useful for measuring short durations of time, but over longer (macroscopic) timeframes, it should be rebaselined against currentTimeMillis().

In order to get the most out of performance tuning, it's useful to have a grounding in some measurement theory as well as the implementation details.

6.4.3   *The role of time in performance tuning*

Performance tuning requires you to understand how to interpret the measurements recorded during code execution, which means you also need to understand the limitations inherent in any measurement of time on the platform.

PRECISION

Quantities of time are usually quoted to the nearest unit on some scale. This is referred to as the *precision* of the measurement. For example, times are often measured to millisecond precision. A timing is precise if repeated measurements give a narrow spread around the same value.

Precision is a measure of the amount of random noise contained in a given measurement. We'll assume that the measurements made of a particular piece of code are normally distributed. In that case, a common way of quoting the precision is to quote the width of the 95 percent confidence interval.

ACCURACY

The *accuracy* of a measurement (in our case, of time) is the ability to obtain a value close to the true value. In reality, you won't normally know the true value, so the accuracy may be harder to determine than the precision.

Accuracy measures the systematic error in a measurement. It's possible to have accurate measurements that aren't very precise (so the basic reading is sound, but there is random environmental noise). It's also possible to have precise results that aren't accurate.

> **Understanding measurements**
>
> An interval quoted at nanosecond precision as 5945 ns that came from a timer accurate to 1 μs is really somewhere between 3945–7945 ns (with 95 percent probability). Beware of performance numbers that seem overly precise—always check the precision and accuracy of the measurements.

GRANULARITY

The true *granularity* of the system is that of the frequency of the fastest timer—likely the interrupt timer, in the 10 ns range. This is sometimes called the *distinguishability*, the shortest interval between which two events can be definitely said to have occurred "close together but at different times."

As we progress through layers of OS, VM, and library code, the resolution of these extremely short times becomes basically impossible. Under most circumstances, these very short times aren't available to the application developer.

NETWORK-DISTRIBUTED TIMING

Most of our discussion of performance tuning centers on systems where all the processing takes places on a single host. But you should be aware that there are a number of special problems that arise when doing performance tuning of systems spread over a network. Synchronization and timing over networks is far from easy, and not only over the internet. Even Ethernet networks will show these issues.

A full discussion of network-distributed timing is outside the scope of this book, but you should be aware that it's, in general, difficult to obtain accurate timings for workflows that extend over several boxes. In addition, even standard protocols such as NTP can be too inaccurate for high-precision work.

Before we move on to discuss garbage collection, let's look at an example we referred to earlier—the effects of memory caches on code performance.

6.4.4 *A case study—understanding cache misses*

For many high-throughput pieces of code, one of the main factors reducing performance is the number of L1 cache misses that are involved in executing application code.

Listing 6.2 runs over a 1 MB array and prints the time taken to execute one of two loops. The first loop increments 1 in every 16 entries of an int[]. There are usually 64 bytes in an L1 cache line (and Java ints are 4 bytes wide on a 32-bit JVM), so this means touching each cache line once.

Note that before you can get accurate results, you need to warm up the code, so that the JVM will compile the methods you're interested in. We'll talk about the need for warmup more in section 6.6.

Listing 6.2   Understanding cache misses

```
public class CacheTester {
  private final int ARR_SIZE = 1 * 1024 * 1024;
  private final int[] arr = new int[ARR_SIZE];          Touch every
                                                         item
  private void doLoop2() {
    for (int i=0; i<arr.length; i++) arr[i]++;      ◁──
  }

  private void doLoop1() {                               Touch each
    for (int i=0; i<arr.length; i += 16) arr[i]++;   ◁── cache line
  }

  private void run() {
    for (int i=0; i<10000; i++) {              ◁───────  Warm up
      doLoop1();                                         the code
      doLoop2();
    }
    for (int i=0; i<100; i++) {
      long t0 = System.nanoTime();
      doLoop1();
      long t1 = System.nanoTime();
      doLoop2();
      long t2 = System.nanoTime();
      long el = t1 - t0;
      long el2 = t2 - t1;
      System.out.println("Loop1: "+ el +" nanos ; Loop2: "+ el2);
    }
  }

  public static void main(String[] args) {
    CacheTester ct = new CacheTester();
    ct.run();
  }
}
```

The second function, loop2(), increments every byte in the array, so it looks like it does 16 times as much work as loop1(). But here are some sample results from a typical laptop:

```
Loop1: 634000 nanos ; Loop2: 868000
Loop1: 801000 nanos ; Loop2: 952000
Loop1: 676000 nanos ; Loop2: 930000
Loop1: 762000 nanos ; Loop2: 869000
Loop1: 706000 nanos ; Loop2: 798000
```

Timing subsystems gotcha

Notice that in the results all the nanos values are neat, round thousands. This means the underlying system call (which is what System.nanoTime() is ultimately calling) is only returning a whole number of microseconds—a microsecond is 1000 nanos. As this example is from a Mac laptop, we can guess that the underlying system call only has microsecond precision on OS X—in fact, it's gettimeofday().

The results of this code show that `loop2()` doesn't take 16 times as long to run as `loop1()`. This means that it's the memory accesses that come to dominate the overall performance profile. `loop1()` and `loop2()` have the same number of cache line reads, and the cycles spent on actually modifying the data are but a small percentage of the overall time needed.

Before moving on, let's recap the most important points about Java's timing systems:

- Most systems have several different clocks inside them
- Millisecond timings are safe and reliable
- Higher-precision time needs careful handling to avoid drift
- You need to be aware of the precision and accuracy of timing measurements

Our next topic is a discussion of the garbage collection subsystem of the platform. This is one of the most important pieces of the performance picture, and it has a great many tunable parts that can be very important tools for the developer doing performance analysis.

6.5 *Garbage collection*

Automatic memory management is one of the most important parts of the Java platform. Before managed platforms such as Java and .NET, developers could expect to spend a noticeable percentage of their careers hunting down bugs caused by imperfect memory handling.

In recent years, however, automatic allocation techniques have become so advanced and reliable that they have become part of the furniture—a large number of Java developers are unaware of how the memory management capabilities of the platform work, what options are available to the developer, and how to optimize within the constraints of the framework.

This is a sign of how successful Java's approach has been. Most developers don't know about the details of the memory and GC systems because they often don't need to know. The VM can do a pretty good job of handling most applications without special tuning, so most apps never get tuned.

In this section, we'll talk about what you can do when you're in a situation where you do need to do some tuning. We'll cover basic theory, explain how memory is handled for a running Java process, explore the basics of mark-and-sweep collection, and discuss a couple of useful tools—`jmap` and VisualVM. We'll round off by describing two common alternative collectors—Concurrent Mark-Sweep (CMS) and the new Garbage First (G1) collector.

Perhaps you have a server-side application that is running out of memory or is suffering long pauses. In the section 6.5.3 on `jmap`, we'll show you a simple way to see if any of your classes are using a lot of memory. We'll also teach you about the switches you can use to control the VM's memory profile.

Let's start with the basics.

6.5.1   *Basics*

The standard Java process has both a stack and a heap. The *stack* is where local variables holding primitives are created (but local variables of reference type will point at heap-allocated memory). The *heap* is where objects will be created. Figure 6.4 shows where storage for variables of various types is created.

Note that the primitive fields of an object are still allocated at addresses within the heap. The basic algorithm by which the platform recovers and reuses heap memory that is no longer in use by application code is called *mark and sweep*.

6.5.2   *Mark and sweep*

Mark and sweep is the simplest garbage collection algorithm, and it was the first to be developed. There are other automatic memory management techniques, such as the reference-counting schemes used by languages like Perl and PHP, which are arguably simpler, but they aren't schemes that require garbage collection.

In its simplest form, the mark-and-sweep algorithm pauses all running program threads and starts from the set of objects that are known to be "live"—objects that have a reference in any stack frame (whether that reference is the content of a local variable, method parameter, temporary variable, or some rarer possibility) of any user thread. It then walks through the tree of references from the live objects, marking as live any object found en route. When this has completed, everything left is garbage and can be collected (swept). Note that the swept memory is returned to the JVM, not necessarily to the OS.

The Java platform provides an enhancement to the basic mark-and-sweep approach. This is the addition of "generational GC." In this approach, the heap isn't a uniform area of memory—there are a number of different areas of heap memory that participate in the lifecycle of a Java object. Depending on how long an object lives, references to it can point to several different areas of memory during the lifespan of the object (as illustrated in figure 6.5). The object can be moved from area to area during collections.

The reason for this arrangement is that analysis of running systems shows that objects tend to have either brief lives or be very long lived. The different areas of heap memory are designed to allow the platform to exploit this property of the lifecycle of objects.

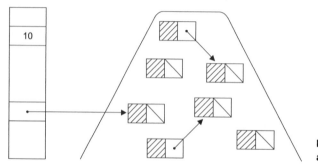

Figure 6.4   Variables in the stack and heap

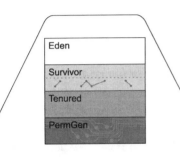

Figure 6.5　The Eden, survivor, tenured, and PermGen areas of memory

---

What about the non-deterministic pause?

One of the criticisms often leveled at Java and .NET is that the mark-and-sweep form of garbage collection inevitably leads to stop-the-world—states in which all user threads must be stopped briefly. This can cause pauses that go on for some non-deterministic amount of time.

This issue is frequently overstated. For server software, there are very few applications that have to care about the pause times displayed by Java. Elaborate schemes to avoid a pause, or a full collection of memory, are sometimes dreamed up—these should be avoided unless careful analysis has shown that there are genuine issues to do with the full collection times.

AREAS OF MEMORY

The JVM has different areas of memory that are used to store objects during their natural lifecycle:

- *Eden*—Eden is the area of the heap where all objects are initially allocated, and for many objects this will be the only part of memory that they ever reside in.

- *Survivor*—There are typically two survivor spaces (or you can think of it as one space split in half). These spaces are where objects that survive from Eden (hence the name) are moved. They are sometimes referred to as *From* and *To*. For reasons explained later, one of the survivor spaces is always empty unless a collection is under way.

- *Tenured*—The tenured space (a.k.a. old generation) is where surviving objects deemed to be "old enough" are moved to (escaping from the survivor spaces). Tenured memory isn't collected during young collections.

- *PermGen*—This is where memory for internal structures is allocated, such as the definitions of classes. PermGen isn't strictly part of the heap proper, and ordinary objects don't ever end up here.

As noted, these areas of memory also participate in collections in different ways. Specifically, there are two types of collections: young and full.

YOUNG COLLECTIONS

A *young collection* only attempts to clear the "young" spaces (Eden and survivor). The process is relatively simple:

- All live young objects found during the marking phase are moved:
  - Objects that are sufficiently old (ones that have survived enough previous GC runs) go into tenured.
  - All other young, live objects go into the empty survivor space.
- At the end, Eden and the recently vacated survivor space are ready to be over-written and reused, as they contain nothing but garbage.

A young collection is triggered when Eden is full. Note that the marking phase must traverse the entire live object graph. That means that if a young object has a reference to a tenured object, the references held by the tenured object must still be scanned and marked. Otherwise the situation could arise where a tenured object holds a reference to an object in Eden but nothing else does. If the mark phase doesn't fully traverse, this Eden object would never been seen and would not be correctly handled.

FULL COLLECTIONS

When a young collection can't promote an object to tenured (due to lack of space), a full collection is triggered. Depending on the collector used in the old generation, this may involve moving around objects within the old generation. This is done to ensure that the old generation has enough space to allocate a large object if necessary. This is called compacting.

SAFEPOINTS

Garbage collection can't take place without at least a short pause of all application threads. But threads can't be stopped at any arbitrary time for GC. Instead, there are certain special times when GC can take place—these are called *safepoints*. The usual example of a safepoint is a point where a method is called (a "call site"), but there are others. For garbage collection to take place, all application threads must be stopped at a safepoint.

Let's take a brief timeout and introduce a simple tool, jmap, which can help you to understand the memory utilization of your live applications, and where all that memory goes. Later in the chapter we'll introduce a more advanced GUI tool, but many problems can be triaged by using the very simple command-line tools, so you should definitely know how to drive them (rather than automatically reaching for the GUI tool).

6.5.3   *jmap*

The standard Oracle JVM ships with simple tools to help you get some insight into your running processes. The simplest one, jmap, shows memory maps of Java processes (it can also work on a Java core file or even connect to a remote debug server). Let's return to our example of a server-side ecommerce application and use jmap to explore it while it's running.

DEFAULT VIEW

jmap's simplest form shows native libraries linked in to a process. This isn't usually of great interest unless you've got a lot of JNI code in your application, but we'll demonstrate it anyway so it doesn't confuse you if you ever forget to specify which view you want jmap to display:

```
$ jmap 19306
Attaching to process ID 19306, please wait...
Debugger attached successfully.
Server compiler detected.
JVM version is 20.0-b11
0x08048000    46K      /usr/local/java/sunjdk/1.6.0_25/bin/java
0x55555000    108K     /lib/ld-2.3.4.so
... some entries omitted
0x563e8000    535K     /lib/libnss_db.so.2.0.0
0x7ed18000    94K      /usr/local/java/sunjdk/1.6.0_25/jre/lib/i386/libnet.so
0x80cf3000    2102K    /usr/local/kerberos/mitkrb5/1.4.4/lib/
    libgss_all.so.3.1
0x80dcf000    1440K    /usr/local/kerberos/mitkrb5/1.4.4/lib/libkrb5.so.3.2
```

Far more useful are the -heap and -histo switches, which we'll tackle next.

HEAP VIEW

The -heap switch gives a quick snapshot of the heap as it is at the moment when you run it. In the output from -heap you can see the basic parameters that define the makeup of the Java process's heap memory.

The size of the heap is the size of the young and old generations plus the size of PermGen. But inside the young generation, you have Eden and survivor spaces, and we haven't yet told you how the sizes of these areas are related. There is a number called the survivor ratio, which determines the relative sizes of the areas.

Let's take a look at some sample output. Here you can see Eden, the survivor spaces (labeled From and To), and the tenured space (Old Generation) and related information:

```
$ jmap -heap 22186
Attaching to process ID 22186, please wait...
Debugger attached successfully.
Server compiler detected.
JVM version is 20.0-b11

using thread-local object allocation.
Parallel GC with 13 thread(s)

Heap Configuration:
   MinHeapFreeRatio = 40
   MaxHeapFreeRatio = 70
   MaxHeapSize      = 536870912 (512.0MB)
   NewSize          = 1048576 (1.0MB)
   MaxNewSize       = 4294901760 (4095.9375MB)
   OldSize          = 4194304 (4.0MB)
   NewRatio         = 2
   SurvivorRatio    = 8        ◁————————  Eden = (From + To) *
   PermSize         = 16777216 (16.0MB)              SurvivorRatio
   MaxPermSize      = 67108864 (64.0MB)
```

```
Heap Usage:
PS Young Generation
Eden Space:
   capacity = 163774464 (156.1875MB)
   used     = 58652576 (55.935455322265625MB)
   free     = 105121888 (100.25204467773438MB)
   35.81301661289516% used
From Space:
   capacity = 7012352 (6.6875MB)
   used     = 4144688 (3.9526824951171875MB)
   free     = 2867664 (2.7348175048828125MB)
   59.10553263726636% used
To Space:
   capacity = 7274496 (6.9375MB)
   used     = 0 (0.0MB)
   free     = 7274496 (6.9375MB)
   0.0% used
PS Old Generation
   capacity = 89522176 (85.375MB)
   used     = 6158272 (5.87298583984375MB)
   free     = 83363904 (79.50201416015625MB)
   6.87904637170571% used
PS Perm Generation
   capacity = 30146560 (28.75MB)
   used     = 30086280 (28.69251251220703MB)
   free     = 60280 (0.05748748779296875MB)
   99.80004352072011% used
```

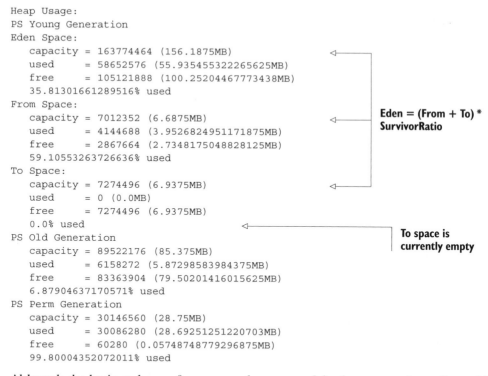

Eden = (From + To) * SurvivorRatio

To space is currently empty

Although the basic makeup of spaces can be very useful, what you can't see from this picture is what's in the heap. Being able to see which objects make up the contents of memory can give you more useful clues about where all the memory is going. Fortunately, jmap comes with a histogram mode that can give you simple statistics on exactly that.

HISTOGRAM VIEW

The histogram view shows the amount of memory occupied by instances of each type in the system (and some internal entries as well). The types are listed in order of how much memory they use, to make it easy to see the biggest memory hogs.

Of course, if all the memory is paying for framework and platform classes, there may not be much you can do. But if one of your classes really stands out, you may be in a much better position to do something about its memory usage.

A bit of warning: jmap uses the internal names for types that you saw in chapter 5. For example, array-of-char is written [C and arrays of class objects will be shown as [Ljava.lang.Class;.

```
$ jmap -histo 22186 | head -30

num    #instances     #bytes   class name
----------------------------------------------
  1:      452779     31712472  [C
  2:       76877     14924304  [B
  3:       20817     12188728  [Ljava.lang.Object;
```

4:	2520	10547976	`com.company.cache.Cache$AccountInfo`
5:	439499	9145560	`java.lang.String`
6:	64466	7519800	`[I`
7:	64466	5677912	`<constMethodKlass>`
8:	96840	4333424	`<methodKlass>`
9:	6990	3384504	`<symbolKlass>`
10:	6990	2944272	`<constantPoolKlass>`
11:	4991	1855272	`<instanceKlassKlass>`
12:	25980	1247040	`<constantPoolCacheKlass>`
13:	17250	1209984	`java.nio.HeapCharBuffer`
14:	13515	1173568	`[Ljava.util.HashMap$Entry;`
15:	9733	778640	`java.lang.reflect.Method`
16:	17842	713680	`java.nio.HeapByteBuffer`
17:	7433	713568	`java.lang.Class`
18:	10771	678664	`[S`
19:	1543	489368	`<methodDataKlass>`
20:	10620	456136	`[[I`
21:	18285	438840	`java.util.HashMap$Entry`
22:	9985	399400	`java.util.HashMap`
23:	13725	329400	`java.util.Hashtable$Entry`
24:	9839	314848	`java.util.LinkedHashMap$Entry`
25:	9793	249272	`[Ljava.lang.String;`
26:	11927	241192	`[Ljava.lang.Class;`
27:	6903	220896	`java.lang.ref.SoftReference`

Internal VM objects and type information (bracket spanning rows 7–19)

We've cut off the display after a couple of dozen lines, because the histogram can output a *lot* of data. You may need to use grep or other tools to look through the histogram view and find the details that interest you.

In this example, you can see that a lot of the memory usage comes from entries like the one for `[C`. Arrays of character data are often found inside `String` objects (where they hold the contents of the string), so this isn't very surprising—strings are really common in most Java programs. But there are other interesting things that you can learn by looking at the histograms. Let's look at two of them.

The `Cache$AccountInfo` entries are the only actual application classes that appear in the top entries—everything else is a platform or a framework type—so they're the most important type that the developer has full control over. The `AccountInfo` objects are occupying a lot of space—10.5 MB for around 2,500 entries (or 4 KB per account). That's quite a lot for some account details.

This information can be really useful. You've already figured out what the largest contribution to memory usage from your code is. Suppose your boss now comes to you and tells you that due to a massive sales promotion, there are going to be 10 times as many customers in the system in a month's time. You know that that's potentially going to add a lot of strain—the `AccountInfo` objects are heavy beasts. You're a little bit worried—but at least you've started analyzing the problem.

The information from `jmap` can be used as input to help govern a decision-making process about how to tackle the potential issue. Should you split up the account cache, look to reduce the information held in the type, or go and buy more RAM for the server. There's more analysis to be done before making any changes, but you have a place to start.

To see another interesting thing, let's rerun the histogram, but specify `-histo:live`. This will tell `jmap` to only do the live objects, not the whole heap (by default, `jmap` will do everything, including garbage that is still in memory and hasn't been collected yet). Let's see what this looks like:

```
$ jmap -histo:live 22186 | head -7

 num     #instances         #bytes  class name
----------------------------------------------
   1:          2520       10547976  com.company.cache.Cache$AccountInfo
   2:         32796        4919800  [I
   3:          5392        4237628  [Ljava.lang.Object;
   4:        141491        2187368  [C
```

Notice how the picture has changed—the amount of character data has dropped from 31 MB to about 2 MB, and about two-thirds of the `String` objects you saw in the first run turn out to be garbage awaiting collection. The account information objects are 100 percent live though, further confirming that they're a source of much memory consumption.

When using these modes of `jmap`, you should always be a bit careful. The JVM is still running when you do this operation (and if you're unlucky, it may have done a GC run in between the snapshots you took), so you should always do several runs, especially if you see any results that seem weird or too good to be true.

PRODUCING OFFLINE DUMP FILES

The final mode of `jmap` we're going to look at is its ability to create a dump file, like this:

```
jmap -dump:live,format=b,file=heap.hprof 19306
```

Dumps are really for offline analysis, either in `jmap` itself at some later date, or in an Oracle-provided tool called `jhat` (Java Heap Analysis Tool) for advanced analysis. Unfortunately, we can't fit in a full discussion of it here.

With `jmap` you can start to see some of the basic settings and memory consumption of your application. For performance tuning, however, it's often necessary to exercise more control over the GC subsystem. The standard way to do this is via command-line parameters, so let's take a look at some of the parameters you can use to control your JVM and change aspects of its behavior to better fit the needs of your application.

6.5.4 *Useful JVM parameters*

The JVM ships with a huge number of useful parameters (at least a hundred) that can be used to customize many aspects of the runtime behavior of the JVM. In this section, we'll discuss some of the switches that pertain to garbage collection; in later sections we'll cover the other switches.

> ## Nonstandard JVM switches
>
> If a switch starts with `-X:` it's a nonstandard switch and may not be portable across JVM implementations.
>
> If it starts with `-XX:` it's an extended switch and isn't recommended for casual use. Many performance-relevant switches are extended switches.
>
> Some switches are Boolean in effect and take a + or - in front of them to turn it on or off. Other switches take a parameter, such as `-XX:CompileThreshold=1000` (which would set the number of times a method needs to be called before being considered for JIT compilation to `1000`). Still others, including many standard ones, take neither.

Table 6.2 lists the basic GC switches and displays the default value (if any) of the switch.

Table 6.2 Basic garbage collection switches

Switch	Effect
`-Xms<size in MB>m`	Initial size of the heap (default 2 MB)
`-Xmx<size in MB>m`	Maximum size of the heap (default 64 MB)
`-Xmn<size in MB>m`	Size of the young generation in the heap
`-XX:-DisableExplicitGC`	Prevent calls to `System.gc()` from having any effect

One very common technique is to set the size of `-Xms` to the same as `-Xmx`. This then means that the process will run with exactly that heap size, and there will be no need to resize during execution (which can lead to unpredictable slowdowns).

The last switch in the list outputs standard information about GC to the log, the interpretation of which is the subject of our next section.

6.5.5 Reading the GC logs

To make the most out of garbage collection, it's often useful to see what the subsystem is doing. As well as the basic `verbose:gc` flag, there are a large number of other switches that control the information being printed.

Reading the GC logs can be a bit of a task—you may find yourself drowning in output at times. As you'll see in the next section, on VisualVM, having a graphical tool to help you visualize the VM's behavior can be very useful. Nevertheless, it's important to be able to read the log formats and to know about the basic switches that affect GC, as there are times when GUI tools may not be available. Some of the most useful GC logging switches are shown in table 6.3.

In combination, these switches will produce log lines like this:

```
6.580: [GC [PSYoungGen: 486784K->7667K(499648K)]
1292752K->813636K(1400768K), 0.0244970 secs]
```

Table 6.3   Additional switches for extended logging

Switch	Effect
`-XX:+PrintGCDetails`	Extended details about GC
`-XX:+PrintGCDateStamps`	Timestamps on GC operations
`-XX:+PrintGCApplicationConcurrentTime`	Time spent on GC with application threads still running

Let's break this apart and see what each piece means:

```
<time>: [GC [<collector name>: <occupancy at start>
➥ -> <occupancy at end>(<total size>)] <full heap occupancy at start>
➥ -> <full heap occupancy at end>(<total heap size>), <pause time> secs
```

The first field shows the time at which the GC occurred, in seconds since the JVM was fired up. Then you have the collector name (PSYoungGen) used to collect the young generation. Then there's the memory used before and after collection in the young generation, and the total young generation size. Then there are the same fields for the full heap.

In addition to the GC logging flags, there's a flag that could potentially be a bit misleading without some explanation. The `-XX:+PrintGCApplicationStoppedTime` flag produces log lines like this:

```
Application time: 0.9279047 seconds
Total time for which application threads were stopped: 0.0007529 seconds
Application time: 0.0085059 seconds
Total time for which application threads were stopped: 0.0002074 seconds
Application time: 0.0021318 seconds
```

These don't refer, necessarily, to how long GC took. Instead, they refer to how long threads were stopped during an operation that was started at a safepoint. This includes GC operations, but there are other safepoint operations (such as biased lock operations in Java 6), so it's impossible to say with certainty that the log message refers to GC.

All this information, while useful for logging and after-the-fact analysis, isn't very easy to visualize. Instead, many developers prefer to use a GUI tool while performing initial analysis. Fortunately, the HotSpot VM (from the standard Oracle installation, which we'll discuss in detail later) ships with a very useful tool.

6.5.6   *Visualizing memory usage with VisualVM*

VisualVM is a visualization tool that ships with the standard Oracle JVM. It has a plugin architecture, and in one standard configuration can be used as a more convenient replacement for the now quite elderly JConsole.

Figure 6.6 shows a standard VisualVM summary screen. This is the view that you'll see if you start up VisualVM and connect it to an application running locally on your machine. (VisualVM can also connect to remote applications, but not all functionality

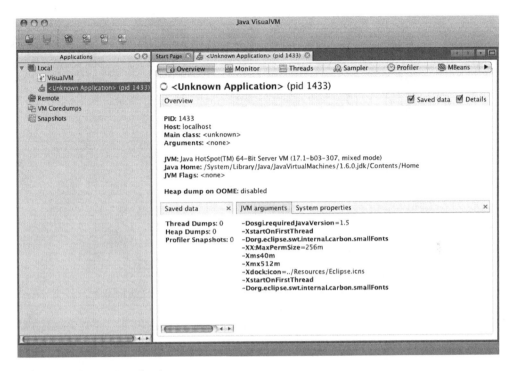

Figure 6.6 VisualVM application summary screen

is available over the network.) Here you can see VisualVM profiling an instance of Eclipse running on a MacBook Pro, which is the very setup that we used to create the code examples in this book.

There are a load of useful tabs across the top of the right panel. We run with the Extensions, Sampler, JConsole, MBeans, and VisualVM plugins, which provides an excellent toolset for really getting to grips with some of the dynamic aspects of the Java runtime. We recommend installing all of these plugins into VisualVM before doing any serious work with it.

In figure 6.7 you can see the "sawtooth" pattern of memory utilization. This is an absolutely classic visualization of how memory is used in the Java platform. It represents objects being allocated in Eden, used, and then collected in young collections.

After each young collection, the amount of memory used falls back to a baseline level. This level is the combined usage of the objects in tenured and survivor, and it can be used to ascertain the health over time of a Java process. If the baseline stays stable (or even decreases over time) while the process is working, the memory utilization should be very healthy.

If the baseline level rises, this doesn't necessarily mean that anything is wrong, just that some objects are living long enough to reach tenure. In this case, a full collection will eventually occur. The full collections will lead to a second sawtooth pattern, with the memory used falling back to a baseline that corresponds to the level with only

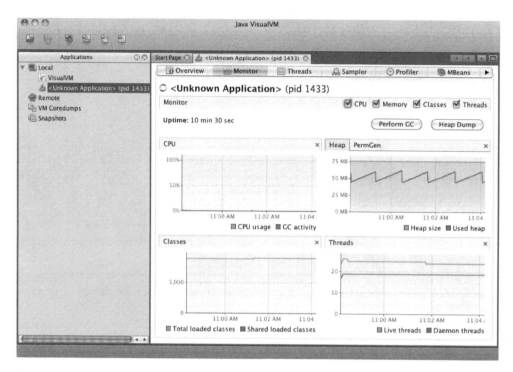

Figure 6.7   VisualVM overview screen

truly live objects in memory. If the full collection baseline is stable over time, the process should not run out of memory.

One key concept is that the gradient of the slope on the saw teeth is the rate at which a process is using young generation (usually Eden) memory. The aim of reducing the frequency of young collections is basically trying to reduce the steepness of the saw teeth.

Another way of visualizing the running memory usage is shown in figure 6.8. Here, you can see Eden, the survivor spaces (S0 and S1), and the old generation and PermGen. As the application runs, you can see the sizes of the generations change. In particular, after a young collection you'll see Eden shrink and the survivor spaces swap roles.

Exploring the memory system and other aspects of the runtime environment will help you understand how your code runs. This, in turn, shows how the services that the VM provides impact performance, so it's definitely worth taking time to experiment with VisualVM, especially in combination with switches such as Xmx and Xms.

Let's move on to the next section, where we'll discuss a new JVM technique to automatically reduce the amount of heap memory that's used during execution.

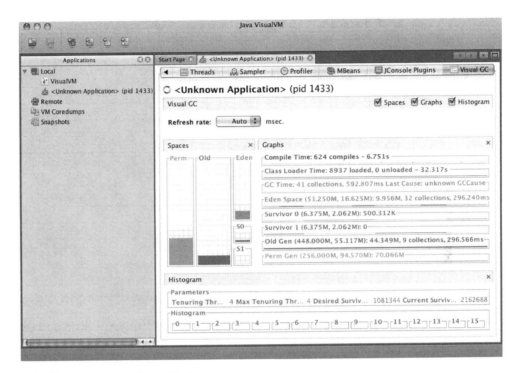

Figure 6.8 VisualVM's Visual GC plugin

6.5.7 *Escape analysis*

This section is largely informational—it describes a recent change to the JVM. This isn't a change that the programmer can directly influence or control, and the optimization is enabled by default on recent releases of Java. For that reason, there aren't many takeaways or examples for this change. So if you're interested in seeing one of the tricks that the JVM plays to improve performance, keep reading. Otherwise, feel free to skip ahead to section 6.5.8, on the concurrent collector.

Escape analysis is, at first sight, quite a surprising idea. The basic idea is to analyze a method and see which local variables (of reference type) are only used inside the method, determining which variables aren't passed in to other methods or returned from the current method.

The JVM is then able to create the object on the stack inside the frame belonging to the current method, rather than using up heap memory. This can improve performance by reducing the number of young collections your program needs to perform. You can see this in figure 6.9.

This means that a heap allocation can be avoided, because when the current method returns, the memory that was used to hold the local variable is automatically freed. This lack of heap allocation means that variables allocated in this way don't contribute to the growth of garbage, or ever need collection.

Escape analysis is a new approach to reducing garbage collection on the JVM. It can have a dramatic effect on the number of young collections that a process undergoes. Experience using the feature shows that, in general, it can provide an overall performance impact of a few percent. That's not a huge amount, but it's worth having, especially if your processes do a lot of garbage collection.

From Java 6u23 onwards, escape analysis is enabled by default, so newer versions of Java get this speed uptick for free.

We'll now turn to look at another aspect that can have a huge impact on your code—the choice of collection strat-

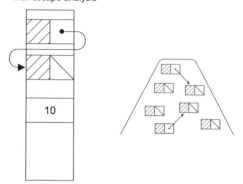

Object allocated on the stack - only possible with escape analysis

Figure 6.9   Escape analysis avoids heap allocation of objects

egy. We'll start with a classic high-performance choice (Concurrent Mark-Sweep) and then take a look at the newest collector—Garbage First.

There are many good reasons for considering a high-performance collector. The application might benefit from shorter GC pauses and be willing to have extra threads running (and consuming CPU) to achieve that. Or you might want to exercise control over how often the GC pauses happen. In addition to the basic collector, it's possible to use switches to force the platform to use a different collection strategy. In the next two sections, we'll cover two collectors that enable these possibilities.

6.5.8   *Concurrent Mark-Sweep*

The Concurrent Mark-Sweep (CMS) collector is the high-performance collector that was the recommended choice for Java 5 and most of the service life of Java 6. It's enabled by a combination of switches, as shown in table 6.4.

Table 6.4   Switches for CMS collector

Switch	Effect
-XX:+UseConcMarkSweepGC	Switch on CMS collection
-XX:+CMSIncrementalMode	Incremental mode (usually required)
-XX:+CMSIncrementalPacing	Incremental mode (usually required)
-XX:+UseParNewGC	Collect young generation concurrently
-XX:ParallelGCThreads=<N>	Number of threads to use for GC

These switches override the default settings for garbage collection and instead configure a CMS garbage collector with *N* parallel threads for GC. This collector will do as much GC work as possible in a concurrent mode.

How does the concurrent approach work? There are three key facts about mark and sweep that are relevant:

- Some sort of stop-the-world pause is unavoidable.
- The GC subsystem must never miss a live object—to do so would cause the JVM to crash (or worse).
- You can only guarantee to collect all the garbage if all the application threads are stopped for the whole collection.

CMS works by exploiting this last point. It makes two, very short, STW pauses, and runs at the same time as application threads for the rest of the GC cycle. This means that it's willing to make the trade-off of "false negatives," failing to identify some garbage due to race conditions (the garbage it misses will be collected on a following GC cycle).

CMS also needs to do more complicated bookkeeping about what is and isn't garbage while it's running. This extra overhead is part of the price of being able to run mostly without stopping application threads. It tends to perform better on machines with more CPU cores, and to produce more frequent, shorter pauses. It produces log lines such as this:

```
2010-11-17T15:47:45.692+0000: 90434.570: [GC 90434.570:
[ParNew: 14777K->14777K(14784K), 0.0000595 secs]90434.570:
[CMS: 114688K->114688K(114688K), 0.9083496 secs] 129465K->117349K(129472K),
[CMS Perm : 49636K->49634K(65536K)] icms_dc=100 , 0.9086004 secs]
[Times: user=0.91 sys=0.00, real=0.91 secs]
```

These lines are similar to the basic unit of GC logging that you saw in section 6.4.4, but with additional sections for the CMS and CMS Perm collectors.

In recent years, a new challenger to CMS as the best high-performance collector has arrived—the Garbage First (G1) collector. Let's look at this upstart, and explain how novel its approach is and why it represents a break with all of the existing Java collectors.

6.5.9 *G1—Java's new collector*

G1 is the brand-new collector for the Java platform. It was originally intended to be introduced as part of Java 7, but it was made available as a prerelease in point releases of Java 6 and reached production status with Java 7. It isn't widely deployed in Java 6 installations, but as Java 7 becomes widespread, it's anticipated that G1 will become the default choice for high-performance (and possibly for all) applications.

The central idea with G1 is the pause goal. This is how long the program can pause for GC while executing (such as 20 ms every 5 minutes). G1 will do everything it can to hit your pause goals. This represents a radical departure from the other collectors we've come across so far, and allows the developer a lot more control over how GC is performed.

G1 isn't really a generational collector (although it still uses the mark-and-sweep approach). Instead, G1 divides the heap into equal-sized regions (such as 1 MB each) that aren't distinguished between young and old regions. During a pause, objects are evacuated to another region (like Eden objects being moved to survivor spaces), and the region is placed back on the free list (of empty regions). The new arrangement of equal-sized regions in the heap is illustrated in figure 6.10.

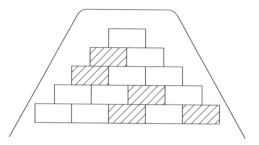

This change to collection strategy allows the platform to collect statistics on how long (on average) a single region takes to collect. This is how you can specify (within reason) a pause goal. G1 will only collect as many regions as it has time for

Figure 6.10   How G1 divides up the heap

(although there may be overruns if the last region takes longer to collect than expected).

To turn on G1, use settings such as those in table 6.5.

Table 6.5   Flags for the G1 collector

Switch	Effect
`-XX:+UseG1GC`	Switch on G1 collection
`-XX:MaxGCPauseMillis=50`	Indicate to G1 that it should try to pause for no more than 50 ms during one collection
`-XX:GCPauseIntervalMillis=200`	Indicate to G1 that it should try to run for at least 200 ms between collections

The switches can be combined, such as to set a maximum pause goal of 50 ms with pauses occurring no closer together than 200 ms. Of course, there's a limit on how hard the GC system can be pushed. There has to be enough pause time to take out the trash. A pause goal of 1 ms per 100 years is certainly not going to be attainable, or honored.

G1 offers great promise as a collector across a wide variety of workloads and application types. If you've reached the point of tuning your application's GC, it's likely to be worth considering.

In the next section, we'll look at JIT compilation. For many (or even most) programs, this is the single biggest contributing factor to producing performant code. We'll look at some of the basics of JIT compilation, and at the end of the section we'll explain to how to switch on logging of JIT compilation to enable you to tell which of your methods are being compiled.

6.6   *JIT compilation with HotSpot*

As we discussed in chapter 1, the Java platform is perhaps best thought of as "dynamically compiled." This means that the application classes undergo further compilation at runtime to transform them into machine code.

This process is called just-in-time (JIT) compilation, or JITing, and it usually occurs on one method at a time. Understanding this process is key to identifying the important parts of any sizable codebase.

Let's look at some good basic facts about JIT compilation:

- Virtually all modern JVMs will have a JIT compiler of some sort.
- Purely interpreted VMs are very slow by comparison.
- Compiled methods run much, much faster than interpreted code.
- It makes sense to compile the most heavily used methods first.
- When doing JIT compilation, it's always important to take the low-hanging fruit first.

This last point means that we should look at the compiled code first, because under normal circumstances, any method that is still in interpreted state hasn't been run as often as one that has been compiled. (Occasionally a method will fail compilation, but this is quite rare.)

Methods start off being interpreted from their bytecode representation, with the JVM keeping track of how many times a method has been called (and a few other statistics). When a threshold value is reached (10,000 times, by default), and if the method is eligible, a JVM thread will compile the bytecode to machine code in the background. If compilation succeeds, all further calls to the method will use the compiled form, unless something happens to invalidate it or otherwise cause deoptimization.

Depending on the exact nature of the code in a method, a compiled method can be up to 100 times faster than the same method in interpreted mode. Understanding which methods are important in a program, and which important methods are being compiled, is very often the cornerstone of improving performance.

Why have dynamic compilation?

A question that is sometimes asked is why does the Java platform bother with dynamic compilation—why isn't all compilation done up front (like C++). The first answer is usually that having platform-independent artifacts (.jar and .class files) as the basic unit of deployment is much less of a headache than trying to deal with a different compiled binary for each platform being targeted.

An alternative, and more ambitious, answer is that languages that use dynamic compilation have more information available to their compiler. Specifically, ahead-of-time (AOT) compiled languages don't have access to any runtime information—such as the availability of certain instructions or other hardware details, or any statistics on how the code is running. This opens the intriguing possibility that a dynamically compiled language like Java could actually run faster than AOT-compiled languages.

For the rest of this discussion of the mechanics of JITing, we'll be speaking specifically about the JVM called HotSpot. A lot of the general discussion will apply to other VMs, but the specifics could vary a lot.

We'll start by introducing the different JIT compilers that ship with HotSpot, and then explain two of the most powerful optimizations available from HotSpot—inlining and monomorphic dispatch. We'll conclude this short section by showing how to turn on logging of method compilation, so that you can see exactly which methods are being compiled. Let's get started by introducing HotSpot.

6.6.1 Introduction to HotSpot

HotSpot is the VM that Oracle acquired when it bought Sun Microsystems (it already owned a VM called JRockit, which was originally developed by BEA Systems). HotSpot is the VM that forms the basis of OpenJDK. It's capable of running in two separate modes—client and server. The mode can be chosen by specifying the `-client` or `-server` switch to the JVM on startup. (This must be the first switch provided on the command line.) Each of these modes has different applications that they can be preferred for.

CLIENT COMPILER

The client compiler is primarily intended for use in GUI applications. This is an arena where consistency of operation is vital, so the client compiler (sometimes called C1) tends to make more conservative decisions when compiling. This means that it can't pause unexpectedly while it backs out an optimization decision that turned out to be incorrect or based on a faulty assumption.

SERVER COMPILER

By contrast, the server compiler (C2) will make aggressive assumptions when compiling. To ensure that the code that's run is always correct, C2 will add a quick runtime check (usually called a guard condition) that the assumption it made is valid. If not, it will back out the aggressive compilation and will often try something else. This aggressive approach can yield far better performance than the rather risk-averse client compiler.

REAL-TIME JAVA

In recent years, there has been a form of Java developed called real-time Java, and some developers wonder why code that has a need for high performance doesn't simply use this platform (which is a separate JVM, not a HotSpot option). The answer is that a real-time system is not, despite common myth, necessarily the fastest system.

Real-time programming is really about the guarantees that can be made. In statistical terms, a real-time system seeks to reduce the variance of the time taken to perform certain operations, and is prepared to sacrifice a certain amount of mean latency to do so. Overall performance may be slightly sacrificed in order to attain more consistent running.

In figure 6.11, you can see two series of points that represent latency. Series 2 (the upper group of points) has an increased mean latency (as it is higher on the latency scale), but a reduced variance, because the points are more closely clustered around their mean than the Series 1 points, which are quite widely scattered by comparison.

Teams in search of higher performance are usually in search of lower mean latency, even at the cost of higher variance, so the aggressive optimizations of the server compiler (which corresponds to Series 1) are the usual choice.

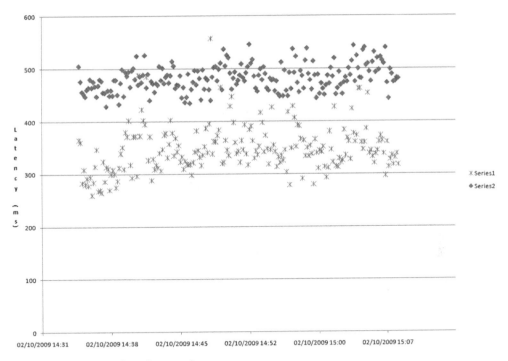

Figure 6.11   Changes in variance and mean

Our next topic is one that is extensively used by all of the runtimes—server, client, and real-time—to great effect.

6.6.2   Inlining methods

Inlining is one of the most powerful techniques that HotSpot has at its disposal. It works by eliminating the call to the inlined method, and instead placing the code of the called method inside the caller.

One of the advantages of the platform is that the compiler can make the decision to inline based on decent runtime statistics about how often the method is called and other factors (for example, will it make the caller method too large and potentially affect code caches). This means that HotSpot's compiler can make much smarter decisions about inlining than ahead-of-time compilers.

Inlining of methods is entirely automatic, and under almost all circumstances the default parameter values are fine. There are switches to control what size of methods will be inlined, and how often a method needs to be called before becoming a candidate. These switches are mostly useful for the curious programmer to get a better understanding of how the inlining part of the internals works. They aren't often useful for production code and should be considered something of a last resort as a performance technique, because they may well have other unpredictable effects on the performance of the runtime system.

What about accessor methods?

Some developers incorrectly assume that an accessor method (a public getter accessing a private member variable) can't be inlined by HotSpot. Their reasoning is that because the variable is private, the method call can't be optimized away, because access to it is prohibited outside the class. This is incorrect. HotSpot can and will ignore access control when compiling methods to machine code and will replace an accessor method with a direct access to the private field. This doesn't compromise Java's security model, because all of the access control was checked at class loading and linking time.

If you still need to be convinced that this behavior occurs, a good exercise is to write a test harness similar to the one in listing 6.2, comparing the speed of a warmed-up accessor method to the speed of access to a public field.

6.6.3   *Dynamic compilation and monomorphic calls*

One example of this type of aggressive optimization is that of the monomorphic call. This is an optimization that's based around the observation that in most circumstances, a method call on an object, like this,

```
MyActualClassNotInterface obj = getInstance();
obj.callMyMethod();
```

will only ever be called by one type of object. Another way of saying this is that the call site `obj.callMyMethod()` will almost never encounter both a class and its subclass. In this case, the Java method lookup can be replaced with a direct call to the compiled code corresponding to `callMyMethod()`.

> **TIP**   Monomorphic dispatch provides an example of the JVM runtime profiling allowing the platform to perform optimizations that an AOT language like C++ simply can't.

There's no technical reason why the `getInstance()` method can't return an object of type `MyActualClassNotInterface` under some circumstances and an object of some subclass under others, but in practice this almost never occurs. But to guard against the possibility that it might, a runtime check to ensure that the type of `obj` is inserted by the compiler, as expected. If this expectation is ever violated, the runtime backs out the optimization without the program ever noticing or ever doing anything incorrect.

This is a fairly aggressive optimization that is only ever performed by the server compiler. The real-time and client compilers would not do this.

6.6.4   *Reading the compilation logs*

Let's take a look at an example to illustrate how you can use the log messages output by the JIT compiler. The Hipparcos star catalog lists details about stars that can be observed from Earth. Our example application processes the catalog to generate star maps of the stars that can be seen on a given night, in a given location.

Let's look at some example output that shows which methods are being compiled when we run our star map application. The key VM flag we're using is -XX:+Print-Compilation. This is one of the extended switches we briefly discussed earlier. Adding this switch to the command line used to start the JVM tells the JIT compilation threads to add messages to the standard log. These messages indicate when methods have passed the compilation threshold and been turned into machine code.

```
  1           java.lang.String::hashCode (64 bytes)
  2           java.math.BigInteger::mulAdd (81 bytes)
  3           java.math.BigInteger::multiplyToLen (219 bytes)
  4           java.math.BigInteger::addOne (77 bytes)
  5           java.math.BigInteger::squareToLen (172 bytes)
  6           java.math.BigInteger::primitiveLeftShift (79 bytes)
  7           java.math.BigInteger::montReduce (99 bytes)
  8           sun.security.provider.SHA::implCompress (491 bytes)
  9           java.lang.String::charAt (33 bytes)
  1% !        sun.nio.cs.SingleByteDecoder::decodeArrayLoop @ 129 (308 bytes)
...
 39           sun.misc.FloatingDecimal::doubleValue (1289 bytes)
 40           org.camelot.hipparcos.DelimitedLine::getNextString (5 bytes)
 41 !         org.camelot.hipparcos.Star::parseStar (301 bytes)
...
  2% !        org.camelot.CamelotStarter::populateStarStore @ 25 (106 bytes)
 65 s         java.lang.StringBuffer::append (8 bytes)
```

This is pretty typical output from PrintCompilation. These lines indicate which methods have been deemed sufficiently "hot" to be compiled. As you might expect, the first methods to be compiled will likely be platform methods (such as String#hashCode). Over time, application methods (such as the org.camelot.hipparcos.Star#parse-Star method, which is used in the example to parse a record from the astronomical catalog) will also be compiled.

The output lines have a number, which indicates in which order the methods are compiled on this run. Note that this order may change slightly between runs due to the dynamic nature of the platform. These are some of the other fields:

- s—Indicates the method is synchronized.
- !—Indicates that the method has exception handlers.
- %—On-stack replacement (OSR). The method was compiled and replaced the interpreted version in running code. Note that OSR methods have their own numbering scheme from 1.

BEWARE OF THE ZOMBIE
When looking at sample output logs on code that is run using the server compiler (C2), you'll occasionally see lines like "made not entrant" and "made zombie." These lines mean that a particular method, which had been compiled, has now been invalidated, usually because of a classloading operation.

DEOPTIMIZATION

HotSpot is capable of deoptimizing code that's based on an assumption that turned out not to be true. In many cases, it will then reconsider and try an alternative optimization. Thus, the same method may be deoptimized and recompiled several times.

Over time, you'll see that the number of compiled methods stabilizes. Code reaches a steady, compiled state and largely remains there. The exact details of which methods get compiled can depend on the exact JVM version and OS platform in use. It's a mistake to assume that all platforms will produce the same set of compiled methods, and that the compiled code for a given method will be roughly the same size across platforms. As with so much else in the performance space, this should be measured, and the results may surprise. Even a fairly innocent looking Java method has proved to have a factor-of-5 difference between Solaris and Linux in terms of the machine code generated by JIT compilation. Measurement is always necessary.

6.7   *Summary*

Performance tuning isn't about staring at your code and praying for enlightenment, or applying canned quick fixes. Instead, it's about meticulous measurement, attention to detail, and patience. It's about persistent reduction of sources of error in your tests, so that the true sources of performance problems emerge.

Let's look at some of the key points that you've learned about performance optimization in the dynamic environment provided by the JVM:

- The JVM is an incredibly powerful and sophisticated runtime environment.
- The JVM's nature can make it sometimes challenging to optimize code within.
- You have to measure to get an accurate idea of where the problems really are.
- Pay particular attention to the garbage collection subsystem and the JIT compiler.
- Monitoring and other tools can really help.
- Learn to read the logs and other indicators of the platform—tools aren't always available.
- You must measure and set goals (this is so important we're saying it twice).

You should now have the basic grounding needed to explore and experiment with the platform's advanced performance features, and to understand how the performance mechanisms will affect your own code. Hopefully, you've also started to gain the confidence and experience to analyze all of this data with an open mind and to apply that insight to solving your own performance problems.

In the next chapter, we'll start to look beyond the Java language to alternatives on the JVM, but many of the performance features of the platform will be very useful in the wider context—especially what you've learned about JIT compilation and GC.

Part 3

Polyglot programming on the JVM

This part of the book is all about exploring new language paradigms and polyglot programming on the JVM.

The JVM is an amazing runtime environment—it provides not only performance and power, but also a surprising amount of flexibility to the programmer. In fact, the JVM is the gateway to exploring other languages beyond Java, and it allows you to try out some different approaches to programming.

If you've programmed only in Java, you may be wondering what you'll gain from learning different languages. As we said in chapter 1, the essence of being a well-grounded Java developer is to have a growing mastery of all aspects of the Java language, platform, and ecosystem. That includes an appreciation of topics that are on the horizon now, but that will be an integral part of the landscape in the near future.

> The future is already here—it's just not evenly distributed.
>
> —William Gibson

It turns out that many of the new ideas that will be needed in the future are present in other JVM languages today, such as functional programming. By learning a new JVM language, you can steal a glimpse into another world—one that may resemble some of your future projects. Exploring an unfamiliar point of view can help you put your existing knowledge into a fresh light. This opens the possibility that by learning a new language you'll discover new talents you didn't know you had and add new skills that will prove useful going forward.

You'll begin with a chapter that explains why Java isn't always the ideal language to solve all problems, why functional programming concepts are useful, and how to choose a non-Java language for a particular project.

Many recent books and blog articles are putting forward the view that functional programming is likely to be a major feature of every working developer's life in the near future. Many of these articles can make functional programming sound quite daunting, and it isn't always made clear how it would manifest itself in a language such as Java.

In fact, functional programming is not a monolithic construct at all. Instead, it's more of a style, and a gradual progression in a developer's way of thinking. In chapter 8, we'll show examples of slightly functional programming, which are just a way to handle collections code in a cleaner, less bug-friendly style using the Groovy language. We'll build up to talking about "object-functional" style in chapter 9 with the Scala language. We'll look at a purer approach to functional programming (one that even leaves behind object orientation) in chapter 10 with the language Clojure.

In part 4, we'll cover a number of real-world use cases where alternative languages provide superior solutions. If you need convincing, peek ahead at part 4, then come back here to learn the languages you need to apply those techniques.

Alternative JVM languages 7

This chapter covers

- Why you should use alternative JVM languages
- Language types
- Selection criteria for alternative languages
- How the JVM handles alternative languages

If you've used Java for any sizable amount of work, you've probably noticed that it tends toward being a bit verbose and clumsy at times. You may even have found yourself wishing that things were different—easier somehow.

Fortunately, as you've seen in the last few chapters, the JVM is awesome! So awesome, in fact, that it provides a natural home for programming languages other than Java. In this chapter, we'll show you why and how you might want to start mixing another JVM programming language into your project.

In this chapter, we'll cover ways of describing the different language types (such as static versus dynamic), why you might want to use alternative languages, and what criteria to look for in choosing them. You'll also be introduced to the three languages (Groovy, Scala, and Clojure) that we'll cover in more depth throughout parts 3 and 4 of this book.

Before we get started on that, however, you might need more convincing about some of Java's shortcomings. The next section is an extended example that highlights some annoyances, and points the way toward the programming language style called *functional programming*.

7.1   *Java too clumsy? Them's fighting words!*

Suppose you're writing a new component in a system that deals with trade (transaction) handling. A simplified view of the system is shown in figure 7.1.

As you can see, the system has two sources of data—the upstream incoming orders system, which you can query via a web service, and the dispatch database, which is further downstream.

This is a real bread-and-butter system, of the kind Java developers build all the time. In this section, we're going to introduce a simple bit of code that reconciles the two sources of data. Then we'll show how it can be a little clumsy to work with. After that, we'll introduce a core concept of functional programming, and show how functional idioms, such as *map* and *filter*, can simplify many common programming tasks. You'll see that Java's lack of direct support for these idioms makes programming harder than it needs to be.

7.1.1   *The reconciliation system*

You need a reconciliation system to check that the data is actually reaching the database. The core of such a system is the `reconcile()` method, which takes two parameters: `sourceData` (data from the web service, boiled down into a `Map`) and `dbIds`.

You need to pull out the `main_ref` key from `sourceData` and compare it to the primary key on the rows you pulled back from the database. Listing 7.1 shows how you can do the comparison.

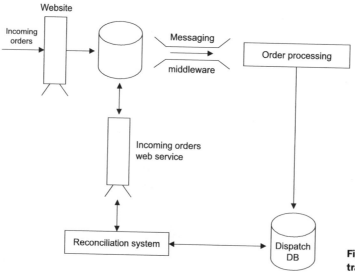

Figure 7.1   An example trade-handling system

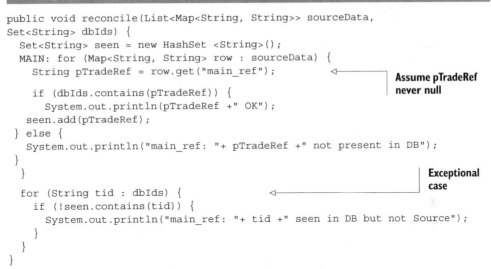

Listing 7.1   Reconciling two data sources

```
public void reconcile(List<Map<String, String>> sourceData,
Set<String> dbIds) {
  Set<String> seen = new HashSet <String>();
  MAIN: for (Map<String, String> row : sourceData) {
    String pTradeRef = row.get("main_ref");          ⟵—————  Assume pTradeRef
                                                              never null
    if (dbIds.contains(pTradeRef)) {
      System.out.println(pTradeRef +" OK");
    seen.add(pTradeRef);
  } else {
    System.out.println("main_ref: "+ pTradeRef +" not present in DB");
  }
  }                                                    ⟵—————  Exceptional
                                                              case
  for (String tid : dbIds) {
    if (!seen.contains(tid)) {
      System.out.println("main_ref: "+ tid +" seen in DB but not Source");
    }
  }
}
```

The main case you need to check is that everything in the incoming orders system made it to the dispatch database. This is handled by the top `for` loop—which is labeled `MAIN` for clarity.

But there is another possibility. Suppose an intern did some test orders via the administration interface (not realizing they were using the live system). Then the orders would show up in the dispatching database but not in the incoming orders system.

To take care of this exceptional case, you have a second loop. It checks to see if the seen set (all the trades that were in both systems) contains all the rows you saw in the database. It will also confirm which ones are missing. Here's some output from a sample run:

```
7172329 OK
1R6GV OK
1R6GW OK
main_ref: 1R6H2 not present in DB
main_ref: 1R6H3 not present in DB
1R6H6 OK
```

What's gone wrong? The answer is that the upstream system is case-insensitive, whereas the downstream one is case-sensitive. `1R6H2` is present in the dispatch database—it's called `1r6h2` instead.

If you examine the code in listing 7.1, you can see that the problem is the use of the `contains()` method. This method checks to see if the argument appears in the collection in question, but it only returns `true` if there's an exact match.

This means that what you really need is a `containsCaseInsensitive()` method, which doesn't exist! So instead you have to replace this bit of code,

```
if (dbIds.contains(pTradeRef)) {
  System.out.println(pTradeRef +" OK");
```

```
    seen.add(pTradeRef);
} else {
    System.out.println("main_ref: "+ pTradeRef +" not present in DB");
}
```

with a loop, like this:

```
for (String id : dbIds) {
    if (id.equalsIgnoreCase(pTradeRef)) {
        System.out.println(pTradeRef +" OK");
        seen.add(pTradeRef);
        continue MAIN;
    }
}
System.out.println("main_ref: "+ pTradeRef +" not present in DB");
```

This seems clunky. You're having to loop over the collection instead of handling it as a whole. The code is less concise and seems more fragile.

As your applications get larger, this difference in conciseness will become more important—you want to write concise code to conserve your mental bandwidth.

7.1.2 *Conceptual basics of functional programming*

There are two ideas in the last example that we want to draw your attention to:

- Operating on collections as a whole is more concise and usually better then iterating through the contents of the collection.
- Wouldn't it be awesome if we could add a tiny bit of logic to tweak the behavior of existing methods on our objects?

If you've ever found yourself writing collections code and getting frustrated because there's a method that almost provides a way to do what you need, but you need to tweak it slightly, then that frustration is an itch that could be scratched by functional programming (FP).

Another way of saying this is that a major limiting factor in writing concise (and safer) object-oriented code is the inability to add additional logic to existing methods. This leads us to the big idea of FP: Suppose you did have some way to tweak the functionality of a method by adding in some new code of your own.

What would that mean? To add in code of your own after the fact, you'd need to pass a representation of your block of code into the method as a parameter. What you really want to be able to write is something like this (we've called out the special con-tains() method in bold):

```
if (dbIds.contains(pTradeRef, matchFunction)) {
    System.out.println(pTradeRef +" OK");
    seen.add(pTradeRef);
} else {
    System.out.println("main_ref: "+ pTradeRef +" not present in DB");
}
```

If you could do this, the contains() method could be customized to use whatever test you wanted—a case-insensitive match in this example. In order to do that, you'd need some way of representing your match function as though it were a value—to be able to write out the bit of code as a "function literal" and then assign it to a variable.

To do functional programming, you need to be able to represent bits of logic (basically methods) as though they were values. This is the central idea of FP, and we'll come back to it, but first, let's look at another Java example that has some new FP ideas buried in it.

7.1.3 Map and filter idioms

Let's expand our example a little, and consider the context in which `reconcile()` gets called:

```
reconcile(sourceData, new HashSet<String>(extractPrimaryKeys(dbInfos)));

private List<String> extractPrimaryKeys(List<DBInfo> dbInfos) {
  List<String> out = new ArrayList<>();
  for (DBInfo tinfo : dbInfos) {
    out.add(tinfo.primary_key);
  }

  return out;
}
```

The `extractPrimaryKeys()` method returns a list of primary key vales (as strings) that have been extracted from the database objects. FP fans would call this a `map()` expression—`extractPrimaryKeys()` takes a `List` and returns a `List` by running an operation on each element in turn. This builds up the new list, which is returned from the method.

Note that the type contained in the returned `List` may be different (`String`) from the incoming `List` (`DBInfo`), and the original list hasn't been affected in any way.

This is where the name "functional programming" comes from—the functions behave like mathematical functions. After all, a function like $f(x) = x * x$ doesn't alter the value 2 when it's passed in. Instead, it returns a different value, 4.

Cheap optimization trick

There's a useful and slightly sneaky trick in the call to `reconcile()`—you pass the returned `List` from `extractPrimaryKeys()` into the constructor for `HashSet` to convert it to a `Set`. This handily de-dups the `List` for you, making the `contains()` call do less work in the `reconcile()` method.

This use of a `map()` is a classic FP idiom. It's often paired with another very well-known pattern, the `filter()` form, which you can see in the next listing.

Listing 7.2 Filter form

```
List<Map<String, String>> filterCancels(List<Map<String, String>> in) {
  List<Map<String, String>> out = new ArrayList<>();              Defensive
  for (Map<String, String> msg : in) {                            copy
    if (!msg.get("status").equalsIgnoreCase("CANCELLED")) {
```

```
        out.add(msg);
      }
    }

  return out;
}
```

Notice the defensive copy—this means that you return a new `List` instance. You don't mutate the existing `List` (so the `filter()` form behaves like a mathematical function). You build up a new `List` by testing each element against a function that returns a `boolean`. If the result of testing an element is `true`, you add it into the output `List`.

For the filter form to work, you need a function that says whether or not a given element should be included. You can think of this function as asking the question, "Should this element be allowed to pass through the filter?" for each element in the collection.

These functions are called *predicate functions*, and we need some way to represent them. Here's one way you could write one in some pseudocode (it's almost Scala):

```
(msg) -> { !msg.get("status").equalsIgnoreCase("CANCELLED")  }
```

This is a function that takes in one argument (called `msg`) and returns a `boolean` result. It returns `false` if the `msg` has been canceled, and `true` otherwise. When used in a filter form, it will filter out any canceled messages.

This is precisely what you want. Before calling the reconciliation code, you need to remove any canceled orders because a canceled order won't be present in the dispatch database.

As it turns out, this syntax is how Java 8 is going to write it (but it was strongly influenced by the Scala and C# syntax). We'll come back to this theme in chapter 14, but we'll meet these function literals (also called *lambda expressions*) in several other contexts first.

Let's move on and discuss some of these other contexts, starting by taking a look at the types of languages available on the JVM—what is sometimes called *language zoology*.

7.2   *Language zoology*

Programming languages come in many different flavors and classifications. Another way of saying this is that there is a wide range of styles and approaches to programming that are embodied in different languages. If you're going to master these different styles and use them to make your life easier, you need to understand the differences and how to classify languages.

> **NOTE**   These classifications are an aid to thinking about the diversity of languages. Some of these divisions provide clearer-cut classifications than others, and none of the classifying schemes is perfect.

In recent years there has also been a trend for languages to add features from across the spectrum of possibilities. This means that it's often helpful to think of a given language as being "less functional" than another language, or "dynamically typed but with optional static typing when needed."

The classifications we'll cover are "interpreted versus compiled," "dynamic versus static," "imperative versus functional," and reimplementations of a language versus the original. In general, these classifications should be used as a useful tool for thinking about the space, rather than as a complete and precise academic scheme.

Java is a runtime-compiled, statically typed, imperative language. It emphasizes safety, code clarity, and performance, and it's happy to accept a certain amount of verbosity and lack of agility (such as in deployment). Different languages may have different priorities; for example, dynamically typed languages may emphasize deployment speed.

Let's get started with the interpreted versus compiled classification.

7.2.1 *Interpreted vs. compiled languages*

An interpreted language is one in which each step of the source code is executed as is, rather than the entire program being transformed to machine code before execution begins. This contrasts with a compiled language, which is one that uses a compiler to convert the human-readable source code into a binary form as an initial task.

This distinction is one that has become less clear recently. In the '80s and early '90s, the divide was fairly clear: C/C++ and the like were compiled languages, and Perl and Python were interpreted languages. But as we alluded to in chapter 1, Java has features of both compiled and interpreted languages. The use of bytecode further muddies the issue. Bytecode is certainly not human readable, but neither is it true machine code.

For the JVM languages we'll study in this part of the book, the distinction we'll make is whether the language produces a class file from the source code, and executes that—or not. In the latter case, there will be an interpreter (probably written in Java) that's used to execute the source code, line by line. Some languages provide both a compiler and an interpreter, and some provide an interpreter and a just-in-time (JIT) compiler that will emit JVM bytecode.

7.2.2 *Dynamic vs. static typing*

In languages with dynamic typing, a variable can contain different types at different times. As an example, let's look at a simple bit of code in a well-known dynamic language, JavaScript. This example should hopefully be comprehensible even if you don't know the language in detail:

```
var answer = 40;
answer = answer + 2;
answer = "What is the answer? " + answer;
```

In this code, the variable answer starts off being set to 40, which is, of course, a numeric value. We then add 2 to it, giving 42. Then we change track slightly and make answer hold a string value. This is a very common technique in a dynamic language, and it causes no syntax errors.

The JavaScript interpreter is also able to distinguish between the two uses of the + operator. The first use of + is numeric addition—adding 2 to 40, whereas in the following line the interpreter figures out from context that the developer meant string concatenation.

> **NOTE** The key point here is that dynamic typing keeps track of information about what sort of values the variables contain (for example, a number or a string), and static typing keeps track of type information about the variables.

Static typing can be a good fit for a compiled language because the type information is all about the variables, not the values in them. This makes it much easier to reason about potential type system violations at compile time.

Dynamically typed languages carry type information on the values held in variables. This means that it's much harder to reason about type violations because the information needed for that reasoning isn't known until execution time.

7.2.3   *Imperative vs. functional languages*

Java 7 is a classic example of an imperative language. Imperative languages can be thought of as languages that model the running state of a program as mutable data and issue a list of instructions that transform that running state. Program state is thus the concept that has center stage in imperative languages.

There are two main subtypes of imperative languages. Procedural languages, such as BASIC and FORTRAN, treat code and data as completely separate, and have a simple code-operates-on-data paradigm. The other subtype is object-oriented (OO) languages, where data and code (in the form of methods) are bundled together into objects. In OO languages, additional structure is imposed to a greater or lesser degree by metadata (such as class information).

Functional languages take the view that computation itself is the most important concept. Functions operate on values, as in procedural languages, but instead of altering their inputs, functions are seen as acting like mathematical functions and return new values.

As illustrated in figure 7.2, functions are seen as "little processing machines" that take in values and output new values. They don't have any state of their own, and it doesn't really make sense to bundle them up with any external state. This means that the object-centered view of the world is somewhat at odds with the natural viewpoint of functional languages.

In each of the next three chapters, we'll focus on a different language and build on the previous treatments of functional programming. We'll start off with Groovy, which enables a "slightly functional style," processing collections in the way we discussed in section 7.1, then Scala which makes more of a big deal out of FP, and finally Clojure (a purer functional language, but no longer OO).

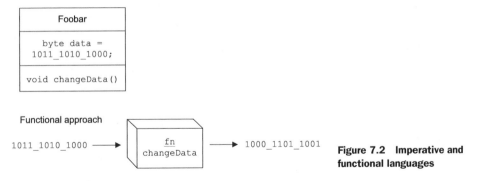

Figure 7.2 Imperative and functional languages

7.2.4 *Reimplementation vs. original*

Another important distinction between JVM languages is the division into those that are reimplementations of existing languages versus those that were specifically written to target the JVM. In general, languages that were specifically written to target the JVM are able to provide a much tighter binding between their type systems and the native types of the JVM.

The following three languages are JVM reimplementations of existing languages:

- *JRuby* is a JVM reimplementation of the Ruby programming language. Ruby is a dynamically typed OO language with some functional features. It's basically interpreted on the JVM, but recent versions have included a runtime JIT compiler to produce JVM bytecode under favorable conditions.

- *Jython* was started in 1997 by Jim Hugunin as a way to use high-performance Java libraries from Python. It's a reimplementation of Python on the JVM, so it's a dynamic, mostly OO language. It operates by generating internal Python bytecode, then translating that to JVM bytecode. This enables it to operate in a manner that looks like Python's typical interpreted mode. It can also work in an ahead-of-time (AOT) compiled mode, by generating the JVM bytecode, and saving the resulting class files to disk.

- *Rhino* was originally developed by Netscape, and later the Mozilla project. It provides an implementation of JavaScript on the JVM. JavaScript is a dynamically typed OO language (but one that takes a very different approach to object orientation than Java does). Rhino supports both a compiled and an interpreted mode and ships with Java 7 (see the com.sun.script.javascript package for details).

The earliest JVM language?

The earliest non-Java JVM language is hard to pin down. Certainly, Kawa, an implementation of Lisp, dates to 1997 or so. In the years since then, we've seen an explosion of languages, to the point that it's almost impossible to keep track of them.

A reasonable guess at time of writing is that there are at least 200 languages that target the JVM. Not all can be considered to be active or widely used, but the large number indicates that the JVM is a very active platform for language development and implementation.

> **NOTE** In the versions of the language and VM spec that debuted with Java 7, all direct references to the Java language have been removed from the VM spec. Java is now simply one language among many that run on the JVM—it no longer enjoys a privileged status.

The key piece of technology that enables so many different languages to target the JVM is the class file format, as we discussed in chapter 5. Any language that can produce a class file is considered a compiled language on the JVM.

Let's move on to discuss how ployglot programming came to be an area of interest for Java programmers. We'll explain the basic concepts, and why and how to choose an alternative JVM language for your project.

7.3   *Polyglot programming on the JVM*

The phrase "polyglot programming on the JVM" is relatively new. It was coined to describe projects that utilize one or more non-Java JVM languages alongside a core of Java code. One common way to think about polyglot programming is as a form of separation of concerns. As you can see in figure 7.3, there are potentially three layers where non-Java technologies can play a useful role. This diagram is sometimes called the polyglot programming pyramid, and it's due to the work of Ola Bini.

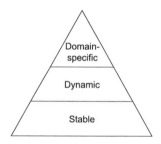

Figure 7.3 The polyglot programming pyramid

Within the pyramid, you can see three well-defined layers—domain-specific, dynamic, and stable.

> ### The secret of polyglot programming
>
> Polyglot programming makes sense because different pieces of code have different lifetimes. A risk engine in a bank may last for five or more years. JSP pages for a website could last for a few months. The most short-lived code for a startup could be live for just a few days. The longer the code lives, the closer to the bottom of the pyramid it is.
>
> This represents a trade-off between concerns like performance and thorough testing at the bottom versus flexibility and rapid deployment at the top.

Table 7.1 shows these three layers in more detail.

As you can see, there are patterns in the layers—the statically typed languages tend to gravitate toward tasks in the stable layer. Conversely, the less-powerful and general-purpose technologies tend to be well-suited to roles at the top of the pyramid.

Table 7.1 Three layers of the polyglot programming pyramid

Name	Description	Examples
Domain-specific	Domain-specific language. Tightly coupled to a specific part of the application domain.	Apache Camel DSL, Drools, Web templating
Dynamic	Rapid, productive, flexible development of functionality.	Groovy, Jython, Clojure
Stable	Core functionality, stable, well-tested, performant.	Java, Scala

In the middle of the pyramid, there is a rich role for languages in the dynamic tier. These are also the most flexible—in many cases there is potential overlap between the dynamic tier and either of the neighboring tiers.

Let's dig a little deeper into this diagram and look at why Java isn't the best choice for everything in the pyramid. We'll begin by discussing why you should consider a non-Java language, then we'll cover some of the major criteria to look at in choosing a non-Java language for your project.

7.3.1 Why use a non-Java language?

Java's nature as a general-purpose, statically typed, compiled language provides many advantages. These qualities make it a great choice for implementing functionality in the stable layer. But these same attributes become a burden in the upper tiers of the pyramid. For example,

- Recompilation is laborious
- Static typing can be inflexible and lead to long refactoring times
- Deployment is a heavyweight process
- Java's syntax isn't a natural fit for producing DSLs

The recompilation and rebuild time of a Java project quickly reaches the 90 seconds to 2 minutes mark. This is a long enough to seriously break a developer's flow, and it's a bad fit for developing code that may live in production for only a few weeks.

A pragmatic solution is to play to Java's strengths, and to take advantage of its rich API and library support to do the heavy lifting for the application—down in the stable layer.

NOTE If you're starting a new project from scratch, you may also find that another stable layer language (such as Scala) has a particular feature (for example, superior concurrency support) that's important to your project. In most cases, however, you should not throw out working stable layer code to rewrite in a different stable language.

At this point, you may be asking yourself, "What type of programming challenges fit inside these layers? Which languages should I choose?" A well-grounded Java developer knows that there is no silver bullet, but we do have criteria that you could consider when evaluating your choices. We can't cover every alternative choice in the book, so for the rest of the chapters, we'll focus on three languages that we think cover a wide spectrum of possible sensible choices for Java shops.

7.3.2 Up-and-coming languages

For the rest of the book, we've picked three languages that we see having the greatest potential longevity and influence. These are the languages on the JVM (Groovy, Scala, and Clojure) that already have well-established mind share among polyglot programmers. So why are these three languages gaining traction. Let's look at each in turn.

GROOVY

The Groovy language was invented by James Strachan in 2003. It's a dynamic, compiled language with syntax very similar to Java's, but more flexible. It's widely used as a scripting and rapid prototyping language, and it's often the first non-Java language that developers or teams investigate on the JVM. Groovy can be seen as sitting in the dynamic layer and is also known for being great for building DSLs. Chapter 8 provides an introduction to Groovy.

SCALA

Scala is an OO language that also supports aspects of functional programming. It traces its origins to 2003, when Martin Odersky began work on it, following his earlier projects related to generics in Java. It's a statically typed, compiled language like Java, but unlike Java it performs a large amount of type inference. This means that it often has the feel of a dynamic language.

Scala has learned a great deal from Java, and its language design "fixes" several long-term annoyances that Java developers have with Java. Scala can be seen as sitting in the stable layer, and some developers argue that it might one day challenge Java as the "next big language on the JVM." Chapter 9 provides an introduction to Scala.

CLOJURE

Clojure, designed by Rich Hickey, is a language from the Lisp family. It inherits many syntactic features (and lots of parentheses) from that heritage. It's a dynamically typed, functional language, as is usual for Lisps. It's a compiled language, but usually distributes code in source form—for reasons we'll see later. It also adds a significant number of new features (especially in the arena of concurrency) to its Lisp core.

Lisps are usually seen as experts-only languages. Clojure is somewhat easier to learn than other Lisps, yet still provides the developer with formidable power (and also lends itself very nicely to the test-driven development style). But it's likely to remain outside the mainstream, for enthusiasts and specialized jobs (for example, some financial applications find its combination of features very appealing).

Clojure is usually seen as sitting in the dynamic layer, but due to its concurrency support and other features can be seen as capable of performing many of the roles of a stable layer language. Chapter 10 provides an introduction to Clojure.

Now that we've outlined some of the possible choices, let's discuss the issues that should drive your decision of which language to choose.

7.4 How to choose a non-Java language for your project

Once you've decided to experiment with non-Java languages in your project, you need to identify which parts of your project naturally fit into the stable, dynamic, or domain-specific layers. Table 7.2 highlights tasks that might be suitable for each layer.

Table 7.2   Project areas suited for domain-specific, dynamic, and stable layers

Name	Example problem domains
Domain-specific	Build, continuous integration, continuous deployment Dev-ops Enterprise Integration Pattern modeling Business rules modeling
Dynamic	Rapid web development Prototyping Interactive administrative and user consoles Scripting Tests (such as for test- and behavior-driven development)
Stable	Concurrent code Application containers Core business functionality

As you can see, there is a wide range of use cases for alternative languages. But identifying a task that could be resolved with an alternative language is just the beginning. You next need to evaluate whether using an alternative language is appropriate. Here are some useful criteria that we take into account when considering technology stacks:

- Is the project area low-risk?
- How easily does the language interoperate with Java?
- What tooling support (for example, IDE support) is there for the language?
- How steep is the learning curve for this language?
- How easy is it to hire developers with experience in this language?

Let's dive into each of these areas so you get an idea of the sorts of questions you need to be asking yourself.

7.4.1 Is the project area low-risk?

Let's say you have a core payment-processing rules engine that handles over one million transactions a day. This is a stable piece of Java software that has been around for over seven years, but there aren't a lot of tests, and there are plenty of dark corners in the code. The core of the payment-processing engine is clearly a high-risk area to bring a new language into, especially when it's running successfully and there's a lack of test coverage and of developers who fully understand it.

But there's more to a system than its core processing. For example, this is a situation where better tests would clearly help. Scala has a great testing framework called

ScalaTest (which we'll meet properly in chapter 11). It enables developers to produce JUnit-like tests for Java or Scala code, but without a lot of the boilerplate that JUnit seems to generate. So once they're over the initial ScalaTest learning curve, developers can be much more productive at improving the test coverage. ScalaTest also provides a great way to gradually introduce concepts like behavior-driven development to the codebase. The availability of modern testing features can really help when the time comes to refactor or replace parts of the core—whether the new processing engine ends up being written in Java or Scala.

Or suppose you need to build a web console so that the operations users can administer some of the noncritical static data behind the payment-processing system. The development team members already know Struts and JSF, but don't feel any enthusiasm for either technology. This is another low-risk area to try out a new language and technology stack. One obvious choice would be Grails (the Groovy-based web framework originally inspired by ideas from Ruby on Rails). Developer buzz, backed up by some studies (including a very interesting one by Matt Raible), says that Grails is the best-available web framework for productivity.

By focusing on a limited pilot in an area that is low-risk, the manager always has the option of terminating the project and porting to a different delivery technology without too much disruption if it turns out that the attempted technology stack was not a good fit for the team or system.

7.4.2   *Does the language interoperate well with Java?*

You don't want to lose the value of all of that great Java code you've already written! This is one of the main reasons organizations are hesitant to introduce a new programming language into their technology stack. But with alternative languages that run on the JVM, you can turn this on its head, so it becomes about maximizing your existing value in the codebase and not throwing away working code.

Alternative languages on the JVM are able to cleanly interoperate with Java and can, of course, be deployed on a preexisting environment. This is especially important when discussing this step with the production management folks. By using a non-Java JVM language as part of your system, you'll be able to make use of their expertise in supporting the existing environment. This can help alleviate any worries they might have about supporting the new solution and help reduce risk.

> **NOTE**   DSLs are typically built using a dynamic (or, in some cases, stable) layer language, so many of them run on the JVM via the languages that they were built in.

Some languages interoperate with Java more easily than others. We've found that most popular JVM alternatives (such as Groovy, Scala, Clojure, Jython, and JRuby) all have good interoperability with Java (and for some of the languages, the integration is excellent, almost completely seamless). If you're a really cautious shop, it's quick and easy to run a few experiments first, and make certain that you understand how the integration can work for you.

Let's take Groovy, for example. You can import Java packages directly into its code via the familiar `import` statement. You can build a quick website using the Groovy-based Grails framework, yet still reference your Java model objects. Conversely, it's very easy for Java to call Groovy code in a variety of ways and receive back familiar Java objects. One example use case here could be calling out to Groovy from Java to process some JSON, and have a Java object returned.

7.4.3 Is there good tooling and test support for the language?

Most developers underestimate the amount of time they save once they've become comfortable in their environment. Their powerful IDEs and build and test tools help them to rapidly produce high quality software. Java developers have benefited from great tooling support for years, so it's important to remember that other languages may not be at quite the same level of maturity.

Some languages (such as Groovy) have had longstanding IDE support for compiling, testing, and deploying the end result. Other languages may have tooling that hasn't matured as fully. For example, Scala's IDEs aren't as polished as Java's, but Scala fans feel that the power and conciseness of Scala more than make up for the imperfections of the current generation of IDEs.

A related issue is that when an alternative language has developed a powerful tool for its own use (such as Clojure's awesome Leiningen build tool), the tool may not be well adapted to handle other languages. This means that the team will need to think carefully about how to divide up a project, especially for deployment of separate but related components.

7.4.4 How hard is the language to learn?

It always takes time to learn a new language, and that time only increases if the paradigm of the language isn't one that your development team is familiar with. Most Java development teams will be comfortable picking up a new language if it's object oriented with a C-like syntax (for example, Groovy).

It gets harder for Java developers as they move further away from this paradigm. Scala tries to bridge the gap between the OO and functional worlds, but the jury is still out on whether this fusion is viable for large-scale software projects. At the extreme of the popular alternative languages, a language such as Clojure can bring incredibly powerful benefits, but can also represent a significant retraining requirement for development teams as they learn Clojure's functional nature and Lisp syntax.

One alternative is to look at the JVM languages that are reimplementations of existing languages. Ruby and Python are well-established languages, with plenty of material available for developers to use to educate themselves. The JVM incarnations of these languages could provide a sweet spot for your teams to begin working with an easy-to-learn non-Java language.

7.4.5   *Are there lots of developers using this language?*

Organizations have to be pragmatic; they can't always hire the top 2 percent (despite what their advertising might say), and their development teams will change throughout the course of a year. Some languages, such as Groovy and Scala, are becoming well-established enough that there is a pool of developers to hire from. But a language such as Clojure is still finding its way to popularity, and finding good Clojure developers is going to be difficult.

> **WARNING**   A warning about the reimplemented languages: many existing packages and applications written in Ruby, for example, are only tested against the original C-based implementation. This means that there may be problems when trying to use them on top of the JVM. When making platform decisions, you should factor in extra testing time if you're planning to leverage an entire stack written in a reimplemented language.

Again, the reimplemented languages (JRuby, Jython, and so on) can potentially help here. Few developers may have JRuby on their CV, but as it's just Ruby on the JVM, there's actually a large pool of developers to hire from—a Ruby developer familiar with the C version can learn the differences induced by running on the JVM very easily.

In order to understand some of the design choices and limitations of alternative languages on the JVM, you need to understand how the JVM supports multiple languages.

7.5   *How the JVM supports alternative languages*

There are two possible ways that a language can run on the JVM:

- Have a compiler that emits class files
- Have an interpreter that is implemented in JVM bytecode

In both cases, it's usual to have a runtime environment that provides language-specific support for executing programs. Figure 7.4 shows the runtime environment stack for Java and for a typical non-Java language.

These runtime support systems vary in complexity, depending on the amount of hand holding that a given non-Java language requires at runtime. In almost all cases, the runtime will be implemented as a set of JARs that an executing program needs to have on its classpath and that will bootstrap before program execution starts.

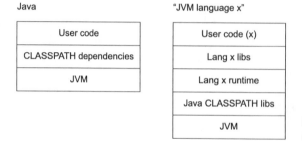

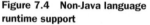

Figure 7.4   Non-Java language runtime support

In this book, our focus is on compiled languages. The interpreted languages—such as Rhino—are mentioned for completeness, but we won't spend too much time on them. In the rest of this section, we'll discuss the need for runtime support for alternative languages (even for compiled languages) and then talk about compiler fictions—language-specific features that are synthesized by the compiler and that may not appear in the low-level bytecode.

7.5.1 Runtime environments for non-Java languages

One simple way to measure the complexity of the runtime environment that a particular language requires is to look at the size of the JAR files that provide the implementation of the runtime. Using this as a metric, we can see that Clojure is a relatively lightweight runtime, whereas JRuby is a language that requires more support.

This isn't a completely fair test, as some languages bundle much larger standard libraries and additional functionality into their standard distributions than others. But it can be a useful (if rough) rule of thumb.

In general, the purpose of the runtime environment is to help the type system and other aspects of the non-Java language achieve the desired semantics. Alternative languages don't always have exactly the same view as Java about basic programming concepts.

For example, Java's approach to OO isn't universally shared by other languages. In Ruby, an individual object instance can have additional methods attached to it at runtime that were not known when the class was defined and that aren't defined on other instances of the same class. This property (which is somewhat confusingly called "open classes") needs to be replicated by the JRuby implementation. This is only possible with some advanced support from the JRuby runtime.

7.5.2 Compiler fictions

Certain language features are synthesized by the programming environment and high-level language and aren't present in the underlying JVM implementation. These are referred to as *compiler fictions*. We've already met one good example in chapter 6—Java's string concatenation.

> **TIP** It helps to have some knowledge of how these features are implemented—otherwise you can find your code running slowly, or in some cases even crashing the process. Sometimes the environment has to do a lot of work to synthesize a particular feature.

Other examples in Java include checked exceptions and inner classes (which are always converted to top-level classes with specially synthesized access methods if necessary, as shown in figure 7.5). If you've ever looked inside a JAR file (using `jar tvf`) and seen a load of classes with $ in their names, then these are the inner classes unpacked and converted to "regular" classes.

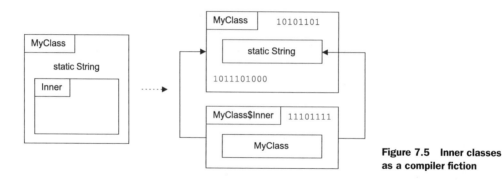

Figure 7.5 Inner classes as a compiler fiction

Alternative languages also have compiler fictions. In some cases, these compiler fictions even form a core part of the language's functionality. Let's take a look at a couple of important examples.

FIRST-CLASS FUNCTIONS

In section 7.1, we introduced the key concept of functional programming—that functions should be values that can be put into variables. The usual way of saying this is that "functions are first-class values." We also showed that Java doesn't have a very good way to model functions.

All of the non-Java languages that we'll consider in part 3 of this book support functions as first-class values. This means that functions can be put into variables, passed to methods, and manipulated in the same ways as any other value. The JVM only handles classes as the smallest unit of code and functionality, so under the hood, all the non-Java languages are creating little anonymous classes to hold the functions (although this may change with Java 8).

The solution to this discrepancy between source code and JVM bytecode is to remember that objects are just bundles of data along with methods to act on that data. Now imagine you had an object that has no state, and just one method—for example, a simple anonymous implementation of Java's `Callable` interface from chapter 4. It wouldn't be at all unusual to put such an object in a variable, pass it around, and then invoke its `call()` method later, like this:

```
Callable<String> myFn = new Callable<String>() {
  @Override
  public String call() {
    return "The result";
  }
};

try {
  System.out.println(myFn.call());
} catch (Exception e) {
}
```

We've omitted exception handling because, in this case, the `call()` method of `myFn` can never throw.

NOTE The `myFn` variable in this example is an anonymous type, so it will show up after compilation as something like `NameOfEnclosingClass$1.class`. The class numbers start at 1 and go up for each anonymous type the compiler encounters. If they're dynamically created, and there are a lot of them (as sometimes happens in languages like JRuby), this can place pressure on the PermGen area of memory where the definitions of classes are stored.

Java programmers use this trick of creating an anonymous implementation a lot, although Java doesn't have any special syntax for it. This means that the result can be a bit long-winded. All of the languages that we're about to meet provide a special syntax for writing out these function values (or "function literals" or "anonymous functions"). They're a major pillar of the functional programming style, which both Scala and Clojure support well.

MULTIPLE INHERITANCE

As another example, in Java (and the JVM), there's no way to express multiple inheritance of implementation. The only way to achieve multiple inheritance is to use interfaces, which don't allow any method bodies to be specified.

By contrast, in Scala, the traits mechanism allows implementation of methods to be mixed into a class, so it provides a different view of inheritance. We'll cover this in full detail in chapter 9. For now, just remember that this behavior has to be synthesized by the Scala compiler and runtime—there's no provision for it at the VM level.

This concludes our introduction to the different types of languages available on the JVM and some of the ways their unique features are implemented.

7.6 Summary

Alternative languages on the JVM have come a long way. They can now offer better solutions than Java for certain problems while retaining compatibility with existing systems and investments made in Java technology. This means that even for Java shops, Java isn't always the automatic choice for every programming task.

Understanding the different ways languages can be classified (static versus dynamic, imperative versus functional, and compiled versus interpreted) gives you the foundation for being able to pick the right language for the right task.

For the polyglot programmer, languages fall roughly into three programming layers: stable, dynamic, and domain-specific. Languages such as Java and Scala are best used for the stable layer of software development, whereas others, such as Groovy and Clojure, are more suited to tasks in the dynamic or domain-specific realms.

Certain programming challenges fit well into particular layers, such as rapid web development in the dynamic layer or modeling enterprise messaging in the domain-specific layer.

It's worth emphasizing again that the core business functionality of an existing production application is almost never the correct place to introduce a new language. The core is where high-grade support, excellent test coverage, and a proven track record of stability are of paramount importance. Rather than start here, choose a low-risk area for your first deployment of an alternative language.

Always remember that each team and project has its own unique characteristics that will impact the decision of which language to choose. There are no universal right answers here. When choosing to implement a new language, managers and senior techs must take into account the nature of their projects and team.

A small team composed exclusively of experienced propeller-heads may choose Clojure for its clean design, sophistication, and power (and never mind the conceptual complexity and possible difficulty of hiring). Meanwhile, a web shop, looking to grow the team quickly and attract young developers, may choose Groovy and Grails for the productivity gains and relatively deep talent pool.

There are three alternative languages on the JVM that we see as leading the pack: Groovy, Scala, and Clojure. By the time you finish this book, you'll have learned the basics of three of the most promising alternative languages on the JVM and will have expanded your programming toolkit in interesting new directions.

In the next chapter, you'll learn about the first of these—Groovy.

Groovy:
Java's dynamic friend

This chapter covers

- Why you should learn Groovy
- Basic Groovy syntax
- Differences between Groovy and Java
- Powerful Groovy features not found in Java
- How Groovy is also a scripting language
- Groovy interoperability with Java

Groovy is an OO, dynamically typed language that, like Java, runs on the JVM. In fact, it can be seen as a language that provides dynamic capabilities to complement the static world of Java. The Groovy project was initially founded by James Strachan and Bob McWhirter in late 2003, with its leadership changed to Guillaume Laforge in 2004. The community based at http://groovy.codehaus.org/ continues to thrive and grow today. Groovy is seen as the most popular language on the JVM after Java itself.

Inspired by Smalltalk, Ruby, and Python, Groovy has implemented several language features that Java doesn't have, such as:

- Function literals
- First-class[1] support for collections

---

[1] By *first-class*, we mean that support is built into the language syntax as opposed to requiring library calls.

- First-class support for regular expressions
- First-class support for XML processing

NOTE In Groovy, *function literals* are called *closures*. As explained in chapter 7, they're functions that can be put into variables, passed to methods, and manipulated in the same ways as any other value.

So why would you want to use Groovy? If you remember back to the polyglot programming pyramid in chapter 7, you'll recall that Java isn't ideal for solving problems in the dynamic layer. These problems include rapid web development, prototyping, scripting, and more. Groovy is designed to solve exactly those problems.

Here's an example of Groovy's usefulness. Imagine that your boss asked you to write a Java routine that turned a bunch of Java beans into XML. With Java, this task is certainly possible, and you have a wide variety of APIs and libraries to choose from:

- Java Architecture for XML Binding (JAXB) with Java API for XML Processing (JAXP) that comes as part of Java 6
- The XStream library hosted at Codehaus
- Apache's XMLBeans library

And the list goes on...

This processing is laborious. For example, to marshal a `Person` object under JAXB, you'd have to write something like this:

```
JAXBContext jc = JAXBContext.newInstance("net.teamsparq.domain");
ObjectFactory objFactory = new ObjectFactory();
Person person = (Person)objFactory.createPerson();
person.setId(2);
person.setName("Gweneth");
Marshaller m = jc.createMarshaller();
m.setProperty(Marshaller.JAXB_FORMATTED_OUTPUT, Boolean.TRUE);
m.marshal(person, System.out);
```

You'd also have to have a full `Person` class coded up with getters and setters to make it a proper Java bean.

Groovy takes a different approach because it treats XML as a first-class citizen in the language. This would be the Groovy equivalent:

```
def writer = new StringWriter();
def xml = new groovy.xml.MarkupBuilder(writer);
xml.person(id:2) {
  name 'Gweneth'
  age 1
}
println writer.toString();
```

As you can see, it's a very quick language to work with, and it's close enough to Java that developers can transition easily to it.

Groovy's features are also aimed at helping you write less boilerplate code; for example, you can deal with XML and loop over collections in a much more concise way than in Java. Groovy interoperates well with Java and so you can use Groovy's dynamic nature and language features and yet still easily interoperate with Java.

Groovy has a very flat learning curve for Java developers as it's syntactically very similar to Java and you only need the Groovy JAR to get started. By the end of this chapter, we expect that you'll be well into the groove with this new language![2]

Groovy is fully parsed, compiled, and generated before execution by the JVM, which leaves some developers wondering, "Why doesn't it pick up obvious errors at compile time?" It always pays to remember that Groovy is a *dynamic* language—that performs its type checking and binding at runtime.

> **Groovy performance**
>
> Groovy isn't always the best choice of language if your software has stringent performance requirements. Groovy objects extend from `GroovyObject`, which contains an `invokeMethod(String name, Object args)` method. Each time you call a Groovy method, that method isn't called directly as it would in Java. Instead, it's executed via the aforementioned `invokeMethod(String name, Object args)`, which itself executes a number of reflection calls and lookups, which of course slows processing. The Groovy language developers have made several optimizations, and more will follow as future versions of Groovy take advantage of the new `invokedynamic` bytecode in the JVM.

Groovy still relies on Java for some of its heavy lifting, and it's very easy to call out to existing Java libraries. This ability to use Java along with Groovy's dynamic typing and new language features makes Groovy an excellent rapid prototyping language. Groovy can also be used as a scripting language, and it therefore has a firmly established reputation as Java's agile and dynamic friend.

In this chapter, you'll start by running some simple Groovy examples. Once you're comfortable with the running of a basic Groovy program, you'll move on to learning Groovy-specific syntax and the parts of Groovy that typically trip up a Java developer. The remainder of the chapter gets into the meat of Groovy, covering several major language features that have no equivalents in Java. Finally, you'll learn to become a polyglot programmer on the JVM by blending Java and Groovy code!

8.1 Getting started with Groovy

If you haven't got Groovy installed, see appendix C for the details of how to get it set up on your machine before you move on to compiling and running the first example in this chapter.

In this section, we'll show you how to run the basic commands to compile and execute Groovy so you can do so comfortably from any OS. We'll also introduce you to

---

[2] Yes, another terrible pun—we warned you, and yet here you are.

the Groovy console, a valuable, OS-independent scratchpad environment ideal for trying out quick bits of Groovy code.

Have it installed? Then let's get started compiling and running some Groovy code!

8.1.1 Compiling and running

There are a number of useful command-line tools that you should get to know with Groovy; in particular, the compiler (`groovyc`) and the runtime executor (`groovy`). These two commands are roughly synonymous with `javac` and `java` respectively.

> **Why is the style of the code examples changing?**
> The syntax and semantics of the code snippets and listings will evolve from Java-like examples to purely idiomatic Groovy examples as you move through this chapter. Our intention here is to ease your transition from Java to Groovy. Another excellent title to assist you is *Making Java Groovy*, by Kenneth A. Kousen (Manning, 2012).

Let's quickly explore these command-line tools by compiling and running a simple Groovy script that will print this line:[3]

```
It's Groovy baby, yeah!
```

Open a command-line prompt and follow these steps.

1 Create a file called HelloGroovy.groovy in any directory you like.
2 Edit the file, adding this line:
```
System.out.println("It's Groovy baby, yeah!");
```
3 Save HelloGroovy.groovy.
4 Compile the file by executing this command:
```
groovyc HelloGroovy.groovy
```
5 Run it by executing this command:
```
groovy HelloGroovy
```

TIP You can skip the compile step if the Groovy source file is in your CLASSPATH. The Groovy runtime will execute `groovyc` on the source file first if need be.

Congratulations, you've run your first line of Groovy code!

Just like Java, you can write, compile, and execute Groovy code from the command line, but that quickly becomes unwieldy when dealing with things such as the CLASSPATH. Groovy is well supported by the major Java IDEs (Eclipse, IntelliJ, and NetBeans) but Groovy also provides a useful console for you to run code in. This console is ideal if you're quickly trying to script up a solution or prototype a small piece of code, as it's much faster to use than a full-fledged IDE.

---

[3] Thank you Austin Powers!

8.1.2   *Groovy console*

We'll use the Groovy console to run the code examples in this chapter, because it's a nice, lightweight IDE to use. To start the console, execute `groovyConsole` on the command line.

A separate window should come up that looks similar to figure 8.1.

First, you'll want to untick the Show Script in Output option under the View menu. This will make the output a little cleaner. Now you can make sure that the console is working correctly by running the same line of Groovy code as in the previous example. In the top panel of the console, enter the following code:

```
System.out.println("It's Groovy baby, yeah!");
```

Then click the Execute Script button or use the Ctrl-R keyboard shortcut. The Groovy console will then show the following output in the bottom panel:

```
It's Groovy baby, yeah!
```

As you can see, the output panel shows you the result of the expression you've just executed.

Now that you know how to execute Groovy code quickly, it's time to move on to learning some Groovy syntax and semantics.

8.2   *Groovy 101—syntax and semantics*

In the previous section, you wrote a one-line Groovy statement with no class or method constructs (which you'd typically need with Java). You were, in fact, writing a Groovy script.

Figure 8.1 The Groovy console

Groovy as a scripting language

Unlike Java, Groovy source code can be executed as a script. For example, if you have code outside of a class definition, that code will still execute. Like other dynamic scripting languages, such as Ruby or Python, a Groovy script is fully parsed, compiled, and generated in memory before execution on the JVM. Any code that you can execute in the Groovy console can also be saved in a .groovy file, compiled, and then run as a script.

Some developers have taken to using Groovy scripts over shell scripts, because they're more powerful, easier to write, and cross-platform as long as there is a JVM installed. A quick performance tip here is to utilize the `groovyserv` library, which starts up the JVM and Groovy extensions, making your scripts run that much faster.

A key feature of Groovy is that you can use the same constructs as in Java, and similar syntax too. In order to highlight this similarity, execute the following Java-like code in the Groovy console:

```
public class PrintStatement
{
  public static void main(String[] args)
  {
    System.out.println("It's Groovy baby, yeah!");
  }
}
```

The result here is the same `"It's Groovy baby, yeah!"` output that you got from the previous one-line Groovy script. As an alternative to using the Groovy console, you could happily place the preceding code into a source file called PrintStatement.groovy, use `groovyc` to compile it, and then execute `groovy` to run it. In other words, you can write Groovy source code with classes and methods just as you would with Java.

> **TIP** You can use almost all of the common Java syntax with Groovy, so your `while`/`for` loops, `if`/`else` constructs, `switch` statements, and so on, will all work as you'd expect them to. Any new syntax and major differences will be highlighted in this and corresponding sections.

We'll introduce you to Groovy-only syntax idioms as the chapter progresses, with the examples shifting from very Java-like syntax to more pure Groovy syntax. You'll see a marked difference between the heavily structured Java code that you're used to and the less verbose script-like Groovy syntax.

The rest of this section will cover the basic syntax and semantics of Groovy and why they'll help you as a developer. In particular, we'll cover

- Default imports
- Numeric handling
- Variables, dynamic versus static types, and scoping
- Syntax for lists and maps

First, it's important to understand what Groovy provides out of the box. Let's look at the language features that are imported by default for a Groovy script or program.

8.2.1 Default imports

Groovy imports some language and utility packages by default to provide the basic language support. Groovy also imports a series of Java packages to give it a wider base of initial functionality. The following list of imports is always implicit in your Groovy code:

- `groovy.lang.*`
- `groovy.util.*`
- `java.lang.*`
- `java.io.*`
- `java.math.BigDecimal`
- `java.math.BigInteger`
- `java.net.*`
- `java.util.*`

In order to utilize further packages and classes, you can use the `import` statement in the same way that you would in Java. For example, to get all of the `Math` classes from Java, you can simply add the `import java.math.*;` line to your Groovy source code.

Setting up optional JAR files

In order to add functionality (like that of an in-memory database and its driver), you'll want to add optional JARs to the Groovy installation. There are Groovy idioms for this—a commonly used one is to use the `@Grab` annotation in your script. Another way (while you're still learning Groovy) is to add the JAR files to your `CLASSPATH`, just like you would with Java.

Let's use some of that default language support and look at the differences between how Java and Groovy deal with numeric handling.

8.2.2 Numeric handling

Groovy can evaluate mathematical expressions on the fly, and its observable effects have been described as the *principle of least surprise*. This principle is especially apparent when you're dealing with literal floating point numbers (for example, 3.2). Java's `BigDecimal` is used to represent the literal floating point number under the hood, but Groovy ensures that the behavior is what will *least surprise* the developer.

JAVA AND BIGDECIMAL

Let's look at a common area where Java developers have been tripped up with regards to numeric handling. In Java, if you were to add 3 and 0.2 using `BigDecimal`, what answer would you expect? The inexperienced Java developer who doesn't check the Javadoc might well execute something like the following code, which would return the truly horrendous result of 3.2000000000000000111022302462515654042363166680908203125.

```
BigDecimal x = new BigDecimal(3);
BigDecimal y = new BigDecimal(0.2);
System.out.println(x.add(y));
```

More experienced Java developers know that the better practice is to use the `BigDecimal` `(String val)` constructor as opposed to using the `BigDecimal` constructor with a numeric literal argument. Writing it the better-practice way would get you the answer of 3.2:

```
BigDecimal x = new BigDecimal("3");
BigDecimal y = new BigDecimal("0.2");
System.out.println(x.add(y));
```

This is a little counterintuitive and Groovy solves this problem by utilizing the better-practice constructor as a default.

GROOVY AND BIGDECIMAL

In Groovy the better-practice constructor is used automatically when dealing with floating point numeric literals (remember these are `BigDecimals` under the hood); 3 + 0.2 will result in 3.2. You can prove this for yourself by executing the following snippet in your Groovy console:

```
3 + 0.2;
```

You'll find that BEDMAS[4] is correctly supported and that Groovy seamlessly swaps between numeric types (such as `int` and `double`) as required.

Already Groovy is helping you perform arithmetic operations just that little bit easier than Java. If you'd like to know what's really going on under the hood in all cases, the page at http://groovy.codehaus.org/Groovy+Math has the complete details.

The next bit of Groovy semantics you'll need to learn about is how Groovy deals with its variables and scoping. Here the rules are a little different from Java, due to Groovy's dynamic nature and script-capable execution.

8.2.3   *Variables, dynamic versus static types, and scoping*

As Groovy is a dynamic language that's capable of being a scripting language, there are some nuances about dynamic versus static types and about how variables are scoped that you need to know about.

> **TIP**   If you intend your Groovy code to interoperate with Java, it can pay to use static types where possible, because it simplifies type overloading and dispatch.

The first step is to understand the difference between Groovy's dynamic and static types.

---

[4] Takes you back to school doesn't it! BEDMAS stands for Brackets, Exponents, Division, Multiplication, Addition, Subtraction—the standard order of operations for arithmetic. Depending on where you grew up, you may remember BODMAS or PEMDAS instead.

DYNAMIC VERSUS STATIC

Groovy is a dynamic language, so you don't have to specify the type of the variable you're declaring (or returning). For example, you can assign a Date to a variable x, and assign a *different* type to x immediately afterward.

```
x = new Date();
x = 1;
```

Using dynamic types can have the benefits of terser code (omitting "obvious" types), faster feedback, and the flexibility to assign different types of objects to a single variable that you want to execute work on. For those who like to be more sure about what type they're using, Groovy does support static types as well. For example:

```
Date x = new Date();
```

The Groovy runtime can detect if you have declared a static type and then try to assign an incorrect type to it, for example.

```
Exception thrown

org.codehaus.groovy.runtime.typehandling.GroovyCastException: Cannot cast
    object 'Thu Oct 13 12:58:28 BST 2011' with class 'java.util.Date' to
    class 'double'
...
```

You can reproduce that output by running the following code in the Groovy console.

```
double y = -3.1499392;
y = new Date();
```

As expected the Date type cannot be assigned to a double. That covers dynamic versus static typing in Groovy, but what about scope?

SCOPES IN GROOVY

For classes in Groovy, scoping works just like it does in Java, with class, method, and loop scoped variables, as you'd expect. It's when you're dealing with a Groovy script that the topic of scoping gets interesting.

> **TIP**   Remember, Groovy code that's not inside the usual class and method constructs is considered to be a Groovy script. You saw an example of this in section 8.1.1.

In simple terms, a Groovy script has two scopes:

- *binding*—The binding is the global scope for the script.
- *local*—The local scope is just that—variables are scoped locally to the block that they're declared in. With regards to a variable declared inside the script block (for example, at the top of a script) the variable is in the local scope if it has been *defined*.

Having the ability to use global variables in a script allows for great flexibility. You can think of it a little like a class-scoped variable in Java. A *defined* variable is one that has a static type declared or that uses the special `def` keyword to indicate that it is a defined variable with no type.

Methods declared in a script don't have access to the local scope. If you call a method that tries to reference a locally scoped variable, it will fail with a message similar to this:

```
groovy.lang.MissingPropertyException: No such property: hello for class:
    listing_8_2
...
```

The following code outputs the preceding exception, highlighting this scoping issue.

```
String hello = "Hello!";
void checkHello()
{
  System.out.println(hello);
}
checkHello();
```

If you were to replace the first line in the preceding code with `hello = "Hello!";` the method would successfully print "Hello." As the variable `hello` is no longer defined as a `String`, it's now in the *binding* scope.

Apart from the differences in writing a Groovy script, dynamic and static types, scoping, and variable declarations work pretty much as you'd expect. Let's move on to Groovy's built-in support for collections (lists and maps).

8.2.4   *Syntax for lists and maps*

Groovy treats lists and maps (including sets) as first-class citizens in the language, so there's no need to explicitly declare a `List` or a `Map` construct like you would in Java. That said, Groovy lists and maps are implemented behind the scenes as the familiar Java `ArrayList` and `LinkedHashMap` constructs.

A massive advantage for you in using the Groovy syntax here is that there is far less boilerplate code to write, and the code is much more concise, yet retains maximum readability.

In order to specify and utilize a list in Groovy, you use square bracket `[]` syntax (reminiscent of Java's native array syntax). The following code demonstrates this behavior, by referencing the first element (`Java`), setting the size of the list (4), and then setting the list to empty `[]`.

```
jvmLanguages = ["Java", "Groovy", "Scala", "Clojure"];
println(jvmLanguages[0]);
println(jvmLanguages.size());
jvmLanguages = [];
println(jvmLanguages);
```

You can see that working with a list as a first-class citizen is more lightweight than having to use `java.util.List` and its implementations!

Groovy's dynamic typing allows you to store values of mixed types in a list (or a map, for that matter), so the following code is also valid:

```
jvmLanguages = ["Java", 2, "Scala", new Date()];
```

Dealing with maps in Groovy is similar, using the [] notation and a colon character (:) to separate key/value pairs. To reference a value in a map, you use the special *map.key* notation. The following code demonstrates this behavior by

- Referencing the value 100 for the key "Java"
- Referencing the value "N/A" for the key "Clojure"
- Changing the value to 75 for the key "Clojure"
- Setting the map to be empty ([:])

```
languageRatings = [Java:100, Groovy:99, Clojure:"N/A"];
println(languageRatings["Java"]);
println(languageRatings.Clojure);
languageRatings["Clojure"] = 75;
println(languageRatings["Clojure"]);
languageRatings = [:];
println languageRatings;
```

TIP   Notice how the keys in the map are strings, but without the quotation marks? Again Groovy makes some syntax optional for conciseness. You can choose to use or not use quotation marks around map keys.

This is all fairly intuitive and comfortable to work with. Groovy takes this concept of first-class support of maps and lists further.

You can perform a few syntax tricks such as referencing a range of items in a collection or even referencing the last item using a special negative index. The following code demonstrates this behavior by referencing the first three elements in the list ([Java, Groovy, Scala]) and the last element (Clojure).

```
jvmLanguages = ["Java", "Groovy", "Scala", "Clojure"];
println(jvmLanguages[0..2]);
println(jvmLanguages[-1]);
```

You've now seen some of the basic syntax and semantics that Groovy has to offer. But there's more to explore in this area before you can use Groovy effectively. The next section covers further syntax and semantics, with a particular emphasis on things that can trip up a Java developer new to Groovy.

8.3   *Differences from Java—traps for new players*

By now you should be quite comfortable with the basic syntax of Groovy, in part due to its syntactic similarity with Java. But that similarity can sometimes trip you up, and this section will cover further syntax and semantics that commonly confuse Java developers.

Groovy has a great deal of syntax that isn't required, such as

- Semicolons at the end of a statement
- return statements
- Parentheses for method parameters
- public access modifiers

This is all designed to make your source code more concise, an advantage when you're rapidly prototyping a piece of software.

Other changes include their being no difference between checked and unchecked exceptions, an alternative way of dealing with the concept of equality, and the idiom of no longer using inner classes. Let's begin with the simplest change: optional semicolons and optional `return` statements.

8.3.1   Optional semicolons and return statements

In Groovy, semicolon characters (`;`) at the end of a statement are optional, unless you have several statements on one line.

Another optional piece of syntax is that you don't need to specify the `return` keyword when returning an object or value from a method. Groovy will automatically return the result of the last evaluated expression.

The following listing demonstrates these optional behaviors and returns 3 as the last expression evaluated in the method.

Listing 8.1   Semicolons and returns are optional

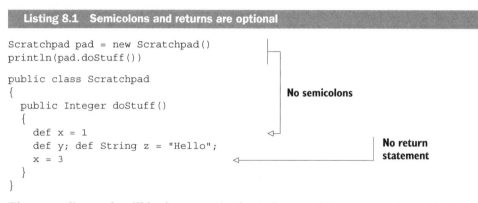

```
Scratchpad pad = new Scratchpad()
println(pad.doStuff())

public class Scratchpad
{
  public Integer doStuff()
  {
    def x = 1
    def y; def String z = "Hello";
    x = 3
  }
}
```

No semicolons

No return statement

The preceding code still looks pretty similar to Java, and Groovy continues this theme of less verbose code even further. Next up, you'll see how Groovy has optional parentheses for method parameters.

8.3.2   Optional parentheses for method parameters

Method calls in Groovy can omit the parentheses if there is at least one parameter and there is no ambiguity. This means that the following code

```
println("It's Groovy baby, yeah!")
```

can be written as

```
println "It's Groovy baby, yeah!"
```

Again, the code is becoming slightly less verbose yet still retains its readability.

The next aspect that makes Groovy code look less like Java is the optional `public` access modifier.

8.3.3   *Access modifiers*

The well-grounded Java developer knows that determining the level of access to your classes, methods, and variables is an important part of your OO design. Groovy provides the same `public`, `private`, and `protected` levels as Java, but unlike Java, its default access modifier is `public`. So let's alter the previous listing (8.1) by removing some of the `public` modifiers and adding a few `private` modifiers to clarify this change.

> **Listing 8.2   `public` is the default access modifier**

```
Scratchpad2 pad = new Scratchpad2()
println(pad.doStuff())

class Scratchpad2                          ◁──────────────────    No public access
{                                                                 modifier
  def private x;
  Integer doStuff()
  {
    x = 1
    def y; def String z = "Hello";
    x = 3
  }
}
```

Continuing with the theme of reducing the amount of syntax, what about those familiar `throws` clauses that you, as a Java developer, use in your method signatures for throwing checked exceptions?

8.3.4   *Exception handling*

Unlike Java, there is no difference between checked and unchecked exceptions in Groovy. Any `throws` clauses in method signatures are ignored by the Groovy compiler.

Groovy utilizes certain syntax shortcuts to make your source code more concise while still maintaining readability. Now it's time to look at a syntax change that has some serious semantic impact—the equality operator.

8.3.5   *Equality in Groovy*

Following the principle of least surprise, Groovy treats `==` as the equivalent of the `equals()` method in Java. Again, this is a benefit to the intuitive developer; you don't have to remember to swap between `==` and `equals()` for primitives and objects like you do in Java.

If you want to check for actual object identity equality, you need to use Groovy's built-in `is()` function. There is an exception to this rule, in that you can still use `==` when checking to see if an object is `null`. The following listing demonstrates these behaviors.

> **Listing 8.3   Equality in Groovy**

```
Integer x = new Integer(2)
Integer y = new Integer(2)
Integer z = null
```

```
if (x == y)
{
  println "x == y"
}
```
Implicit equals() called

```
if (!x.is(y))
{
  println "x is not y"
}
```
Object identity check

```
if (z.is(null))
{
  println "z is null"
}
```
Check for null with is()

```
if (z == null)
{
  println "z is null"
}
```
Check for null

You can, of course, use the `equals()` method to check for equality, if that's what you're more comfortable with.

There is one last Java construct that's worth mentioning briefly—inner classes, which are pretty much replaced by a new language construct in Groovy.

8.3.6   *Inner classes*

Inner classes are supported in Groovy, but in most cases you'll be using the concept of a function literal instead. We'll cover function literals in the next section, because it's a powerful modern programming construct that deserves fuller treatment.

Groovy syntax and semantics allow you to write less code while retaining decent readability, and you can (mostly) keep using the Java syntax constructs that you feel comfortable with. Next up, you'll see some of the language features of Groovy that Java doesn't have yet. Some of these features are likely to be the tipping point for your project in choosing Groovy for a particular task, such as XML processing.

8.4   *Groovy features not (yet) in Java*

There are some major language features in Groovy that Java (as of version 7) doesn't yet have. It's here that a well-grounded Java developer can really reach out to a new language in order to solve certain problems in a more elegant fashion. In this section we'll explore a number of these features, including:

- GroovyBeans—beans made simpler
- Safe navigation of `null` objects using the `?.` operator
- Elvis operator—an even shorter way of writing if/else constructs
- Groovy strings, a more powerful string abstraction
- Function literals (a.k.a. closures)—passing around functions
- Native support for regular expressions
- XML handling made easy

We'll start with GroovyBeans, because you'll see them regularly in Groovy code. As a Java developer, you may perhaps look upon them with slight suspicion, as they never seem to be quite as complete as JavaBeans. But rest assured; GroovyBeans are every bit as complete and they're more convenient to use as well.

8.4.1 GroovyBeans

GroovyBeans are much like JavaBeans, except they omit the explicit getters and setters, provide auto constructors, and allow you to reference member variables using dot (.) notation. If you need to make a particular getter or setter `private`, or wish to change the default behavior, you can explicitly provide that method and change it accordingly. Auto constructors simply allow you to construct a GroovyBean, passing in a map of parameters that correspond to the member variables of that GroovyBean.

All of this saves you from having to deal with an awful lot of boilerplate code generation that comes with writing JavaBeans, whether you laboriously type the getters and setters by hand or your IDE generates them for you.

Let's explore how a GroovyBean behaves using a `Character` class for a role-playing game (RPG).[5] The following code listing will produce an output of `STR[18]`, `WIS[15]`, which represents the strength and wisdom member variables of the GroovyBean.

Listing 8.4 Exploring the GroovyBean

```
class Character
{
  private int strength
  private int wisdom
}
def pc = new Character(strength: 10, wisdom: 15)
pc.strength = 18
println "STR [" + pc.strength + "] WIS [" + pc.wisdom + "]"
```

The behavior here is very similar to an equivalent JavaBean in Java (encapsulation is preserved), yet the syntax is more concise.

> **TIP** You can use the `@Immutable` annotation to make a GroovyBean immutable (meaning its state can't change). This can be useful for passing around thread-safe data constructs, which is much safer for use with concurrent code. This concept of immutable data structures is explored further in chapter 10, which discusses Clojure.

Next we'll move on to Groovy's ability to help you with checking for `null`. Again, more boilerplate code is reduced, so that you can prototype your ideas more quickly.

---

[5] A shout out to PCGen (http://pcgen.sf.net) belongs here—a truly useful open source project for us RPGers!

8.4.2   *The safe-dereference operator*

The NullPointerException[6] (NPE) is something that all Java developers will be (unfortunately) well acquainted with. In order to avoid the NPE, the Java developer typically has to check for null before referencing an object, especially if they can't guarantee that the object they're dealing with isn't null. If you were to carry over that development style into Groovy, in order to iterate over a list of Person objects, you'd probably write null-safe code as follows (the code simply prints out "Gweneth").

```
List<Person> people = [null, new Person(name:"Gweneth")]
for (Person person: people) {
  if (person != null) {
    println person.getName()
  }
}
```

Groovy helps you reduce some of the boilerplate "if object is null" checking code by introducing a safe-dereference syntax, using the ?. notation. By using this notation, Groovy introduces a special *null* construct that effectively represents "do nothing" as opposed to an actual null reference.

In Groovy, you could rewrite the previous snippet with the safe-dereference syntax as follows:

```
people = [null, new Person(name:"Gweneth")]
for (Person person: people) {
  println person?.name
}
```

This safe-dereference support is extended to Groovy function literals, so default Groovy collection methods such as the max() method automatically play nicely with null references.

Next up is the Elvis operator, which looks like the safe-dereference operator, but has a particular use case to reduce the syntax of certain if/else constructs.

8.4.3   *The Elvis operator*

The Elvis operator (?:) allows you to write if/else constructs that have a default value in extremely short syntax. Why Elvis? Because the symbol apparently looks like his wavy hair back when Elvis was at his peak.[7] The Elvis operator allows you to omit the explicit null check as well as avoiding any repetition of variables.

Assume you were checking whether Austin Powers was an active agent. In Java you might use the ternary operator as follows:

```
String agentStatus = "Active";
String status = agentStatus != null ? agentStatus : "Inactive";
```

Groovy can shorten this because it coerces types to boolean values as needed, such as in conditional checks like if statements. In the preceding code snippet, Groovy

---

[6]   One of the greatest shames of Java is that this is not called a NullReferenceException, which is what this actually is. This still causes one of the authors to rant on demand!

[7]   The authors will stringently deny knowing what Elvis looked like in his heyday. We're not that old, seriously!

coerces the `String` into a `boolean`; assuming the `String` was `null`, it will convert to the Boolean value of `false`, so you can omit the `null` check. You can then write the previous snippet as follows:

```
String agentStatus = "Active"
String status = agentStatus ? agentStatus : "Inactive"
```

But the `agentStatus` variable is still repeated, and Groovy can save you extra syntax typing here. The Elvis operator can be used to remove the need to duplicate the variable name:

```
String agentStatus = "Active"
String status = agentStatus ?: "Inactive"
```

The second occurrence of the `agentStatus` variable is removed to reduce the code to a more concise form.

It's now time to look at strings in Groovy and how they're a little different from the regular `String` in Java.

8.4.4 Enhanced strings

There is an extension to the Java `String` class in Groovy known as `GString`, which has slightly more power and flexibility than the standard Java `String`.

By convention, ordinary strings are defined by an opening and closing single quote, although double quotes are also valid. For example:

```
String ordinaryString = 'ordinary string'
String ordinaryString2 = "ordinary string 2"
```

GStrings on the other hand *must* be defined with double quotes. Their main benefit to the developer is that they can contain expressions (using ${} syntax) that can be evaluated at runtime. If the `GString` is subsequently converted to an ordinary `String` (that is, if it's passed to a `println` call) any expressions contained within the `GString` are evaluated. For example:

```
String name = 'Gweneth'
def dist = 3 * 2
String crawling = "${name} is crawling ${dist} feet!"
```

The expressions are evaluated down to either an `Object`, which `toString()` can be called on, or a function literal. (See http://groovy.codehaus.org/Strings+and+GString for details on the complex rules around function literals and `GString`.)

> **WARNING** GStrings are *not* Java `Strings` under the covers! In particular, you should not use `GStrings` as keys in maps or try to compare their equality. Results are likely to be unexpected!

One other slightly useful construct in Groovy is the triple-quoted `String` or triple-quoted `GString`, which allows you to wrap a string across multiple lines in your source code.

```
"""This GString
wraps over two lines!"""
```

We'll now move on to function literals, a coding technique that has become a hot topic again in recent years due to the rise of interest in functional languages. Understanding function literals can take a little bit of a mind shift, if you're not used to them, so if this is your first time, now is probably a good time for a Duke mug full of your favorite brew before you get going.

8.4.5   *Function literals*

A function literal is a representation of a block of code that can be passed around as a value and can be manipulated just like any other value. It can be passed in to methods, assigned to variables, and so on. As a language feature, they have been heavily debated in the Java community, but they're a standard tool in the Groovy programmer's kit.

As usual, working through examples is often the best way to learn a new concept, so we'll walk you through a few!

Imagine you have an ordinary static method that builds out a `String` with a greeting to authors or readers. You call that static method from outside the utility class in the usual manner, as in the following code listing.

Listing 8.5   A simple static function

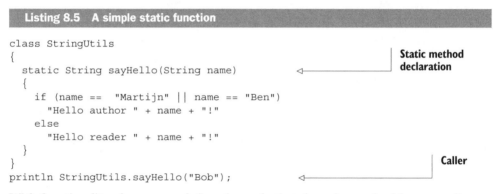

```
class StringUtils
{
  static String sayHello(String name)          ⟵    Static method
  {                                                  declaration
    if (name ==  "Martijn" || name == "Ben")
      "Hello author " + name + "!"
    else
      "Hello reader " + name + "!"
  }
}                                                ⟵    Caller
println StringUtils.sayHello("Bob");
```

With function literals, you can define the code that does the work without needing to use method or class structures so you can provide the same functionality as the `sayHello(String name)` method, but in a function literal. That function literal, in turn, can be assigned to a variable, which can be passed around and executed.

The following listing prints "Hello author Martijn!" as a result of passing the function literal assigned to `sayHello`, with the variable `"Martijn"` passed in.

Listing 8.6   Utilizing a simple function literal

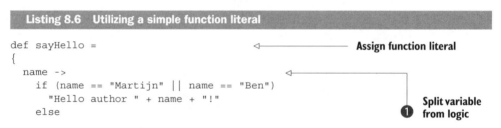

```
def sayHello =                    ⟵    Assign function literal
{
  name ->
    if (name == "Martijn" || name == "Ben")
      "Hello author " + name + "!"
    else
```
                                        ❶ Split variable
                                           from logic

```
           "Hello reader " + name + "!"
    }
    println(sayHello("Martijn"))
```

Print result

Notice the use of the { syntax that opens the function literal. The arrow syntax (->) ❶ separates the parameters being passed into the function literal from the logic being performed. Lastly, the } character closes off the function literal.

In listing 8.6, we've treated the function literal pretty much like we would a method. You might therefore be thinking, "They still don't seem that useful!" It's only when you start getting creative with them (thinking in a functional way) that you start to see their benefits. For example, function literals are especially powerful when combined with the first-class support Groovy provides for collections.

8.4.6   *First-class support for manipulating collections*

Groovy has several built-in methods that can be utilized with collections (lists and maps). This language level support for collections, combined with function literals, results in a significant reduction of the sort of boilerplate code you'd typically have to write in Java. It's important to note that readability isn't sacrificed, ensuring that your code stays maintainable.

A useful subset of the built-in functions that utilize function literals are listed in table 8.1.

Table 8.1   Subset of Groovy functions on collections

Method	Description
each	Iterates over a collection applying a function literal
collect	Collects the return value of the function literal call on each item in a collection (equivalent to map in the map/reduce pairing in other languages)
inject	Processes the collection with a function literal and builds up a return value (equivalent to reduce in the map/reduce pairing in other languages)
findAll	Finds all of the items in the collection matching the function literal
max	Returns the maximum value in that collection
min	Returns the minimum value in that collection

A fairly typical coding task in Java is when you have to iterate over a collection of objects and perform some sort of action on each object in that collection. For example, using Java 7, if you wanted to print movie titles, you'd probably write code similar to the next listing.[8]

---

[8] No, we're not going to tell you who picked Snow White as his favorite movie (it was the other author!)

Listing 8.7   Printing out a collection in Java 7

```java
List<String> movieTitles = new ArrayList<>();
movieTitles.add("Seven");
movieTitles.add("Snow White");
movieTitles.add("Die Hard");

for (String movieTitle : movieTitles)
{
  System.out.println(movieTitle);
}
```

There are some syntactical tricks you can play in Java to reduce the amount of source code, but the fact remains that you have to manually iterate over the List of movie titles using some sort of a loop construct.

With Groovy, you can use its first-class support for collections, built-in functionality for iterating over a collection (the each function), and a function literal to radically reduce the amount of source code you need to write. In doing so, you also invert the relationship between the list and the algorithm you want to execute. Instead of passing the collection into a method, you effectively pass the method into the collection!

The following code performs exactly the same work as listing 8.7, but it's reduced to just two lines of easily readable code:

```groovy
movieTitles = ["Seven", "SnowWhite", "Die Hard"]
movieTitles.each({x -> println x})
```

In fact, you can make this even more concise by using the implicit it variable, which can be used with single-argument function literals, as follows:[9]

```groovy
movieTitles = ["Seven", "SnowWhite", "Die Hard"]
movieTitles.each({println it})
```

As you can see, the code is concise, easy to read, and has the same observable effect as the Java 7 version.

> **TIP** There's only so much room in this chapter, so for more examples we recommend you check out the collections section on the Groovy website (http://groovy.codehaus.org/JN1015-Collections) or the excellent *Groovy in Action*, second edition, by Dierk König, Guillaume Laforge, Paul King, Jon Skeet, and Hamlet D'Arcy (Manning, 2012).

The next language feature that might take some getting used to is Groovy's built-in regular expression support, so while you've still got that coffee going it's best to jump straight in!

---

[9] Groovy gurus will also point out that this can be reduced to one line of code!

8.4.7   First-class support for regular expressions

Groovy treats regular expressions as a built-in part of the language, making activities such as text processing much simpler than in Java. Table 8.2 shows the regular expression syntax you can use in Groovy, with the Java equivalent.

Table 8.2   Groovy regular expression syntax

Method	Description and Java equivalent
~	Creates a pattern (creates a compiled Java `Pattern` object)
=~	Creates a matcher (creates a Java `Matcher` object)
==~	Evaluates the string (effectively calls Java's `match()` on the `Pattern`)

Say you want to partially match on some incorrect log data that you've received from a piece of hardware. In particular, you're looking for instances of the pattern `1010`, which you're then looking to flip around to `0101`. In Java 7, you'd probably write code similar to the following.

```
Pattern pattern = Pattern.compile("1010");
String input = "1010";
Matcher matcher = pattern.matcher(input);
if (input.matches("1010"))
{
  input = matcher.replaceFirst("0101");
  System.out.println(input);
}
```

In Groovy, the individual lines of code are shorter, because the `Pattern` and `Matcher` objects are built into the language. The output (`0101`), of course, stays the same, as the following code demonstrates.

```
def pattern = /1010/
def input = "1010"
def matcher = input =~ pattern
if (input ==~ pattern)
{
  input = matcher.replaceFirst("0101")
  println input
}
```

Groovy supports the full semantics of regular expressions in the same way that Java does, so you should have the full flexibility you're used to there.

Regular expressions can also be combined nicely with function literals. For example, you could print out the details of a person by parsing a `String` and pulling out the name and age.

```
("Hazel 1" =~ /(\w+) (\d+)/).each {full, name, age
                        -> println "$name is $age years old."}
```

Now is probably a good time to take a mental breather, because you'll be exploring a quite different concept next—XML handling.

8.4.8   *Simple XML handling*

Groovy has the concept of *builders*, abstractions that help you deal with arbitrary tree-like data structures using native Groovy syntax. Examples of this can include HTML, XML, and JSON. Groovy understands the need to be able to process this type of data easily and provides out-of-the-box builders to do this.

> ### XML—a widely abused language
> XML is an excellent, verbose data exchange language that has become much maligned these days. Why? Because software developers have attempted to treat XML as a programming language, something it isn't suited for because it isn't a Turing complete language.[9] Hopefully in your projects, XML is being used as it was intended, to exchange data in a human-readable format.

In this section, we'll focus on XML, a common format for exchanging data. Although the core Java language (via JAXB and JAXP) and a virtual army of third-party Java libraries (XStream, Xerces, Xalan, and so on) do give you a lot of power with XML processing, deciding which solution to pick can often be confusing, and the Java code to utilize those solutions can become quite verbose.

This section will take you through creating XML from Groovy and show how you can parse that XML back into GroovyBeans.

CREATING XML

Groovy can make it very simple for you to build up your XML documents, such as a person:

```
<person id='2'>
  <name>Gweneth</name>
  <age>1</age>
</person>
```

Groovy can produce this XML structure using its built-in `MarkupBuilder` for XML. The following code listing will produce the `person` XML record.

Listing 8.8   Producing simple XML

```
def writer = new StringWriter()
def xml = new groovy.xml.MarkupBuilder(writer)
xml.person(id:2) {
  name 'Gweneth'
  age 1
```

---

[10] For a language to be Turing complete, it must at least be able to conditionally branch and have the ability to change memory locations.

```
}
println writer.toString()
```

Notice how the starting `person` element (with the `id` attribute set to 2) is simply created without having to define what a `Person` object is. Groovy doesn't force you to have an explicit GroovyBean backing this XML creation, again saving you time and effort.

Listing 8.8 is a fairly simple example. You can experiment further by changing the output type from `StringWriter`, and you can try different builders such as `groovy.json.JsonBuilder()` to instantly create JSON.[11] When dealing with more complex XML structures, there is also extra help to deal with namespaces and other specific constructs.

You'll also want to be able to perform the reverse operation, reading in some XML and parsing it into a useful GroovyBean.

PARSING XML

There are several ways that Groovy can parse incoming XML. Table 8.3 lists three methods and is derived from the official Groovy documentation (http://docs.codehaus.org/display/GROOVY/Processing+XML).

Table 8.3   Groovy XML parsing techniques

Method	Description
XMLParser	Supports GPath expressions for XML documents
XMLSlurper	Similar to XMLParser but does so in a lazy loading manner
DOMCategory	Low-level parsing of the DOM with some syntax support

All three are quite simple to use, but for this section we'll focus on using a `XMLParser`.

> **NOTE**   GPath is an expression language. You can read all about it in the Groovy documentation: http://groovy.codehaus.org/GPath.

Let's take the XML representing "Gweneth" (a person) produced in listing 8.8 and parse it back into a `Person` GroovyBean. The following code listing demonstrates this.

Listing 8.9   Parsing XML with XMLParser

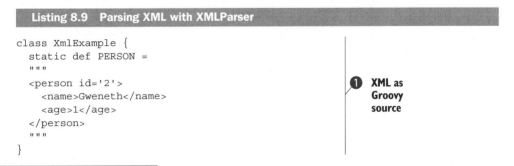

```
class XmlExample {
  static def PERSON =
  """
  <person id='2'>
    <name>Gweneth</name>
    <age>1</age>
  </person>
  """
}
```

❶ XML as Groovy source

---

[11] Dustin has a great post on this, titled "Groovy 1.8 Introduces Groovy to JSON" in his *Inspired by Actual Events* blog at http://marxsoftware.blogspot.com/.

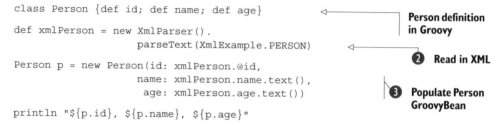

```
class Person {def id; def name; def age}

def xmlPerson = new XmlParser().
                parseText(XmlExample.PERSON)

Person p = new Person(id: xmlPerson.@id,
              name: xmlPerson.name.text(),
               age: xmlPerson.age.text())

println "${p.id}, ${p.name}, ${p.age}"
```

Person definition in Groovy

2 Read in XML

3 Populate Person GroovyBean

You begin by taking a slight shortcut and rendering the XML document in code so that it's already nicely on your CLASSPATH **1**. The first real step is to use the parse-Text() method of the XMLParser to read in the XML data **2**. A new Person object is then created, values are assigned to it **3**, and the Person is finally printed out for an eyeball check.

That completes your introduction to Groovy. By now, you're probably itching to use some of Groovy's features alongside one of your Java projects! In the next section, we'll take you through how you can interoperate between Java and Groovy. You'll take that first important step for a well-grounded Java developer, becoming a polyglot programmer on the JVM.

8.5   *Interoperating between Groovy and Java*

This section is deceptively small, but its importance can't be overstated! Assuming you have been reading the material in this book in order, this is the part where you take the leap into becoming more than just a Java developer on the JVM. The well-grounded Java developer needs to be capable of utilizing more than one language on the JVM to complement Java, and Groovy is a great language to start with!

First, you'll revisit how trivial it is to call out to Java from Groovy. Following on from that, you'll work through the three common ways to interface with Groovy from Java, using GroovyShell, GroovyClassLoader, and GroovyScriptEngine.

Let's start with a recap of how you call Java from Groovy.

8.5.1   *Calling Java from Groovy*

You remember how we told you that calling Java from Groovy is as simple as providing the JAR on the CLASSPATH and using the standard import notation? Here's an example of importing the classes from the org.joda.time package that belongs to the popular Joda date and time library:[12]

```
import org.joda.time.*;
```

You use the classes as you would in Java. The following code snippet will print the numerical representation of the current month.

```
DateTime dt = new DateTime()
int month = dt.getMonthOfYear()
println month
```

---

[12] Joda is the de facto date and time library for Java until Java 8 is delivered.

Hmm, surely it has to be more complicated than this right?

Admiral Ackbar: "It's a Trap!"[13]

Only joking, there's no trap! It really is that simple, so let's look at the more difficult case shall we? Calling Groovy from Java and getting back some meaningful results is a little more tricky.

8.5.2 Calling Groovy from Java

Calling Groovy from inside a Java application requires the Groovy JAR and other related JARs to be put into your Java application's CLASSPATH, as they're runtime dependencies.

> **TIP** Simply put the GROOVY_HOME/embeddable/groovy-all-1.8.6.jar file into your CLASSPATH.

There are several ways you can call Groovy code from inside a Java application:

- Using the Bean Scripting Framework (BSF)—a.k.a. JSR 223
- Using GroovyShell
- Using GroovyClassLoader
- Using GroovyScriptEngine
- Using the embedded Groovy console

In this section, we'll focus on the most commonly used ways (GroovyShell, Groovy-ClassLoader, and GroovyScriptEngine), starting with the simplest, the GroovyShell.

GROOVYSHELL

The GroovyShell can be invoked on a temporary basis to quickly call out to Groovy and evaluate some expressions or script-like code. For example, some developers who may prefer Groovy's handling of numeric literals could call out to the GroovyShell to perform some mathematical arithmetic. The following Java code listing will return the value of 10.4 by using Groovy's numeric literals to perform the addition.

Listing 8.10 Using GroovyShell to execute Groovy from Java

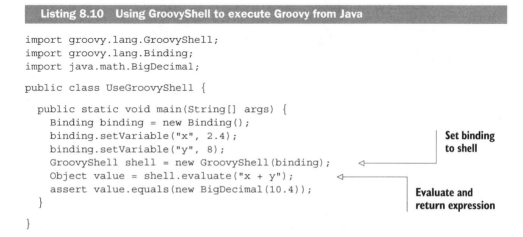

```java
import groovy.lang.GroovyShell;
import groovy.lang.Binding;
import java.math.BigDecimal;

public class UseGroovyShell {

  public static void main(String[] args) {
    Binding binding = new Binding();
    binding.setVariable("x", 2.4);                           Set binding
    binding.setVariable("y", 8);                             to shell
    GroovyShell shell = new GroovyShell(binding);    ◄──
    Object value = shell.evaluate("x + y");          ◄──
    assert value.equals(new BigDecimal(10.4));              Evaluate and
  }                                                          return expression

}
```

---

[13] Star Wars fans will be familiar with this internet meme!

This use of the GroovyShell covers the case where you want to execute a quick bit of Groovy code, but what if you have a full-fledged Groovy class that you want to interact with? In that case, you can look at using the GroovyClassLoader.

GROOVYCLASSLOADER

From a developer's perspective, the GroovyClassLoader behaves much like a Java Class-Loader. You look up the class and the method that you want to call, and simply call it!

The following code snippet contains a simple CalculateMax class that contains a getMax method, which in turn uses Groovy's built-in max function. To run this from Java via the GroovyClassLoader, you need create a Groovy file (CalculateMax.groovy) with the following source code:

```
class CalculateMax {
  def Integer getMax(List values) {
    values.max();
  }
}
```

Now that you have the Groovy script that you want to execute, you can call that from Java. The following listing has Java call out to the CalculateMax getMax function, which returns 10 as the maximum value of the arguments passed in.

> **Listing 8.11   Using `GroovyClassLoader` to execute Groovy from Java**

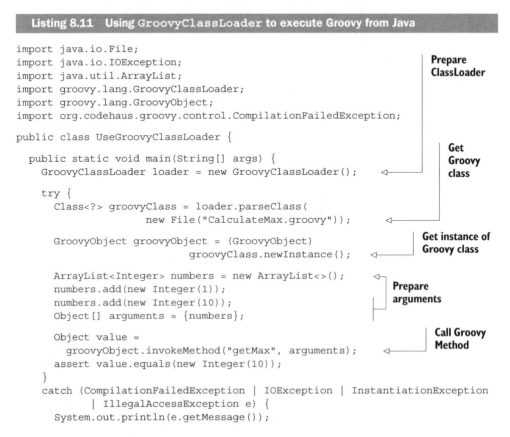

```
import java.io.File;
import java.io.IOException;                                          Prepare
import java.util.ArrayList;                                          ClassLoader
import groovy.lang.GroovyClassLoader;
import groovy.lang.GroovyObject;
import org.codehaus.groovy.control.CompilationFailedException;

public class UseGroovyClassLoader {

  public static void main(String[] args) {                          Get
    GroovyClassLoader loader = new GroovyClassLoader();      ◁──     Groovy
                                                                     class
    try {
      Class<?> groovyClass = loader.parseClass(
                  new File("CalculateMax.groovy"));      ◁──

      GroovyObject groovyObject = (GroovyObject)                    Get instance of
                  groovyClass.newInstance();      ◁──               Groovy class

      ArrayList<Integer> numbers = new ArrayList<>();      ◁──
      numbers.add(new Integer(1));                                  Prepare
      numbers.add(new Integer(10));                                 arguments
      Object[] arguments = {numbers};

      Object value =                                               Call Groovy
        groovyObject.invokeMethod("getMax", arguments);      ◁──   Method
      assert value.equals(new Integer(10));
    }
    catch (CompilationFailedException | IOException | InstantiationException
           | IllegalAccessException e) {
      System.out.println(e.getMessage());
```

```
      }
    }
  }
```

This technique will probably be useful if you have a few Groovy utility classes that you want to call out to. But if you have a larger amount of Groovy code that you need to access, using the complete `GroovyScriptEngine` is the recommended option.

GROOVYSCRIPTENGINE

When you use the `GroovyScriptEngine`, you specify the URL or directory location of your Groovy code. The engine then loads and compiles those scripts as necessary, including dependent scripts. For example, if you change script B and script A is reliant on B, the engine will recompile the whole lot.

Let's say that you have a Groovy script (Hello.groovy) that defines a simple statement of "Hello" followed by a name (a parameter that you want to be supplied by your Java application).

```
def helloStatement = "Hello ${name}"
```

Your Java application then uses the `GroovyScriptEngine` to utilize Hello.groovy and prints out a greeting, as in the following code listing.

Listing 8.12 Using `GroovyScriptEngine` to execute Groovy from Java

```
import groovy.lang.Binding;
import groovy.util.GroovyScriptEngine;
import groovy.util.ResourceException;
import groovy.util.ScriptException;
import java.io.IOException;
                                                              Set
public class UseGroovyScriptEngine {                          roots
  public static void main(String[] args)
  {
    try {
      String[] roots = new String[] {"/src/main/groovy"};    ◁────┐   Initialize
      GroovyScriptEngine gse =                                         Engine
                   new GroovyScriptEngine (roots);           ◁────
      Binding binding = new Binding();
      binding.setVariable("name", "Gweneth");                         Run
      Object output = gse.run("Hello.groovy", binding);      ◁───────  script
      assert output.equals("Hello Gweneth");
    }
    catch (IOException | ResourceException | ScriptException e) {
      System.out.println(e.getMessage());
    }
  }
}
```

Remember that any Groovy script that's being monitored by the `GroovyScriptEngine` can now be changed by you at whim. For example, if you were to change the Hello.groovy script to this,

```
def helloStatement = "Hello ${name}, it's Groovy baby, yeah!"
```

then the next time that bit of Java code ran, it would use that new, longer message. This gives your Java applications a dynamic flexibility that was not possible before. This can be invaluable in situations such as debugging production code, altering properties of a system at runtime, and more!

That completes your introduction to Groovy. There's been a lot to go over!

8.6   *Summary*

Groovy has several compelling features that make it a great language to use alongside Java. You can write syntax that's very similar to that of Java, but you also have the choice of writing the same logical code in a more concise manner. Readability isn't sacrificed with this conciseness, and Java developers will have no trouble in picking up the new shortened syntax related to collections, null reference handling, and Groovy-Beans. There are a few traps awaiting the Java developer in Groovy, but you've now worked through most of the common cases, and you'll hopefully be able to pass this newfound knowledge on to your colleagues.

Groovy has several new language features that many Java developers hope to see in the Java language itself one day. The most difficult to grasp, yet most powerful, of these is function literals, a powerful programming technique that (amongst other capabilities) helps you execute operations over collections with ease. Collections, of course, are treated as first-class citizens, and you're able to create, alter, and generally manipulate them with short, easy to use syntax.

Most Java developers have to either generate or parse XML in their Java programs, and you can get assistance from Groovy, which takes much of the heavy burden with its built-in XML support.

You took your first steps toward becoming a polyglot programmer by making use of various techniques to integrate your Java and Groovy code so that they can work together to solve your coding challenges.

Your journey doesn't stop here. You'll continue to use and explore more Groovy in chapter 13, which discusses rapid web development.

Next up, we have Scala, another language on the JVM that's causing a bit of a stir in the industry. Scala is a language that's both object oriented and functional, making it a language worth looking at to solve modern programming dilemmas.

Scala: powerful
and concise

This chapter covers

- Scala is not Java
- Scala syntax and more functional style
- Match expressions and patterns
- Scala's type system and collections
- Concurrent Scala with actors

Scala is a language that came out of the academic and programming language research community. It has gained a certain amount of adoption, due to its very powerful type system and advanced features, which have proved to be useful for elite teams.

There is currently a lot of interest in Scala, but it's too early to tell whether it's a language that will fully permeate the Java ecosystem and challenge Java as a primary development language.

Our best guess is that Scala is going to filter down into more teams, and that some projects are going to end up deploying it. Our prediction is that a larger pool of developers will see some Scala in one of their projects over the next 3-4 years. This means that the well-grounded Java developer should be aware of it, and be able to determine whether it's right for their projects.

EXAMPLE   A financial risk modeling application might want to make use of Scala's novel approach to object-orientation, type inference, and flexible syntax capabilities, new collections classes (including natural functional programming style, such as the map/filter idioms), and the actor-based concurrency model.

When arriving from Java, there are some aspects of Scala that a new developer needs to keep uppermost in mind—most importantly the simple fact that *Scala is not Java*.

This seems like a pretty obvious point. After all, every language is different, so of course Scala is a different beast from Java. But as we discussed in chapter 7, some languages are more similar to each other than others. When we introduced Groovy in chapter 8, we emphasized the similarities it has to Java. This hopefully helped with your first exploration of a non-Java JVM language.

In this chapter, we want to do something a little different—we'll start by highlighting some Scala features that are quite specific to the language. We like to think of it as "Scala in its natural habitat"—a tour of how to start writing Scala that doesn't look like translated Java. After that, we'll discuss project aspects—how to figure out if Scala is right for your project. Then, we'll look at some of Scala's syntax innovations that can make Scala code concise and beautiful. Next up is Scala's approach to object orientation, and then a section on collections and data structures. We'll conclude with a section on Scala's approach to concurrency and its powerful actor model.

As we go over our featured aspects of Scala, we'll explain the syntax (and any other necessary concepts) as we go. Scala is quite a large language compared to Java—there are more basic concepts and more syntax points to be aware of. This means you should expect that as you're exposed to more Scala code, you'll need to explore more of the language on your own.

Let's take a peek ahead at some of the themes we'll be encountering in full later on. This will help you get used to Scala's different syntax and mindset, and will help pave the way for what's to come.

9.1   *A quick tour of Scala*

These are the main aspects that we want to showcase:

- The use of Scala as a concise language, including the power of type inference
- Match expressions, and associated concepts like patterns and case classes
- Scala's concurrency, which is based on messages and actors, rather than on the locks of old-school Java code

These topics won't teach you the entire language, or make you a full-fledged Scala developer. What they can do is whet your appetite and start to show you concrete examples of where Scala might be applicable. To go further, you'll need to explore the language more deeply—either by finding some online resources or a book that provides a full treatment of Scala, such as Joshua Suereth's *Scala in Depth* (Manning, 2012).

The first and most visible aspect of Scala's difference that we want to explain is the conciseness of Scala's syntax, so let's head straight there.

9.1.1 Scala as a concise language

Scala is a compiled, statically typed language. This means that developers sometimes expect the same sort of verbose code that you sometimes see in Java. Fortunately, Scala is much more succinct—so much so that it can almost feel like a scripting language. This can make the developer much faster and more productive, picking up some of the speed gains that can come when working in a dynamically typed language.

Let's look at some very simple sample code and examine Scala's approach to constructors and classes. For example, consider writing a simple class to model a cash flow. This needs the user to supply two pieces of information—the amount of the cash flow and the currency. In Scala, you'd do it like this:

```
class CashFlow(amt : Double, curr : String) {
  def amount() = amt
  def currency() = curr
}
```

This class is just four lines (and one of those is the terminating right brace). Nevertheless, it provides getter methods (but no setters) for the parameters, and a single constructor. This is considerably more bang for the buck (or line of code) than the corresponding Java code:

```
public class CashFlow {
  private final double amt;
  private final String curr;

  public CashFlow(double amt, String curr) {
    this.amt = amt;
    this.curr = curr;
  }

  public double getAmt() {
    return amt;
  }

  public String getCurr() {
    return curr;
  }
}
```

The Java version is much more repetitive than the Scala code, and this repetition is one of the causes of verbosity.

By taking the Scala path of trying not to make the developer repeat information, more code will fit on an IDE screen at any one time. This means that when faced with a complex bit of logic, the developer can see more of it, and hopefully get additional clues toward understanding it.

Want to save $1,500?

The Scala version of the `CashFlow` class is almost 75 percent shorter than the Java version. One estimate for the cost of code is $32 per line per year. If we assume a five-year lifespan for this piece of code, the Scala version will cost $1,500 less in maintenance than the Java code over the lifetime of the project.

While we're here, let's have a look at some of the syntax points can we glean from this first example:

- The definition of a class (in terms of its parameters) and the constructor for a class are one and the same. Scala does allow additional "auxiliary constructors"—we'll talk about those later.
- Classes are public by default, so there's no need for a `public` keyword.
- Return types of methods are type-inferred, but you need the equals sign in the `def` clause that defines them to tell the compiler to type-infer.
- If a method body is just a single statement (or expression), it doesn't need braces around it.
- Scala doesn't have primitive types in the same way that Java does. Numeric types are objects.

Conciseness doesn't stop there. You can even see it in as simple a program as the classic Hello World:

```
object HelloWorld {
  def main(args : Array[String]) {
    val hello = "Hello World!"

    println(hello)
  }
}
```

There are a few features that help reduce boilerplate even in this most basic example:

- The `object` keyword tells the Scala compiler to make this class a singleton.
- The call to `println()` doesn't need to be qualified (thanks to default imports).
- `main()` doesn't need to have the keywords `public` or `static` applied to it.
- You don't have to declare the type of `hello`—the compiler just works it out.
- You don't have to declare the return type of `main()`—it's automatically `Unit` (Scala's equivalent of `void`).

There are some other useful syntax facts that are relevant in this example:

- Unlike Java and Groovy, the type of the variable comes after the variable name.
- Square brackets are used by Scala to indicate a generic type, so the type of `args` is specified as `Array[String]` instead of `String[]`.
- `Array` is a genuine generic type.
- Generics are mandatory for collection types (you can't have the equivalent of a Java raw type).

- Semicolons are pretty much optional.
- `val` is the equivalent of a `final` variable in Java—it declares an immutable variable.
- Initial entry points to Scala applications are always contained in an `object`.

In the sections to come, we'll explain in more detail how the syntax we've met so far works, and we'll cover a selection of Scala's other finger-saving innovations. We'll also discuss Scala's approach to functional programming, which helps considerably with writing concise code. For now, let's move on to discuss a very powerful "native Scala" feature.

9.1.2   Match expressions

Scala has a very powerful construct called a `match` expression. The simple cases of `match` are related to Java's `switch`, but `match` has forms that are far more expressive. The form of a `match` expression depends on the structure of the expression in the `case` clause. Scala calls the different types of `case` clauses *patterns*, but be careful to note that these are distinct from the "patterns" found in regular expressions (although you can use a regexp pattern in a `match` expression, as you'll see).

Let's start by looking at an example that comes from familiar ground. The following code snippet shows the strings-in-switch example we met way back in section 1.3.1, but freely translated into Scala code.

```
var frenchDayOfWeek = args(0) match {
  case "Sunday"    => "Dimanche"
  case "Monday"    => "Lundi"
  case "Tuesday"   => "Mardi"
  case "Wednesday" => "Mercredi"
  case "Thursday"  => "Jeudi"
  case "Friday"    => "Vendredi"
  case "Saturday"  => "Samedi"
  case _           => "Error: '"+ args(0) +"' is not a day of the week"
}
println(frenchDayOfWeek)
```

In this example, we're only exhibiting the two most basic patterns—the constant patterns for the days of the week, and the _ pattern, which handles the default case. We'll meet others later in the chapter.

From a language purity point of view, we could note that Scala's syntax is cleaner and more regular than Java's in at least two ways:

- The default case doesn't require the use of a different keyword.
- Individual cases don't fall through into the next case as they do in Java, so there's no need for the `break` keyword either.

Some other syntax points to take away from this example:

- The `var` keyword is used to declare a mutable (nonfinal) variable. Try not to use it unless necessary, but it is needed some of the time.
- Array access uses round brackets; for example, `args(0)` for the first argument to `main()`.

- A default case should always be included. If Scala fails to find a match with any case at runtime, a MatchError will be thrown. This is pretty much never what you want to happen.
- Scala supports *indirect method call* syntax, so you can write args(0) match { ... } as an equivalent to args(0).match({ ... }).

So far, so good. The match construct looks like a slightly cleaner switch statement. But this is only the most Java-like of many possible patterns. Scala has a large number of language constructions that use different sorts of patterns. As an example, let's consider a typed pattern, which is a useful way of handling data of uncertain provenance, without a lot of messy casts or Java-style instanceof tests:

```
def storageSize(obj: Any) = obj match {
  case s: String => s.length
  case i: Int    => 4
  case _         => -1
}
```

This very simple method takes in a value of type Any (that is, of unknown type). Then, patterns are used to handle values of type String and Int separately. Each case binds a temporary alias for the value under consideration to allow methods to be called on the value if necessary.

A syntax form that is very similar to the variable pattern is used in Scala's exception handling code. Let's look at classcoding code that is lightly adapted from the ScalaTest framework we'll meet in chapter 11:

```
def getReporter(repClassName: String, loader: ClassLoader): Reporter = {
  try {
    val reporterCl: java.lang.Class[_] = loader.loadClass(repClassName)
    reporterCl.newInstance.asInstanceOf[Reporter]
  }
  catch {
    case e: ClassNotFoundException => {
      val msg = "Can't load reporter class"
      val iae = new IllegalArgumentException(msg)
      iae.initCause(e)
      throw iae
    }
    case e: InstantiationException => {
      val msg = "Can't instantiate Reporter"
      val iae = new IllegalArgumentException(msg)
      iae.initCause(e)
      throw iae
    }
    ...
  }
}
```

In getReporter(), you're attempting to load a custom reporter class (via reflection) to report on a test suite as it runs. A number of things can go wrong with the class load and instantiation, so you have a try-catch block protecting execution.

The catch blocks are very similar to match expressions with a match on the type of the exception seen. This idea can be extended even further with the concept of case classes, which is where we'll turn next.

9.1.3 Case classes

One of the most powerful ways to use match expressions is with Scala's case classes (which can be thought of as similar to object-oriented extensions of the concept of enums). Let's examine an example—an alarm signal that indicates that a temperature has gone too high:

```scala
case class TemperatureAlarm(temp : Double)
```

This single line of code defines a perfectly valid case class. A roughly equivalent class in Java would look something like this:

```java
public class TemperatureAlarm {
  private final double temp;
  public TemperatureAlarm(double temp) {
    this.temp = temp;
  }

  public double getTemp() {
    return temp;
  }

  @Override
  public String toString() {
    return "TemperatureAlarm [temp=" + temp + "]";
  }

  @Override
  public int hashCode() {
    final int prime = 31;
    int result = 1;
    long temp;
    temp = Double.doubleToLongBits(this.temp);
    result = prime * result + (int) (temp ^ (temp >>> 32));
    return result;
  }

  @Override
  public boolean equals(Object obj) {
    if (this == obj)
        return true;
    if (obj == null)
        return false;
    if (getClass() != obj.getClass())
        return false;
    TemperatureAlarm other = (TemperatureAlarm) obj;
    if (Double.doubleToLongBits(temp) !=
        Double.doubleToLongBits(other.temp))
        return false;
    return true;
  }
}
```

Just adding the single keyword `case` causes the Scala compiler to create these additional methods. It also creates a lot of additional scaffolding methods. Most of the time, these other methods aren't directly used by the developer. Instead, they exist to provide runtime support for certain Scala features—to enable the case class to be used in a "naturalistic Scala" manner.

Case classes can be created without needing the `new` keyword, like this:

```
val alarm = TemperatureAlarm(99.9)
```

This reinforces the view of case classes as being similar to "parametrized enums" or a form of value type.

Equality in Scala
Scala regards Java's use of `==` to mean "reference equality" as a mistake. Instead, in Scala, `==` and `.equals()` are equivalent. If reference equality is required, then `===` can be used. Case classes have an `.equals()` method that returns `true` if and only if two instances have exactly the same values for all parameters.

Case classes fit very naturally into the constructor pattern, as you can see:

```
def ctorMatchExample(sthg : AnyRef) = {
  val msg = sthg match {
    case Heartbeat => 0
    case TemperatureAlarm(temp) => "Tripped at temp "+ temp
    case _ => "No match"
  }
  println(msg)
}
```

Let's move on to look at the final feature we want to address in our introductory tour of Scala—the concurrency construct known as *actors*.

9.1.4   *Actors*

Actors are Scala's alternative take on concurrent programming. They provide an asynchronous model of concurrency, which is based on passing messages between executing units of code. This is a different high-level concurrency model that many developers find easier to use than the lock-based, shared-by-default model that Java provides (although Scala is, of course, built on the same low-level model—the JMM).

Let's look at an example. Suppose the veterinarian we met in chapter 4 needs to monitor the health (and especially the body temperature) of the animals in the clinic. We can imagine that the hardware temperature sensors will send messages containing their readings to a central piece of monitoring software.

We can model this setup in Scala via an actor class, `TemperatureMonitor`. This will expect two different sorts of messages—a standard "heartbeat" message, and a `TemperatureAlarm` message. The second of these will take a parameter indicating the temperature at which the alarm went off. The following listing shows these classes.

Listing 9.1 Simple communication with an actor

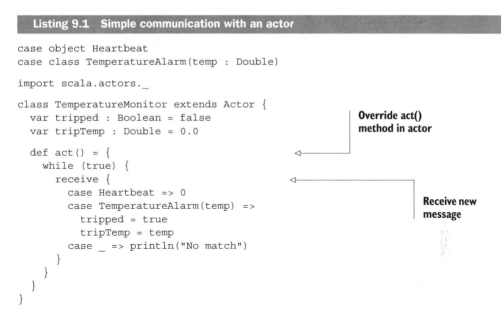

```
case object Heartbeat
case class TemperatureAlarm(temp : Double)

import scala.actors._

class TemperatureMonitor extends Actor {
  var tripped : Boolean = false
  var tripTemp : Double = 0.0

  def act() = {
    while (true) {
      receive {
        case Heartbeat => 0
        case TemperatureAlarm(temp) =>
          tripped = true
          tripTemp = temp
        case _ => println("No match")
      }
    }
  }
}
```

Override act()
method in actor

Receive new
message

You have three separate cases that the monitoring actor can respond to (via `receive`). The first is a heartbeat message, which tells you only that all is well. Because this case class takes no parameters, it's technically a singleton, so it's referred to as a case object. The actor doesn't need to take any action when it receives a heartbeat.

If you receive a `TemperatureAlarm` message, the actor will save the temperature at which the alarm was tripped. You can imagine that the veterinarian will have another piece of code that periodically checks the `TemperatureMonitor` actor to see if it's been tripped.

Finally, there's a default case. This is a catch-all just in case any unexpected messages leak into the actor's environment. Without this catch-all, the actor would throw an exception if an unexpected message type was seen. We'll come back to actors at the end of this chapter and look at a little more of the detail, but Scala concurrency is a huge subject, and we give you more than a taste in this book.

We've had a very quick spin through some of the highlights of Scala. Hopefully you've seen some features that have sparked your interest. In the next section, we'll spend a bit of time talking about the reasons why you might (and might not) choose to use Scala for some part of your project.

9.2   *Is Scala right for my project?*

The decision to start using an additional language in your Java project should always be driven by sound reasoning and evidence. In this section, we want you to think about those reasons and how they apply to your project.

We'll start by having a quick look at how Scala compares to Java, then move on to the when and how of starting to use Scala. To round out this short section, we'll look at some telltale signs that Scala may not be the language best suited for your project.

9.2.1   *Comparing Scala and Java*

Key differences between the languages are summarized in table 9.1. The "surface area" of a language is the number of keywords and independent language constructs that the working developer must master to be productive in the language.

Table 9.1   Comparing Java and Scala

Feature	Java	Scala
Type system	Static, quite verbose	Static, heavily type-inferred
Polyglot layer	Stable	Stable, dynamic
Concurrency model	Lock-based	Actor-based
Functional programming	Requires disciplined special coding style, not a natural fit	Built-in support, natural part of the language
Surface area	Small/medium	Large/very large
Syntax style	Simple, regular, relatively verbose	Flexible, concise, many special cases

These differences can provide some reasons why Scala might be attractive to the well-grounded Java developer as an alternative language for some projects or components. Let's draw out in more detail how you might start bringing Scala into a project.

9.2.2   *When and how to start using Scala*

As we discussed in chapter 7, it's always better to start introducing a new language to low-risk areas if you're working on an existing project. An example of a low-risk area might be the ScalaTest testing framework we'll meet in chapter 11. If the experiment with Scala doesn't go well all it has cost is wasted developer time (the unit tests can probably be salvaged and turned into regular JUnit tests).

In general, a good introductory component for Scala within an existing project will have most or all of these characteristics:

- You can estimate effort required with some degree of confidence.
- There is a bounded, well-defined problem area.
- You have properly specified requirements.
- There are known interoperability requirements with other components.
- You have identified developers who are motivated to learn the language.

When you've thought about the area, you can move into implementing your first Scala component. The following guidelines have proved to be very useful in ensuring that the initial component remains on track:

- Produce a quick spike to start with.
- Test interoperation with existing Java components early.
- Have gating criteria (based on requirements) that define the success or failure of the spike.

- Have a plan B for use if the spike fails.
- Budget additional refactoring time for the new component. (A first project in a new language will almost certainly acquire higher technical debt than the same project written in the team's existing languages.)

The other angle that you should also consider when evaluating Scala is to check whether there are any obvious aspects that may make the language a less than ideal fit for your project.

9.2.3 Signs that Scala may not be right for your current project

There are a number of signs that Scala may not be right for your current project. If your team shows signs of one or more of these, you should carefully consider whether this is the right time to introduce Scala to your project. If two or more of these are in evidence, this is a big red flag.

- Resistance or lack of buy-in from operations and other groups who need to support your application
- No clear buy-in from the development team to learn Scala
- Divided or politically polarized views in the group
- Lack of support from senior technologists in the group
- Very tight deadlines (no time to learn a new language)

One other factor to consider closely is the global distribution of your team. If you have staff in several locations who will need to develop (or support) Scala code, this will increase the cost and burden of reskilling staff in Scala.

Now that we've discussed the mechanics of introducing Scala into your project, let's move on to look at some of Scala's syntax. We'll focus on features that will make the Java developer's life easier, encouraging much more compact code, with less boilerplate and no lingering aftertaste of verbosity.

9.3 Making code beautiful again with Scala

In this section, we'll start by introducing the Scala compiler and interactive environment (REPL). Then we'll discuss type inference, followed by method declarations (which may be slightly less Java-like than you're used to). Together, these two features will help you to write a lot less boilerplate code and thus improve your productivity.

We'll cover Scala's approach to code packages and its more powerful `import` statement, and then we'll take a close look at loops and control structures. These are rooted in a very different programming tradition than Java, so we'll use this as an opportunity to discuss some of Scala's functional programming aspects. These include a functional approach to looping constructs, match expressions, and function literals.

All of this will set you up to be able to make the most of the rest of the chapter and build your confidence and skill as a Scala programmer. Let's get under way by discussing the compiler and built-in interactive environment.

9.3.1   *Using the compiler and the REPL*

Scala is a compiled language, so the usual way of executing Scala programs is to first compile them into .class files, then execute them in a JVM environment that includes scala-library.jar (the runtime library for Scala) on the classpath.

If you haven't got Scala installed yet, see appendix C for details of how to get it set up on your machine before moving on. An example program (the HelloWorld example from section 9.1.1) can be compiled with scalac HelloWorld.scala (assuming you're currently in the directory where you saved the HelloWorld.scala file).

Once you have a .class file, you can kick it off by using the command scala HelloWorld. This command will launch a JVM with the Scala runtime environment on the classpath, and then enter at the main method of the class file specified.

In addition to these options for compiling and running, Scala has a built-in interactive environment—a bit like Groovy's console, which you saw in the last chapter. But unlike Groovy, Scala implements this within a command-line environment. This means that in a typical Unix/Linux environment (with a correctly set up Path), you can type scala, and this will open within the terminal window rather than spawning a new window.

> **NOTE**   Interactive environments of this sort are sometimes called Read-Eval-Print loops, or REPLs for short. They're quite common in languages that are more dynamic than Java. In a REPL environment, the results of previous lines of input remain around and can be reused in later expressions and calculations. In the rest of the chapter, we'll make occasional use of the REPL environment to illustrate more of Scala's syntax.

Now, let's move on to the next big feature that we want to discuss—Scala's advanced type inference.

9.3.2   *Type inference*

In the code snippets you've seen so far, you may have noticed that when we declared hello as a val, we didn't need to tell the compiler what type it was. It was "obvious" that it was a string. On the surface, this looks a bit like Groovy, where variables don't have types (Groovy is dynamically typed), but something very different is happening with Scala code.

Scala is a statically typed language (so variables do have definite types), but its compiler is able to analyze source code and in many cases is able to work out what the types ought to be from context. If Scala can work the types out, you don't need to provide them.

This is *type inference*, a feature we've mentioned in several places already. Scala has very advanced capabilities in this area—so much so that the developer can often forget the static types and the code just flows. This can give the language more of a dynamic language "feel" most of the time.

You've already seen the simplest example of these features—the var and val keywords, which cause a variable to infer its type from the value being assigned to it. Another important aspect of Scala's type inference involves method declarations. Let's look at an example (and keep in mind that the Scala type AnyRef is the same as Java's Object):

```
def len(obj : AnyRef) = {
  obj.toString.length
}
```

This is a type-inferred method. The compiler can figure out that it returns Int by examining the return code of java.lang.String#length, which is int. Notice that there is no explicit return type specified, and that we didn't need to use the return keyword. In fact, if you include an explicit return, like this,

```
def len(obj : AnyRef) = {
  return obj.toString.length
}
```

you'll get a compile-time failure:

```
error: method len has return statement; needs result type
      return obj.toString.length
      ^
```

If you omit the = from a def altogether, the compiler will assume that this is a method that returns Unit (the Scala equivalent of a method that returns void in Java).

In addition to the previous restrictions, there are two main areas where type inference is limited:

- *Parameter types in method declarations*—Parameters to methods must always have their types specified.
- *Recursive functions*—The Scala compiler is unable to infer the return type of a recursive function.

We've talked quite a bit about Scala methods, but we haven't covered them in any kind of systematic way, so let's put what you've already learned onto a firmer footing.

9.3.3   *Methods*

You've already seen how to define a method with the `def` keyword. There are some other important facts about Scala methods that you should be aware of as you get more familiar with Scala:

- Scala doesn't have the `static` keyword. The equivalent of static methods in Java must live in Scala's `object` (singleton) constructs. Later on, we'll introduce you to *companion* objects, which are a useful, related concept in Scala.

- The Scala language runtime is quite heavyweight compared to Groovy (or Clojure). Scala classes may have a lot of additional methods that are autogenerated by the platform.

- The concept of method calls is central to Scala. Scala doesn't have operators in the Java sense.

- Scala is more flexible than Java about which characters can appear in method names. In particular, characters that are used as operators in other languages may be legal in Scala method names (such as the plus symbol, +).

The indirect method call syntax (that you met earlier) offers a clue as to how Scala is able to merge the syntax of method calls and operators. As an example, consider addition of two integers. In Java, you'd write an expression like a + b. You can also use this syntax in Scala, but additionally, you can write a.+(b). In other words, you call the +() method on a and pass it b as a parameter. This is how Scala is able to get rid of operators as a separate concept.

> **NOTE**   You may have noticed that the form a.+(b) involves calling a method on a. But what if a is a variable of a primitive type? The full explanation is in section 9.4, but for now, you should know that Scala's type system basically regards everything as an object, so you can call methods on anything—even variables that would be primitives in Java.

You've already seen one example of using the `def` keyword to declare a method. Let's look at another example, of a simple recursive method to implement the factorial function:

```
def fact(base : Int) : Int = {
  if (base <= 0)
    return 1
  else
    return base * fact(base - 1)
}
```

This function slightly cheats by returning 1 for all negative numbers. In fact, the factorial of a negative number doesn't exist, but we're among friends here. It looks a bit Java-like—it has a return type (`Int`, in this case) and uses the `return` keyword to indicate which value to hand back to the caller. The only additional thing to notice is the use of the = sign before the block defining the function body.

Scala permits another concept that isn't present in Java—the local function. This is a function that is defined (and is only in scope) within another function. This can be a simple way to have a helper function that the developer doesn't want to expose to the outside world. In Java there would be no recourse but to use a private method and have the function visible to other methods within the same class. But in Scala you can simply write this:

```
def fact2(base : Int) : Int = {

  def factHelper(n : Int) : Int = {
    return fact2(n-1)
  }

  if (base <= 0)
    return 1
  else
    return base * factHelper(base)
}
```

`factHelper()` will never be visible outside of the enclosing scope of `fact2()`.

Next, let's look at how Scala handles code organization and imports.

9.3.4 *Imports*

Scala uses packages in the same way as Java, and it uses the same keywords: `package` and `import`. Scala can import and use Java packages and classes without an issue. A Scala `var` or `val` can hold an instance of any Java class, without any special syntax or treatment:

```
import java.io.File
import java.net._
import scala.collection.{Map, Seq}
import java.util.{Date => UDate}
```

The first two of these code lines are the equivalent of a standard import and a wild-card import in Java. The third allows multiple classes from a single package to be imported with a single line. The last shows aliasing of a class's name at import time (to prevent unfortunate shortname clashes).

Unlike in Java, imports in Scala can appear anywhere in the code (not just at the top of the file), so you can isolate the import to just a subset of the file. Scala also provides default imports; in particular, `scala._` is always imported into every .scala file. This contains a number of useful functions, including some we've already discussed, such as `println`. For all of the default imports, the full details are available in the API documentation at www.scala-lang.org/.

Let's move on and discuss how you can control the execution flow of a Scala program. This can be a little different from what you may be familiar with from Java and Groovy.

9.3.5   *Loops and control structures*

Scala introduces a few novel twists on control and looping constructs. But before we meet the unfamiliar forms, let's look at a few old friends, such as the standard while loop:

```
var counter = 1
while (counter <= 10) {
  println("." * counter)
  counter = counter + 1
}
```

And here's the do-while form:

```
var counter = 1
do {
  println("." * counter)
  counter = counter + 1
} while (counter <= 10)
```

Another familiar-seeming form is the basic for loop:

```
for (i <- 1 to 10) println(i)
```

So far, so good. But Scala has additional flexibility, such as the conditional for loop:

```
for (i <- 1 to 10; if i %2 == 0) println(i)
```

The for loop is also able to accommodate looping over multiple variables, like this:

```
for (x <- 1 to 5; y <- 1 to x)
  println(" " * (x - y) + x.toString * y)
```

These more flexible forms of the for loop come from a fundamental difference in the way that Scala approaches the construct. Scala uses a concept from functional programming, called a *list comprehension*, to implement for.

The general idea of a list comprehension is that you start with a list and apply a transformation (or filter, in the case of the conditional for loop) to the elements of the list. This generates a new list, which you then run the body of the for loop on, one element at a time.

It's even possible to split up the definition of the filtered list from the execution of the for body, using the yield keyword. For example, this bit of code:

```
val xs = for (x <- 2 to 11) yield fact(x)
for (factx <- xs) println(factx)
```

This sets up xs as the new collection before looping over the elements of it in the second for loop, which prints the values out. This alternative syntax can be extremely useful if you want to make a collection once, and use it multiple times.

This construction is due to Scala's support for functional programming, so let's move on to see how Scala implements functional ideas.

9.3.6   *Functional programming in Scala*

As we mentioned in section 7.5.2, Scala supports functions as first-class values. This means that the language allows you to write functions in a way that can be put into vars or vals and treated as any other value. These are called *function literals* (or *anonymous functions*) and they're very much part of the Scala worldview.

Scala provides a very simple way of writing function literals. The key piece of syntax is the arrow, =>, which Scala uses to express taking in the list of parameters and passing them to a block of code:

```
(<list of function parameters>) => { ... function body as a block ... }
```

Let's use the Scala interactive environment to demonstrate this. This simple example defines a function that takes in an Int and doubles it:

```
scala> val doubler = (x : Int) => { 2 * x }
doubler: (Int) => Int = <function1>

scala> doubler(3)
res4: Int = 6

scala> doubler(4)
res5: Int = 8
```

Notice how Scala infers the type of doubler. Its type is "function that takes in an Int and returns an Int." This isn't a type that Java's type system has an entirely satisfactory way of expressing. As you can see, to call doubler with a value, you use the standard call syntax with brackets.

Let's take this concept a little further. In Scala, function literals are just values. And values are returned from functions. This means you could have a function-making function—a function literal that takes in a value and returns a new function as a value.

For example, you can define a function literal called adder. The purpose of adder() is to make functions that add a constant to their argument:

```
scala> val adder = (n : Int) => { (x : Int) => x + n }
adder: (Int) => (Int) => Int = <function1>

scala> val plus2 = adder(2)
plus2: (Int) => Int = <function1>

scala> plus2(3)
res2: Int = 5

scala> plus2(4)
res3: Int = 6
```

As you've seen, Scala has good support for function literals. In fact, Scala can generally be written using a very functional programming view of the world, as well as by using the more imperative style that you've seen so far. We won't do much more than dip a toe into Scala's functional programming capabilities, but it's important to know that they're there.

In the next section, we'll cover Scala's object model and approach to OO in some detail. Scala has a number of advanced features that make the treatment of OO quite different from Java in some important respects.

9.4   Scala's object model—similar but different

Scala is sometimes referred to as a "pure" object-oriented language. This means that all values are objects, so you can't get very far without encountering OO concepts. We'll start this section by exploring the consequences of "everything is an object." This leads very naturally into a consideration of Scala's hierarchy of types.

This hierarchy differs in a couple of important ways from Java's, and also encompasses Scala's approach to the handling of primitive types, such as boxing and unboxing. From there, we'll consider Scala constructors and class definitions and how they can help you write a lot less code. The important topic of traits is next, and then we'll look at Scala's singleton, companion, and package objects. We'll round out the section by seeing how case classes can reduce boilerplate still further, and we'll conclude with a cautionary tale of Scala syntax.

Let's get started.

9.4.1   Everything is an object

Scala takes the view that every type is an object type. This includes what Java regards as primitive types. Figure 9.1 shows Scala's inheritance of types, including the equivalent of both value (aka primitive) and reference types.

As you can see, the `Unit` type is a proper type in Scala, along with the other value types. The `AnyRef` class is Scala's name for `java.lang.Object`. Every time you see `AnyRef`, you should mentally translate it to `Object`. The reason why it has a separate name is that at one time Scala also targeted the .NET runtime, so it made sense to have a separate name for the concept.

Scala uses the `extends` keyword for class inheritance, and it behaves very similarly to Java—all nonprivate members will be inherited, and the superclass/subclass relationship will be set up between the two types. If a class definition doesn't explicitly extend another class, the compiler will assume the class is a direct subclass of `AnyRef`.

The "everything is an object" principle explains a Scala syntax point that you've already met—the infix notation for method calls. You saw in section 9.3.3 that `obj.meth(param)` and `obj meth param` were equivalent ways of calling a method. Now you can see that the expression `1 + 2`, which in Java would be an expression about numeric primitives and the addition operator, is in Scala equivalent to: `1.+(2)`, which uses a method call on the `scala.Int` class.

Scala does away with some of the confusion around boxed numerics that Java can sometimes cause. Consider this bit of Java code:

```
Integer one = new Integer(1);
Integer uno = new Integer(1);
System.out.println(one == uno);
```

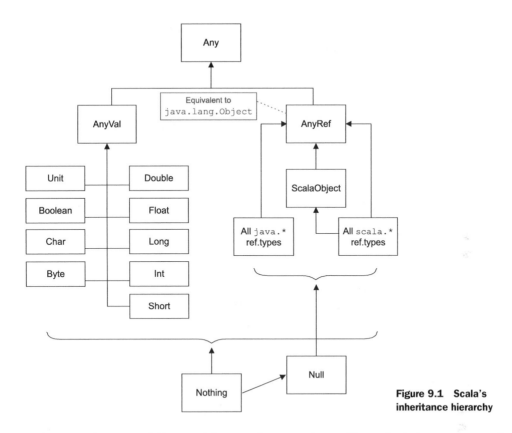

Figure 9.1 Scala's inheritance hierarchy

This prints the potentially surprising result `false`. As you'll see, Scala has an approach to boxed numerics, and equality in general, that helps in several ways:

- Numeric classes can't be instantiated from constructors. They're effectively `abstract` and `final` (this combination would be illegal in Java).
- The only way to get a new instance of a numeric class is as a literal. This ensures that 2 is always the same 2.
- Equality using the `==` method is defined to be the same as `equals()`—it isn't reference equality.
- `==` can't be overridden, but `equals()` can.
- Scala provides the `eq` method for reference equality. It isn't very often needed.

Now that we've covered some of the most basic Scala OO concepts, we need to introduce a little more of Scala's syntax. The simplest place to start is with Scala's constructors.

9.4.2 *Constructors*

Scala classes must have a primary constructor that defines the parameters for the class. In addition, a class may have additional auxiliary constructors. These are denoted using the `this()` syntax, but they're more restrictive than Java's overloaded constructors.

A Scala auxiliary constructor must, as its first statement, call another constructor in the same class (either the primary, or another auxiliary constructor). This restriction serves to funnel the control flow towards the primary constructor, which is the only true entrance point to the class. This means that the auxiliary constructors really act like providers of default parameters to the primary constructor.

Consider these auxiliary constructors added to `CashFlow`:

```
class CashFlow(amt : Double, curr : String) {
  def this(amt : Double) = this(amt, "GBP")
  def this(curr : String) = this(0, curr)

  def amount = amt
  def currency = curr
}
```

The auxiliary constructors in this example allow you to specify just an amount, in which case the `CashFlow` class will assume that the user intended for the cash flow to be in British pounds. The other auxiliary constructor allows construction with just a currency; the amount in that case is assumed to be 0.

Note that we've also defined `amount` and `currency` as methods without including brackets or a parameter list (even an empty one). This tells the compiler that, when using this class, the code may call `amount` or `currency` without needing parentheses, like this:

```
val wages = new CashFlow(2000.0)
println(wages.amount)
println(wages.currency)
```

Scala's definitions of classes broadly map to those of Java. But there are some significant differences in terms of how Scala approaches the inheritance aspects of OO. That's the subject of the next section.

9.4.3 *Traits*

Traits are a major part of Scala's approach to object-oriented programming. Broadly, they play the same role that interfaces do in Java. But unlike with Java interfaces, you can include the implementation of methods in a trait, and have that code be shared by different classes that have the trait.

To see the problem in Java that this solves, consider figure 9.2, which shows two Java classes that derive from different base classes. If these two classes both want to display additional, common functionality, this is done by declaring that they both implement a common interface.

Listing 9.2 shows a simple Java example that implements this in code. Recall the example of a veterinarian's office that you saw in section 4.3.6. Many animals brought to the office will be microchipped for identification. For example, cats and dogs almost certainly will be, but other species may not.

The capability of being chipped needs to be factored out into a separate interface. Let's update the Java code from listing 4.11 to incorporate this capability (and we'll omit the `examine()` method for clarity).

Java   Scala

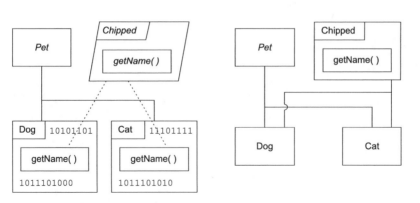

Figure 9.2   Duplication of implementation in Java's model

Listing 9.2   Demonstrating implementation code duplication

```
public abstract class Pet {
  protected final String name;

  public Pet(String name_) {
    name = name_;
  }
}

public interface Chipped {
  String getName();
}

public class Cat extends Pet implements Chipped {
  public Cat(String name_) {
    super(name_);
  }

  public String getName() {
    return name;
  }
}

public class Dog extends Pet implements Chipped {
  public Dog(String name_) {
    super(name_);
  }

  public String getName() {
    return name;
  }
}
```

As you can see, both `Dog` and `Cat` need to duplicate the code that implements `getName()` because Java interfaces can't contain implementation code. The following listing shows how you could implement this in Scala using traits.

Listing 9.3   Pets in Scala

```scala
class Pet(name : String)

trait Chipped {
  var chipName : String
  def getName = chipName
}

class Cat(name : String) extends Pet(name : String) with Chipped {
  var chipName = name
}

class Dog(name : String) extends Pet(name : String) with Chipped {
  var chipName = name
}
```

Scala requires you to assign a value to each parameter present in a superclass constructor clause in every subclass. But the method declarations that are present in the trait are inherited by each subclass. This reduces implementation duplication. You can see this in action where the name parameter must be handled by both Cat and Dog. Both subclasses have access to the implementation provided by Chipped—in this case, there's a parameter called chipName that can be used to store the name written on the microchip.

9.4.4   *Singleton and companion objects*

Let's take a look at how Scala's singletons (that is, classes that start with the keyword object) are implemented. Recall the code for our very first Hello World example in section 9.1.1:

```scala
object HelloWorld {
  def main(args : Array[String]) {
    val hello = "Hello World!"
    println(hello)

  }
}
```

If this were Java, you'd expect this code to be turned into a single file called HelloWorld .class. In fact, Scala compiles it to two files: HelloWorld.class and HelloWorld$.class.

As these are ordinary class files, you can use the javap decompilation tool that you met in chapter 5 to look at the bytecode that the Scala compiler has produced. This will give you a number of insights into the Scala type model and how it's implemented. The following listing shows the result of running javap -c -p on the two class files:

Listing 9.4   Decompiling Scala's singleton objects

```
Compiled from "HelloWorld.scala"
public final class HelloWorld extends java.lang.Object {
  public static final void main(java.lang.String[]);
    Code:
      0: getstatic     #11
```

```
// Field HelloWorld$.MODULE$:LHelloWorld$;          ◄──────┐   Get companion
    3: aload_0                                               │   singleton MODULE$
    4: invokevirtual #13
// Method HelloWorld$.main:([Ljava/lang/String;)V   ◄────┐  Call main() on
    7: return                                               │  companion
}
```

```
Compiled from "HelloWorld.scala"
public final class HelloWorld$ extends java.lang.Object
implements scala.ScalaObject {
  public static final HelloWorld$ MODULE$;          ◄──────┐   Singleton
                                                             │   companion instance
  public static {};
    Code:
      0: new          #9    // class HelloWorld$
      3: invokespecial #12  // Method "<init>":()V
      6: return

  public void main(java.lang.String[]);
    Code:
      0: getstatic    #19   // Field scala/Predef$.MODULE$:Lscala/Predef$;
      3: ldc          #22   // String Hello World!
      5: invokevirtual #26
// Method scala/Predef$.println:(Ljava/lang/Object;)V
      8: return                                    ┌──────── Private
                                                   │         constructor
  private HelloWorld$();                      ◄────┘
    Code:
      0: aload_0
      1: invokespecial #33  // Method java/lang/Object."<init>":()V
      4: aload_0
      5: putstatic    #35   // Field MODULE$:LHelloWorld$;
      8: return
}
```

You can see where the statement that "Scala doesn't have static methods or fields" comes from. Instead of these constructs, the Scala compiler has automatically generated code corresponding to the Singleton pattern (immutable static instance, and private constructor) and inserted it into the .class file that ends with "$". The main() method is still a regular instance method, but it's being called on the HelloWorld$ class, which is a singleton.

This means that there's a duality between a pair of .class files—one with the same name as the Scala file, and the other with a "$" added. The static methods and fields have been placed into this second, singleton class.

It's very common for there to be both a Scala class and object with the same name. In this case, the singleton class is referred to as a *companion object*. The relationship between the Scala source file and the two VM classes (the primary class and the companion object) is shown in figure 9.3.

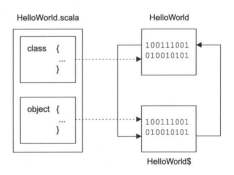

Figure 9.3 Scala singleton objects

You've already met companion objects, although you didn't know it. In our Hello World example, you didn't have to specify which class the `println()` method was contained in. It looks like a static method, so you'd expect that it's a method that belongs to a companion object.

Let's have another look at the bytecode from listing 9.2 that corresponds to the `main()` method:

```
public void main(java.lang.String[]);
  Code:
     0: getstatic     #19 // Field scala/Predef$.MODULE$:Lscala/Predef$;
     3: ldc           #22 // String Hello World!
     5: invokevirtual #26
➥ // Method scala/Predef$.println:(Ljava/lang/Object;)V
     8: return
```

From this, you can see that `println()`, and the other always-available Scala functions, are contained in the companion object to the `Scala.Predef` class.

A companion object has a privileged relationship to its class. In particular, it can access private methods of the class. This allows Scala to define private auxiliary constructors in a sensible way. The Scala syntax for a private constructor is to include the keyword `private` before the parameter list of the constructor, like this:

```
class CashFlow private (amt : Double, curr : String) {
   ...
}
```

If the constructor that is made private is the primary, there will be only two ways to construct new instances of this class: either via a factory method contained in the companion object (which is able to access the private constructor), or by calling a public auxiliary constructor.

Let's move on to look at our next topic—Scala's case classes. You've already met them, but to refresh your memory, these are a useful way to reduce boilerplate code by automatically providing a number of basic methods.

9.4.5 Case classes and match expressions

Consider modeling a simple entity in Java, such as the `Point` class.

Listing 9.5 Simple class implementation in Java

```
public class Point {
  private final int x;
  private final int y;

  public Point(int x, int y) {              ◁┐
    this.x = x;                              │  Boilerplate
    this.y = y;                              │  code
  }                                          │
                                             │
  public String toString() {                ◁┘
    return "Point(x: " + x + ", y: " + y + ")";
  }
```

```
  @Override
  public boolean equals(Object obj) {           ◄──────────┐
    if (!(obj instanceof Point)) {                         │
      return false;                                        │
    }                                                      │
    Point other = (Point)obj;                   Boilerplate│
    return other.x == x && other.y == y;        code       │
  }                                                        │
                                                           │
  @Override                                                │
  public int hashCode() {                       ◄──────────┘
    return x * 17 + y;
  }
}
```

This has an enormous amount of boilerplate code, and what's worse, methods such as hashCode(), toString(), equals(), and any getters will usually be autogenerated by the IDE. Wouldn't it be nicer if the language permitted a simpler syntax, and the autogeneration was handled within the language core?

Scala does indeed have such support in the form of a language feature called *case classes*. You can rewrite listing 9.5 into a very simple form:

```
case class Point(x : Int, y : Int)
```

This provides all of the functionality of the longer Java example, but has additional other benefits as well as being much shorter.

For example, with the Java version, if you were to change the code (say by adding a z coordinate), you'd have to update toString() and the other methods. In practice, you'd do this by deleting the entire existing method and regenerating the method from the IDE.

With the Scala version, this is simply not necessary because there is no explicit method definition that needs to be kept up to date. This boils down to a very powerful principle— you can't introduce bugs into code that doesn't exist in the source-level representation.

When creating new instances of a case class, the new keyword can be omitted. You can write code like this:

```
val pythag = Point(3, 4)
```

This syntax reinforces the view that case classes are like enums with one or more free parameters. Under the hood, what's actually happening is that the case class definition is providing a factory method that will make new instances.

Let's take a look at a major use of case classes: patterns and match expressions. Case classes can be used in a Scala pattern type called a Constructor pattern. Consider the following code.

Listing 9.6 Constructor pattern in match expression

```
val xaxis = Point(2, 0)
val yaxis = Point(0, 3)
val some  = Point(5, 12)
```

```
val whereami = (p : Point) => p match {
  case Point(x, 0) => "On the x-axis"
  case Point(0, y) => "On the y-axis"
  case _           => "Out in the plane"
}
println(whereami(xaxis))
println(whereami(yaxis))
println(whereami(some))
```

We'll revisit Constructor patterns and case classes in section 9.6 when we discuss actors and Scala's view of concurrency.

Before we leave this section, we want to sound a note of caution. The richness of Scala's syntax and the cleverness of its parser can produce some very concise and elegant ways to represent complex code. But Scala doesn't have a formal language specification, and new features are added fairly often. You should take extra care—even experienced Scala coders are sometimes caught out by language features not always behaving the way they expected. This is especially true when syntax features are combined with each other.

Let's look at an example of this—a way to simulate operator overloading in Scala syntax.

9.4.6   A cautionary tale

Let's consider the Point case class we just introduced. You may want a simple way to represent the adding of coordinates, or linear scaling of coordinates. If you have a mathematical background, then you'll probably recognize that these are the vector space properties of coordinates in a plane.

The next listing shows a simple way to define methods that will look like operators in normal usage.

Listing 9.7   Simulating operator overloading

```
case class Point(x : Int, y : Int) {
  def *(m : Int) = Point(this.x * m, this.y * m)
  def +(other : Point) = Point(this.x + other.x, this.y + other.y)
}
var poin = Point(2, 3)
var poin2 = Point(5, 7)
println(poin)
println(poin 2)
println(poin * 2)
println(poin + poin2)
```

If you run this bit of code, you'll see some output like this:

```
Point(2,3)
Point(5,7)
Point(4,6)
Point(7,10)
```

This shows how much nicer it is to work with the Scala case classes than the Java equivalents. With very little code, you've generated a friendly class that produces sensible output. With the method definitions for + and *, you've been able to simulate aspects of operator overloading.

But there's a problem with this approach. Consider this bit of code:

```
var poin = Point(2, 3)
println(2 * poin)
```

This will produce a compile-time error:

```
error: overloaded method value * with alternatives:
  (Double)Double <and>
  (Float)Float <and>
  (Long)Long <and>
  (Int)Int <and>
  (Char)Int <and>
  (Short)Int <and>
  (Byte)Int
cannot be applied to (Point)
              println(2 * poin)
                          ^
one error found
```

The reason for this error is that although you've defined a method *(m : Int) on the case class Point, that isn't the method that Scala is looking for. For the previous code to compile, you'd need to supply a method *(p : Point) on the standard Int class. This isn't feasible, so the illusion of operator overloading is left incomplete.

This illustrates an interesting point about Scala—many of the syntactic features have limitations that may cause surprise in some circumstances. Scala's language parser and runtime do a lot of work under the hood, but this hidden machinery largely works on the basis of trying to do the right thing.

This concludes our introductory survey of Scala's approach to object orientation. There are many advanced features we didn't cover. Scala has implemented a lot of modern ideas about the ways that type systems and objects should behave, so if you're interested in those areas, there's plenty to explore. Consult Joshua Suereth's *Scala in Depth* (Manning Publications, 2012) or another dedicated Scala book if what you've read so far has got you fired up about Scala's approach to type systems and OO.

One important application of this part of language theory is, as you might expect, the subject of data structures and collections in Scala. This is the focus of our next section.

9.5 *Data structures and collections*

You've already met a simple example of Scala's data structures—the List. This is a fundamental data structure in any programming language, and it's no less important in Scala. We'll spend some time looking at List in detail, and then move on to studying Scala's Map.

Next, we'll make a serious study of Scala's generics, including the differences and additional power that Scala gives over Java's implementation. This discussion relies on your having seen some of the earlier examples of standard Scala collections to ground the theory.

Let's get started with a few general remarks about Scala's collections—especially concerning immutability and interoperability with Java's collections.

9.5.1 *List*

Scala's approach to collections is quite different from Java's. This can be quite surprising, as in many other areas Scala reuses and extends Java components and concepts. Let's take a look at the largest differences that the Scala philosophy brings:

- Scala collections are usually immutable.
- Scala decomposes the many aspects of a `List`-like collection into separate concepts.
- Scala builds up the core of its `List` from a very small number of concepts.
- Scala's approach to collections is to provide a consistent experience across different types of collections.
- Scala encourages developers to build their own collections that feel like the built-in collection classes.

We'll look at each of these major differences in turn.

IMMUTABLE AND MUTABLE COLLECTIONS

One of the first things you need to know is that Scala has both immutable and mutable versions of its collections, and that the immutable versions are the default (and are always available to every Scala source file).

We need to draw an essential distinction between mutability of the collection and mutability of the contents. Let's look at this in action.

Listing 9.8 Mutable and immutable

```scala
import scala.collection.mutable.LinkedList
import scala.collection.JavaConversions._
import java.util.ArrayList

object ListExamples {
  def main(args : Array[String]) {
    var list = List(1,2,3)
    list = list :+ 4
    println(list)

    val linklist = LinkedList(1,2,3)
    linklist.append(LinkedList(4))
    println(linklist)

    val jlist = new ArrayList[String]()
    jlist.add("foo")
    val slist = jlist.toList
    println(slist)
  }
}
```

Append methods

As you can see, `list` is a mutable reference (it's a `var`). It points at an instance of an immutable list, so you can reassign it to point at a new object. The `:+` method returns a new (immutable) `List` instance, with the additional element appended.

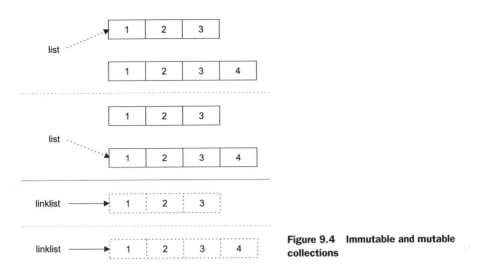

Figure 9.4   Immutable and mutable collections

By contrast, `linklist` is an immutable reference (a `val`) to a `LinkedList`, which is mutable. You can change the contents of `linklist` in place; for example, by calling `append()` on it. This distinction is illustrated in figure 9.4.

We also demonstrated a useful group of conversion functions in listing 9.8—the `JavaConversions` class, which is used to convert Java collections to and from their Scala equivalents.

TRAITS FOR LIST

One other important way in which Scala is different is that it chooses to emphasize the traits and behavioral aspects of its collections. As an example, consider Java's `Array-List`. Leaving aside `Object`, this class directly or indirectly extends

- `java.util.AbstractList`
- `java.util.AbstractCollection`

There are also interfaces to consider. `ArrayList` or one of its superclasses implements the interfaces shown in table 9.2.

Table 9.2   Java interfaces implemented by `ArrayList`

Serializable	Cloneable	Iterable
Collection	List	RandomAccess

For Scala, the situation is a bit more complicated. Consider the `LinkedList` class. It derives from 27 other classes or traits, as shown in table 9.3.

Scala's collections aren't as distinctively different from each other as Java's are. In Java, `List`, `Map`, `Set`, and so on, are treated with slightly different patterns depending on the specific type in use. But in Scala, the use of traits makes the types much more fine-grained than in Java. This allows you to focus on one or more aspects of the collection's

Table 9.3   Scala interfaces implemented by `LinkedList`

Serializable	LinkedListLike	LinearSeq
LinearSeqLike	Cloneable	Seq
SeqLike	GenSeq	GenSeqLike
PartialFunction	Function1	Iterable
IterableLike	Equals	GenIterable
GenIterableLike	Mutable	Traversable
GenTraversable	GenTraversableTemplate	TraversableLike
GenTraversableLike	Parallelizable	TraversableOnce

nature and to express your intent more precisely by using a type that closely corresponds to the aspect that's under consideration.

For this reason, collection handling code in Scala can seem a lot more uniform than the corresponding Java code would be.

Sets in Scala

As you might expect by now, Scala includes support for both immutable and mutable sets. Typical usage of the sets follows the same pattern as you see in Java—using an intermediate object to act sequentially over the collection. But where Java would use an `Iterator` or `Iterable`, Scala uses a `Traversable`, which isn't interoperable with the Java types.

Lists can be built up from a couple of simple conceptual basics: `Nil`, which represents the empty list, and the `::` operator, which makes new lists from old ones. The `::` operator is pronounced "cons," and it's related to Clojure's `(concat)` form, which you'll meet in chapter 10. These are both illustrations of Scala's roots in more functional programming—roots that ultimately go back to Lisp.

The cons operator takes two arguments—an element of type `T` and an object of type `List[T]`. It creates a new value of type `List[T]` that contains the contents of the two arguments pushed together:

```
scala> val x = 2 :: 3 :: Nil
x: List[Int] = List(2, 3)
```

Alternatively, you can write this directly:

```
scala> val x = List(2, 3)
x: List[Int] = List(2, 3)

scala> 1 :: x
res0: List[Int] = List(1, 2, 3)
```

The cons operator and brackets

The definition of the cons operator means that `A :: B :: C` is unambiguous. It means `A :: (B :: C)`. The reason for this is that the first argument of `::` is a single value of type `T`. But `A :: B` is a value of type `List[T]`, so `(A :: B) :: C` doesn't make any sense as a possible value. Academic computer scientists would say that `::` is right-associative.

This also explains why you need to say `2 :: 3 :: Nil` rather than just `2 :: 3`. You need the second argument to `::` to be a value of type `List`, and `3` isn't a `List`.

As well as `List`, Scala has its own forms of other familiar collections. The next one we'll consider is `Map`.

9.5.2 *Map*

The `Map` collection is another classic data structure. In Java it's most often seen in its `HashMap` guise. Scala provides the immutable `Map` class as its default and provides `HashMap` as the standard mutable form.

In the following listing you can see some simple standard ways of defining and working with maps.

Listing 9.9　Maps in Scala

```
import scala.collection.mutable.HashMap

var x = Map(1 -> "hi", 2 -> "There")
for ((key, vau) <- x) println(key + ": " + vau)
x = x + (3 -> "bye")

val hm = HashMap(1 -> "hi", 2 -> "There")
hm += (3 -> "bye")
println(hm)
```

As you can see, Scala has a lovely compact syntax for defining a map literal: `Map(1 -> "hi", 2 -> "There")`. The arrow notation shows visually which value each key "points at." To get values back from maps, the `get()` method is used, just like in Java.

Both mutable and immutable maps use + to denote adding to a map (and - for removing). But there are some subtleties involved in this. When used on a mutable map, + alters the map and returns it. On an immutable instance, a new map containing the new key/value pair is returned. This leads to the following corner case involving the += operator:

```
scala> val m = Map(1 -> "hi", 2 -> "There", 3 -> "bye", 4 -> "quux")
m: scala.collection.immutable.Map[Int,java.lang.String]
⇒ = Map(1 -> hi, 2 -> There, 3 -> bye, 4 -> quux)

scala> m += (5 -> "Blah")
<console>:10: error: reassignment to val
       m += (5 -> "Blah")
         ^
```

```
scala>  val hm = HashMap(1 -> "hi", 2 -> "There", 3 -> "bye", 4 -> "quux")
hm: scala.collection.mutable.HashMap[Int,java.lang.String]
➥ = Map(3 -> bye, 4 -> quux, 1 -> hi, 2 -> There)

scala> hm += (5 -> "blah")
res6: hm.type = Map(5 -> blah, 3 -> bye, 4 -> quux, 1 -> hi, 2 -> There)
```

The reason for this is that += is implemented differently for an immutable and a mutable map. For a mutable map, += is a method that alters the map in place. This means that this method can quite legally be called on a val (just like calling put() on a final HashMap in Java). For the immutable case, += decomposes to a combination of = and +, just like in listing 9.9; it can't be used on a val, as reassignment isn't allowed.

Another nice piece of syntax illustrated in listing 9.9 is the for loop syntax. This uses the idea of the list comprehension (which you saw in section 9.3.5), but combines it with splitting each key/value pair into a key and value. This is called a destructuring of the pair—another concept from Scala's functional heritage.

We've only scratched the surface of Scala's maps and their power, but we need to move on to take a look at our next topic—generic types.

9.5.3 *Generic types*

You've already seen that Scala uses square brackets to indicate parameterized types, and you've met some of Scala's basic data structures. Let's dig deeper and look at how Scala's approach to generics differs from Java's.

First off, let's see what happens if you try to ignore generics when defining a function parameter's type:

```
scala> def junk(x : List) = println("hi")
<console>:5: error: type List takes type parameters
       def junk(x : List) = println("hi")
                     ^
```

In Java, this would be completely legal. The compiler might complain, but it would allow it. In Scala, this is a hard compile-time failure. Lists (and other generic types) must be parameterized—end of story. There's no equivalent of Java's "raw type" concept.

TYPE INFERENCE FOR GENERIC TYPES

When assigning to a variable of a generic type, Scala provides suitable type inference around type parameters. This is in accordance with Scala's general effort to provide useful type inference and a lack of boilerplate wherever possible:

```
scala> val x = List(1, 2, 3)
x: List[Int] = List(1, 2, 3)
```

One feature of Scala's generics that may seem strange at first sight can be demonstrated using the ::: concat operator, which joins lists together to make a new list:

```
scala> val y = List("cat", "dog", "bird")
y: List[java.lang.String] = List(cat, dog, bird)
scala> x ::: y
res0: List[Any] = List(1, 2, 3, cat, dog, bird)
```

This means that rather than cause an error when trying to make a new `List` in this way, the runtime produced a list with the smallest common supertype of `Int` and `String`, which is `Any`.

GENERICS EXAMPLE—WAITING PETS

Suppose you have pets that need to be seen by a veterinarian, and you want to model the queue in the waiting room. The following listing shows some familiar basic classes and a helper function that can be used as a starting point.

Listing 9.10   Pets waiting to be seen

```
class Pet(name : String)
class Cat(name : String) extends Pet(name : String)
class Dog(name : String) extends Pet(name : String)
class BengalKitten(name : String) extends Cat(name : String)

class Queue[T](elts : T*) {
  var elems = List[T](elts : _* )                    ◁────────────────  Need type
                                                                        hint
  def enqueue(elem : T) = elems ::: List(elem)

  def dequeue = {
    val result = elems.head
    elems = elems.tail
    result
  }
}

def examine(q : Queue[Cat]) {
  println("Examining: " + q.dequeue)
}
```

Let's now consider how you might use these classes from the Scala prompt. These are the simplest examples:

```
scala> examine(new Queue(new Cat("tiddles")))
Examining: line5$object$$iw$$iw$Cat@fb0d6fe

scala> examine(new Queue(new Pet("george")))
<console>:10: error: type mismatch;
 found    : Pet
 required: Cat
       examine(new Queue(new Pet("george")))
                 ^
```

So far, so Java-like. Let's do a couple more simple examples:

```
scala> examine(new Queue(new BengalKitten("michael")))
Examining: line7$object$$iw$$iw$BengalKitten@464a149a

scala> var kitties = new Queue(new BengalKitten("michael"))
kitties: Queue[BengalKitten] = Queue@2976c6e4

scala> examine(kitties)
<console>:12: error: type mismatch;
 found    : Queue[BengalKitten]
 required: Queue[Cat]
```

```
examine(kitties)
           ^
```

This is also relatively unsurprising. In the example where you don't create `kitties` as a temporary variable, Scala type-infers the type of the queue to be `Queue[Cat]`, and then accepts `michael` as being of a suitable type—`BengalKitten`—to be added to the queue. In the second example, you explicitly provide the type of `kitties`. This means that Scala is unable to use type inference and so can't make the parameters match.

Next, we'll look at how to fix some of these type problems by using the *type variance* of a language's type system—in particular, the form called *covariance*. (There are other possible forms of type variance, but covariance is the most commonly used.) In Java, this is very flexible, but it can also be somewhat arcane. We'll show you how this works in both Scala and Java.

COVARIANCE

Have you ever found yourself wondering things like, "Is `List<String>` a subtype of `List<Object>` in Java?" If so, then this topic is for you.

By default, Java's answer to that question, is "No," but you can set things up to make it "Yes." To see how, consider this bit of code:

```
public class MyList<T> {
  private List<T> theList;
}

MyList<Cat> katzchen = new MyList<Cat>();
MyList<? extends Pet> petExt = pet1;
```

The `? extends Pet` clause means that `petExt` is a variable of a type that is partly unknown (the `?` in a Java type is always read as "unknown"). What you do know is that the type parameter to `MyList` must be a `Pet` or a subtype of `Pet`. The Java compiler then allows `petExt` to have a value assigned to it where the type parameter is a subtype.

This is effectively saying that `MyList<Cat>` is a subtype of `MyList<? extends Pet>`. Notice how this subtyping relationship was set up when you used the `MyList` type, not when you defined it. This property of types is called *covariance*.

Scala does things differently than Java. Rather than have the type variance defined at the point of use of a type, Scala allows you to make covariance explicit at the point where the type is declared. This has some advantages:

- The compiler can check for usage that doesn't fit with covariance at compile time.
- Any conceptual burden is placed on the writer of a type, not on the users of that type.
- It allows intuitive relationships to be built into basic collection types.

This does produce the theoretical disadvantage that it's technically not as flexible as Java's use site variance, but in practice the benefits of Scala's approach usually outweigh this concern. The really advanced features of Java's generics are rarely used by most programmers.

The standard Scala collections, such as `List`, implement covariance. This means that `List[BengalKitten]` is a subtype of `List[Cat]`, which is a subtype of `List[Pet]`. To see this in action, let's fire up the interpreter:

```
scala> val kits = new BengalKitten("michael") :: Nil
kits: List[BengalKitten] = List(BengalKitten@71ed5401)

scala> var katzen : List[Cat] = kits
katzen: List[Cat] = List(BengalKitten@71ed5401)

scala> var haustieren : List[Pet] = katzen
haustieren: List[Pet] = List(BengalKitten@71ed5401)
```

We're using explicit types on the `vars` to ensure that Scala doesn't infer the types too narrowly.

This concludes our brief look at Scala's generics. The next big topic we want to address is Scala's novel approach to concurrency, which makes use of the actors model as an alternative approach to explicit management of multiple threads.

9.6   *Introduction to actors*

Java's model of explicit locks and synchronization is showing its age. It was a fantastic innovation when the language was first conceived, but it has a big problem. Java's concurrency model is essentially a balancing act between two unwanted outcomes.

Too little locking leads to unsafe concurrent code, which will manifest as race conditions. Too much locking leads to failures of liveness, and the code will grind to a halt, unable to make meaningful forward progress. This is the tension between safety and liveness that we discussed in chapter 4.

The lock-based model requires you to think about all of the concurrent operations that could be in flight at a given time. This means that as applications become larger, it becomes more and more difficult to think about all of the things that could go wrong. Although there are things that Java can do to mitigate some of these issues, the core problem remains and can't be completely fixed within the Java language without a backwards-incompatible release.

Non-Java languages have an opportunity to start again. Instead of exposing the low-level details of locks and threads to the programmer, alternative languages can provide features in their language runtimes that provide extra support for concurrency.

This should not be an unusual idea. After all, when Java first appeared, the idea that the runtime would manage memory and the developer would be kept away from the details was considered odd by many C and C++ developers.

Let's take a look at how Scala's concurrency model, based on a technology called actors, can provide a different (and simpler) approach to concurrent programming.

9.6.1   *All the code's a stage*

An actor is an object that extends `scala.actors.Actor` and implements the `act()` method. This should hopefully echo the definition of a thread in Java in your mind. The most important difference is that Scala actors don't communicate using explicit shared data under most circumstances.

Note that the shared data part is some-thing the programmer must do as part of best practices. There is nothing in Scala stopping you from sharing state between actors if you want to. It's just considered bad style to do so. Instead, actors have a communication channel called a mailbox, which is used to send a mes-sage (a work item) into an actor from another context. Figure 9.5 shows how.

Figure 9.5   Scala actors and mailboxes

To implement an actor, you could simply extend the `Actor` class:

```
import scala.actors._

class MyActor extends Actor {
  def act() {
    ...
  }
}
```

This looks a lot like the way that Java code would declare a subclass of `Thread`. Just as with threads, you need to tell the actor to start and put itself into a state where it can start to receive methods. This is done with the `start()` method.

As you might expect by now, Scala also provides a handy factory method, `actor`, to help with creating new actors (the equivalent Java concept might be a static factory method that produces anonymous implementations of `Runnable`). That allows con-cise Scala code like this:

```
val myactor = actor {
    ...
}
```

The contents of the block being passed to actor are turned into the contents of the `act()` method. In addition, actors that are created this way don't need to be started with a separate `start()` call—they automatically start.

That's a neat bit of syntactic sugar, but we still need to introduce the heart of the Scala concurrency model—the mailbox. Let's move on to look at that now.

9.6.2   *Communicating with actors via the mailbox*

Sending a message into an actor from another object is very simple—you just call the `!` method on the actor object.

On the receiving end, however, you need some code to handle the messages or they'll just pile up in the mailbox. In addition, the body of the actor method usually needs to loop, so that it can handle an entire stream of incoming messages. Let's see some of this in action at the Scala REPL:

```scala
scala> import scala.actors.Actor._
       val myact = actor {
         while (true) {
           receive {
             case incoming => println("I got mail: "+ incoming)
           }
         }
       }
myact: scala.actors.Actor = scala.actors.Actor$$anon$1@a760bb0

scala> myact ! "Hello!"
I got mail: Hello!

scala> myact ! "Goodbye!"
I got mail: Goodbye!

scala> myact ! 34
I got mail: 34
```

This example uses the `receive` method to make the actor handle a message. This takes a block as an argument, which is the body of the processing method that Scala will use to handle the method.

> **NOTE** Overall, the Scala model is similar to a processing pattern that we discussed in chapter 4 (listing 4.13) with the Java processing threads playing the role of actors, and the `LinkedBlockingQueue` playing the role of the Scala mailbox. Scala provides language and library level support for this pattern in a very straightforward way, which really helps to reduce the amount of boilerplate that needs to be written.

Despite being a very simple example, this demonstrates a lot of the basics of working with actors:

- Use a loop in the `actor` method to handle a stream of incoming messages.
- Use `receive` to handle incoming messages.
- Use a set of cases as the body of `receive`.

This last point is worth further discussion. The set of cases defines what is called a *partial function*. This is useful, because of another aspect of Scala's actors that's more convenient than the Java equivalent. Specifically, Scala's mailboxes as set up here are untyped. This means that you can send a message of any type into an actor, and set up patterns to receive messages of different types by using the typed patterns and the constructor patterns that you saw earlier in the chapter.

In addition to these basics, there are a number of best practices for using actors. Here are some of the main ones that you should try to adhere to in your own code:

- Make incoming messages immutable.
- Consider making message types case classes.
- Don't do any blocking operations within an actor.

Not every application is in a position to follow all of these best practices, but most apps should strive to use as many as possible.

For more sophisticated actors, it's often necessary to control the startup and shutdown of actors. This is often done with a loop that uses a Boolean condition to control shutting down the actor. Depending on your preferred style, you may also like to write the actor in a functional style so that it has no state that's affected by incoming messages.

Scala provides a lot more support for concurrent programming in the actor style. We're only just scratching the surface here. For a comprehensive treatment, we recommend *Scala in Action* by Nilanjan Raychaudhuri (Manning, 2010).

9.7   *Summary*

Scala is a language that differs significantly from Java:

- Functional techniques can be used to provide a more flexible style of programming.
- Type inference can make a statically typed language feel like a dynamic language.
- Scala's advanced type system can extend the notion of object orientation that you see in Java.

In the next chapter, we'll meet the last of our non-Java languages—the Lisp dialect called Clojure. This is probably the language that is least like Java in most ways. We'll build on the discussions of immutability, functional programming, and alternative concurrency from this chapter and show how Clojure takes all of these ideas and builds an incredibly powerful and beautiful programming environment from them.

Clojure: safer programming

10

This chapter covers

- Clojure's concept of identity and state
- The Clojure REPL
- Clojure syntax, data structures, and sequences
- Clojure interoperability with Java
- Multithreaded development with Clojure
- Software transactional memory

Clojure is a very different style of language from Java and the other languages we've studied so far. Clojure is a JVM reboot of one of the oldest programming languages—Lisp. If you're not familiar with Lisp, don't worry. We'll teach you everything you need to know about the Lisp family of languages to get you started with Clojure.

In addition to its heritage of powerful programming techniques from classic Lisp, Clojure adds amazing cutting-edge technology that's very relevant to the modern Java developer. This combination makes Clojure a standout language on the JVM and an attractive choice for application development.

Particular examples of Clojure's new tech are its concurrency toolkits and data structures. The concurrency abstractions enable programmers to write much safer multithreaded code. These can be combined with Clojure's seq abstraction (a different take on collections and data structures) to provide a very powerful developer toolbox.

To access all of this power, some important language concepts are approached in a fundamentally different way from Java. This difference in approach makes Clojure interesting to learn, and it will probably also change the way you think about programming. Learning Clojure can help to make you a better programmer in any language.

We'll kick off with a discussion of Clojure's approach to state and variables. After some simple examples, we'll introduce the basic vocabulary of the language—the special forms that can be used to build up the rest of the language. We'll also delve into Clojure's syntax for data structures, loops, and functions. This will allow us to introduce sequences, which are one of Clojure's most powerful abstractions. We'll conclude the chapter by looking at two very compelling features: tight Java integration and Clojure's amazing concurrency support.

10.1   *Introducing Clojure*

Let's get started by looking at one of Clojure's most important conceptual differences from Java. This is the treatment of state, variables, and storage. As you can see in figure 10.1, Java (like Groovy and Scala) has a model of memory and state that involves a variable being a "box" (really a memory location) with contents that can change over time.

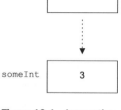

Figure 10.1   Imperative language memory use

Clojure is a little bit different—the important concept is that of a *value*. Values can be numbers, strings, vectors, maps, sets, or a number of other things. Once created, values never alter. This is really important, so we'll say it again. *Once created, Clojure values can't be altered*—they're *immutable*.

This means that the imperative language model of a box that has contents that change isn't the way Clojure works. Figure 10.2 shows how Clojure deals with state and memory. It creates an association between a name and a value.

Figure 10.2   Clojure memory use

This is called *binding*, and it's done using the special form (def). Special forms are the Clojure equivalent of Java keywords, but be aware that Clojure has a different meaning for the term "keyword," which we'll encounter later.

The syntax for (def) is

```
(def <name> <value>)
```

Don't worry that the syntax looks a little weird—this is entirely normal for Lisp syntax, and you'll get used to it really quickly. For now you can pretend that the brackets are arranged slightly differently and that you're calling a method like this:

```
def(<name>, <value>)
```

Let's demonstrate (def) with a time-honored example that uses the Clojure interactive environment.

10.1.1 Hello World in Clojure

If you haven't already installed Clojure, check out appendix D. Then change into the directory where you installed Clojure and run this command:

```
java -cp clojure.jar clojure.main
```

This brings up the user prompt for the Clojure read-evaluate-print loop (REPL). This is the interactive session, which is where you'll typically spend quite a lot of time when developing Clojure code.

The user=> part is the Clojure prompt for the session, which can be thought of as a bit like an advanced debugger or a command line:

```
user=> (def hello (fn [] "Hello world"))
#'user/hello
user=> (hello)
"Hello world"
```

In this code, you start off by binding the identifier hello to a value. (def) always binds identifiers (which Clojure calls *symbols*) to values. Behind the scenes, it will also create an object, called a *var*, that represents the binding (and the name of the symbol).

What is the value you're binding to? It's the value:

```
(fn [] "Hello world")
```

This is a function, which is a genuine value (and so therefore immutable) in Clojure. It's a function that takes no arguments and returns the string "Hello world".

After binding it, you execute it via (hello). This causes the Clojure runtime to print the results of evaluating the function, which is "Hello world."

At this point, you should enter the Hello World example (if you haven't already), and see that it behaves as described. Once you've done that, we can explore a little further.

10.1.2 Getting started with the REPL

The REPL allows you to enter Clojure code and execute Clojure functions. It's an interactive environment, and the results of earlier evaluations are still around. This enables a type of programming called *exploratory programming*, which we'll discuss in section 10.5.4—it basically means that you can experiment with code. In many cases the right thing to do is to play around in the REPL, building up larger and larger functions once the building blocks are correct.

Let's look at an example of that right now. One of the first things to point out is that the binding of a symbol to a value can be changed by another call to def, so let's see that in action in the REPL—we'll actually use a slight variant of (def) called (defn):

```
user=> (hello)
"Hello world"
user=> (defn hello [] "Goodnight Moon")
#'user/hello
user=> (hello)
"Goodnight Moon"
```

Notice that the original binding for `hello` is still in play until you change it—this is a key feature of the REPL. There is still state, in terms of which symbols are bound to which values, and that state persists between lines the user enters.

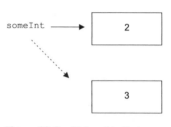

someInt

2

3

The ability to change which value a symbol is bound to is Clojure's alternative to mutating state. Rather than allowing the contents of a "memory box" to change over time, Clojure allows a symbol to be bound to different immutable values at different

Figure 10.3   Clojure bindings changing over time

points in time. Another way of saying this is that the `var` can point to different values during the lifetime of a program. An example can be seen in figure 10.3.

> **NOTE**   This distinction between mutable state and different bindings at different times is subtle, but it's a very important concept to grasp. Remember, *mutable state* means the contents of the box change, whereas *rebinding* means pointing at different boxes at different points in time.

We've also slipped in another Clojure concept in the last code snippet—the `(defn)` "define function" macro. Macros are one of the key concepts of Lisp-like languages. The central idea is that there should be as little distinction between built-in constructs and ordinary code as possible.

Macros allow you to create forms that behave like built-in syntax. The creation of macros is an advanced topic, but mastering their creation will allow you to produce incredibly powerful tools.

This means that the true language primitives of the system (the special forms) can be used to build up the core of the language in such a way that you don't really notice the difference between the two. The `(defn)` macro is an example of this. It's just a slightly easier way to bind a function value to a symbol (and create a suitable `var`, of course).

10.1.3   *Making a mistake*

What happens if you make a mistake? Say you leave out the `[]` (which is the part of the function declaration that says that this function takes no arguments):

```
user=> (defn hello "Goodnight Moon")
#'user/hello
user=> (hello)
java.lang.IllegalArgumentException: Wrong number of args (0) passed to:
user$hello (NO_SOURCE_FILE:0)
```

All that's happened is that you've got your `hello` identifier bound to something that doesn't make a lot of sense. In the REPL, you can fix this by simply rebinding it:

```
user=> (defn hello [] (println "Dydh da an Nor"))
  ; "Hello World" in Cornish
#'user/hello
user=> (hello)
```

```
Dydh da an Nor
nil
user=>
```

As you might guess from the preceding snippet, the semicolon (;) character means that everything to the end of the line is a comment, and (println) is the function that prints a string. Notice that (println), like all functions, returns a value, which is echoed back to the REPL at the end of the function's execution. That value is nil, which is basically the Clojure equivalent of Java's null.

10.1.4 *Learning to love the brackets*

The culture of programmers has always had a large element of whimsy and humor. One of the oldest jokes is that Lisp is an acronym for Lots of Irritating Silly Parentheses (instead of the more prosaic truth—that it's an abbreviation for List Processing). This rather self-deprecating joke is popular with some Lisp coders, partly because it points out the unfortunate truth that Lisp syntax has a reputation for being difficult to learn.

In reality, this hurdle is rather exaggerated. Lisp syntax is different from what most programmers are used to, but it isn't the obstacle that it's sometimes presented as. In addition, Clojure has several innovations that reduce the barrier to entry even further.

Let's take another look at the Hello World example. To call the function that returns the value "Hello World", you wrote this:

```
(hello)
```

If you were writing this in Java, it would look something like the following (assuming you had a function called hello defined somewhere in the class):

```
hello();
```

But Clojure is different. Rather than having expressions such as myFunction(someObj), this is written in Clojure as (myFunction someObj). This syntax is called *Polish notation*, as it was developed by Polish mathematicians in the 19th century.

If you've studied compiler theory, you might wonder if there's a connection here to concepts like the abstract syntax tree (AST). The short answer is yes, there is. A Clojure (or other Lisp) program that is written in Polish notation (usually called an *s-expression* by Lisp programmers) can be shown to be a very simple and direct representation of the AST of that program.

You can think of a Lisp program as being written in terms of its AST directly. There's no real distinction between a data structure representing a Lisp program and the code, so code and data are very interchangeable. This is the reason for the slightly strange notation—it's used by Lisp-like languages to blur the distinction between built-in primitives and user and library code. This power is so great that it far outweighs the slight oddity of the syntax to the eyes of a newly arrived Java programmer.

Let's dive into some more of the syntax and start using Clojure to build real programs.

10.2 Looking for Clojure—syntax and semantics

In the previous section, you met the (def) and (fn) special forms. There are a small number of other special forms that you need to know immediately to provide a basic vocabulary for the language. In addition, there are a large number of useful forms and macros, of which a greater awareness will develop with practice.

Clojure is blessed with a very large number of useful functions for doing a wide range of conceivable tasks. Don't be daunted by this—embrace it. Be happy that for many practical programming tasks you may face in Clojure, somebody else has already done the heavy lifting for you.

In this section, we'll cover the basic working set of special forms, then progress to Clojure's native data types (the equivalent of Java's collections). After that, we'll progress to a natural style for writing Clojure—one in which functions rather than variables have center stage. The object-oriented nature of the JVM will still be present beneath the surface, but Clojure's emphasis on functions has a power that isn't as obviously present in purely OO languages.

10.2.1 Special forms bootcamp

Table 10.1 covers the definitions of some of Clojure's most commonly used special forms. To get best use of the table, skim through it now and refer back to it as necessary when you reach some of the examples in sections 10.3 onwards.

Table 10.1   Some of Clojure's basic special forms

Special form	Meaning
(def <symbol> <value?>)	Binds a symbol to a value (if provided). Creates a var corresponding to the symbol if necessary.
(fn <name>? [<arg>*] <expr>*)	Returns a function value that takes the specified args, and applies them to the exprs. Often combined with (def) into forms like (defn).
(if <test> <then> <else>?)	If test evaluates to logical-true, evaluate and yield then. Otherwise, evaluate and yield else, if present.
(let [<binding>*] <expr>*)	Aliases values to a local name and implicitly defines a scope. Makes the alias available inside all exprs within the scope of let.
(do <expr>*)	Evaluates the exprs in order and yields the value of the last.
(quote <form>)	Returns form as is (without evaluation). It only takes a single form and ignores all other arguments.
(var <symbol>)	Returns the var corresponding to symbol (returns a Clojure JVM object, not a value).

This isn't an exhaustive list of special forms, and a high percentage of them have multiple ways of being used. Table 10.1 is a starter collection of basic use cases, and not anything comprehensive.

Now that you have an appreciation of the syntax for some basic special forms, let's turn to Clojure's data structures and start to see how the forms can operate on data.

10.2.2 *Lists, vectors, maps, and sets*

Clojure has several native data structures. The most familiar is the list, which in Clojure is a singly linked list.

Lists are typically surrounded with parentheses, which presents a slight syntactic hurdle because round brackets are also used for general forms. In particular, parentheses are used for evaluation of function calls. This leads to the following common beginner's syntax error:

```
1:7 user=> (1 2 3)
java.lang.ClassCastException: java.lang.Integer cannot be cast to
clojure.lang.IFn (repl-1:7)
```

The problem here is that, because Clojure is very flexible about its values, it's expecting a function value (or a symbol that resolves to one) as the first argument, so it can call that function and pass 2 and 3 as arguments; 1 isn't a value that is a function, so Clojure can't compile this form. We say that this *s*-expression is invalid. Only valid *s*-expressions can be Clojure forms.

The solution is to use the (quote) form that you met in the last section. This has a handy short form, which is '. This gives us these two equivalent ways of writing this list:

```
1:22 user=> '(1 2 3)
(1 2 3)
1:23 user=> (quote (1 2 3))
(1 2 3)
```

Note that (quote) handles its arguments in a special way. In particular, there is no attempt made to evaluate the argument, so there's no error arising from a lack of a function value in the first slot.

Clojure has vectors, which are like arrays (in fact, it's not too far from the truth to think of lists as being basically like Java's LinkedList and vectors as like ArrayList). They have a convenient literal form that makes use of square brackets, so all of these are equivalent:

```
1:4 user=> (vector 1 2 3)
[1 2 3]
1:5 user=> (vec '(1 2 3))
[1 2 3]
1:6 user=> [1 2 3]
[1 2 3]
```

We've already met vectors. When we declared the Hello World function and others, we used a vector to indicate the parameters that the declared function takes. Note that the form (vec) accepts a list and creates a vector from it, whereas (vector) is a form that accepts multiple individual symbols and returns a vector of them.

The function (nth) for collections takes two parameters: a collection and an index. It can be thought of as similar to the get() method from Java's List interface. It can be used on vectors and lists, but also on Java collections and even strings, which are treated as collections of characters. Here's an example:

```
1:7 user=> (nth '(1 2 3) 1)
2
```

Clojure also supports maps (which you can think of as being very similar to Java's HashMap), with this simple literal syntax:

```
{key1 value1 key2 "value2}
```

To get a value back out of a map, the syntax is very simple:

```
user=> (def foo {"aaa" "111" "bbb" "2222"})
#'user/foo
user=> foo
{"aaa" "111", "bbb" "2222"}
user=> (foo "aaa")
"111"
```

One very useful stylistic point is the use of keys that have a colon in front of them. These are what Clojure refers to as "keywords":

```
1:24 user=> (def martijn {:name "Martijn Verburg",
    :city "London", :area "Highbury"})
#'user/martijn
1:25 user=> (:name martijn)
"Martijn Verburg"
1:26 user=> (martijn :area)
"Highbury"
1:27 user=> :area
:area
1:28 user=> :foo
:foo
```

Here are some useful points about keywords and maps to keep in mind:

- A keyword in Clojure is a function that takes one argument, which must be a map.
- Calling a keyword function on a map returns the value that corresponds to the keyword function in the map.
- When using keywords, there's a useful symmetry in the syntax, as (my-map :key) and (:key my-map) are both legal.
- As a value, a keyword returns itself.
- Keywords don't need to be declared or def'd before use.
- Remember that Clojure functions are values, and therefore are eligible to be used as keys in maps.

- Commas can be used (but aren't necessary) to separate key/value pairs, as Clojure considers them whitespace.
- Symbols other than keywords can be used as keys in Clojure maps, but the keyword syntax is extremely useful and is worth emphasizing as a style in your own code.

In addition to map literals, Clojure also has a (map) function. But don't be caught out. Unlike (list), the (map) function doesn't produce a map. Instead, (map) applies a supplied function to each element in a collection in turn, and builds a new collection (actually a Clojure sequence, which you'll meet in detail in section 10.4) from the new values returned.

```
1:27 user=> (def ben {:name "Ben Evans", :city "London", :area "Holloway"})
#'user/ben
1:28 user=> (def authors [ben martijn])
#'user/authors
1:29 user=> (map (fn [y] (:name y)) authors)
("Ben Evans" "Martijn Verburg")
```

There are additional forms of (map) that are able to handle multiple collections at once, but the form that takes a single collection as input is the most common.

Clojure also supports sets, which are very similar to Java's HashSet. They also have a short form for data structures:

```
#{"apple" "pair" "peach"}
```

These data structures provide the fundamentals for building up Clojure programs.

One thing that may surprise the Java native is the lack of any immediate mention of objects as first-class citizens. This isn't to say that Clojure isn't object-oriented, but it doesn't see OO in quite the same way as Java. Java chooses to see the world in terms of statically typed bundles of data and code in explicit class definitions of user-defined data types. Clojure emphasizes the functions and forms instead, although these are implemented as objects on the JVM behind the scenes.

This philosophical distinction between Clojure and Java manifests itself in how code is written in the two languages, and to fully understand the Clojure viewpoint, it's necessary to write programs in Clojure and understand some of the advantages that deemphasizing Java's OO constructs brings.

10.2.3 Arithmetic, equality, and other operations

Clojure has no operators in the sense that you might expect them in Java. So how would you, for example, add two numbers? In Java it's easy:

```
3 + 4
```

But Clojure has no operators. We'll have to use a function instead:

```
(add 3 4)
```

That's all well and good, but we can do better. As there aren't any operators in Clojure, we don't need to reserve any of the keyboard's characters to represent them. That means our function names can be more outlandish than in Java, so we can write this:

```
(+ 3 4)
```

Clojure's functions are in many cases *variadic* (they take a variable number of inputs), so you can, for example, write this:

```
(+ 1 2 3)
```

This will give the value 6.

For the equality forms (the equivalent of equals() and == in Java), the situation is a little more complex. Clojure has two main forms that relate to equality: (=) and (identical?). Note that these are both examples of how the lack of operators in Clojure means that more characters can be used in function names. Also, (=) is a single equals sign, because there's not the same notion of assignment as in Java-like languages.

This bit of REPL code sets up a list, list-int, and a vector, vect-int, and applies equality logic to them:

```
1:1 user=> (def list-int '(1 2 3 4))
#'user/list-int
1:2 user=> (def vect-int (vec list-int))
#'user/vect-int
1:3 user=> (= vect-int list-int)
true
1:4 user=> (identical? vect-int list-int)
false
```

The key point is that the (=) form on collections checks to see whether the collections comprise the same objects in the same order (which is true for list-int and vect-int), whereas (identical?) checks to see if they're really the same object.

You might also notice that our symbol names don't use camel-case. This is usual for Clojure. Symbols are usually all in lowercase, with hyphens between words.

True and false in Clojure

Clojure provides two values for logical false: false and nil. Anything else is logical true. This parallels the situation in many dynamic languages, but it's a bit strange for Java programmers encountering it for the first time.

With basic data structures and operators under our belts, let's put together some of the special forms and functions we've seen and write slightly longer example Clojure functions.

10.3 *Working with functions and loops in Clojure*

In this section, we'll start dealing with some of the meat of Clojure programming. We'll start writing functions to act on data and bring Clojure's focus on functions to the fore. Next up are Clojure's looping constructs, then reader macros and dispatch forms. We'll round out the section by discussing Clojure's approach to functional programming, and its take on closures.

The best way to start doing all of this is by example, so let's get going with a few simple examples and build up toward some of the powerful functional programming techniques that Clojure provides.

10.3.1 Some simple Clojure functions

Listing 10.1 defines three functions. Two of which are very simple functions of one argument; the third is a little more complex.

Listing 10.1   Defining simple Clojure functions

```
(defn const-fun1 [y] 1)

(defn ident-fun [y] y)

(defn list-maker-fun [x f]
  (map (fn [z] (let [w z]
    (list w (f w))
)) x))
```

In this listing, (const-fun1) takes in a value and returns 1, and (ident-fun) takes in a value and returns the very same value. Mathematicians would call these a *constant function* and the *identity function*. You can also see that the definition of a function uses vector literals to denote the arguments to a function, and for the (let) form.

The third function is more complex. The function (list-maker-fun) takes two arguments: first a vector of values to operate on, which is called x, and second a value that must be a function.

Take a look at how list-maker-fun works:

Listing 10.2   Working with functions

```
user=> (list-maker-fun ["a"] const-fun1)
(("a" 1))
user=> (list-maker-fun ["a" "b"] const-fun1)
(("a" 1) ("b" 1))
user=> (list-maker-fun [2 1 3] ident-fun)
((2 2) (1 1) (3 3))
user=> (list-maker-fun [2 1 3] "a")
java.lang.ClassCastException: java.lang.String cannot be cast to
clojure.lang.IFn
```

Note that when you're typing these expressions into the REPL, you're interacting with the Clojure compiler. The expression (list-maker-fun [2 1 3] "a") fails to compile because (list-maker-fun) expects the second argument to be a function, which a string isn't. In section 10.5 you'll learn that, to the VM, Clojure functions are objects that implement clojure.lang.IFn.

This example shows that when interacting with the REPL, you still have a certain amount of static typing in play. This is because Clojure isn't an interpreted language. Even in the REPL, every Clojure form that is typed is compiled to JVM bytecode and linked into the running system. The Clojure function is compiled to JVM bytecode when it's defined, so the ClassCastException occurs because of a static typing violation in the VM.

Listing 10.3 shows a longer piece of Clojure code, the Schwartzian transform. This is a piece of programming history, made popular by the Perl programming language in the 1990s. The idea is to do a sort operation on a vector, based not on the provided vector, but on some property of the elements of the vector. The property values to sort on are found by calling a *keying function* on the elements.

The definition of the Schwartzian transform in listing 10.3 calls the keying function key-fn. When you actually want to call the (schwartz) function, you need to supply a function to use for keying. In listing 10.3, you use our old friend, (ident-fun), from listing 10.1.

Listing 10.3   Schwartzian transform

```
1:65 user=> (defn schwartz [x key-fn]                          Step 3
  (map (fn [y] (nth y 0))              <───────────────┐
      (sort-by (fn [t] (nth t 1))      <──────────────────────── Step 2
              (map (fn [z] (let [w z]  <───────┐
                    (list w (key-fn w)))
              ) x))))                                             Step 1
#'user/schwartz
1:66 user=> (schwartz [2 3 1 5 4] ident-fun)
(1 2 3 4 5)
1:67 user=> (apply schwartz [[2 3 1 5 4] ident-fun])
(1 2 3 4 5)
```

This code is performing three separate steps:

- Create a list consisting of pairs.
- Sort the pairs based on the values of the keying function.
- Construct a new list by taking only the original value from each pair in the sorted list of pairs (and discarding the keying function values).

This is shown in figure 10.4.

Note that in listing 10.3 we introduced a new form: (sort-by). This is a function that takes two arguments: a function to use to do the sorting, and a vector to be sorted. We've also showcased the (apply) form, which takes two arguments: a function to call, and a vector of arguments to pass to it.

One amusing aspect of the Schwartzian transform is that the person for whom it was named (Randall Schwartz) was deliberately aping Lisp when he came up with the Perl version. Representing it in the Clojure code here means we've come full circle—back to a Lisp again!

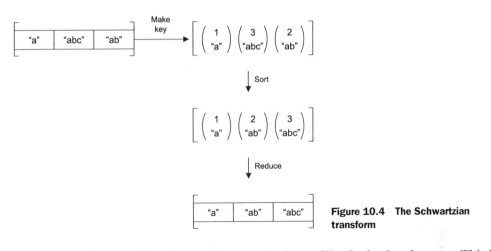

Figure 10.4 The Schwartzian transform

The Schwartzian transform is a useful example that we'll refer back to later on. This is because it contains just enough complexity to demonstrate quite a few useful concepts.

Now, let's move on to discuss loops in Clojure, which work a bit differently than you may be used to.

10.3.2 Loops in Clojure

Loops in Java are a fairly straightforward proposition—the developer can choose from a `for`, a `while`, and a couple of other loop types. Usually central is the concept of repeating a group of statements until a condition (often expressed in terms of a mutable variable) is met.

This presents us with a slight conundrum in Clojure: how can we express a `for` loop, for example, when there are no mutable variables to act as the loop index? In more traditional Lisps, this is often solved by rewriting iterative loops into a form that uses recursion. But the JVM doesn't guarantee to optimize tail recursion (as is required by Scheme and other Lisps), so using recursion can cause the stack to blow up.

Instead, Clojure provides useful constructions to allow looping without increasing the size of the stack. One of the most common is `loop-recur`. The next snippet shows how `loop-recur` can be used to build up a simple construction similar to a Java `for` loop.

```
(defn like-for [counter]
(loop [ctr counter]
  (println ctr)
  (if (< ctr 10)
     (recur (inc ctr))
     ctr
)))
```

The `(loop)` form takes a vector of arguments of local names for symbols—effectively aliases as `(let)` does. Then, when execution reaches the `(recur)` form (which it will only do in this example if the `ctr` alias is less than 10), the `(recur)` causes control to branch back to the (loop) form, but with the new value specified. This allows us to build up iteration-style constructs (such as for and while loops), but to still have a recursive flavor to the implementation.

We'll now turn to our next topic, which is a look at useful shorthand in Clojure syntax, to help make your programs even shorter and less verbose.

10.3.3 Reader macros and dispatch

Clojure has syntax features that surprise many Java programmers. One of them is the lack of operators. This has the side effect of relaxing Java's restrictions on which characters can be used in function names. You've already met functions such as (identical?), which would be illegal in Java, but we haven't addressed the issue of exactly which characters aren't allowed in symbols.

Table 10.2 lists the characters that aren't allowed in Clojure symbols. These are all characters that are reserved by the Clojure parser for its own use. They're usually referred to as reader macros.

Table 10.2   Reader macros

Character	Name	Meaning
'	Quote	Expands to (quote). Yields the unevaluated form.
;	Comment	Marks a comment to end of line. Like // in Java.
\	Character	Produces a literal character.
@	Deref	Expands to (deref), which takes in a var object and returns the value in that object (the opposite action of the (var) form). Has additional meaning in a transactional memory context (see section 10.6).
^	Metadata	Attaches a map of metadata to an object. See the Clojure documentation for details.
`	Syntax-quote	Form of quote often used in macro definitions. Not really suitable for beginners. See the Clojure documentation for details.
#	Dispatch	Has several different subforms. See table 10.3

The dispatch reader macro has several different subforms, depending on what follows the # character. Table 10.3 shows the different possible forms.

Table 10.3   The subforms of the dispatch reader macro

Dispatch form	Meaning
#'	Expands to (var).
#{}	Creates a set literal, as discussed in section 10.2.2.
#()	Creates an anonymous function literal. Useful for single uses where (fn) is too wordy.

Table 10.3 The subforms of the dispatch reader macro *(continued)*

Dispatch form	Meaning
`#_`	Skips the next form. Can be used to produce a multiline comment, via `#_ ( . . . multi-line . . . )`.
`#"<pattern>"`	Creates a regular expression literal (as a `java.util.regex.Pattern` object).

Here are a couple of additional points that follow from the dispatch forms. The var-quote, `#'`, form explains why the REPL behaves as it does after a `(def)`:

```
1:49 user=> (def someSymbol)
#'user/someSymbol
```

The `(def)` form returns the newly created var object named `someSymbol`, which lives in the current namespace (which is `user` in the REPL), so `#'user/someSymbol` is the full value of what's returned from `(def)`.

The anonymous function literal also has an innovation to reduce verboseness. This is to omit the vector of arguments, and instead use a special syntax to allow the Clojure reader to infer how many arguments are required for the function literal. Let's rewrite the Schwartzian transform to see how to use this syntax.

Listing 10.4 Rewritten Schwartzian transform

```
(defn schwartz [x f]
  (map #(nth %1 0)
       (sort-by #(nth %1 1)             Anonymous
                (map #(let [w %1]        function literals
                       (list w (f w))
                       ) x))))
```

The use of `%1` as a placeholder for a function literal's argument (and `%2`, `%3`, and so on for subsequent arguments) makes the usage really stand out, and makes the code a lot easier to read. This visual clue can be a real help for the programmer, similar to the arrow symbol used in function literals in Scala, which you saw in section 9.3.6.

As you've seen, Clojure relies heavily on the concept of functions as the basic unit of computation, rather than on objects, which are the staple of languages like Java. The natural setting for this approach is functional programming, which is our next topic.

10.3.4 *Functional programming and closures*

We're now going to turn to the scary world of functional programming in Clojure. Or rather, we're *not*, because it's not that scary. In fact, we've been doing functional programming for this entire chapter; we just didn't tell you, in order to not put you off.

As we mentioned in section 7.3.2, functional programming means a function is a value. A function can be passed around, placed in Vars and manipulated, just like 2 or "hello." But so what? We did that back in our very first example: `(def hello (fn []`

"Hello world")). We created a function (one that takes no arguments and returns the string "Hello world") and bound it to the symbol hello. The function was just a value, not fundamentally different for a value like value 2.

In section 10.3.1, we introduced the Schwartzian transform as an example of a function that takes another function as an input value. Again, this is just a function taking a particular type as one of its input arguments. The only thing that's slightly different about is that the type it's taking is a function.

What about closures? Surely they're really scary, right? Well, not so much. Let's take a look at a simple example that should hopefully remind you of some of the examples we did for Scala in chapter 9:

```
1:5 user=> (defn adder [constToAdd] #(+ constToAdd %1))
#'user/adder
1:6 user=> (def plus2 (adder 2))
#'user/plus2
1:7 user=> (plus2 3)
5
1:8 user=> 1:9 user=> (plus2 5)
7
```

You first set up a function called (adder). This is a function that makes other functions. If you're familiar with the Factory Method pattern in Java, you can think of this as kind-of a Clojure equivalent. There's nothing strange about functions that have other functions as their return values—this is a key part of the concept that functions are just ordinary values.

Notice that this example uses the shorthand form #() for an anonymous function literal. The function (adder) takes in a number and returns a function, and the function returned from (adder) takes one argument.

You then use (adder) to define a new form: (plus2). This is a function that takes one numeric argument and adds 2 to it. That means the value that was bound to constToAdd inside (adder) was 2. Now let's make a new function:

```
1:13 user=> (def plus3 (adder 3))
#'user/plus3
1:14 user=> (plus3 4)
7
1:15 user=> (plus2 4)
6
```

This shows that you can make a different function, (plus3), that has a different value bound to constToAdd. We say that the functions (plus3) and (plus2) have captured, or "closed over" a value from their environment. Note that the values that were captured by (plus3) and (plus2) were different, and that defining (plus3) had no effect on the value captured by (plus2).

Functions that "close over" some values in their environment are called *closures*; (plus2) and (plus3) are examples of closures. The pattern whereby a function-making function returns another function that has closed over something is a very common one in languages that have closures.

Now let's turn to a powerful Clojure feature—sequences. These are used something like Java's collections or iterators, but they have somewhat different properties. Sequences are a major part of writing Clojure code that utilizes the strengths of the language, and they'll provide a fresh look at how Java handles similar concepts.

10.4 Introducing Clojure sequences

Consider the Java `Iterator`, as shown in the next code snippet. This is a slightly old-school way of using an iterator. In fact, this is what a Java 5 `for` loop is turned into under the covers:

```
Collection<String> c = ...;

for (Iterator<String> it = c.iterator(); it.hasNext();) {
  String str = it.next();
  ...
}
```

This is fine for looping over a simple collection, such as a `Set` or `List`. But the `Iterator` interface only has the `next()` and `hasNext()` methods, plus an optional `remove()` method.

CONCEPTUAL PROBLEMS WITH JAVA ITERATORS

There is a problem with Java iterators, however. The `Iterator` interface doesn't provide as rich a set of methods for interacting with a collection as you might want. With the Java `Iterator`, you can only do two things:

- Check to see whether the collection has any more elements in it
- Get the next element, and advance the iterator

The key to the problems with the `Iterator` is that getting the next element and advancing the iterator are combined into a single operation (figure 10.5). This means that there's no way of examining the next element in a collection, deciding that it needs special handling, and handing it off intact.

The very act of getting the next element from the iterator alters it. That is, mutation is built into Java's approach to collections and iterators, and it makes constructing a robust multipass solution all but impossible.

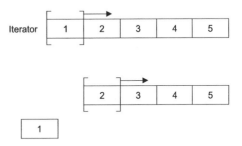

Figure 10.5   The nature of Java iterators

CLOJURE'S KEY ABSTRACTION

Clojure's approach to this subject differs. It has a powerful core abstraction that corresponds to collections and iterators in Java. This is the *sequence*, or seq. It essentially merges some of the features of both Java classes into one concept. This is motivated by wanting three things:

- More robust iterators, especially for multipass algorithms
- Immutability, allowing the seqs to be passed around between functions without a problem
- The possibility of lazy sequences (more on these later)

Some core functions that relate to sequences are shown in table 10.4. Note that none of these functions will mutate their input arguments; if they need to return a different value, it will be a different seq.

Table 10.4 Basic sequence functions

Function	Effect
(seq <coll>)	Returns a seq that acts as a "view" onto the collection acted upon.
(first <coll>)	Returns the first element of the collection, calling (seq) on it first if necessary. Returns nil if the collection is nil.
(rest <coll>)	Returns a new seq, made from the collection, minus the first element. Returns nil if the collection is nil.
(seq? <o>)	Returns true if o is a seq (meaning, if it implements ISeq).
(cons <elt> <coll>)	Returns a seq made from the collection, with the additional element prepended.
(conj <coll> <elt>)	Returns a new collection with the new element added to the appropriate end—the end for vectors and the head for lists.
(every? <pred-fn> <coll>)	Returns true if (pred-fn) returns logical-true for every item in the collection.

Here are a few examples:

```
1:1 user=> (rest '(1 2 3))
(2 3)
1:2 user=> (first '(1 2 3))
1
1:3 user=> (rest [1 2 3])
(2 3)
1:13 user=> (seq ())
nil
1:14 user=> (seq [])
nil
1:15 user=> (cons 1 [2 3])
(1 2 3)
1:16 user=> (every? is-prime [2 3 5 7 11])
true
```

One important point to note is that Clojure lists are their own seqs, but vectors aren't. In theory, that would mean that you shouldn't be able to call (rest) on a vector. The reason you're able to is that (rest) acts by calling (seq) on the vector before operating on it. This is a very common property of the seq construct—many of the sequence functions take more general objects than seqs, and will call (seq) on them before they begin.

In this section, we're going to explore some of the basic properties and uses of the seq abstraction, paying special attention to lazy sequences and variadic functions. The first of these concepts, laziness, is a programming technique that isn't often exploited in Java, so it may be new to you. Let's take a look at it now.

10.4.1 *Lazy sequences*

Laziness in programming languages is a powerful concept. Essentially, laziness allows an expression to be delayed in computation until it's required. In Clojure this means that rather than having a complete list of every value that's in a sequence, values can instead be obtained when they're required (such as by calling a function to generate them on demand).

In Java, such an idea would require something like a custom implementation of List, and there would be no convenient way to write it without large amounts of boilerplate code. Clojure comes with powerful macros designed to help you create lazy seqs with only a small amount of effort.

Consider how you could represent a lazy, potentially infinite sequence. One obvious choice would be to use a function to generate items in the sequence. The function should do two things:

- Return the next item in a sequence
- Take a fixed, finite number of arguments

Mathematicians would say that such a function defines a recurrence relation, and the theory of such relations immediately suggests that recursion is an appropriate way to proceed.

Imagine you have a machine in which stack space and other constraints aren't present, and suppose that you can set up two threads of execution: one will prepare the infinite sequence, and the other will use it. Then you could use recursion to define the lazy seq in the generation thread with something like the following snippet of pseudocode:

```
(defn infinite-seq <vec-args>
(let [new-val (seq-fn <vec-args>)]
  (cons new-val (infinite-seq <new-vec-args>))))
```

In actual Clojure, this doesn't work, because the recursion on (infinite-seq) blows the stack up. But by adding a construct that tells Clojure not to go crazy on the recursion, instead only proceeding as needed, you can do it.

Not only that, but you can do it within a single thread of execution, as the next example shows. The following listing defines the lazy sequence k, k+1, k+2, ... for some number k.

Listing 10.5 Lazy sequence example

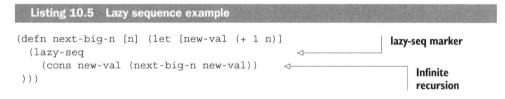

```
(defn next-big-n [n] (let [new-val (+ 1 n)]
  (lazy-seq                                        ⟵──  lazy-seq marker
    (cons new-val (next-big-n new-val))    ⟵────
)))                                                         Infinite
                                                            recursion
```

```
(defn natural-k [k]
  (concat [k] (next-big-n k)))      ◁──────────────────────
1:57 user=> (take 10 (natural-k 3))
(3 4 5 6 7 8 9 10 11 12)
```

**concat constrains
recursion**

The key points are the form (lazy-seq), which marks a point where an infinite recursion could occur, and the (concat) form, which handles it safely. You can then use the (take) form to pull the required number of elements from the lazy sequence, which is essentially defined by the form (next-big-n).

Lazy sequences are an extremely powerful feature, and with practice you'll find them a very useful tool in your Clojure arsenal.

10.4.2 Sequences and variable-arity functions

There is one powerful feature of Clojure's approach to functions that we've delayed discussing fully until now. This is the natural ability to easily have variable numbers of arguments to functions, sometimes called the *arity* of functions. Functions that accept variable numbers of parameters are called *variadic*.

As a trivial example, consider the constant function (const-fun1) that we discussed in listing 10.1. This function takes in a single argument and discards it, always returning the value 1. But consider what happens when you pass more than one argument to (const-fun1):

```
1:32 user=> (const-fun1 2 3)
java.lang.IllegalArgumentException: Wrong number of args (2) passed to:
user$const-fun1 (repl-1:32)
```

The Clojure compiler is still enforcing some runtime checks on the number (and types) of arguments passed to (const-fun1). For a function that simply discards all of its arguments and returns a constant value, this seems overly restrictive. What would a function that could take any number of arguments look like in Clojure?

Listing 10.6 shows how to do this for a version of the (const-fun1) constant function from earlier in the chapter. We've called it (const-fun-arity1), for *const-fun1* with variable *arity*. This is a homebrewed version of the (constantly) function provided in the Clojure standard function library.

Listing 10.6   Variable arity function

```
1:28 user=> (defn const-fun-arity1
  ([] 1)
  ([x] 1)
  ([x & more] 1)
 )
#'user/const-fun-arity1
1:33 user=> (const-fun-arity1)
1
1:34 user=>  (const-fun-arity1 2)
1
1:35 user=>  (const-fun-arity1 2 3 4)
1
```

**Multiple defns with
different signatures**

The key is that the function definition is followed not by a vector of function parameters and then a form defining the behavior of the function. Instead, there is a list of pairs, with each pair consisting of a vector of parameters (effectively the signature of this version of the function) and the implementation for this version of the function. This can be thought of as a similar concept to method overloading in Java. The usual convention is to define a few special-case forms (that take none, one, or two parameters) and an additional form that has as its last parameter a seq. In listing 10.6 this is the form that has the parameter vector of [x & more]. The & sign indicates that this is the variadic version of the function.

Sequences are a very powerful Clojure innovation. In fact, a large part of learning to think in Clojure is to start thinking about how the seq abstraction can be put to use to solve your specific coding problems.

Another important innovation in Clojure is the integration between Clojure and Java, which is the subject of the next section.

10.5 Interoperating between Clojure and Java

Clojure was designed from the ground up to be a JVM language and to not attempt to completely hide the JVM character from the programmer. These specific design choices are apparent in a number of places. For example, at the type-system level, Clojure's lists and vectors both implement List—the standard interface from the Java collections library. In addition, it's very easy to use Java libraries from Clojure and vice versa.

These properties are extremely useful, as it means that Clojure programmers can make use of the rich variety of Java libraries and tooling, as well as the performance and other features of the JVM. In this section, we'll cover a number of aspects of this interoperability decision, specifically

- Calling Java from Clojure
- How Java sees the type of Clojure functions
- Clojure proxies
- Exploratory programming with the REPL
- Calling Clojure from Java

Let's start exploring this integration by looking at how to access Java methods from Clojure.

10.5.1 Calling Java from Clojure

Consider this piece of Clojure code being evaluated in the REPL:

```
1:16 user=> (defn lenStr [y] (.length (.toString y)))
#'user/lenStr
1:17 user=> (schwartz ["bab" "aa" "dgfwg" "droopy"] lenStr)
("aa" "bab" "dgfwg" "droopy")
1:18 user=>
```

In this snippet, we've used the Schwartzian transform to sort a vector of strings by their lengths. To do that, we've used the forms (.toString) and (.length), which are Java methods. They're being called on the Clojure objects. The period at the start of the symbol means that the runtime should invoke the named method on the next argument. This is achieved by the use of the (.) macro under the covers.

All Clojure values defined by (def) or a variant of it are placed into instances of clojure.lang.Var, which can house any java.lang.Object, so any method that can be called on java.lang.Object can be called on a Clojure value. Some of the other forms for interacting with the Java world are

```
(System/getProperty "java.vm.version")
```

for calling static methods (in this case the System.getProperty() method) and

```
Boolean/TRUE
```

for accessing static public variables (such as constants). In these last two examples, we've implicitly used Clojure's namespaces concept. These are similar to Java packages, and have mappings from shorthand forms to Java package names for common cases, such as the preceding ones.

> **The nature of Clojure calls**
>
> A function call in Clojure is a true JVM method call. The JVM does not guarantee to optimize away tail recursion, which Lisps (especially Scheme implementations) usually do. Some other Lisp dialects on the JVM take the viewpoint that they want true tail recursion and so are prepared to have a Lisp function call not be exactly equivalent to a JVM method call under all circumstances. Clojure, however, fully embraces the JVM as a platform, even at the expense of full compliance with usual Lisp practice.

If you want to create a new instance of a Java object and manipulate it in Clojure, you can easily do so by using the (new) form. This has an alternative short form, which is the class name followed by the full stop, which boils down to another use of the (.) macro:

```
(import '(java.util.concurrent CountDownLatch LinkedBlockingQueue))
(def cdl (new CountDownLatch 2))
(def lbq (LinkedBlockingQueue.))
```

Here we're also using the (import) form, which allows multiple Java classes from a single package to be imported in just one line.

We mentioned earlier that there's a certain amount of alignment between Clojure's type system and that of Java. Let's take a look at this concept in a bit more detail.

10.5.2 *The Java type of Clojure values*

From the REPL, it's very easy to take a look at the Java types of some Clojure values:

```
1:8 user=> (.getClass "foo")
java.lang.String
```

```
1:9 user=> (.getClass 2.3)
java.lang.Double
1:10 user=> (.getClass [1 2 3])
clojure.lang.PersistentVector
1:11 user=> (.getClass '(1 2 3))
clojure.lang.PersistentList
1:12 user=> (.getClass (fn [] "Hello world!"))
user$eval110$fn__111
```

The first thing to notice is that all Clojure values are objects; the primitive types of the JVM aren't exposed by default (although there are ways of getting at the primitive types for the performance-conscious). As you might expect, the string and numeric values map directly onto the corresponding Java reference types (`java.lang.String`, `java.lang.Double`, and so on).

The anonymous `"Hello world!"` function has a name that indicates that it's an instance of a dynamically generated class. This class will implement the interface `clojure.lang.IFn`, which is the interface that Clojure uses to indicate that a value is a function, and it can be thought of as Clojure's equivalent to the `Callable` interface in `java.util.concurrent`.

Seqs will implement the `clojure.lang.ISeq` interface. They will typically be one of the concrete subclasses of the abstract `ASeq` or the single lazy implementation, `LazySeq`.

We've looked at the types of various values, but what about the storage for those values? As we mentioned at the start of this chapter, `(def)` binds a symbol to a value, and in doing so creates a var. These vars are objects of type `clojure.lang.Var` (which implements `IFn` amongst other interfaces).

10.5.3 Using Clojure proxies

Clojure has a powerful macro called `(proxy)` that enables you to create a bona fide Clojure object that extends a Java class (or implements an interface). For example, the next listing revisits an earlier example (listing 4.13), but the heart of the execution example is now done in a fraction of the code, due to Clojure's more compact syntax.

Listing 10.7   Revisiting scheduled executors

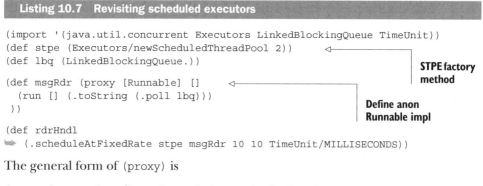

```
(import '(java.util.concurrent Executors LinkedBlockingQueue TimeUnit))
(def stpe (Executors/newScheduledThreadPool 2))        STPE factory
(def lbq (LinkedBlockingQueue.))                        method

(def msgRdr (proxy [Runnable] []
  (run [] (.toString (.poll lbq)))                      Define anon
  ))                                                    Runnable impl

(def rdrHndl
  (.scheduleAtFixedRate stpe msgRdr 10 10 TimeUnit/MILLISECONDS))
```

The general form of `(proxy)` is

```
(proxy [<superclass/interfaces>] [<args>] <impls of named functions>+)
```

The first vector argument holds the interfaces that this proxy class should implement. If the proxy should also extend a Java class (and it can, of course, only extend one Java class), that class name must be the first element of the vector.

The second vector argument comprises the parameters to be passed to a superclass constructor. This is quite often the empty vector, and it will certainly be empty for all cases where the (proxy) form is just implementing Java interfaces.

After these two arguments come the forms that represent the implementations of individual methods, as required by the interfaces or superclasses specified.

The (proxy) form allows for the simple implementation of any Java interface. This leads to an intriguing possibility—that of using the Clojure REPL as an extended playpen for experimenting with Java and JVM code.

10.5.4 *Exploratory programming with the REPL*

The key concept of exploratory programming is that with less code to write, due to Clojure's syntax, and the live, interactive environment that the REPL provides, the REPL can be a great environment for exploring not only Clojure programming, but for learning about Java libraries as well.

Let's consider the Java list implementations. They have an iterator() method that returns an object of type Iterator. But Iterator is an interface, so you might be curious about what the real implementing type is. Using the REPL, it's easy to find out:

```
1:41 user=> (import '(java.util ArrayList LinkedList))
java.util.LinkedList
1:42 user=> (.getClass (.iterator (ArrayList.)))
java.util.ArrayList$Itr
1:43 user=> (.getClass (.iterator (LinkedList.)))
java.util.LinkedList$ListItr
```

The (import) form brings in two different classes from the java.util package. Then you can use the getClass() Java method from within the REPL just as you did in section 10.5.2. As you can see, the iterators are actually provided by inner classes. This perhaps shouldn't be surprising; as we discussed in section 10.4, iterators are tightly bound up with the collections they come from, so they may need to see internal implementation details of those collections.

Notice that in the preceding example, we didn't use a single Clojure construct—just a little bit of syntax. Everything we were manipulating was a true Java construct. Let's suppose, though, that you wanted to use a different approach and use the powerful abstractions that Clojure brings within a Java program. The next subsection will show you just how to accomplish this.

10.5.5 *Using Clojure from Java*

Recall that Clojure's type system is closely aligned with Java's. The Clojure data structures are all true Java collections that implement the whole of the mandatory part of the Java interfaces. The optional parts aren't usually implemented, as they're often about mutation of the data structures, which Clojure doesn't support.

This alignment of type systems opens the possibility of using Clojure data structures in a Java program. This is made even more viable by the nature of Clojure itself—it's a compiled language with a calling mechanism that matches that of the JVM. This minimizes the runtime aspects and means a class obtained from Clojure can be treated almost like any other Java class. Interpreted languages would find it a lot harder to interoperate and would typically require a minimal non-Java language runtime for support.

The next example shows how Clojure's seq construct can be used on an ordinary Java string. For this code to run, clojure.jar will need to be on the classpath:

```
ISeq seq = StringSeq.create("foobar");
while (seq != null) {
  Object first = seq.first();
  System.out.println("Seq: "+ seq +" ; first: "+ first);
  seq = seq.next();
}
```

The preceding code snippet uses the factory method `create()` from the `StringSeq` class. This provides a seq view on the character sequence of the string. The `first()` and `next()` methods return new values, as opposed to mutating the existing seq, just as we discussed in section 10.4.

So far we've dealt solely with single-threaded Clojure code. In the next section, we'll move on to talk about concurrency in Clojure. In particular, we'll talk about Clojure's approach to state and mutability, which allows a model of concurrency that's quite different from Java's.

10.6 Concurrent Clojure

Java's model of state is based fundamentally around the idea of mutable objects. As we saw in chapter 4, this leads directly to problems with safety in concurrent code. We needed to introduce quite complicated locking strategies in order to prevent other threads from seeing intermediate (meaning *inconsistent*) objects states while a given thread was working on mutating an object's state. These strategies were hard to come up with, hard to debug, and harder to test.

Clojure's abstractions for concurrency aren't as low-level as Java's in some respects. For example, the use of threadpools that are managed by the Clojure runtime (and over which the developer has little or no control) may seem strange. But the power gained comes from allowing the platform (in this case, the Clojure runtime) to meticulously perform bookkeeping for you, to free up your mind for much more important tasks, such as overall design.

The philosophy guiding Clojure is to isolate threads from each other by default, which goes a long way to making the language concurrently type safe by default. By assuming a baseline of "nothing needs to be shared" and having immutable values, Clojure sidesteps a lot of Java's issues, and instead can focus on ways to share state safely for concurrent programming.

NOTE To help promote safety, Clojure's runtime provides mechanisms for coordinating between threads, and it's very strongly recommended that you use these mechanisms rather than trying to use Java idioms or making your own concurrency constructs.

In fact, there are several different methods that Clojure uses to provide different sorts of concurrency models—futures and pcalls, refs, and agents. Let's look at each in turn, starting with the simplest.

10.6.1 Futures and pcalls

The first, and most obvious, way to share state is not to. In fact, the Clojure construct that we've been using up until now, the var, isn't really able to be shared. If two different threads inherit the same name for a var, and rebind it in-thread, then those rebindings are only visible within those individual threads and can never be shared by other threads.

You can start new threads by exploiting Clojure's tight binding to Java. This means that you can write concurrent Java code very easily in Clojure. But some of these abstractions have a cleaned-up form within Clojure. For example, Clojure provides a very clean approach to the Future concept that we encountered in Java in chapter 4. The following listing shows a simple example.

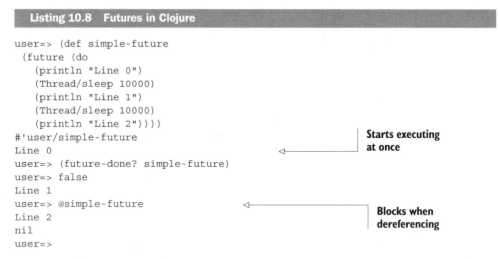

Listing 10.8 Futures in Clojure

```
user=> (def simple-future
  (future (do
    (println "Line 0")
    (Thread/sleep 10000)
    (println "Line 1")
    (Thread/sleep 10000)
    (println "Line 2"))))
#'user/simple-future
Line 0                                          Starts executing
                                                at once
user=> (future-done? simple-future)
user=> false
Line 1
user=> @simple-future
Line 2                                          Blocks when
nil                                             dereferencing
user=>
```

In this listing, you set up a Future with (future). As soon as this is created, it begins to run on a background thread, which is why you see the printout of Line 0 (and later Line 1) on the Clojure REPL—the code has started to run on another thread. You can then test to see whether the code has completed using (future-done?), which is a nonblocking call. The attempt to dereference the future, however, causes the calling thread to block until the function has completed.

This is effectively a thin Clojure wrapper over a Java Future, with some slightly cleaner syntax. Clojure also provides useful helper forms that can be very useful to the concurrent programmer. One simple function is (pcalls), which takes in a variable number of 0-argument functions and executes them in parallel. They're executed on a runtime-managed threadpool and will return a lazy seq of the results. Trying to access any elements of the seq that haven't yet completed will cause the accessing thread to block.

The next listing sets up a 1-argument function called (wait-with-for). This uses a loop form similar to the one introduced in section 10.3.2. From this, you create a number of 0-argument functions (wait-1), (wait-2), and so on, which you can feed to (pcalls).

Listing 10.9 Parallel calls in Clojure

```
user=> (defn wait-with-for [limit]
  (let [counter 1]
    (loop [ctr counter]
      (Thread/sleep 500)
      (println (str "Ctr=" ctr))
      (if (< ctr limit)
          (recur (inc ctr))
          ctr))))
#'user/wait-with-for
user=> (defn wait-1 [] (wait-with-for 1))
user=> #'user/wait-1
user=> (defn wait-2 [] (wait-with-for 2))
user=> #'user/wait-2
user=> (defn wait-3 [] (wait-with-for 3))
user=> #'user/wait-3
user=> (def wait-seq (pcalls wait-1 wait-2 wait-3))
#'user/wait-seq
Ctr=1
Ctr=1
Ctr=1
Ctr=2
Ctr=2
Ctr=3

user=> (first wait-seq)
1
user=> (first (next wait-seq))
2
```

With a thread sleep value of only 500 ms, the wait functions complete very quickly. By playing with the timeout (such as by extending it to 10 s), it's easy to verify that the lazy sequence called wait-seq that is returned by (pcalls) has the described blocking behavior.

This access to simple multithreaded constructs is fine for the case where you don't need to share state, but in many applications different processing threads need to communicate in flight. Clojure has a couple of models for handling this, so let's look at one of these next: the shared state enabled by the (ref) form.

10.6.2 Refs

Clojure's refs are a way of sharing state between threads. They rely on a model provided by the runtime for state changes that need to be seen by multiple threads. This model introduces an additional level of indirection between a symbol and a value. That is, a symbol is bound to a reference to a value, rather than directly to a value. The system is essentially transactional and is coordinated by the Clojure runtime. This is illustrated in figure 10.6.

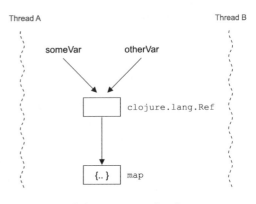

Figure 10.6 Software transactional memory

This indirection means that before a ref can be altered or updated, it has to be placed inside a transaction. When the transaction is completed, either all or none of the updates will take effect. This can be thought of as being like a transaction in a database.

This can seem a bit abstract, so let's look at an example and model an ATM. In Java, you're required to protect every sensitive bit of data with locks. The following listing shows a simple example of one way to model a cash machine, including the locks.

Listing 10.10 Modeling an ATM in Java

```
public class Account {
  private double balance = 0;
  private final String name;
  private final Lock lock = new ReentrantLock();

  public Account(String name_, double initialBal_){
    name = name_;
    balance = initialBal_;
  }

  public synchronized double getBalance(){
    return balance;
  }

  public synchronized void debit(double debitAmt_) {
    balance -= debitAmt_;
  }

  public String getName() {
    return name;
  }

  public String toString() {
    return "Account [balance=" + balance + ", name=" + name + "]";
  }

  public Lock getLock() {
    return lock;
```

```
      }
  }

public class Debitter implements Runnable {
  private final Account acc;
  private final CountDownLatch cdl;

  public Debitter(Account account_, CountDownLatch cdl_) {
    acc = account_;
    cdl = cdl_;
  }

  public void run() {
    double bal = acc.getBalance();
    Lock lk = acc.getLock();

    while (bal > 0) {
      try {
        Thread.sleep(1);
      } catch (InterruptedException e) { }
      lk.lock();
      bal = acc.getBalance();
      if (bal > 0) {
        acc.debit(1);
        bal--;
      }
      lk.unlock();
    }
    cdl.countDown();
  }
}

Account myAcc = new Account("Test Account", 500 * NUM_THREADS);
CountDownLatch stopl = new CountDownLatch(NUM_THREADS);

for (int i=0; i<NUM_THREADS; i++) {
  new Thread(new Debitter(myAcc, stopl)).start();
}
stopl.await();
System.out.println(myAcc);
```

Annotations in code:
- **Could synchronize on acc** → (points to `lk.lock();`)
- **Must re-get balance** → (points to `bal = acc.getBalance();`)

Let's see how you could rewrite this in Clojure. Let's start with a single-threaded version. Then we can develop a concurrent version and compare it to the single-threaded code. This should make the concurrent code easier to understand.

The following listing contains a simple single-threaded version.

Listing 10.11 Simple ATM model in Clojure

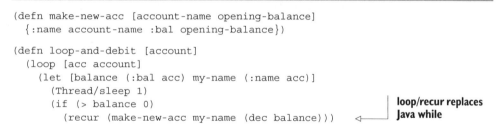

```
(defn make-new-acc [account-name opening-balance]
  {:name account-name :bal opening-balance})

(defn loop-and-debit [account]
  (loop [acc account]
    (let [balance (:bal acc) my-name (:name acc)]
      (Thread/sleep 1)
      (if (> balance 0)
        (recur (make-new-acc my-name (dec balance)))))
```

Annotation: **loop/recur replaces Java while** → (points to `(recur (make-new-acc my-name (dec balance)))`)

```
        acc
    ))))

(loop-and-debit (make-new-acc "Ben" 5000))
```

Notice how compact this code is compared to the Java version. Admittedly, this is still single-threaded, but it's a lot less code than was needed for Java. Running the code will give you the expected result—you end up with a map called acc with a zero balance. Now let's move to a concurrent form.

To make this code concurrent, you need to introduce Clojure's refs. These are created with the (ref) form and are JVM objects of type clojure.lang.Ref. Usually they're set up with a Clojure map to hold the state. You'll also need the (dosync) form, which sets up a transaction. Within this transaction, you'll also use the (alter) form, which can be used to modify a ref. The functions that make use of refs for this multithreaded ATM are shown in the following listing.

Listing 10.12   Multithreaded ATM

```
(defn make-new-acc [account-name opening-balance]
  (ref {:name account-name :bal opening-balance}))

(defn alter-acc [acc new-name new-balance]
  (assoc acc :bal new-balance :name new-name))        ◁————————  Must return
                                                                 value, not ref
(defn loop-and-debit [account]
  (loop [acc account]
    (let [balance (:bal @acc)
          my-name (:name @acc)]
      (Thread/sleep 1)
      (if (> balance 0)
        (recur (dosync (alter acc alter-acc my-name (dec balance)) acc))
        acc
    ))))

(def my-acc (make-new-acc "Ben" 5000))

(defn my-loop [] (let [the-acc my-acc]
  (loop-and-debit the-acc)
))

(pcalls my-loop my-loop my-loop my-loop my-loop)
```

As noted, the (alter-acc) function acts on a value and must return a value. The value acted upon is the local value visible to this thread during the transaction. This is called the *in-transaction value*. The value returned is the new value of the ref after the alter function returns. This value isn't visible outside the altering thread until you exit the transaction block defined by (dosync).

Other transactions may be proceeding at the same time as this one. If so, the Clojure STM system will keep track of that and will only allow a transaction to commit if it's consistent with other transactions that have committed since it started. If it's inconsistent, it will be rolled back and may be retried with an updated view of the world.

This retry behavior can cause problems if the transaction does anything that produces side effects (such as a log file or other output). It's up to you to keep the transactional parts as simple and as pure in the functional programming sense (meaning as side-effect free) as possible.

For some multithreaded approaches, this optimistic-transactional behavior can seem a rather heavyweight approach. Some concurrent applications only need to communicate between threads occasionally, and in a rather asymmetric fashion. Fortunately, Clojure provides another concurrency mechanism that is much more fire-and-forget, and it's the topic of our next section.

10.6.3 Agents

Agents are Clojure's asynchronous, message-oriented concurrency primitive. Instead of having shared state, a Clojure agent is a bit of state that belongs to another thread, but it will accept messages (in the form of functions) from another thread. This can seem like a strange idea at first, although perhaps less so after thinking about Scala's actors from section 9.5.

> "They must go by the carrier," she thought; "and how funny it'll seem, sending presents to one's own feet! And how odd the directions will look!"
>
> —Lewis Carroll, *Alice's Adventures in Wonderland*

The functions that are applied to the agent execute on the agent's thread. This thread is managed by the Clojure runtime, in a threadpool that isn't usually accessible to the programmer. The runtime also ensures that the values of the agent that are seen from outside are isolated and atomic. This means that user code will only see the value of the agent in its before or after state.

The following listing shows a simple example of agents, similar to the example used to discuss futures.

Listing 10.13 Clojure agents

```
(defn wait-and-log [coll str-to-add]
  (do (Thread/sleep 10000)
    (let [my-coll (conj coll str-to-add)]
      (Thread/sleep 10000)
      (conj my-coll str-to-add))))

(def str-coll (agent []))

(send str-coll wait-and-log "foo")

@str-coll
```

The send call dispatches a (wait-and-log) call to the agent, and by using the REPL to dereference it, you can see that, as promised, you never see an intermediate state of the agent—only the final state appears (where the "foo" string has been added twice).

In fact, the (send) call in listing 10.13 is rather reminiscent of the directions to Alice's feet. They could almost be written as Clojure code, because Carroll gives them as

```
Alice's Right Foot, Esq.
  Hearthrug,
    Near the Fender,
      (with Alice's love)
```

They do seem odd when you think that one's feet are an integral part of one's body. Similarly, it could seem odd that you'd send a message to an agent that's scheduled on a thread in a Clojure-managed threadpool, when both threads share an address space. But one of the themes in concurrency that you've now encountered several times is that additional complexity can be a good thing if it enables a simpler and clearer usage.

10.7   *Summary*

As a language, Clojure is arguably the most different from Java of the languages we've looked at. Its Lisp heritage, emphasis on immutability, and different approaches seem to make it into an entirely separate language. But its tight integration with the JVM, alignment of its type system (even when it provides alternatives, such as seqs), and the power of exploratory programming make it a very complementary language to Java.

Nowhere is this synergy clearer than in Clojure's delegation of many low-level aspects of threading and concurrency control to the runtime. This frees the programmer to focus on good multithreaded design and higher-level concerns. This is similar to the way in which Java's garbage collection facilities allow you to free yourself from the details of memory management.

The differences between the languages we've studied in this part clearly show the power of the Java platform to evolve, and to continue to be a viable destination for application development. This is also a testament to the flexibility and capability of the JVM.

In the final part of the book, we'll show how our three new languages provide new approaches to software engineering practices. The next chapter is all about test-driven development—a subject you may well have encountered in the Java world. But Groovy, Scala, and Clojure provide a brand-new perspective and will hopefully strengthen and reinforce what you already know.

Part 4

Crafting the polyglot project

In this final part of the book, we'll apply what we've learned about the platform and polyglot programming to some of the most common and important techniques in modern software development.

Being a well-grounded Java developer isn't simply about mastering the JVM and the languages that run on top of it. In order to successfully deliver software development projects, you should also follow the most important industry best practices. Fortunately, quite a few of these practices started out in the Java ecosystem, so there's plenty to talk about.

We'll devote an entire chapter to the fundamentals of test-driven development (TDD) and discuss how to apply the concept of test doubles to complex testing scenarios. Another chapter will be dedicated to the important practice of introducing a formal build lifecycle into your build process, including the technique of continuous integration. In those two chapters, you'll meet some standard tools, such as JUnit for testing, Maven for the build lifecycle, and Jenkins for continuous integration.

We'll also discuss web development for the Java 7 age, covering how you can decide which framework will work best for your project and how to develop with speed in this environment.

Following on from part 3, you'll learn that the non-Java languages we discussed have a huge role to play in the areas of TDD, build lifecycles, and rapid web development. Be it the ScalaTest framework for TDD or Grails (Groovy) and

Compojure (Clojure) frameworks for building web apps, many areas of the Java/JVM ecosystem are being affected by the arrival of these new languages.

We'll show you how to put the strengths of these new languages to work on familiar aspects of the software development craft. Combined with the solid foundations of the JVM and the Java ecosystem as a whole, you'll find that there are potentially big gains to be made by the developer who fully embraces the polyglot viewpoint.

In the concluding chapter of the book, we'll look into the future of the platform and make some predictions about what might lie ahead. Part 4 is all about frontiers, so turn the page, and let's start our push to the horizon.

Test-driven development

11

This chapter covers

- The benefits of practicing test-driven development (TDD)
- The red-green-refactor lifecycle at the heart of TDD
- A brief intro to JUnit, the de facto Java testing framework
- The four types of test double: dummy, fake, stub, and mock
- Testing against an in-memory database for your DAO code
- Mocking subsystems with Mockito
- Using ScalaTest, the testing framework for Scala

Test-driven development (TDD) has been part of the software development industry for quite some time. Its basic premise is that you write a test before writing the code that actually provides the implementation, and then you refactor that implementation as needed. For example, in order to write an implementation of concatenating two String objects ("foo" and "bar"), you'd write the test first (testing the result must equal `"foobar"`) to ensure that you know your implementation is correct.

Many developers already know about the JUnit testing framework and use it on a semi-regular basis. But more often than not, they're writing tests after they've written the implementation, and therefore are losing out on some of the major benefits of TDD.

Despite its seeming pervasiveness, many developers don't understand why they should be doing TDD. The question for many developers remains, "Why write test-driven code? What's the benefit?"

We believe that *eliminating fear and uncertainty* is the overriding reason you should write test-driven code. Kent Beck (co-inventor of the JUnit testing framework) also sums this up nicely in his book, *Test-Driven Development: by Example* (Addison-Wesley Professional, 2002):

- Fear makes you tentative.
- Fear makes you want to communicate less.
- Fear makes you shy away from feedback.
- Fear makes you grumpy.

TDD takes away the fear, making the well-grounded Java developer a more confident, communicative, receptive, and happier developer. In other words, TDD helps you break free from the mindset that leads to statements like these:

- When starting a new piece of work, "I don't know where to start, so I'll just start hacking."
- When changing existing code, "I don't know how the existing code is going to behave, so I'm secretly too scared to change it."

TDD brings many other benefits that aren't always immediately obvious:

- *Cleaner code*—You write only the code you need
- *Better design*—Some developers call TDD *test-driven design*
- *Greater flexibility*—TDD encourages coding to interfaces
- *Fast feedback*—You learn about bugs *now*, not in production

One barrier for developers who are just getting started is that TDD can sometimes be viewed as a technique that isn't used by "ordinary" developers. The perception can be that only practitioners of some imaginary "Church of Agile" or other esoteric movement use TDD. This perception is completely false, as we'll demonstrate. TDD is a technique for every developer.

In addition, agile approaches and the software craftsmanship movement are all about making life easier for developers. They're certainly not out to exclude others from using TDD or any other technique.

This chapter will begin by explaining the basic idea behind TDD—the red-green-refactor loop. Then we'll introduce the workhorse of Java testing, JUnit, and look at a simple example that illustrates the principles.

The Agile Manifesto and the Software Craftsmanship movement

The Agile movement (http://agilemanifesto.org/) has been around for a long time and has arguably changed parts of our software development industry for the better. Many great techniques, such as TDD, were championed as part of this movement. Software Craftsmanship is a newer movement that encourages its practitioners to write clean code (http://manifesto.softwarecraftsmanship.org/).

We like to tease our Agile and Software Craftsmanship practicing brethren. Heck, we even champion these practices ourselves (most of the time). But let's not lose sight of what is useful for you, the well-grounded Java developer. TDD is a software development technique, nothing more, nothing less.

Next, we'll move on to covering the four main types of make-believe objects that are used in TDD. These are important because they simplify the process of isolating the code under test versus the code in a third-party library or the behavior of a subsystem such as a database. As these dependencies become more complicated, you need smarter and smarter pretend objects to help you. At the extreme end, we'll introduce mocking and the Mockito library, a popular mocking tool that works with Java to help you isolate your tests from these external influences.

The Java testing frameworks (especially JUnit) are pretty well known to developers, and you'll probably have some experience in writing tests with them. But you may not be familiar with how to test drive new languages such as Scala and Clojure. We'll make sure that you can apply a TDD methodology to your development by introducing you to ScalaTest, the testing framework for Scala.

Let's begin with an introduction to TDD with a bit of a twist.

11.1 TDD in a nutshell

TDD can be applied at many levels. Table 11.1 lists the four levels of testing that the TDD approach is usually applied to.

Table 11.1 Levels of TDD testing

Level	Description	Example
Unit	Tests to verify code contained in a class	Test methods in the `BigDecimal` class.
Integration	Tests to verify interaction between classes	Test the `Currency` class and how it interacts with `BigDecimal`.
System	Tests to verify a running system	Test the accounting system from the UI through to the `Currency` class.
System integration	Tests to verify a running system, including third-party components	Test the accounting system, including its interactions with the third-party reporting system.

It's easiest to use TDD at the unit testing level, and if you're unfamiliar with TDD, this is a good place to start. This section will mainly deal with using TDD at the unit test level. Later sections will cover other levels, when discussing testing against third-parties and subsystems.

> **TIP** Dealing with existing code that has very few or no tests can be a daunting task. It's almost impossible to retroactively fill in all of the tests. Instead, you should simply add tests for each new bit of functionality that you add. See Michael Feathers' excellent book *Working Effectively with Legacy Code* (Prentice Hall, 2004) for further help.

We'll start with brief coverage of the red-green-refactor premise behind TDD, using JUnit to test drive code for calculating sales revenue for selling theater tickets.[1] As long as you follow this red-green-refactor premise, you're fundamentally practicing TDD! We'll then go into some of the philosophical ideas behind red-green-refactor that will make clear why you should use that technique. Last, we'll introduce JUnit, the de facto testing framework for Java developers; we'll cover the basics of using this library.

Let's start with a working example of the three basic steps of TDD—the red-green-refactor loop—by calculating the revenue when selling theater tickets.

11.1.1 *A TDD example with a single use case*

If you're an experienced TDD practitioner, you may want to skip this small example, although we'll offer insights that are likely to be new. Suppose you've been asked to write a rock-solid method to calculate the revenue generated by selling a number of theater tickets. The initial business rules from the theater company's accountant are simple:

- The baseline price of a ticket is $30.
- Total revenue = number of tickets sold * price.
- The theater seats 100 people.

As the theater doesn't have very good point of sale software, the user currently has to manually enter the number of tickets sold.

If you have practiced TDD, you'll be familiar with the three basic steps of TDD: red, green, refactor. If you're new to TDD or are looking for a little refresher, let's take a look at Kent Beck's definition of those steps, from *Test-Driven Development: by Example*.

1 *Red*—Write a little test that doesn't work (*failing test*).
2 *Green*—Make that test pass as quickly as possible (*passing test*).
3 *Refactor*—Eliminate the duplication (*refined passing test*).

To give you an idea of the `TicketRevenue` implementation that we're trying to achieve, here is some pseudocode you might have in your head.

```
estimateRevenue(int numberOfTicketsSold)

if (numberOfTicketsSold is less than 0 OR greater than 100)
then
```

---

[1] Selling theater tickets is big business in London, our home while writing this book.

```
      Deal with error and exit
else
    revenue = 30 * numberOfTicketsSold;
    return revenue;
endif
```

Note that it's important that you don't think too deeply about this. The tests will end up driving your design and partly your implementation too.

> **NOTE** In section 11.1.2, we'll cover the ways in which you can start with a failing test, but a key concept for this example is that we're going to write a test that won't even compile!

Let's begin by writing a failing unit test using the popular JUnit framework. If you aren't familiar with JUnit, jump forward and to section 11.1.4, then return here.

WRITING A FAILING TEST (RED)

The point in this step is to start with a test that fails. In fact, the test won't even compile, because you haven't even written a `TicketRevenue` class yet!

After a brief whiteboard session with the accountant, you realize that you'll want to write tests for five cases: ticket sales that are negative, 0, 1, 2–100, and > 100.

> **TIP** A good rule of thumb when writing tests (especially involving numbers) is to think of the zero/null case, the one case, and the many (*N*) case. A step beyond that is to think about other constraints on *N*, such as a negative amount or an amount beyond a maximum limit.

To begin, you decide to write a test that covers the revenue received from one ticket sale. Your JUnit test would look similar to the following code (remember we're not writing a perfect, passing test at this stage).

Listing 11.1 Failing unit test for `TicketRevenue`

```java
import java.math.BigDecimal;
import static junit.framework.Assert.*;
import org.junit.Before;
import org.junit.Test;
public class TicketRevenueTest {

  private TicketRevenue venueRevenue;
  private BigDecimal expectedRevenue;

  @Before
  public void setUp() {
    venueRevenue = new TicketRevenue();
  }

  @Test
  public void oneTicketSoldIsThirtyInRevenue() {          ⟵────────  One sold case
    expectedRevenue = new BigDecimal("30");
    assertEquals(expectedRevenue, venueRevenue.estimateTotalRevenue(1));
  }
}
```

As you can see from the code, the test quite clearly expects the revenue from one ticket sale to equal 30 in revenue.

But as it stands, this test won't compile, because you haven't written a TicketRevenue class with the estimateTotalRevenue(int numberOfTicketsSold) method. In order to make the compilation error go away so that you can run the test, you can add a random implementation so that the test will compile.

```
public class TicketRevenue {
  public BigDecimal estimateTotalRevenue(int i) {
      return BigDecimal.ZERO;
  }
}
```

Now that the test compiles, you can run it from your favorite IDE. Each IDE has its own way of running JUnit tests, but generally speaking they all allow you to right-click on the test class and select a Run Test option. Once you do that, the IDE will generally update a window or section that informs you that your test has failed, because the expected value of 30 was not returned by the call to estimateTotalRevenue(1); instead 0 was returned.

Now that you have a failing test, the next step is to make the test pass (go green).

WRITING A PASSING TEST (GREEN)

The point in this step is to make the test pass, but the implementation doesn't have to be perfect. By providing the TicketRevenue class with a better implementation of estimateTotalRevenue (an implementation that doesn't just return 0), you'll make the test pass (go green).

Remember, at this stage, you're trying to make the test pass without necessarily writing perfect code. Your initial solution might look something like the following code.

> **Listing 11.2   First version of `TicketRevenue` that passes the test**

```
import java.math.BigDecimal;

public class TicketRevenue {

  public BigDecimal estimateTotalRevenue(int numberOfTicketsSold) {
    BigDecimal totalRevenue = BigDecimal.ZERO;
    if (numberOfTicketsSold == 1) {
      totalRevenue = new BigDecimal("30");       ◁─────────────┐  Implementation
    }                                                          │  that passes test
    return totalRevenue;
  }
}
```

When you now run the test, it will pass, and in most IDEs that will be indicated with a green bar or tick. Figure 11.1 shows how a passing test looks in the Eclipse IDE.

The next question is, should you then say "I'm done!" and move on to the next bit of work? The resounding answer here should be "No!" Like us, you'll be itching to tidy up the previous code listing, so let's get into that right now.

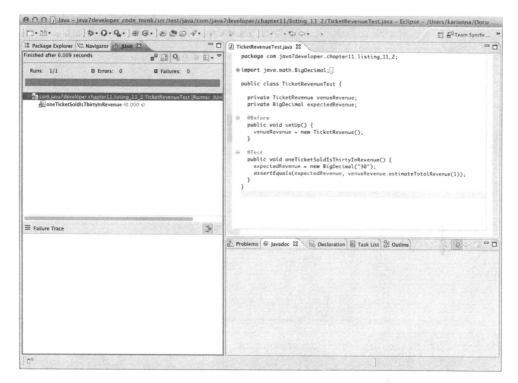

Figure 11.1 A green bar, shown in the print book in medium gray, indicates a passing test in the Eclipse IDE

REFACTORING THE TEST

The point of this step is to look at the quick implementation you wrote in order to pass the test and make sure that you're following accepted practice. Clearly the code in listing 11.2 isn't as clean and tidy as it could be. You can certainly refactor it and reduce technical debt for yourself and others in the future.

> **TECHNICAL DEBT** A metaphor coined by Ward Cunningham that refers to the extra cost (effort) that you pay later when you make a quick and dirty design or code decision now.

Remember, now that you have a passing test, you can *refactor without fear.* There's no chance of losing sight of the business logic that you're supposed to implement.

> **TIP** Another benefit that you've given yourself and the broader team by writing the initial passing test is a faster overall development process. The rest of the team can immediately take this first version of the code and begin to test it alongside the larger codebase (for integration tests and beyond).

In this example, you don't want to be using magic numbers—you want to make sure that the ticket price of 30 is a named concept in the code.

Listing 11.3 Refactored version of `TicketRevenue` that passes the test

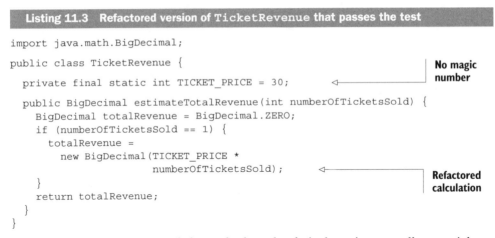

```
import java.math.BigDecimal;

public class TicketRevenue {

  private final static int TICKET_PRICE = 30;          ◄──────── No magic
                                                                 number
  public BigDecimal estimateTotalRevenue(int numberOfTicketsSold) {
    BigDecimal totalRevenue = BigDecimal.ZERO;
    if (numberOfTicketsSold == 1) {
      totalRevenue =
        new BigDecimal(TICKET_PRICE *
                      numberOfTicketsSold);            ◄──────── Refactored
    }                                                            calculation
    return totalRevenue;
  }
}
```

The refactoring has improved the code, but clearly it doesn't cover all potential use cases (negative, 0, 2–100, and > 100 ticket sales). Instead of trying to guess what the implementation should look like for the other use cases, you should have further tests drive the design and the implementation. The next section follows test-driven design by taking you through more use cases in this ticket revenue example.

11.1.2 *A TDD example with multiple use cases*

If you're following a particular style of TDD, you'll continue to add one test at a time for the negative, 0, 2–100, and > 100 ticket sale test cases. But another valid approach can be to write a set of test cases up front, especially if they're related to the original test.

Note that it's still very important to follow the red-green-refactor lifecycle here. After adding all of these use cases, you might end up with a test class with failing tests (red) as follows.

Listing 11.4 Failing unit tests for `TicketRevenue`

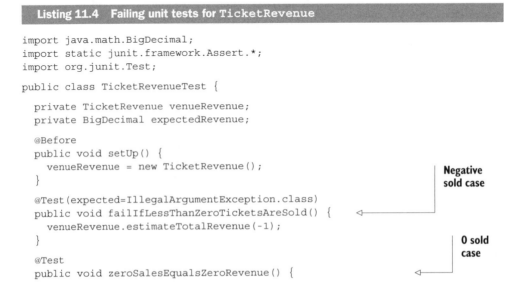

```
import java.math.BigDecimal;
import static junit.framework.Assert.*;
import org.junit.Test;

public class TicketRevenueTest {

  private TicketRevenue venueRevenue;
  private BigDecimal expectedRevenue;

  @Before
  public void setUp() {
    venueRevenue = new TicketRevenue();               ◄──────── Negative
  }                                                              sold case

  @Test(expected=IllegalArgumentException.class)
  public void failIfLessThanZeroTicketsAreSold() {    ◄─────
    venueRevenue.estimateTotalRevenue(-1);
  }                                                             0 sold
                                                                case
  @Test
  public void zeroSalesEqualsZeroRevenue() {          ◄─────
```

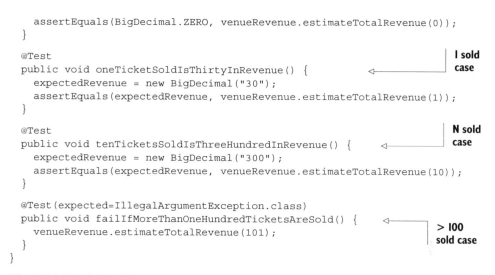

```
    assertEquals(BigDecimal.ZERO, venueRevenue.estimateTotalRevenue(0));
  }

  @Test                                                                    I sold
  public void oneTicketSoldIsThirtyInRevenue() {           ◄───────┘       case
    expectedRevenue = new BigDecimal("30");
    assertEquals(expectedRevenue, venueRevenue.estimateTotalRevenue(1));
  }

  @Test                                                                    N sold
  public void tenTicketsSoldIsThreeHundredInRevenue() {    ◄───────┘       case
    expectedRevenue = new BigDecimal("300");
    assertEquals(expectedRevenue, venueRevenue.estimateTotalRevenue(10));
  }

  @Test(expected=IllegalArgumentException.class)
  public void failIfMoreThanOneHundredTicketsAreSold() {   ◄─────┐         > 100
    venueRevenue.estimateTotalRevenue(101);                      │         sold case
  }
}
```

The initial basic implementation in order to pass all of those tests (green) would then look something like the following listing.

Listing 11.5   First version of `TicketRevenue` that passes the tests

```
import java.math.BigDecimal;

public class TicketRevenue {

  public BigDecimal estimateTotalRevenue(int numberOfTicketsSold)
    throws IllegalArgumentException {

    BigDecimal totalRevenue = null;
    if (numberOfTicketsSold < 0) {
      throw new IllegalArgumentException("Must be > -1");      ◄─┐
    }
    if (numberOfTicketsSold == 0) {
      totalRevenue = BigDecimal.ZERO;
    }
    if (numberOfTicketsSold == 1) {                                Exceptional
      totalRevenue = new BigDecimal("30");                         cases
    }
    if (numberOfTicketsSold == 101) {
      throw new IllegalArgumentException("Must be < 101");     ◄─┘
    }
    else {
      totalRevenue =
          new BigDecimal(30 * numberOfTicketsSold);           ◄─────┐    N sold
    }                                                                │    case
    return totalRevenue;
  }
}
```

With the implementation just completed, you now have passing tests.

Again, by following the TDD lifecycle, you'll now refactor that implementation. For example, you could combine the illegal `numberOfTicketsSold` cases (< 0 or > 100) into one `if` statement and use a formula (`TICKET_PRICE * numberOfTicketsSold`) to return the revenue for all other legal values of `numberOfTicketsSold`. The following code listing should be similar to what you would come up with.

Listing 11.6   `TicketRevenue`, refactored

```java
import java.math.BigDecimal;

public class TicketRevenue {

  private final static int TICKET_PRICE = 30;

  public BigDecimal estimateTotalRevenue(int numberOfTicketsSold)
    throws IllegalArgumentException {

    if (numberOfTicketsSold < 0 || numberOfTicketsSold > 100) {      ◁————————  Exceptional
      throw new IllegalArgumentException                                        case
              ("# Tix sold must == 1..100");
    }

    return new BigDecimal                                            ◁————————  All other
            (TICKET_PRICE * numberOfTicketsSold);                               cases
  }
}
```

The `TicketRevenue` class is now far more compact and yet still passes all of the tests! Now you've completed the full red-green-refactor cycle and can confidently move on to your next piece of business logic. Alternatively, you can start the cycle again, should you (or the accountant) spot any edge cases you've missed, such as having a variable ticket price.

We highly recommend understanding the reasoning behind using the red-green-refactor TDD approach, which we'll discuss next. But if you're impatient, you can jump to section 11.1.4 to learn more about JUnit, or section 11.2 to learn about test doubles for testing with third-party code.

11.1.3   *Further thinking on the red-green-refactor lifecycle*

This section builds on top of the working example and explores some of the thinking behind TDD. Once more, we'll cover the red-green-refactor lifecycle, and as you'll recall, the first step is to write a failing test. But there are a couple of approaches you can take.

FAILING TEST (RED)

Some developers prefer to write a test that actually fails compilation, preferring to wait for the green step before providing any implementation code. Other developers prefer to at least stub out the methods that the test is calling so that the test compiles, yet still fails. We find either style is fine. Choose what you feel most comfortable with.

> **TIP**   These tests are the first client for your code, so you should think carefully about their design—what the method definitions should look like. Some questions you should ask yourself are what parameters do you want to pass in?

What are the expected return values? Will there be any exceptional cases? Also, don't forget to have tests for the all-important domain object `equals()` and `hashCode()` methods.

Once you've written your failing test, it's time to move on to the next stage: getting it to pass.

PASSING TEST (GREEN)

In this step, you should be trying to write the minimal code required to make the test pass. This doesn't mean you need to write the perfect implementation! That comes in the refactoring stage.

Once the test passes, you can indicate to others in your team that your code does what it says on the tin, and that they can start to use it.

REFACTOR

In this step, you should start by refactoring your implementation code. There's an infinite number of categories that you can refactor on. There are some obvious refactorings, such as removing hardcoded variables or splitting a method into two. If you're developing object-oriented code, the SOLID principles are a good guideline to follow.

Coined by Robert "Uncle Bob" Martin, the SOLID principles are summarized in table 11.2. See his article, "The Principles of OOD" (http://butunclebob.com/ArticleS.UncleBob.PrinciplesOfOod), for further details on the SOLID principles.

Table 11.2 Principles of SOLID object-oriented code

Principle	Description
Single responsibility principle (SRP)	Each object should do one thing, and one thing only.
Open/closed principle (OCP)	Objects should be extensible but not modifiable.
Liskov substitution principle (LSP)	Objects should be replaceable by their subtypes.
Interface segregation principle (ISP)	Small specific interfaces are better.
Dependency inversion principle (DIP)	Don't depend on concrete implementations. (See chapter 3, on Dependency Injection, for further details.)

TIP We also recommend using static code analysis tools such as Checkstyle and FindBugs (more on these in chapter 12). Another useful resource is Joshua Bloch's *Effective Java*, second edition (Addison-Wesley, 2008), which is full of tips and tricks for dealing with the Java language.

An area that's often forgotten is the refactoring of the test itself. You'll more often than not be able to extract some common setup and teardown code, rename the test so that it more accurately reflects the test's intent, and make other small fixes recommended by static analysis tools.

Now that you're up to speed with the three steps of TDD, it's time to get familiar with JUnit, the default tool you'll reach for when writing TDD code in Java.

11.1.4 JUnit

JUnit is the de facto testing framework for Java projects. There are alternatives to JUnit, such as TestNG, which has vocal adherents, but the simple fact is that the majority of Java shops run on JUnit.

NOTE   If you're already familiar with JUnit, you can jump to section 11.2.

JUnit provides the following three main features:

- Assertions to test for expected results and exceptions, such as `assertEquals()`.
- The ability to set up and tear down common test data, such as `@Before` and `@After`.
- Test runners for running suites of tests.

As you can see, JUnit makes use of a simple annotation-driven model that provides much of the important functionality.

Most IDEs (such as Eclipse, IntelliJ, and NetBeans) have JUnit built in, so you won't have to download, install, or configure JUnit if you're using one of those IDEs. If your IDE doesn't support JUnit out of the box, you can visit www.junit.org for instructions on downloading and installing it.[2]

NOTE   For the purposes of the examples in this chapter, we used JUnit 4.8.2. We recommend you use the same version if you are following the examples.

A basic JUnit test is laid out with the following elements.

- An `@Before` annotated method for setting up test data before each test run
- An `@After` annotated method that tears down the test data after each test run
- The tests themselves (marked by the `@Test` annotation)

To highlight these elements, we'll look at a couple of very basic JUnit tests.

Let's say you're helping the OpenJDK team write unit tests against the `BigDecimal` class. There's one test to check the use case of the `add` method (`1.5 + 1.5 == 3.0`) and a second test to check that a `NumberFormatException` gets thrown when trying to create a `BigDecimal` with a value that isn't a number.

NOTE   For the code examples in this chapter, we often show more than one failing test, implementation (green), and refactoring at a time. This goes against the pure TDD approach of going through the red-green-refactor cycle for a *single* test, but it allows us to fit more examples in the chapter. We recommend that, in your coding, you try to follow the single test model of development as much as possible.

You can run the code in the following listing in your IDE by right-clicking on the source code and selecting the run or test option (remember, the three major IDEs all have an obvious option that's something like Run Test or Run File).

---

[2]   We cover integrating JUnit with the Maven build tool in chapter 12.

Listing 11.7   Basic JUnit test structure

```
import java.math.BigDecimal;
import org.junit.*;                           Standard JUnit
import static org.junit.Assert.*;             imports

public class BigDecimalTest {

  private BigDecimal x;

  @Before
  public void setUp() { x = new BigDecimal("1.5"); }    ❶ Set up before
                                                           each test
  @After
  public void tearDown() { x = null; }                  ❷ Tear down after
                                                           each test
  @Test
  public void addingTwoBigDecimals() {                  ❸ Perform
    assertEquals(new BigDecimal("3.0"), x.add(x));         test
  }

  @Test(expected=NumberFormatException.class)
  public void numberFormatExceptionIfNotANumber() {     Deal with expected
    x = new BigDecimal("Not a number");               ❹ exception
  }

}
```

Before each test is run, x is set to BigDecimal("1.5") in the @Before section ❶. This ensures that each test is dealing with a known value of x, as opposed to an intermediate value of x altered by one of the previous running tests. After each test is run, you make sure that x is set to null in the @After section ❷ (so that x can be garbage-collected). You then test that BigDecimal.add() works as expected using assertEquals() ❸ (one of JUnit's many static assertX methods). In order to deal with expected exceptions, you add the optional expected parameter to the @Test annotation ❹.

The best way to get into the TDD groove is to start practicing. With the TDD principles firmly in your mind, and with an understanding of the practical JUnit framework, you can get started! As you've seen in the examples, TDD at the unit-testing level is fairly easy to grasp.

But all TDD practitioners eventually run across the problem of testing code that utilizes a dependency or subsystem. The next section will cover techniques you can use to effectively test those.

11.2   Test doubles

As you continue to write code in a TDD style, you'll quickly run into the situation where your code references some (often third-party) dependency or subsystem. In this situation, you'll typically want to ensure that the code under test is isolated from that dependency to ensure that you're only writing test code against what you're actually building. You'll also want the tests to run as quickly as possible. Invoking a third-party dependency or subsystem, such as a database, can take a lot of time, which means you lose the fast feedback benefit that TDD gives you (this is especially true of unit-test level testing). *Test doubles* are the solution to this problem.

In this section, you'll learn how a test double can help you to effectively isolate dependencies and subsystems. You'll work through examples that use the four types of test double (dummy, stub, fake, and mock).

At the most complex end of the spectrum, where you're testing against external dependencies (such as distributed or networked services), the technique of Dependency Injection (discussed in chapter 3) in combination with test doubles can come to your rescue, even for systems that seem dauntingly large.

> ### Why aren't you using Guice?
>
> If chapter 3 is fresh in your mind, you'll remember Guice—the reference implementation DI framework for Java. As you read through this section, you'll likely ask yourself, "Why don't they use Guice here?"
>
> The simple answer is that the code listings don't warrant the extra complexity that even a simple framework like Guice adds. Remember, DI is a technique. You don't always need to introduce a framework in order to apply it.

We like Gerard Meszaros's simple explanation of a test double in his *xUnit Test Patterns* book (Addison-Wesley Professional, 2007), so we'll gladly quote him here: "A *Test Double* (think Stunt Double) is the generic term for any kind of pretend object used in place of a real object for testing purposes."

Meszaros continues to define four kinds of test doubles, which are outlined table 11.3.

Table 11.3   **The four types of test double**

Type	Description
Dummy	An object that is passed around but never used. Typically used to fulfill the parameter list of a method.
Stub	An object that always returns the same canned response. May also hold some dummy state.
Fake	An actual working implementation (not of production quality or configuration) that can replace the real implementation.
Mock	An object that represents a series of expectations and provides canned responses.

The four types of test doubles are far easier to understand when you work through code examples that use them. Let's go do that now, starting with the dummy object.

11.2.1 *Dummy object*

A *dummy* object is the easiest of the four test double types to use. Remember, it's designed to help fill parameter lists or fulfill some mandatory field requirements where you know the object will never get used. In many cases, you can even pass in an empty or `null` object.

Let's go back to the theater tickets scenario. It's all very well having an estimate of the revenue coming in from your single kiosk, but the owners of the theater have started to think a bit bigger. Better modeling of the tickets sold and the revenue expected is needed, and you're hearing murmurings of more requirements and complexity coming down the pipe.

You've been asked to keep track of the tickets sold, and to allow for a 10 percent discounted price on some tickets. It looks like you're going to need a `Ticket` class that provides a discounted price method. You start the familiar TDD cycle with a failing test, focusing on a new `getDiscountPrice()` method. You also know that there will need to be a couple of constructors—one for a regular priced ticket, and one where the face value of the ticket may vary. The `Ticket` object will ultimately expect two arguments:

- The client name—A `String` that won't be referenced at all for this test
- The normal price—A `BigDecimal` that will get used for this test

You're pretty sure that the client name won't be referenced in the `getDiscount-Price()` method. This means you can pass the constructor a dummy object (in this case, the arbitrary string `"Riley"`) as shown in the following code.

> **Listing 11.8 `TicketTest` implementation using a dummy object**

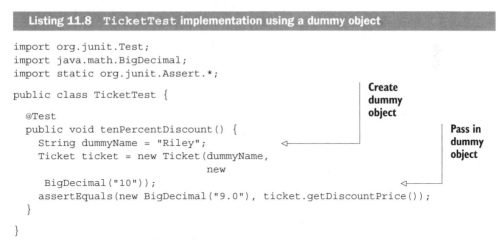

```
import org.junit.Test;
import java.math.BigDecimal;
import static org.junit.Assert.*;

public class TicketTest {

  @Test
  public void tenPercentDiscount() {
    String dummyName = "Riley";                  ← Create dummy object
    Ticket ticket = new Ticket(dummyName,
                        new
      BigDecimal("10"));                          ← Pass in dummy object
    assertEquals(new BigDecimal("9.0"), ticket.getDiscountPrice());
  }

}
```

As you can see, the concept of a dummy object is trivial.

To make the concept extremely clear, the code in the following listing has a partial implementation of the `Ticket` class.

> **Listing 11.9 `Ticket` class to test against using a dummy object**

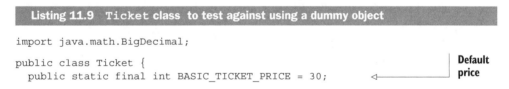

```
import java.math.BigDecimal;

public class Ticket {
  public static final int BASIC_TICKET_PRICE = 30;     ← Default price
```

```
private static final BigDecimal DISCOUNT_RATE =
                        new BigDecimal("0.9");              ◄───────┐   Default
                                                                   │   discount
private final BigDecimal price;
private final String clientName;

public Ticket(String clientName) {
  this.clientName = clientName;
  price = new BigDecimal(BASIC_TICKET_PRICE);
}

public Ticket(String clientName, BigDecimal price) {
  this.clientName = clientName;
  this.price = price;
}

public BigDecimal getPrice() {
  return price;
}

public BigDecimal getDiscountPrice() {
  return price.multiply(DISCOUNT_RATE);
}
}
```

Some developers become confused by dummy objects—they look for complexity that doesn't exist. Dummy objects are very straightforward—they're any old object used to avoid NullPointerException and to get the code to run.

Let's move on to the next type of test double. The next step up (in terms of complexity) is the stub object.

11.2.2 Stub object

You typically use a *stub* object when you want to replace a real implementation with an object that will return the same response every time. Let's return to our theater ticket pricing example to see this in action.

You've come back from a well-deserved holiday after implementing the Ticket class, and the first thing in your inbox is a bug report stating that your tenPercent-Discount() test from listing 11.8 is now failing intermittently. When you look into the codebase, you see that the tenPercentDiscount() method has been altered. The Ticket instance is now created using a concrete HttpPrice class that implements a newly introduced Price interface.

Upon further investigation, you discover that a getInitialPrice() method on the HttpPrice class is called in order to get the initial price from an external website via the third-party HttpPricingService class.

This call to getInitialPrice() can therefore return a different price each time, and it can also fail intermittently for a number of reasons. Sometimes the company firewall rules change, and other times the third-party website is simply unavailable.

Your test is therefore failing, and the purpose of the test has unfortunately been polluted. Remember, all you wanted the unit test to do was to calculate the 10 percent discount!

NOTE Calling a third-party pricing site is certainly not part of the test's responsibility. But you could think of having separate system integration tests that cover the HttpPrice class and its third-party HttpPricingService.

Before you replace the HttpPrice class with a stub, take a look at the current state of the code, as shown in the three following code listings (listings 11.10–11.12). In addition to the changes involving the Price interface, the theater owners have changed their minds and no longer want to record the names of people who purchase tickets, as the following listing demonstrates.

Listing 11.10   `TicketTest` implementation with new requirements

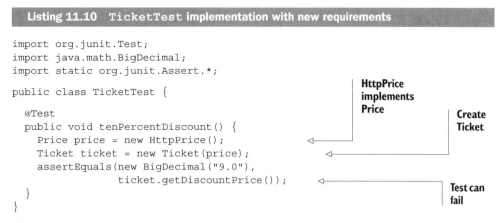

```
import org.junit.Test;
import java.math.BigDecimal;
import static org.junit.Assert.*;

public class TicketTest {

  @Test
  public void tenPercentDiscount() {
    Price price = new HttpPrice();
    Ticket ticket = new Ticket(price);
    assertEquals(new BigDecimal("9.0"),
              ticket.getDiscountPrice());
  }
}
```

HttpPrice implements Price

Create Ticket

Test can fail

The next listing shows the new implementation of Ticket, which now includes a private class, FixedPrice, to deal with the simple case where a price is known and fixed, rather than derived from some external source.

Listing 11.11   `Ticket` implementation with new requirements

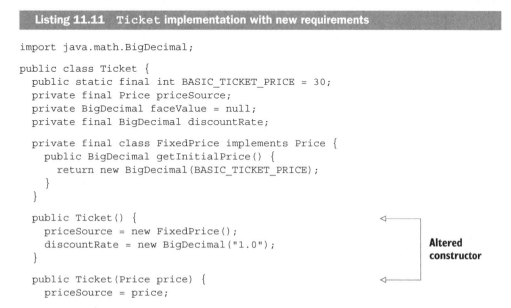

```
import java.math.BigDecimal;

public class Ticket {
  public static final int BASIC_TICKET_PRICE = 30;
  private final Price priceSource;
  private BigDecimal faceValue = null;
  private final BigDecimal discountRate;

  private final class FixedPrice implements Price {
    public BigDecimal getInitialPrice() {
      return new BigDecimal(BASIC_TICKET_PRICE);
    }
  }

  public Ticket() {
    priceSource = new FixedPrice();
    discountRate = new BigDecimal("1.0");
  }

  public Ticket(Price price) {
    priceSource = price;
```

Altered constructor

```
      discountRate = new BigDecimal("1.0");
  }
  public Ticket(Price price,
                BigDecimal specialDiscountRate) {          Altered
    priceSource = price;                                   constructor
    discountRate = specialDiscountRate;
  }
  public BigDecimal getDiscountPrice() {
    if (faceValue == null) {                               New getInitialPrice
      faceValue = priceSource.getInitialPrice();           call
    }
    return faceValue.multiply(discountRate);               Unchanged
  }                                                        calculation
}
```

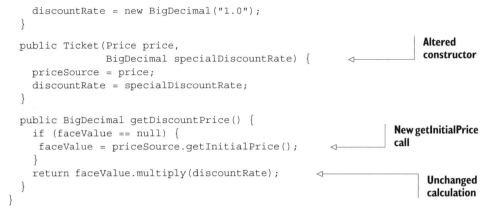

Providing a full implementation of the HttpPrice class would take us too far afield, so let's just suppose that it calls out to another class, HttpPricingService.

Listing 11.12 Price interface and HttpPrice implementation

```
import java.math.BigDecimal;

public interface Price {
  BigDecimal getInitialPrice();
}

public class HttpPrice implements Price {
  @Override
  public BigDecimal getInitialPrice() {                       Returns
    return HttpPricingService.getInitialPrice();              random
  }                                                           results
}
```

So how can you provide the equivalent of what HttpPricingService provides? The trick is to think carefully about what it is you're really trying to test. In this example, you want to test that the multiplication in the Ticket class's getDiscountPrice() method works as expected.

You can therefore replace the HttpPrice class with a StubPrice stub implementation that will reliably return a consistent price for the call to getInitialPrice(). This isolates the test from the inconsistent and intermittently failing HttpPrice class. The test will pass with the implementation in the following code.

Listing 11.13 TicketTest implementation using a stub object

```
import org.junit.Test;
import java.math.BigDecimal;
import static org.junit.Assert.*;

public class TicketTest {

  @Test
  public void tenPercentDiscount() {                        StubPrice
    Price price = new StubPrice();                          stub
```

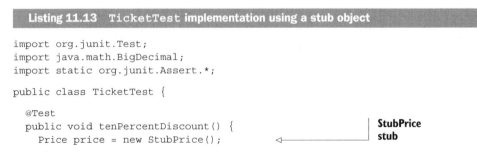

```
        Ticket ticket = new Ticket(price);                      ◄─────────────┐   Create
        assertEquals(9.0,                                                     │   Ticket
                    ticket.getDiscountPrice().doubleValue(),
                    0.0001);                                    ◄─────────────┐   Check
    }                                                                         │   price
}
```

The StubPrice class is a simple little class that consistently returns the initial price of 10.

Listing 11.14 `StubPrice` stub implementation

```
import java.math.BigDecimal;

public class StubPrice implements Price {

  @Override
  public BigDecimal getInitialPrice() {                                       Return
    return new BigDecimal("10");            ◄─────────────┘                   consistent price
  }

}
```

Phew! Now the test passes again, and, equally important, you can look at refactoring the rest of the implementation details without fear.

Stubs are a useful type of test double, but sometimes it's desirable to have the stub perform some real work that's as close to the production system as possible. For that, you use a fake object as your test double.

11.2.3 *Fake object*

A *fake* object can be seen as an enhanced stub that almost does the same work as your production code, but that takes a few shortcuts in order to fulfill your testing requirements. Fakes are especially useful when you'd like your code to run against something that's very close to the real third-party subsystem or dependency that you'll use in the live implementation.

Most well-grounded Java developers will sooner or later have to write code that interacts with a database, typically performing CRUD operations on Java objects. Proving that your Data Access Object (DAO) code works before running it against the production database is often left until the system integration test phase, or it isn't checked at all! It would be of great benefit if you could check that the DAO code works during your unit test or integration test phase, giving you that all important, fast feedback.

A fake object could be used in this case—one that represents the database you're interacting with. But writing your own fake object representing a database would be quite difficult! Luckily, over recent years, in-memory databases have become small enough, lightweight enough, and feature-rich enough to act as a fake object for you. HSQLDB (www.hsqldb.org) is a popular in-memory database used for this purpose.

The theater ticket application is coming along nicely, and the next stage of work is to store the tickets in a database so that they can be retrieved later. The most common Java framework used for database persistence is Hibernate (www.hibernate.org).

Hibernate and HSQLDB

If you're unfamiliar with Hibernate or HSQLDB, don't panic! Hibernate is an object-relational mapping (ORM) framework that implements the Java Persistence API (JPA) standard. In short, it means you can call simple `save`, `load`, `update`, and many other Java methods to perform CRUD operations. This is opposed to using raw SQL and JDBC, and it abstracts away database-specific syntax and semantics.

HSQLDB is simply a Java in-memory database. To use it, all you need is the hsqldb.jar file in your CLASSPATH. It pretty much behaves like your regular RDBMS, although when you shut it down you'll lose your data. (This data loss can be mitigated—see the HSQLDB website for more details.)

Although we're throwing potentially two new technologies at you, the build scripts provided with this book's source code will ensure that you have the correct JAR dependencies and configuration files in the right place.

To begin, you'll need a Hibernate configuration file to define the connection to the HSQLDB database.

Listing 11.15   Hibernate configuration for HSQLDB

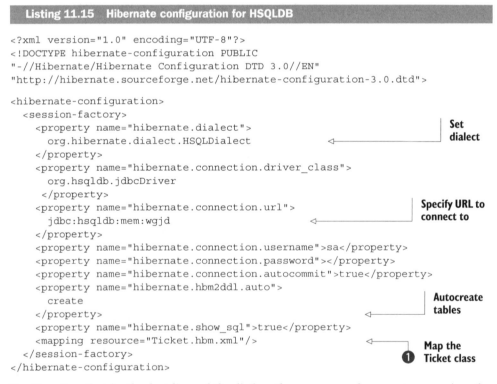

```xml
<?xml version="1.0" encoding="UTF-8"?>
<!DOCTYPE hibernate-configuration PUBLIC
"-//Hibernate/Hibernate Configuration DTD 3.0//EN"
"http://hibernate.sourceforge.net/hibernate-configuration-3.0.dtd">

<hibernate-configuration>
  <session-factory>
    <property name="hibernate.dialect">                          Set
      org.hibernate.dialect.HSQLDialect          <————|          dialect
    </property>
    <property name="hibernate.connection.driver_class">
      org.hsqldb.jdbcDriver
    </property>
    <property name="hibernate.connection.url">                   Specify URL to
      jdbc:hsqldb:mem:wgjd                        <————|          connect to
    </property>
    <property name="hibernate.connection.username">sa</property>
    <property name="hibernate.connection.password"></property>
    <property name="hibernate.connection.autocommit">true</property>
    <property name="hibernate.hbm2ddl.auto">                     Autocreate
      create                                                      tables
    </property>                                     <————|
    <property name="hibernate.show_sql">true</property>
    <mapping resource="Ticket.hbm.xml"/>            <————       Map the
  </session-factory>                                      ❶     Ticket class
</hibernate-configuration>
```

You'll notice that in the last line of the listing there was a reference to mapping the Ticket class as a resource (`<mapping resource="Ticket.hbm.xml"/>`) ❶. This tells Hibernate how to map the Java files to the database columns. Along with the dialect information provided in the Hibernate configuration file (HSQLDB in this case) that's all Hibernate needs to automatically construct SQL for you behind the scenes.

Although Hibernate allows you add mapping information directly to the Java class via annotations, we prefer the XML mapping style shown in the following listing.

> **WARNING** Many a war has erupted over this annotations versus XML mapping choice on mailing lists, so it's best to pick the style you're comfortable with and leave it at that.

Listing 11.16 Hibernate mapping for `Ticket`

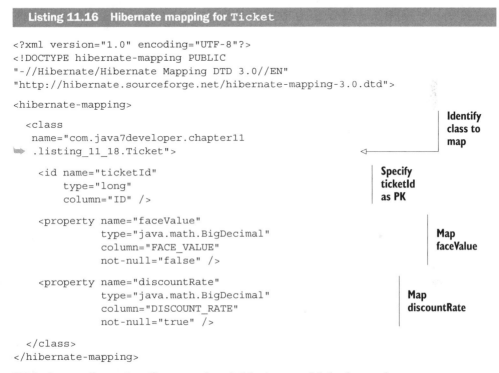

```xml
<?xml version="1.0" encoding="UTF-8"?>
<!DOCTYPE hibernate-mapping PUBLIC
"-//Hibernate/Hibernate Mapping DTD 3.0//EN"
"http://hibernate.sourceforge.net/hibernate-mapping-3.0.dtd">

<hibernate-mapping>
  <class
   name="com.java7developer.chapter11          ◄─── Identify class to map
.listing_11_18.Ticket">

    <id name="ticketId"                         Specify ticketId as PK
        type="long"
        column="ID" />

    <property name="faceValue"                  Map faceValue
              type="java.math.BigDecimal"
              column="FACE_VALUE"
              not-null="false" />

    <property name="discountRate"               Map discountRate
              type="java.math.BigDecimal"
              column="DISCOUNT_RATE"
              not-null="true" />

  </class>
</hibernate-mapping>
```

With the configuration files completed, it's time to think about what you want to test. The business wants to be able to retrieve the `Ticket` by a unique ID. In order to support this (and the Hibernate mapping), you'll have to modify the `Ticket` class as follows.

Listing 11.17 `Ticket` with ID

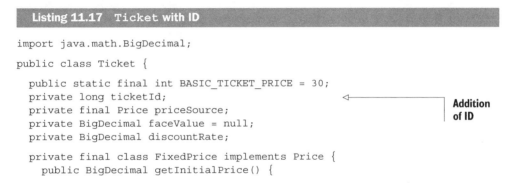

```java
import java.math.BigDecimal;

public class Ticket {

  public static final int BASIC_TICKET_PRICE = 30;
  private long ticketId;                        ◄─── Addition of ID
  private final Price priceSource;
  private BigDecimal faceValue = null;
  private BigDecimal discountRate;

  private final class FixedPrice implements Price {
    public BigDecimal getInitialPrice() {
```

```
      return new BigDecimal(BASIC_TICKET_PRICE);
    }
  }
  public Ticket(long id) {
    ticketId = id;
    priceSource = new FixedPrice();
    discountRate = new BigDecimal("1.0");
  }
  public void setTicketId(long ticketId) {
    this.ticketId = ticketId;
  }
  public long getTicketId() {
    return ticketId;
  }
  public void setFaceValue(BigDecimal faceValue) {
    this.faceValue = faceValue;
  }
  public BigDecimal getFaceValue() {
    return faceValue;
  }
  public void setDiscountRate(BigDecimal discountRate) {
    this.discountRate = discountRate;
  }
  public BigDecimal getDiscountRate() {
    return discountRate;
  }
  public BigDecimal getDiscountPrice() {
    if (faceValue == null) faceValue = priceSource.getInitialPrice();
    return faceValue.multiply(discountRate);
  }
}
```

Now that you have the Ticket mapping and the altered Ticket class, you can start
with a test that will invoke the findTicketById method on the TicketHibernateDao
class. There's additional JUnit test setup scaffolding to put in place, as follows.

Listing 11.18   `TicketHibernateDaoTest` test class

```
import java.math.BigDecimal;
import org.hibernate.cfg.Configuration;
import org.hibernate.SessionFactory;
import org.junit.*;
import static org.junit.Assert.*;

public class TicketHibernateDaoTest {

  private static SessionFactory factory;
  private static TicketHibernateDao ticketDao;
  private Ticket ticket;
  private Ticket ticket2;
```

```
@BeforeClass
public static void baseSetUp() {
  factory =
    new Configuration().
      configure().buildSessionFactory();        ① Use Hibernate
  ticketDao = new TicketHibernateDao(factory);      configuration
}

@Before
public void setUpTest()
{
  ticket = new Ticket(1);
  ticketDao.save(ticket);                        ② Set up test
  ticket2 = new Ticket(2);                           Ticket data
  ticketDao.save(ticket2);
}

@Test
public void findTicketByIdHappyPath() throws Exception {
  Ticket ticket = ticketDao.findTicketById(1);
  assertEquals(new BigDecimal("30.0"),           ③ Find
        ticket.getDiscountPrice());                  Ticket
}

@After
public static void tearDown() {
  ticketDao.delete(ticket);                      Clear
  ticketDao.delete(ticket2);                     data
}

@AfterClass
public static void baseTearDown() {             Close
  factory.close();                              off
}

}
```

Before any tests are run, you use the Hibernate configuration to create the DAO that you want to test ①. Following from there, before each test is run, you save a couple of tickets into the HSQLDB database (as test data) ②. The test is run, and the DAO's findTicketById method is tested ③.

The test will initially fail because you haven't written the TicketHibernateDao class and its corresponding methods. By using the Hibernate framework, there's no need for SQL or to refer to the fact that you're running against the HSQLDB database. Therefore, your DAO implementation will look something like the following listing.

Listing 11.19 The `TicketHibernateDao` class

```
import java.util.List;
import org.hibernate.Criteria;
import org.hibernate.Session;
import org.hibernate.SessionFactory;
import org.hibernate.criterion.Restrictions;

public class TicketHibernateDao {
```

```
private static SessionFactory factory;
private static Session session;

public TicketHibernateDao(SessionFactory factory)
{
  TicketHibernateDao.factory = factory;               Set factory
  TicketHibernateDao.session = getSession();          and session
}

public void save(Ticket ticket)
{
  session.save(ticket);                           ❶  Save a
  session.flush();                                    Ticket
}

public Ticket findTicketById(long ticketId)
{
  Criteria criteria =
      session.createCriteria(Ticket.class);
  criteria.add(Restrictions.eq("ticketId", ticketId));  ❷  Find Ticket
  List<Ticket> tickets = criteria.list();                  by ID
  return tickets.get(0);
}

public void delete(Ticket ticket) {
  session.delete(ticket);
  session.flush();
}

private static synchronized Session getSession() {
  return factory.openSession();
}

}
```

The DAO's save method is fairly trivial, simply invoking the Hibernate framework's save method, followed by a flush to ensure the object is stored in the HSQLDB database ❶. In order to retrieve the `Ticket`, you use Hibernate's `Criteria` functionality (equivalent to constructing a WHERE clause in SQL) ❷.

With the DAO complete, the test now passes. You may have noticed that the save method has also been partly tested. You can now go on to write more thorough tests, checking cases such as whether tickets are coming back from the database with the correct `discountRate`. Your database access code can now be tested much earlier in the testing cycle, so your data access layer gains all of the benefits of a TDD approach.

Let's now turn to discussing the next type of test doubles—mock objects.

11.2.4　*Mock object*

Mock objects are related to the stub test doubles that you've already met, but stub objects are usually pretty dumb beasts. For example, stubs typically fake out methods so that they always give the same result when you call them. This doesn't provide any way to model state-dependent behavior.

As an example: You're trying to follow TDD, and you're writing a text analysis system. One of your unit tests instructs the text analysis classes to count the number of occurrences of the phrase "Java7" for a particular blog post. But as the blog post is a third-party resource, there are a number of possible failure scenarios that have very little to do with the counting algorithm you're writing. In other words, the code under test isn't isolated, and calling the third-party resource could be time-consuming. Here are some common failure scenarios:

- Your code might not be able to go out to the internet to query the blog post, due to firewall restrictions in your organization.
- The blog post may have been moved and there's no redirect.
- The blog post might be edited to increase or decrease the number of times "Java7" appears!

Using stubs, this test would be almost impossible to write, and it would be incredibly verbose for each test case. Enter the *mock object*. This is a special kind of test double, which you can think of as a preprogrammable stub or superstub. Using the mock object is very simple—when you're preparing the mock for use, you tell it the sequence of calls to expect and how it should respond to each one. The mock will combine well with DI; it allows you to inject a pretend object that will behave in precisely known ways.

Let's see this in action by looking at a simple example for the theater tickets use case. We'll be using the popular mocking library, Mockito (available from http://mockito.org/). The following listing shows how to use it.

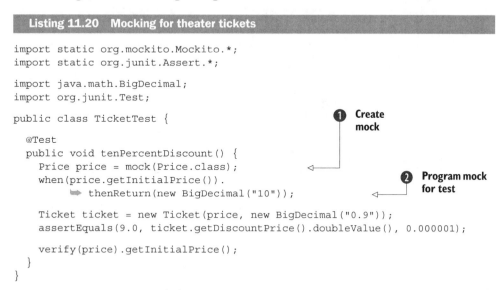

Listing 11.20 Mocking for theater tickets

```java
import static org.mockito.Mockito.*;
import static org.junit.Assert.*;

import java.math.BigDecimal;
import org.junit.Test;

public class TicketTest {                              ❶ Create
                                                          mock
  @Test
  public void tenPercentDiscount() {
    Price price = mock(Price.class);
    when(price.getInitialPrice()).                     ❷ Program mock
        thenReturn(new BigDecimal("10"));                 for test

    Ticket ticket = new Ticket(price, new BigDecimal("0.9"));
    assertEquals(9.0, ticket.getDiscountPrice().doubleValue(), 0.000001);

    verify(price).getInitialPrice();
  }
}
```

To create a mock object, you call the static `mock()` method ❶ with the class object of the type you want to mock up. Then you "record" the behavior that you want your mock to display by calling the `when()` method to indicate which method you want to record behavior for, and `thenReturn()` to specify what the expected result should be ❷. Lastly you verify that you've called the expected methods on the mocked object. This ensures that you didn't get to the correct result via an incorrect path.

You can use the mock just like a regular object, and pass it to your call to the Ticket constructor without any further ceremony. This makes mock objects a very powerful tool for TDD, and some practitioners don't really use the other types of test doubles, preferring to do almost everything with mocks.

Whether or not you choose this "mockist" style of TDD, a thorough knowledge of test doubles (plus a little DI if needed) will let you continue refactoring and coding without fear, even when you're dealing with complex dependencies and third-party subsystems.

As a Java developer, you'll find working in a TDD manner is relatively easy to pick up. But there is the recurring problem that often comes with Java—it can be a bit verbose. Doing TDD in a pure-Java project can lead to a lot of boilerplate code. Fortunately, now that you've studied some other JVM languages, you can potentially use them to do more concise TDD. In fact, one of the classic ways to bring in a non-Java language and start moving toward a polyglot project is to start with tests.

In the next section, we'll discuss ScalaTest—a testing framework that can be used for a wide range of testing purposes. We'll start by introducing ScalaTest and show how it can be used to run JUnit tests against Java classes.

11.3   *Introducing ScalaTest*

In section 7.4, if you recall, we talked about TDD being an ideal use case for a dynamic language. In fact, Scala has many of the same benefits for testing because of Scala's advanced type inference, which often makes the language feel dynamic, despite Scala's static type system.

Scala's Premier test framework is ScalaTest. It provides a number of extremely useful traits and classes for doing all kinds of testing—from JUnit style unit tests through to full-scale integration and acceptance tests. Let's look at an example of ScalaTest in action by rewriting some of the tests from earlier in this chapter in ScalaTest.

The next listing shows the tests from listing 11.4 rewritten in ScalaTest, and it adds a new test of the sellTicket() method—the fiftyDiscountTickets() test.

Listing 11.21   JUnit tests in ScalaTest style

```
import java.math.BigDecimal
import java.lang.IllegalArgumentException
import org.scalatest.junit.JUnitSuite
import org.scalatest.junit.ShouldMatchersForJUnit
import org.junit.Test
import org.junit.Before
import org.junit.Assert._

class RevenueTest extends JUnitSuite with ShouldMatchersForJUnit {

  var venueRevenue: TicketRevenue = _

  @Before def initialize() {
    venueRevenue = new TicketRevenue()
  }
```

```
  @Test def zeroSalesEqualsZeroRevenue() {
    assertEquals(BigDecimal.ZERO, venueRevenue estimateTotalRevenue 0);
  }

  @Test def failIfTooManyOrTooFewTicketsAreSold() {
    evaluating { venueRevenue.estimateTotalRevenue(-1) }
  should produce [IllegalArgumentException]
    evaluating { venueRevenue.estimateTotalRevenue(101) }
  should produce [IllegalArgumentException]
  }

  @Test def tenTicketsSoldIsThreeHundredInRevenue() {
    val expected = new BigDecimal("300");
    assert(expected == venueRevenue.estimateTotalRevenue(10));
  }

  @Test def fiftyDiscountTickets() {
    for (i <- 1 to 50)
  venueRevenue.sellTicket(new Ticket())
    for (i <- 1 to 50)
  venueRevenue.sellTicket(new Ticket(new StubPrice(),
  new BigDecimal(0.9)))
    assert(1950.0 ==
  venueRevenue.getRevenue().doubleValue());
  }
}
```

Exception expected (annotation pointing to the `should produce [IllegalArgumentException]` lines)

Scala-style assertion (annotation pointing to the `venueRevenue.getRevenue().doubleValue());` line)

One of the points about Scala that we haven't mentioned yet is how Scala handles annotations. As you can see, they look just like Java annotations. Not much drama here. Your tests also live in a class that extends `JUnitSuite`—this means that ScalaTest will recognize this class as being something that it can run.

You can easily run ScalaTest from the command line, using a native ScalaTest runner like this:

```
ariel:scalatest boxcat$ scala -cp /Users/boxcat/projects/tickets.jar:/Users/
    boxcat/projects/wgjd/code/lib/scalatest-1.6.1.jar:/Users/boxcat/
    projects/wgjd/code/lib/junit-4.8.2.jar org.scalatest.tools.Runner -o -s
    com.java7developer.chapter11.scalatest.RevenueTest
```

In this run, the Java classes you're testing are in tickets.jar, so you need this file on the classpath along with the ScalaTest and JUnit JARs.

The preceding command specifies the specific test suite to run with the -s switch (omitting the -s switch runs all of the tests in all test suites). The -o switch sends the test output to standard out (use -e to send it to standard error instead). ScalaTest refers to this as configuring a reporter for the output (it includes others, such as a graphical reporter). The preceding example produces output like this:

```
Run starting. Expected test count is: 4
RevenueTest:
- zeroSalesEqualsZeroRevenue
- failIfTooManyOrTooFewTicketsAreSold
- tenTicketsSoldIsThreeHundredInRevenue
- fiftyDiscountTickets
Run completed in 820 milliseconds.
```

```
Total number of tests run: 4
Suites: completed 1, aborted 0
Tests: succeeded 4, failed 0, ignored 0, pending 0
All tests passed.
```

Note that the tests have been compiled to a class file. As long as you have JARs for both JUnit and ScalaTest on the classpath, you can use `scala` to run these tests from within a JUnit runner instead:

```
ariel:scalatest boxcat$ scala -cp /Users/boxcat/projects/tickets.jar:/Users/
    boxcat/projects/wgjd/code/lib/scalatest-1.6.1.jar:/Users/boxcat/
    projects/wgjd/code/lib/junit-4.8.2.jar org.junit.runner.JUnitCore
    com.java7developer.chapter11.scalatest.RevenueTest
JUnit version 4.8.2
...
Time: 0.096

OK (4 tests)
```

This, of course, leads to slightly different output, because you're using a different tool (a JUnit runner) to execute the tests.

> **NOTE**   We'll use this JUnit runner when utilizing Maven to build the java7developer project in chapter 12.

Testing Scala code with ScalaTest

In this section, we're mostly talking about using ScalaTest to test Java code. But what if the project you're working on uses Scala as its main coding language?

Scala is usually thought of as a stable layer language, so if you're working with a code-base of Scala code, your code should be as well tested as Java code. This makes it a perfect candidate for using a TDD approach, with ScalaTest in place of JUnit.

This quick look at ScalaTest completes our treatment of TDD. In chapter 14, we'll build on these ideas when we discuss behavior-driven development (BDD), which can be seen as the next logical step after TDD.

11.4 Summary

Test-driven development is about eliminating or reducing fear in the development process. By following the practices of TDD, such as the red-green-refactor loop for unit tests, you can free yourself of the mindset that leads to just hacking code together.

JUnit is the de facto testing library for Java developers. It provides support for running a suite of independent tests by allowing you to specify setup and teardown hooks. JUnit's assert mechanism ensures that the desired result is met when calling your logic.

Different types of test doubles can help you write tests that zero in on just the right amount of system behavior. The four types of test doubles (dummy, stub, fake, and mock) allow you to replace a dependency with a test double that allows your test to run quickly and accurately. Mocks can provide the ultimate flexibility when writing tests.

ScalaTest holds out the promise of substantially reducing boilerplate testing code, and it gives you an insight into the behavior-driven development style of testing.

In the next chapter, we'll discuss automated builds and the methodology called continuous integration (CI), which builds on TDD. The CI approach allows you to get immediate, automatic feedback on every new change, and it encourages radical transparency among the members of a development team.

Build and
continuous integration

The story we're about to tell you is based on true events at MegaCorp, although the names of the parties have been changed to protect the innocent! Our protagonists are:

- Riley, the new graduate
- Alice and Bob, two existing "experienced" developers
- Hazel, their stressed project manager

It's 2:00 p.m. Friday, and Sally's new payment feature needs to go into production before the weekend batch runs.

Riley:	Can I help with the release?
Alice:	Sure, I think Bob built the last release. Bob?
Bob:	Oh yeah, that was generated from my Eclipse IDE a couple of weeks ago.
Riley:	Um, but we all use the IntelliJ IDE now—how shall we do the build?
Bob:	Well, that's where experience comes in! We'll make it work somehow kid!
Riley:	Well, OK. I'm new at this, but the payment feature should build OK, right?
Alice:	Oh sure, I only forked the code from two weeks ago. The rest of the team can't have changed the code that much, surely.
Bob:	Well, actually, you know we added in the Generics change, right?
	[Cue awkward silence.]
Hazel:	You guys need to try your changes together more often. We've talked about this!
Riley:	Shall I order the pizza? Sounds like we're not going home on time tonight.
Hazel:	You got that right! You're learning fast kid.
Alice:	Actually, I've got them on speed dial—this happens all the time!
Hazel:	Just get it sorted—we've lost thousands on late, buggy releases—senior management is looking for heads to roll!

Clearly Alice, Bob, and Riley don't have good build and continuous integration (CI) practices in place, but what does "build and CI" really mean?

BUILD AND CONTINUOUS INTEGRATION   The practice of rapidly and repeatedly producing high quality binary artifacts for deployment to your various environments.

Development teams often talk about "the build" or a "build process."[1] For the purposes of this chapter, when we

Figure 12.1   A simplified typical build lifecycle

talk about *building*, we're talking about using a build tool to transform your source code into a binary artifact by following a build lifecycle. Build tools such as Maven have a very long, detailed build lifecycle, most of which is hidden from the developer's sight. A fairly basic, typical build lifecycle is outlined in figure 12.1.

Continuous integration is where individuals in a development team integrate their work frequently, following the mantra of "commit early, commit often." Each developer will commit their code to version control at least daily, and the CI server will run regular automated builds to detect integration errors as quickly as possible.[2] Feedback is often displayed to the team with a happy/sad display on a large screen.

So why are build and CI important? Each section of this chapter will highlight individual benefits, but a few overriding themes are outlined in table 12.1.

---

[1] If your team does so in a hushed, reverent, or fearful tone, this is the chapter for you!

[2] This is configurable—you can run builds every so many minutes, on commit, or at other specified times.

Table 12.1   Common themes of why build and CI is important

Theme	Explanation
Repeatability	Anyone can run the build, any time, anywhere. It means your whole development team can comfortably run the build as opposed to needing a dedicated "build master" to do it. If the newest team member needs to run the build at 3 a.m. on a Sunday, they can do so with confidence.[3]
Early feedback	You are informed immediately when something breaks. This is especially pertinent to CI when developers are working on code that needs to integrate.
Consistency	You know what versions of your software are deployed and exactly what code is in each version.
Dependency management	Most Java projects have several dependencies, such as log4j, Hibernate, Guice, and so on. Managing these manually can be very difficult, and a change in version can mean broken software. Good build and CI ensures that you're always compiling and running against the same third-party dependencies.

In order to be deployed to an environment, your source code needs to go through a build lifecycle and be turned into a binary artifact (JAR, WAR, RAR, EAR, and so on). Older Java projects typically use the Ant build tool, with newer projects utilizing Maven or Gradle. Many development teams also have a nightly integration build, and some have evolved to using a CI server to perform regular builds.

> **WARNING**   If you're building JAR files or other artifacts from your IDE, you're looking for trouble. When you build from your IDE, you don't have a repeatable build that's independent of *your* local IDE settings, and that's a disaster waiting to happen. We can't state this strongly enough—friends don't let friends build artifacts from the IDE!

But most developers don't see build and CI as an exciting or rewarding area to put their efforts into. Build tools and CI servers are often set up at the start of the project and promptly forgotten. Over the years we've heard many variations on the following comment: "Why should we spend extra time on the build and CI server? What we've got in place kind of works. It's good enough, right?"

We strongly believe that having good build and CI in place means that you can write code more quickly, with a higher quality bar. In conjunction with TDD (discussed in chapter 11) build and CI means you can *rapidly refactor without fear*. Think of it as having a mentor looking over your shoulder, providing a safe environment in which you can code quickly and make bold changes.

We'll start this chapter by introducing you to Maven 3, a popular (yet polarizing— some developers loathe it) build tool that forces you to work within its strict definition of a build lifecycle. As part of the Maven 3 introduction, you'll build Groovy and Scala code alongside the more common Java code.

---

[3]   Extremely slick project teams get it to a state where their nontechnical teammates run builds.

Jenkins is a hugely popular CI server that can be configured in a multitude of ways (via its plugin system) to continuously execute builds and produce quality metrics. As part of learning about Jenkins, we'll dive into the code quality metrics that can be reported by looking at the FindBugs and Checkstyle plugins.

After learning about Maven and Jenkins, you'll be comfortable with the end-to-end flow of a typical Java-based build and CI process. Lastly, we'll take a completely different look at build and deployment tools by focusing on the Leiningen build tool for Clojure. You'll see how it can enable a very rapid, hands-on style of TDD while still providing industrial-strength build and deployment capabilities.

Let's get started with your build and CI journey by meeting Maven 3!

12.1 Getting started with Maven 3

Maven is a popular, yet hugely polarizing, build tool for Java and related JVM languages. Its underlying premise is that a strict build lifecycle backed up with powerful dependency management is essential for successful builds. Maven goes beyond being merely a build tool. It's more of a project management tool for the technical components of your project. In fact, Maven calls its build scripts Project Object Model (POM) files. These POM files are in XML, and each Maven project or module will have an accompanying pom.xml file.

> **NOTE** Alternative language support is coming for POM files, which should give users full flexibility should they require it (much like what's available for the Gradle build tool).

What about Ant and Gradle?

Ant is a popular build tool, especially on older Java projects. It was the de facto standard for a long time. We're not covering it here because it has been covered a hundred times before. More crucially, we feel that Ant doesn't enforce a common build lifecycle and it doesn't have a set of common (enforced) build targets. This means that developers have to learn the details of each Ant build they come across. If you need to use Ant, the Ant site (http://ant.apache.org) has all of the details you need.

Gradle is the new cool kid on the block. It deliberately takes the opposite approach of Maven, freeing you from tight constraints and allowing you to specify the build your way. Like Maven, it provides dependency management and a host of other features. If you'd like to try Gradle, the Gradle site (www.gradle.org) is where you'll find the details.

For the purposes of learning about good build practices, we think that Maven is still the best tool to use. It forces you to adhere to the build lifecycle and allows you to run the build for any Maven project in the world.

Maven favors convention over configuration, expecting you to fit into its world view of how your source code should be laid out, how to filter properties, and so on. This can be frustrating for some developers, but an awful lot of deep thought about build lifecycles has gone into Maven over the years, and more often than not it's forcing you down a sensible path. For those who rail against conventions, Maven does allow you to override its defaults, but that makes for a more verbose and less standard set of build scripts.

In order to execute builds with Maven, you ask it to run one or several *goals*, which represent specific tasks (compiling your code, running tests, and more). Goals are all tied into the default build lifecycle, so if you ask Maven to run some tests (for example, `mvn test`), it'll compile your code and your test code before trying to run the tests. In short, it forces you to adhere to a correct build lifecycle.

If you haven't already downloaded and installed Maven 3, turn to section A.2 in appendix A. Once you've completed the download and installation, come back here to create your first Maven project.

12.2 *Maven 3—a quick-start project*

Maven follows convention over configuration, and its project structure conventions become quickly evident when you create a quick-start project. The typical project structure it prefers looks similar to the following layout.

```
project
|-- pom.xml
`-- src
    |-- main
    |   `-- java
    |       `-- com
    |           `-- company
    |               `-- project
    |                   `-- App.java
    |   `-- resources
    `-- test
        `-- java
            `-- com
                `-- company
                    `-- project
                        `-- AppTest.java
        `-- resources
`-- target
```

As part of its conventions, Maven splits your *main* code from your *test* code. It also has a special resources directory for any other files that need to be included as part of the build (such as log4.xml file for logging, Hibernate configuration files, and other similar resources). The pom.xml file is the build script for Maven. It's covered in full detail in appendix E.

If you're a polyglot programmer, your Scala and Groovy source code follows the same structure as the Java source code (in the java directory), except that the root folders are called scala and groovy respectively. Java, Scala, and Groovy code can happily sit side by side in a Maven project.

The target directory doesn't get created until a build is run. All classes, artifacts, reports, and other files that the build produces will appear under this directory. For a full listing of the project structure that Maven expects, see the "Introduction to the Standard Directory Layout" page on the Maven website (http://maven.apache.org/guides/introduction/introduction-to-the-standard-directory-layout.html).

To create this conventional structure for a new project, execute the following goal with the specified parameters:

```
mvn archetype:generate
   -DgroupId=com.mycompany.app
   -DartifactId=my-app
   -DarchetypeArtifactId=maven-archetype-quickstart
   -DinteractiveMode=false
```

At this point you'll see your console filling up with output from Maven stating that it's downloading plugins and third-party libraries. Maven needs these plugins and libraries in order to run this goal, and by default it downloads these from Maven Central—the de facto online repository for these artifacts.

Why does Maven seem to download the internet?

"Oh, there goes Maven again, downloading the internet" is a common meme among those involved in building Java projects. But is this really Maven's fault? We think that there are two root causes of this behavior. One is poor packaging and dependency management by third-party library developers (for example, specifying a dependency in their pom.xml file that isn't actually required). The other is the inherent weaknesses in the JAR-based packaging system itself, which doesn't allow for a more fine-grained set of dependencies.

Apart from the "Downloading..." information, you should also see a statement similar to the following one in your console:

```
[INFO] ------------------------------------------------------------
[INFO] BUILD SUCCESS
[INFO] ------------------------------------------------------------
[INFO] Total time: 1.703s
[INFO] Finished at: Fri Jun 24 13:51:58 BST 2011
[INFO] Final Memory: 6M/16M
[INFO] ------------------------------------------------------------
```

If this step fails, it's likely that your proxy server is blocking access to Maven Central, where the plugins and third-party libraries are held. To resolve this issue, simply edit the settings.xml file (mentioned in section A.2 of appendix A) and add the following section, filling out the appropriate values for the various elements:

```
<proxies>
  <proxy>
    <active>true</active>
    <protocol></protocol>
    <username></username>
    <password></password>
    <host></host>
```

```
    <port></port>
  </proxy>
</proxies>
```

Rerun the goal and you should see the my-app project created in your directory.

> **TIP**   Add the proxy configuration in $M2_HOME/conf/settings.xml if every-
> one in your team is suffering from the same problem.

Maven supports an almost limitless bunch of archetypes (project layouts). If you want
to generate a specific type of project, such as a JEE6 project, you can execute the mvn
archetype:generate goal and simply follow the prompts it gives you.

To explore Maven in more detail, let's look at a project that already has source
code and tests ready so we can take you through the build lifecycle.

12.3   *Maven 3—the Java7developer build*

Remember the build lifecycle in figure 12.1? Maven follows a similar build lifecycle, and you're now going to build the source code that comes with this book,
working through those build lifecycle phases. Despite the fact that the source code
for the book doesn't turn into a single application, we'll refer to the project as the
java7developer project.

This section will focus on

- Exploring the basics of a Maven POM file (that is, your build script)
- How to compile, test, and package your code (including Scala and Groovy)
- How to deal with multiple environments using profiles
- How to generate a website containing various reports

First you need to understand the pom.xml file that defines the java7developer project.

12.3.1   *The POM*

The pom.xml file represents the java7developer project, including all of the plugins,
resources, and other elements required to build it. You can find the pom.xml file at
the base of where you unzipped or checked out the project code for this book (we'll
call this location $BOOK_CODE from now on). The POM has four main sections:

- Basic project information
- Build configuration
- Dependency management
- Profiles

It's a fairly long file, but it's much simpler than it first appears. If you want the full gory
details of what can go in a POM see the "POM Reference" on the Maven website (http://
maven.apache.org/pom.html).

We'll split the explanation of the pom.xml file for the java7developer project into
the four parts, starting with the basic project information.

BASIC PROJECT INFORMATION

Maven allows you to include a host of basic project information in the pom.xml file. The following listing contains what we feel is a minimum to get started.

Listing 12.1   POM—basic project information

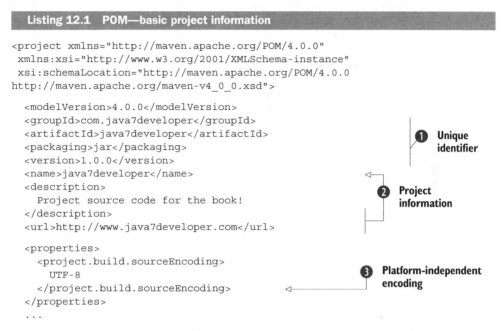

```
<project xmlns="http://maven.apache.org/POM/4.0.0"
 xmlns:xsi="http://www.w3.org/2001/XMLSchema-instance"
 xsi:schemaLocation="http://maven.apache.org/POM/4.0.0
http://maven.apache.org/maven-v4_0_0.xsd">

  <modelVersion>4.0.0</modelVersion>
  <groupId>com.java7developer</groupId>
  <artifactId>java7developer</artifactId>
  <packaging>jar</packaging>
  <version>1.0.0</version>
  <name>java7developer</name>
  <description>
    Project source code for the book!
  </description>
  <url>http://www.java7developer.com</url>

  <properties>
    <project.build.sourceEncoding>
      UTF-8
    </project.build.sourceEncoding>
  </properties>
  ...
```

① Unique identifier

② Project information

③ Platform-independent encoding

The <groupId> element value of com.java7developer makes up the first part of the unique identifier for this artifact in a Maven repository **①**. The <artifactId> element value of java7developer is the second part of that unique identifier. The <packaging> element value of jar tells Maven you're trying to build a JAR file (as you'd expect war, ear, rar, sar, and har are all possible values here). And the final piece of the unique identification comes from the <version> element value of 1.0.0,[4] which specifies what version you're building (this value changes to an incremented SNAPSHOT version when you perform Maven releases).

The <projectName> and <url> are also specified, along with a host of other optional project information **②**. You ensure that the build is consistent across all platforms by specifying the <sourceEncoding> as UTF-8 **③**.

To put this into further context, this configuration will guide Maven to building the java7developer-1.0.0.jar artifact that will be stored in the Maven repository under com/java7developer/1.0.0.

---

[4]   This follows the Major.Minor.Trivial versioning scheme, our personal favorite!

Maven versions and SNAPSHOTs

As part of its convention over configuration, Maven prefers to have your version numbers in the *major.minor.trivial* format. It deals with artifacts of a temporary nature by the convention of adding a -SNAPSHOT suffix to that version number. For example, if your team is constantly building a JAR for an upcoming 1.0.0 release, by convention you'd have the version set to 1.0.0-SNAPSHOT. That way, various Maven plugins know that it isn't the production version yet and will treat it appropriately. When you release the artifact to production, you'd release it as 1.0.0, with the next version for bug fixes starting at 1.0.1-SNAPSHOT.

Maven helps automate all this through its Release plugin. For more details, see the Release plugin's page (http://maven.apache.org/plugins/maven-release-plugin/). Now that you understand the basic project information section, let's take a look at the <build> section.

BUILD CONFIGURATION

The build section contains the plugins[5] and their respective configurations needed to execute the Maven build lifecycle goals. For many projects, this section is quite small, because the default plugins and their default settings are usually adequate.

For the java7developer project, the <build> section contains several plugins that override some of the defaults. This is so that the java7developer project can do several things:

- Build the Java 7 code
- Build the Scala and Groovy code
- Run Java, Scala, and Groovy tests
- Provide Checkstyle and FindBugs code metric reports

Plugins are JAR-based artifacts (mainly written in Java). To configure a build plugin, you need to place it inside the <build><plugins> section of your pom.xml file. Like all Maven artifacts, each plugin is uniquely identified, so you need to specify the <groupId>, <artifactId>, and <version> information. Any extra configuration for the plugin then goes into the <configuration> section, and these details are specific to each plugin. For example, the compiler plugin has configuration elements such as <source>, <target>, and <showWarnings>, which is configuration information that's unique to a compiler.

The following listing shows a section of the build configuration for the java7developer project (the complete listing, with the corresponding explanations, is in appendix E).

---

[5] If you need to configure aspects of your build, you can check out the full list of plugins on Maven's plugins page (http://maven.apache.org/plugins/index.html).

Listing 12.2   POM—build information

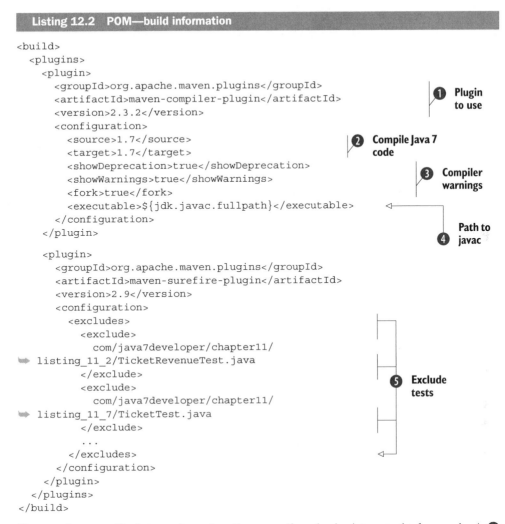

```
<build>
  <plugins>
    <plugin>
      <groupId>org.apache.maven.plugins</groupId>
      <artifactId>maven-compiler-plugin</artifactId>
      <version>2.3.2</version>
      <configuration>
        <source>1.7</source>
        <target>1.7</target>
        <showDeprecation>true</showDeprecation>
        <showWarnings>true</showWarnings>
        <fork>true</fork>
        <executable>${jdk.javac.fullpath}</executable>
      </configuration>
    </plugin>

    <plugin>
      <groupId>org.apache.maven.plugins</groupId>
      <artifactId>maven-surefire-plugin</artifactId>
      <version>2.9</version>
      <configuration>
        <excludes>
          <exclude>
            com/java7developer/chapter11/
   listing_11_2/TicketRevenueTest.java
          </exclude>
          <exclude>
            com/java7developer/chapter11/
   listing_11_7/TicketTest.java
          </exclude>
          ...
        </excludes>
      </configuration>
    </plugin>
  </plugins>
</build>
```

1 Plugin to use

2 Compile Java 7 code

3 Compiler warnings

4 Path to javac

5 Exclude tests

You need to specify that you're using the compiler plugin (at a particular version) **1** as you want to change the default behavior of compiling Java 1.5 code to that of Java 1.7 **2**.

Because you've already broken from convention, you might as well add a few other useful compiler warning options **3**. Next, you make sure that you can specify where your Java 7 installation is **4**. Simply copy over the sample_<os>_build.properties file for your OS to build.properties and edit the value of the `jdk.javac.fullpath` property in order for this property to be picked up.

The Surefire plugin allows you to configure the tests. In the configuration for this project we're excluding several tests **5** that deliberately fail (you'll remember these two tests from chapter 11 on TDD).

Now that you've covered the build section, you can move on to a vital part of the POM, the dependency management.

DEPENDENCY MANAGEMENT

The list of dependencies for most Java projects can be quite long, and the java7developer project is no different. Maven helps you manage those dependencies with its vast store of third-party libraries in the Maven Central Repository. Crucially, those third-party libraries have their own pom.xml files that declare their respective dependencies, allowing Maven to figure out and download any further libraries you require.

There are two main scopes (`compile` and `test`) that you'll initially use.[6] These pretty much correspond to putting the JAR files on your CLASSPATH for compiling your code and running your tests. The following listing shows the `<dependencies>` section for the java7developer project. You'll find the full listing with the corresponding explanations in appendix E.

Listing 12.3 POM—dependencies

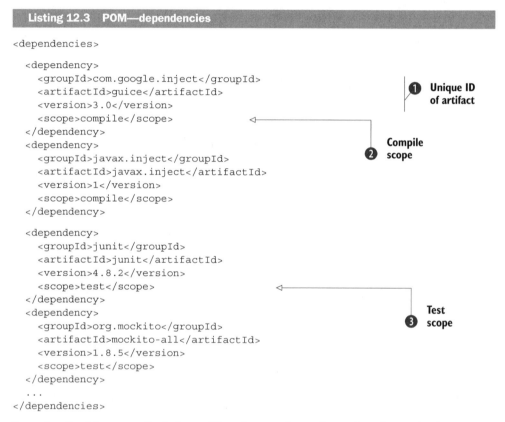

```
<dependencies>

  <dependency>
    <groupId>com.google.inject</groupId>
    <artifactId>guice</artifactId>
    <version>3.0</version>
    <scope>compile</scope>
  </dependency>
  <dependency>
    <groupId>javax.inject</groupId>
    <artifactId>javax.inject</artifactId>
    <version>1</version>
    <scope>compile</scope>
  </dependency>

  <dependency>
    <groupId>junit</groupId>
    <artifactId>junit</artifactId>
    <version>4.8.2</version>
    <scope>test</scope>
  </dependency>
  <dependency>
    <groupId>org.mockito</groupId>
    <artifactId>mockito-all</artifactId>
    <version>1.8.5</version>
    <scope>test</scope>
  </dependency>
  ...
</dependencies>
```

1 Unique ID of artifact

2 Compile scope

3 Test scope

In order for Maven to find the artifact that you're referencing, it needs the correct `<groupId>`, `<artifactId>`, and `<version>` **1**. As we alluded to earlier, setting the `<scope>` to `compile` **2** will add those JARs to the CLASSPATH for the compilation of the code. Setting the `<scope>` to `test` **3** will ensure that those JARs are added to the CLASSPATH when Maven compiles and runs the tests.

---

[6] J2EE/JEE projects also typically have some dependencies declared with a `runtime` scope.

But how do you know what `<groupId>`, `<artifactId>`, and `<version>` to specify? The answer is almost always that you can search for these values at the Maven Central Repository—http://search.maven.org/.

If you can't find the appropriate artifact, you can manually download and install the plugin yourself by using the `install:install-file` goal. Here's an example of installing the asm-4.0_RC1.jar library.

```
mvn install:install-file
-Dfile=asm-4.0_RC1.jar
-DgroupId=org.ow2.asm
-DartifactId=asm
-Dversion=4.0_RC1
-Dpackaging=jar
```

After running this command, you should find that this artifact has been installed into your local repository at $HOME/.m2/repository/org/ow2/asm/asm/4.0_RC1/, just as if Maven had downloaded it itself!

Artifact manager

When you manually install a third-party library, you're only installing it for yourself, but what about the rest of your team? The same issue occurs when you've produced an artifact that you want to share with your colleagues, but can't put into Maven Central (because it's proprietary code).

The solution for this is to use a binary artifact manager, such as Nexus (http://nexus.sonatype.org/). An artifact manager acts as a local Maven Central for you and your team, allowing you to share artifacts with each other, but not with the outside world. Most artifact managers also cache Maven Central and other repositories, making it a one-stop shop for your development team.

The last part of the POM to understand is the profiles section, which effectively deals with the environmentalization of your builds.

PROFILES

Profiles are how Maven deals with environmentalization (for example, your UAT as opposed to your production environment) or other slight variations from your normal build. As an example in the java7developer project, there's a profile that switches off the compiler and deprecation warnings, as the next listing demonstrates.

Listing 12.4   POM—profiles

```
<profiles>
  <profile>
    <id>ignore-compiler-warnings</id>                    ◀————————  ❶ ID for this
    <build>                                                             profile
      <plugins>
        <plugin>
          <groupId>org.apache.maven.plugins</groupId>
```

```
        <artifactId>maven-compiler-plugin</artifactId>
        <version>2.3.2</version>
        <configuration>
          <source>1.7</source>
          <target>1.7</target>
          <showDeprecation>false</showDeprecation>
          <showWarnings>false</showWarnings>
          <fork>true</fork>
          <executable>${jdk.javac.fullpath}</executable>
        </configuration>
      </plugin>
    </plugins>
  </build>
</profile>
</profiles>
```

❷ **Switch off warnings**

You reference the profile that you want to use with the -P <id> parameter when you execute Maven (for example, mvn compile -P ignore-compile-warnings) ❶. When this profile is activated, this version of the compiler plugin is used, and the deprecation and other compiler warnings are switched off ❷.

You can find out more about profiles and how to use them for other environmentalization purposes at Maven's "Introduction to Build Profiles" page (http://maven.apache.org/guides/introduction/introduction-to-profiles.html).

Now that you've finished taking the tour of the pom.xml file for the java7developer project, you're probably itching to build it, right?

12.3.2 *Running the examples*

Hopefully you've already downloaded the code listings for this book. You'll notice that there were also some pom.xml files. It's these files that control the Maven build.

In this section you'll go through the most common Maven build lifecycle goals (clean, compile, test, and install). The first build lifecycle goal is to clean up any leftover artifacts from a previous build.

CLEAN

The Maven clean goal deletes the *target* directory. To see this in action, change to the $BOOK_CODE directory and execute the Maven clean goal.

```
cd $BOOK_CODE
mvn clean
```

Unlike the other Maven build lifecycle goals you'll be using, clean isn't automatically called. If you want the previous build artifacts cleaned up, you always need to include the clean goal.

Now that you've removed any leftover remnants from the previous build, the next build lifecycle goal you typically want to execute is to compile your code.

COMPILE

The Maven compile goal uses the compiler plugin configuration in the pom.xml file to compile the source code under src/main/java, src/main/scala, and src/main/groovy.

This effectively means executing the Java, Scala, and Groovy compilers (javac, scalac, and groovyc) with the compile-scoped dependencies added to the CLASSPATH. Maven will also process the resources under src/main/resources, ensuring that they're part of the CLASSPATH for compilation.

The resulting compiled classes end up under the target/classes directory. To see this in action, execute the following Maven goal:

```
mvn compile
```

The compile goal should execute pretty quickly, and in your console you'll see something similar to the following output.

```
...
[INFO] [properties:read-project-properties {execution: default}]
[INFO] [groovy:generateStubs {execution: default}]
[INFO] Generated 22 Java stubs
[INFO] [resources:resources {execution: default-resources}]
[INFO] Using 'UTF-8' encoding to copy filtered resources.
[INFO] Copying 2 resources
[INFO] [compiler:compile {execution: default-compile}]
[INFO] Compiling 119 source files to
    C:\Projects\workspace3.6\code\trunk\target\classes
[INFO] [scala:compile {execution: default}]
[INFO] Checking for multiple versions of scala
[INFO] includes = [**/*.scala,**/*.java,]
[INFO] excludes = []
[INFO] C:\Projects\workspace3.6\code\trunk\src\main\java:-1: info: compiling
[INFO] C:\Projects\workspace3.6\code\trunk\target\generated-sources\groovy-
    stubs\main:-1: info: compiling
[INFO] C:\Projects\workspace3.6\code\trunk\src\main\groovy:-1: info:
    compiling
[INFO] C:\Projects\workspace3.6\code\trunk\src\main\scala:-1: info: compiling
[INFO] Compiling 143 source files to
    C:\Projects\workspace3.6\code\trunk\target\classes at 1312716331031
[INFO] prepare-compile in 0 s
[INFO] compile in 12 s
[INFO] [groovy:compile {execution: default}]
[INFO] Compiled 26 Groovy classes
[INFO] ------------------------------------------------------------------------
[INFO] BUILD SUCCESSFUL
[INFO] ------------------------------------------------------------------------
[INFO] Total time: 43 seconds
[INFO] Finished at: Sun Aug 07 12:25:44 BST 2011
[INFO] Final Memory: 33M/79M
[INFO] ------------------------------------------------------------------------
```

At this stage, your test classes under src/test/java, src/test/scala, and src/test/groovy haven't been compiled. Although there is a specific test-compile goal for this, the most typical approach is to simply ask Maven to run the test goal.

TEST

The test goal is where you really see Maven's build lifecycle in action. When you ask Maven to run the tests, it knows it needs to execute all of the earlier build lifecycle goals in order to run the test goal successfully (including `compile`, `test-compile`, and a host of others).

Maven will run the tests via the Surefire plugin, using the test provider (in this case JUnit) that you've supplied as one of the `test`-scoped dependencies in the pom.xml file. Maven not only runs the test but produces report files that can be analyzed later to investigate failing tests and to gather test metrics.

To see this in action, execute the following Maven goals:

```
mvn clean test
```

Once Maven has completed compiling the tests and running them, you should see it report something similar to the following output.

```
...
Running com.java7developer.chapter11.listing_11_3.TicketRevenueTest
Tests run: 5, Failures: 0, Errors: 0, Skipped: 0, Time elapsed: 0 sec
Running com.java7developer.chapter11.listing_11_4.TicketRevenueTest
Tests run: 5, Failures: 0, Errors: 0, Skipped: 0, Time elapsed: 0 sec
Running com.java7developer.chapter11.listing_11_5.TicketTest
Tests run: 1, Failures: 0, Errors: 0, Skipped: 0, Time elapsed: 0.015 sec

Results :

Tests run: 20, Failures: 0, Errors: 0, Skipped: 0

[INFO] ------------------------------------------------------------------
[INFO] BUILD SUCCESSFUL
[INFO] ------------------------------------------------------------------
[INFO] Total time: 16 seconds
[INFO] Finished at: Wed Jul 06 13:50:07 BST 2011
[INFO] Final Memory: 24M/58M
[INFO] ------------------------------------------------------------------
```

The results of the tests are stored at target/surefire-reports. You can take a look at the text files there now. Later on you'll be viewing these results through a nicer web frontend.

> **TIP** You'll notice that we also included the `clean` goal. We do this out of habit, just in case there's some old cruft lying about.

Now that you have compiled and tested code, it's ready to be packaged up. Although you can use the `package` goal to do this directly, we'll use the `install` goal. Read on to find out why!

INSTALL

The `install` goal performs two major tasks. It packages up the code as specified by the `<packaging>` element in the pom.xml file (in this case, a JAR file). It installs that artifact into your local Maven repository (under $HOME/.m2/repository) so that it can be used as a dependency by your other projects. As usual, if it detects that earlier build lifecycle steps haven't been executed, it will executed those relevant goals as well.

To see this in action, execute the following Maven goal:

```
mvn install
```

Once Maven has completed the `install` goal, you should see it report something similar to the following output.

```
...
[INFO] [jar:jar {execution: default-jar}]
[INFO] Building jar: C:\Projects\workspace3.6\code\trunk\target\
java7developer-1.0.0.jar
[INFO] [install:install {execution: default-install}]
[INFO] Installing C:\Projects\workspace3.6\code\trunk\target\java7developer-
      1.0.0.jar
to C:\Documents and Settings\Admin\.m2\repository\com\java7developer\
java7develope
r\1.0.0\java7developer-1.0.0.jar
[INFO] -----------------------------------------------------------------
[INFO] BUILD SUCCESSFUL
[INFO] -----------------------------------------------------------------
[INFO] Total time: 17 seconds
[INFO] Finished at: Wed Jul 06 13:53:04 BST 2011
[INFO] Final Memory: 28M/66M
[INFO] -----------------------------------------------------------------
```

You be able to look at the java7developer-1.0.0.jar artifact in the target directory (the result of the `package` goal) as well as in your local Maven repository under $HOME/ .m2/repository/com.java7developer/1.0.0.

> **TIP** You may wish to split your Scala and Groovy code into their own JAR files. Maven supports this, but you have to remember that for Maven, each separate JAR artifact should be a project in its own right. This means you'll have to use the Maven concept of a *multimodule* project. See Maven's "Guide to Working with Multiple Modules" page for details (http://maven.apache .org/guides/mini/guide-multiple-modules.html for further details).

Most of us work in teams and often share a codebase, so how can we ensure that we still have quick, reliable builds for everyone to share? This is where a CI server comes into play, and by far the most popular one out there for Java developers today is Jenkins.

12.4 Jenkins—serving your CI needs

Having a successful CI build requires a combination of developer discipline and the right tooling. In order to support the hallmarks of a good CI process, Jenkins provides much of the tooling support required, as table 12.2 shows.

Table 12.2 Hallmarks of a good CI build and how Jenkins fulfills those

Hallmark	Jenkins fulfillment
Automatic builds	Jenkins will run builds anytime you want it to. It can do so automatically via build triggers.
Always tested	Jenkins will run any goals you like, including the Maven `test` goal. It has powerful trend reporting on test failures and can report a build as failing if the tests don't all pass.

Table 12.2   Hallmarks of a good CI build and how Jenkins fulfills those (*continued*)

Hallmark	Jenkins fulfillment
Regular commits	This one is up to the developers!
Build each commit	Jenkins can perform a build each time it detects a new commit to the version control repository.
Fast builds	This is more important for your unit-test based builds, because you want these to have a fast turnaround time. Jenkins can help here by sending off jobs to slave nodes, but more often it's up to the developers to have a lean, mean build script and to configure Jenkins to call the right build lifecycle goals when executing a build.
Visible results	Jenkins has a web-based dashboard as well as a host of notification methods.

All CI servers are capable of polling a version control repository and executing `compile` and `test` build lifecycle goals. What makes Jenkins stand out is its easy-to-use UI and its extensive plugin ecosystem.

The UI is extremely helpful when you're configuring Jenkins and its plugins, often using Ajax-style calls to check the sanity of your input as you complete each field. There's also plenty of context-sensitive help content on offer; it doesn't take a specialist to get Jenkins up and running.

Jenkins' plugin ecosystem is vast and allows you to poll almost any type of version control repository, run builds for multiple languages, and view a host of valuable reports about your code.

Jenkins and Hudson

In literature around the internet and in certain books, you'll see some confusion over the name of this CI server. Jenkins is actually a recent fork of the Hudson project, taking with it the majority of the developers and active community. Hudson continues as a great CI server project in its own right, but for now Jenkins is the more active project of the two.

Jenkins is free and open source, and it has a very active community willing to help new practitioners.

Refer to appendix D for information on how to download and install Jenkins. Once you've completed the download and installation, come back here to continue!

> **WARNING**   We're assuming that you'll install Jenkins as a WAR file on your favorite web server and that the base URL for the Jenkins install will be http://localhost:8080/jenkins/. If you're running the WAR file directly, the base URL will be http://localhost:8080/.

This section will cover the basics of configuring a basic Jenkins install, followed by how to set up, then execute a build job. We'll be using the java7developer project as an example, but feel free to follow along with your own favorite project.

In order to get Jenkins to monitor your source code repository and to execute your builds, you need to set up basic configuration first.

12.4.1 Basic configuration

You'll start at the Jenkins home page at http://localhost:8080/jenkins/. To start configuring Jenkins, click on the Manage Jenkins link in the menu at the left (http://localhost:8080/jenkins/manage). Listed on the management page are a variety of setup options you can explore.

For now, select the Configure System link (http://localhost:8080/jenkins/configure). You should arrive at a screen whose top section is similar to figure 12.2.

At the top of this screen, you'll notice that Jenkins tells you where its home directory is. If you ever need to perform configuration outside of the UI, you can go there.

TIP If you're installing Jenkins for your team and need to think about security, you should check the Enable Security and Prevent Cross Site Request Forgery Exploits check boxes and configure accordingly. To begin, it's easiest to use Jenkins' own database. You can always swap to your enterprise LDAP or Active Directory–based authentication and authorization later.

In order to execute builds, Jenkins will need to know where your build tool is located. This is located further down the configuration page. Look for the word "Maven".

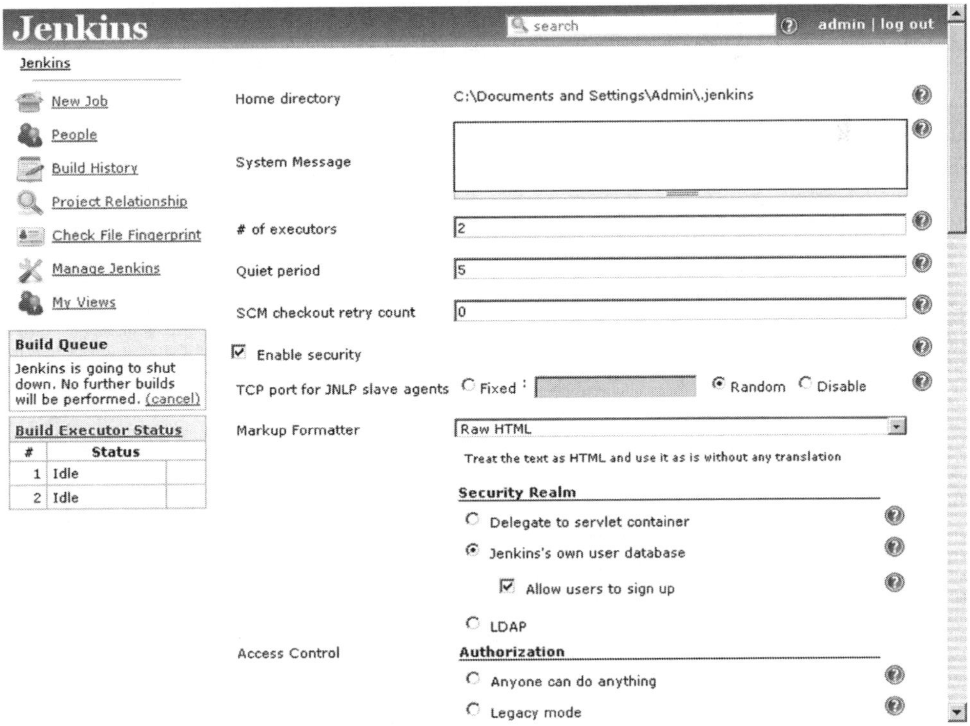

Figure 12.2 Jenkins configuration page

BUILD TOOL CONFIGURATION

Out of the box, Jenkins supports both Ant and Maven (you can get other build tool support via plugins). In the case of the java7developer project, we're using Maven (on Windows), so we have Jenkins configured as shown in figure 12.3.

Note that Jenkins gives you the option to automatically install Maven, which is handy if you're installing on a clean machine.

Now that you have Maven configured, you need to tell Jenkins what type of version control repository you're going to use. This is located further down the configuration page. Look for the word SVN.

VERSION CONTROL CONFIGURATION

Out of the box, Jenkins supports both CVS and Subversion (SVN). Other version control systems such as Git and Mercurial can be supported via plugins. We're using version 1.6 of SVN for the java7developer project, and its configuration can be seen in figure 12.4.

At the end of setting up this configuration, click the Save button at the bottom of the screen to ensure that the configuration is kept.

Now that you have the basics of Jenkins configured, it's time to create your first job.

12.4.2 Setting up a job

To begin setting up a new job, go back to the dashboard and click the New Job link on the left-hand menu to get to the job setup page (http://localhost:8080/jenkins/view/All/newJob). There are a bunch of options to choose from.

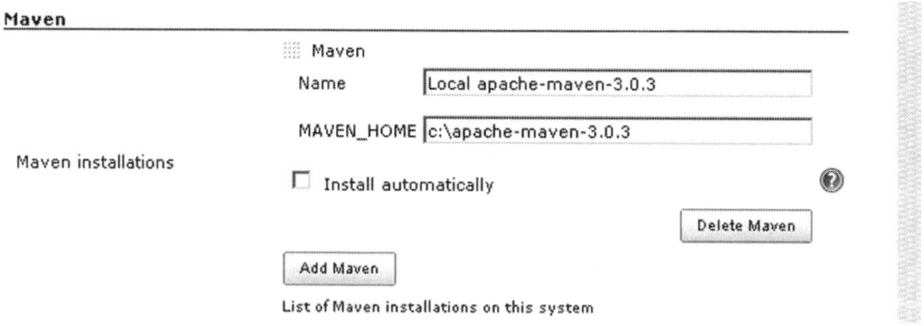

Maven

	Maven	
	Name	Local apache-maven-3.0.3
	MAVEN_HOME	c:\apache-maven-3.0.3
Maven installations	☐ Install automatically	
		Delete Maven
	Add Maven	
	List of Maven installations on this system	

Figure 12.3   Maven build tool configuration

Subversion

Subversion Workspace Version [1.6 (svn:externals to file) ▼]

Exclusion revprop name   [   ]

☑ Validate repository URLs up to the first variable name

☑ Update default Subversion credentials cache after successful authentication

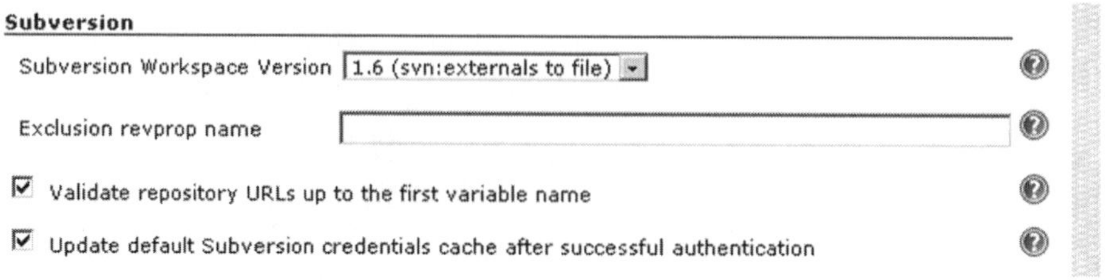

Figure 12.4   SVN version control configuration

To set up a job to build the java7developer project, give the job a title (java7developer), choose the Build a Maven2/3 Project option and click the OK button to continue. You should be taken to a configuration screen whose top section looks similar to figure 12.5.

There are a number of fields you can fill out here, but these are the sections you'll be interested in initially:

- Source Code Management
- Build Triggers
- Build

You begin by specifying the source code management aspects.

SOURCE CODE MANAGEMENT

The source code management section is mainly about specifying which version control branch, tag, or label you're building the source code from. It's the "integration" in continuous integration as your team will be constantly adding new code to version control.

For the java7developer project, we're using SVN and want to build the source code from trunk. Figure 12.6 demonstrates these settings.

Once you've told Jenkins where to get the source code from, the next set of details to configure is how often Jenkins should build for you. This is done via build triggers.

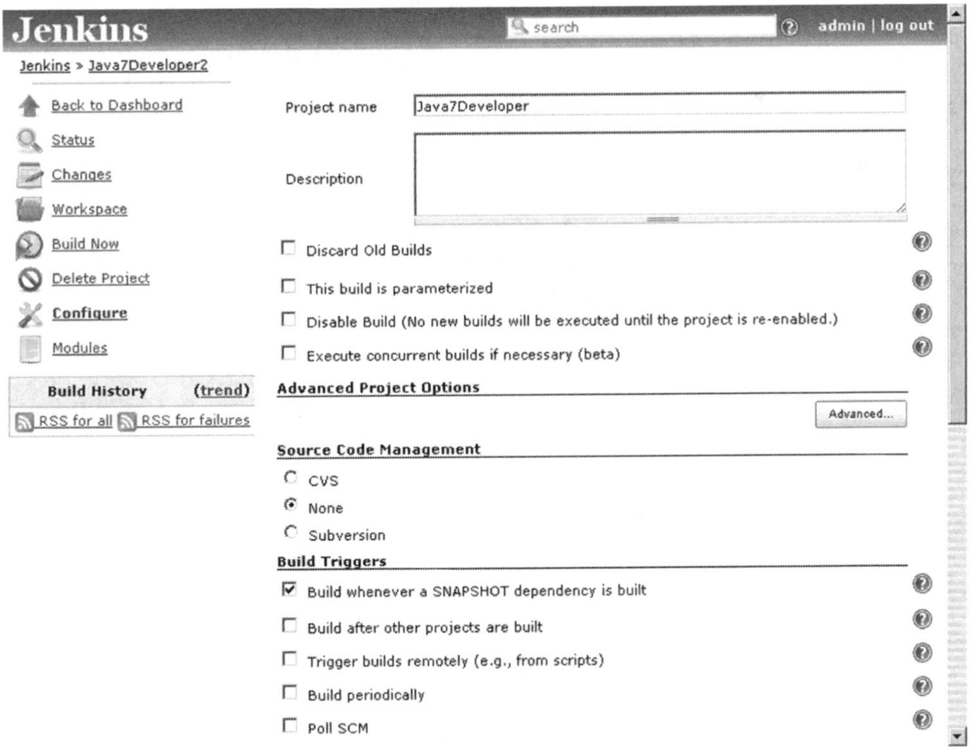

Figure 12.5 Maven 2/3 job configuration page

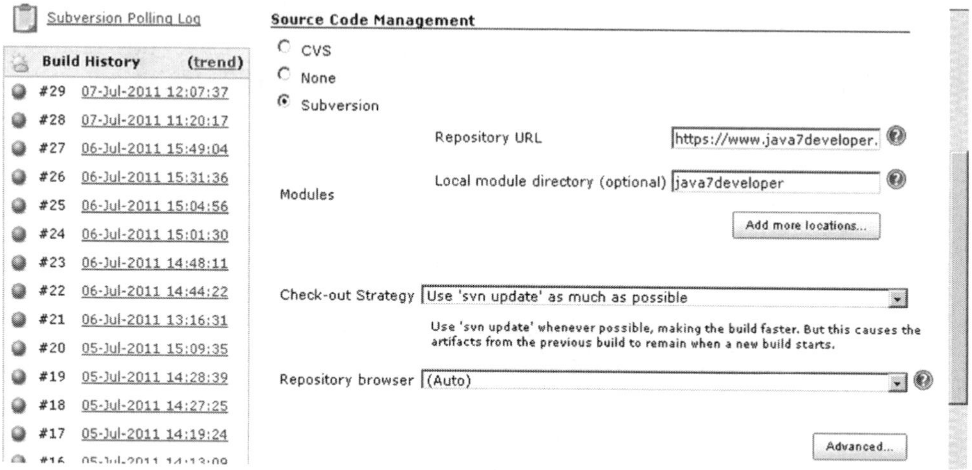

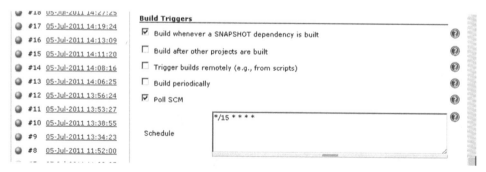

Figure 12.6   Java7developer source code management configuration

BUILD TRIGGERS

Build triggers bring the "continuous" into continuous integration. You can ask Jenkins to build as often as each new commit hits the source control repository or set it for a more leisurely once-a-day build.

For the java7developer project, we simply ask Jenkins to poll SVN every 15 minutes, shown in figure 12.7.

You can find out from Jenkins how to use a particular field by clicking on the help icon (represented by the ? image). In this case, you might want assistance in writing a cron-like expression to specify the polling period.

At this stage Jenkins, knows where to get the code and how often to build it. The next step is to tell Jenkins what build lifecycle phases (goals or targets in your build script) you want it to execute.

BUILD

With Jenkins, you can set up many jobs all executing different parts of the build lifecycle. You might want to have a job that executes the full suite of system integration tests

Figure 12.7   Java7developer build trigger configuration

⊘	# 7	05-Jul-2011 11:08:25
●	#6	05-Jul-2011 11:03:34
●	#5	05-Jul-2011 10:16:13
●	#4	04-Jul-2011 14:30:49
●	#3	04-Jul-2011 11:54:23
●	#2	04-Jul-2011 11:52:37

Build

Root POM   `pom.xml`

Goals and options   `clean install`

Advanced...

Figure 12.8   Java7developer Maven build lifecycle goals to execute (`clean`, `install`)

once a night. More commonly, you'll want a more frequent job that compiles the code and runs the unit tests each time someone commits to version control.

For the java7developer project, we ask Jenkins to execute the familiar Maven `clean` and `install` goals as shown in figure 12.8.

For the java7developer project, Jenkins now has everything it needs in order to poll the trunk of its SVN repository every 15 minutes and execute the Maven `clean` and `install` goals. Don't forget to click the Save button to save your job!

Now you can go back to the dashboard and see your job there, much like in figure 12.9.

In the Last Success (S) column, the circle icon represents the status of the latest build for that job. In the Weather (W) column, the weather icon represents the overall health of the project and is determined by how often your build has failed, whether the tests have passed, and a whole host of other potential scenarios, depending on your configured plugins. For further details on interpreting these icons, you can click the Legend link in the dashboard (http://localhost:8080/jenkins/legend).

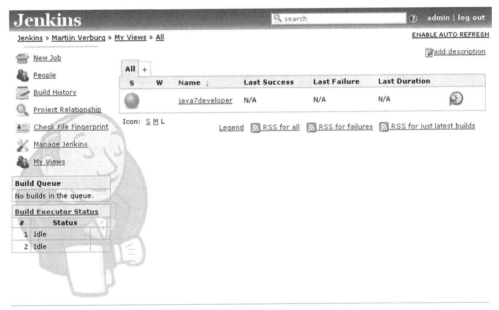

Figure 12.9   Dashboard with java7developer job

Now that you have the job ready to go, you're probably wanting to see it run! You could wait up to 15 minutes for the first poll, or you can simply execute a one-off build.

12.4.3 Executing a job

Forcing the execution of a job is a great way of immediately checking your new configuration. To do so, simply go the dashboard and, for the java7developer job, click the Schedule a Build button (which is the green arrow on the clock image next to the Last Duration field). You can then refresh the page to see the build executing.

> **TIP** By clicking on the Enable Auto Refresh link at the top-right corner of the dashboard, you can automatically keep the dashboard refreshing. This gives you a constantly updated view on the status of all of your builds that are currently in progress.

While the build is executing, you'll see the first icon of the java7developer job flashing to indicate there's a build in progress. You'll also see the Build Executor Status on the left side of the page. Once the build has completed, you'll see that the icon in the Last Success (S) column has gone a red color, indicating that the build has failed!

This failure is due to the missing build.properties file. If you have not done so already in section 12.2, you can fix this quickly by copying over one of the sample build.properties files and editing it, so that your local Java 7 JDK is referenced. Here's an example on a Unix OS:

```
cd $USER/.jenkins/jobs/java7developer/workspace/java7developer
cp sample_build_unix.properties build.properties
```

You can now go back to the dashboard and manually run the build again. This time the build should run successfully and your dashboard should show the java7developer job with a blue icon in the Last Success column, representing a successful build.

Another aspect of the build you can immediately check is a report on the tests, because Jenkins knows how to read the output produced by Maven. To go immediately to the test result, you can click the link in the Last Success column for the java7developer job (http://localhost:8080/jenkins/job/java7developer/lastSuccessfulBuild/). When you follow the link to Latest Test Result, you'll come to a test results screen similar to figure 12.10.

The tests have all passed, which is great! If any of them fail, you can dive into the individual details of each test.

That concludes the basics of running an unsuccessful and then a successful build. For the java7developer project, Jenkins will continue to poll SVN and will execute new builds if it detects a new commit.

You've seen how Jenkins runs a build and how it visually warns you if the build fails for any reason and how it checks on the success or failure of tests. But you can go much further than this. Jenkins can also report on a host of useful code metrics, giving you an insight into the quality of your codebase.

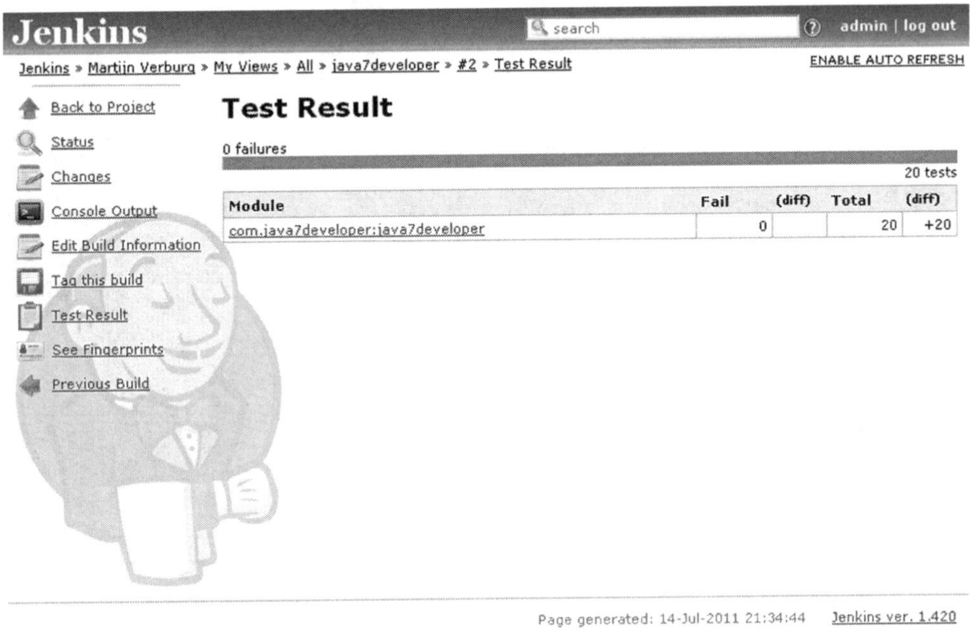

Figure 12.10 Test results for the successful java7developer build

12.5 *Code metrics with Maven and Jenkins*

Java and the JVM have been around for a long time now, and over the years powerful tools and libraries have been developed to guide developers into writing higher quality code. We loosely define this area as *code metrics* or *static code analysis*, and both Maven and Jenkins support the most popular tools out there today. These tools are primarily focused on the Java language itself, although increasingly the more popular tools are also providing support for other languages (or new specific tools are being built).

> **TIP** Several static code analysis tools and libraries are also supported by modern IDEs (such as Eclipse, IntelliJ, and NetBeans) and it's worth spending some time investigating that support as well.

Code metric tooling is primarily aimed at eliminating all of the small, common mistakes that we all make as developers. It helps you set a minimum quality bar for your code, telling you useful things like these:

- How much of your code is being covered by your tests[7]
- Whether the code is formatted cleanly (this aids diff comparisons and readability)
- Whether you're likely to get a NPE
- Whether you've forgotten your `equals()` and `hashCode()` methods on a domain object

---

[7] We do not cover the common code coverage tools in this book as they are not yet compatible with Java 7.

The list of checks that the various tools provide is long, and it's up to each development team to decide what checks they want activated for their project.

> ### The limits of code metrics
>
> Some teams make the mistake of thinking that they have perfect high-quality code base because they've resolved all of the issues that the code metric tooling warned them about. This premise is *false*. Code metric warnings are a useful tool that can help you eliminate lots of low-level bugs and bad coding practices. They don't guarantee quality or tell you whether you got your business logic right or wrong!
>
> Another issue can be that management may be tempted to use these metrics to report on. Do management and yourselves a favor by keeping code metrics at the developer level. They aren't intended to be a project management metric.

Maven and Jenkins combine well in order to give you overviews as well as detailed information on your code metrics. In this section you'll learn two main things:

- How to install and configure Jenkins plugins
- How to configure code consistency (Checkstyle) and bug-finding (FindBugs) plugins

Again, we'll use the java7developer project as an example. Let's begin by looking at how you can install plugins for Jenkins, a prerequisite for getting the code-metrics-reporting functionality.

12.5.1 Installing Jenkins plugins

Installing Jenkins plugins is easy because Jenkins provides a nice UI-based plugin manager to handle the downloading and installing for you. Jenkins needs to perform a restart when you install plugins, so you'll first want to go to the Jenkins management page (http://localhost:8080/jenkins/manage) and click the Prepare to Shutdown link. This halts any jobs that are due to be executed so you can safely install the plugins and restart Jenkins.

Once you've prepared Jenkins for shutdown, it's time to visit the plugin manager. From the management page, click the Manage Plugins link (http://localhost:8080/jenkins/pluginManager/). You should be presented with a screen similar to figure 12.11.

You start on the Updates tab. Swap to the Available tab and you'll be presented with a long list of available plugins. For the purposes of this chapter, you'll want to tick the check box for the following plugins:

- Checkstyle
- FindBugs

Then go to the bottom of the screen and click the Install button to initiate the installation. Once the installation is complete, you can restart Jenkins via the http://localhost:8080/jenkins/restart link.

Figure 12.11   The Jenkins plugin manager

Once Jenkins has restarted, the plugins are installed. Now it's time to configure those plugins, starting with the Checkstyle plugin.

12.5.2   *Making code consistent with Checkstyle*

Checkstyle is a static code analysis tool for Java that focuses on how your source code is laid out, whether you have appropriate levels of Javadocs, and other syntactic sugar checks. It also checks for common coding errors, but FindBugs does a more thorough job of this.

Checkstyle is important for a couple of reasons. First, it can help enforce a minimum set of coding style rules so that your team can easily read each other's code (a major reason why Java is popular is because of its readability). The second benefit is that it's much easier to work with diffs and patches if whitespace and positioning of code elements are consistent.

The Checkstyle plugin has already been configured in the Maven pom.xml, so all you need to do is alter the java7developer job in order to add the `checkstyle:check-style` goal. You can configure the job by clicking on the java7developer link in the job listed on the dashboard, and then in the subsequent screen clicking on the Configure link in the left-hand menu.

Next, you configure the report as well as define whether a build should fail if there are too many violations. Figure 12.12 shows the configuration of the Maven build and the report that we used for the java7developer project.

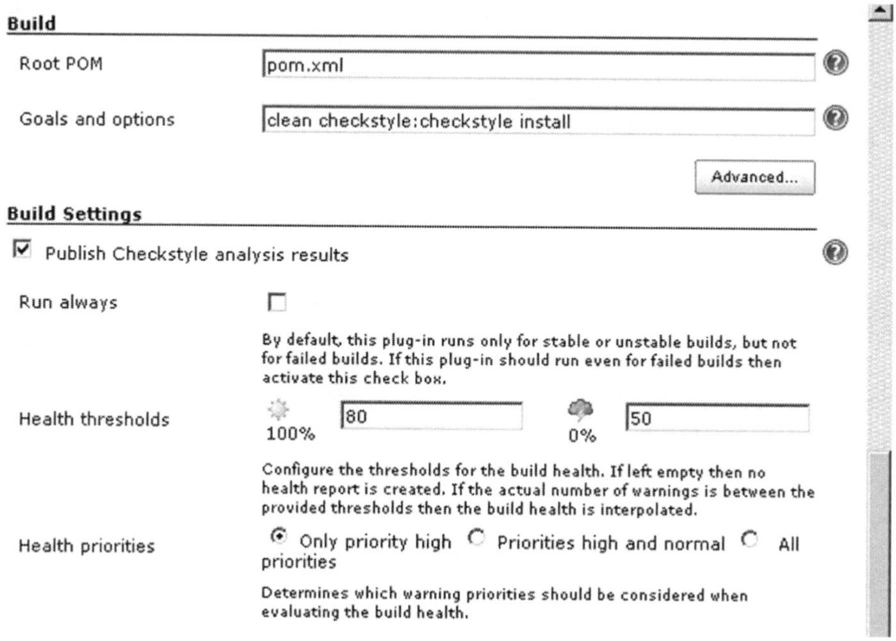

Build

Root POM   pom.xml

Goals and options   clean checkstyle:checkstyle install

                                                        Advanced...

Build Settings

☑ Publish Checkstyle analysis results

Run always   ☐

                        By default, this plug-in runs only for stable or unstable builds, but not
                        for failed builds. If this plug-in should run even for failed builds then
                        activate this check box.

Health thresholds   ☼   80   ☁   50
                        100%   0%

                        Configure the thresholds for the build health. If left empty then no
                        health report is created. If the actual number of warnings is between the
                        provided thresholds then the build health is interpolated.

Health priorities   ⦿ Only priority high   ○ Priorities high and normal   ○ All
                        priorities

                        Determines which warning priorities should be considered when
                        evaluating the build health.

Figure 12.12   Checkstyle configuration

Don't forget to click Save to store this configuration! The default ruleset for Checkstyle is the original Sun Microsystems coding convention for Java. Checkstyle can be tweaked to the nth degree, so that your team's coding conventions are accurately represented.

> **WARNING**   The latest version of Checkstyle may not yet fully support Java 7 syntax, so you may see false positives around try-with-resources, the diamond operator, and other Project Coin syntax elements.

Let's take a look at how the Java7developer project lines up against the default ruleset. As usual, you can go back to the Jenkins dashboard and manually execute the build. Once the build is complete, you can go back to the last successful build page (remember, you can get there via the link in the Last Success column) and click the Checkstyle Warnings link in the left-hand menu to be taken to the page that shows the Checkstyle report. For the java7developer project, this should look similar to figure 12.13.

As you can see, the Java7developer codebase has some valid warnings. Looks like we've still got work to do! You can dive into each of the warnings to get an explanation as to why the violation has occurred and set about correcting it for the next build cycle.

Checkstyle is certainly helpful, but its primary focus isn't on potential code errors. For that type of important detection, it's better to use the FindBugs plugin.

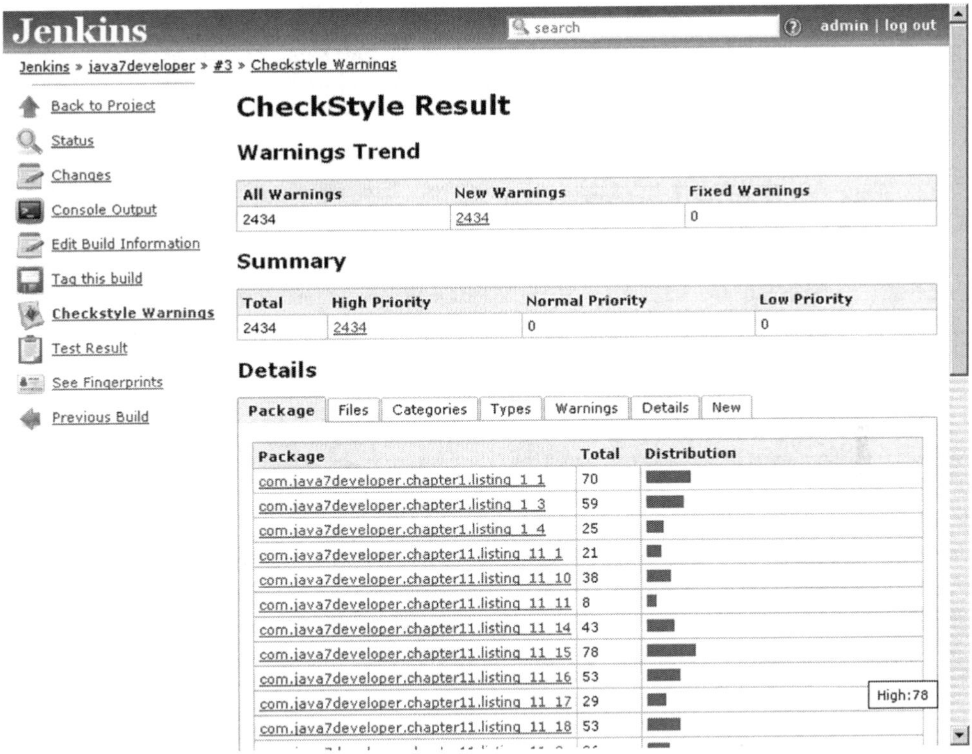

Figure 12.13 Checkstyle report

12.5.3 *Setting the quality bar with FindBugs*

FindBugs (created by Bill Pugh) is a bytecode analysis tool that focuses on finding potential bugs in your code. Its bytecode analysis nature means that FindBugs does work on Scala and Groovy code as well. But the rules are set up for catching Java language bugs, so you need to be careful of false positives in your Groovy and Scala code.

FindBugs has a lot of research behind it, done by developers who are intimately familiar with the Java language. It will detect situations such as:

- Code that will lead to a NPE
- Assigning to a variable that never gets used
- Using == when comparing `String` objects, as opposed to using the `equals` method
- Using basic + `String` concatenation in a loop (as opposed to using `StringBuffer`)

It's worth running FindBugs with its default settings and tweaking which rules you want checked a little later on.

WARNING Even for the Java language, FindBugs can produce false positives. The warnings should be carefully investigated, and if they should be ignored, you can specifically exclude those particular use cases.

FindBugs is important for a couple of reasons. First, it teaches developers good habits by acting as a pair programmer (as far as helping detect potential bugs goes). Second, the overall code quality of the project goes up and your issue tracker will be less full of small annoying bugs, leaving the team to tackle the real issues, such as changes in business logic.

As with the Checkstyle plugin, you can configure the job by clicking on the java7developer link in the job listed on the dashboard, and in the subsequent screen clicking on the Configure link in the left-hand menu.

In order to execute the FindBugs plugin, you need to add the `compile find-bugs:findbugs` goals to the Maven build command in Jenkins (you need `compile` so that FindBugs can work on the bytecode).

You can also configure the report as well as define whether a build fails if there are too many violations. Figure 12.14 shows this configuration.

Don't forget to click Save in order to store your configuration! FindBugs comes with a predefined ruleset that can be extensively tweaked so that your team's coding standards are accurately represented. Let's take a look at how the Java7developer project lines up against the default ruleset.

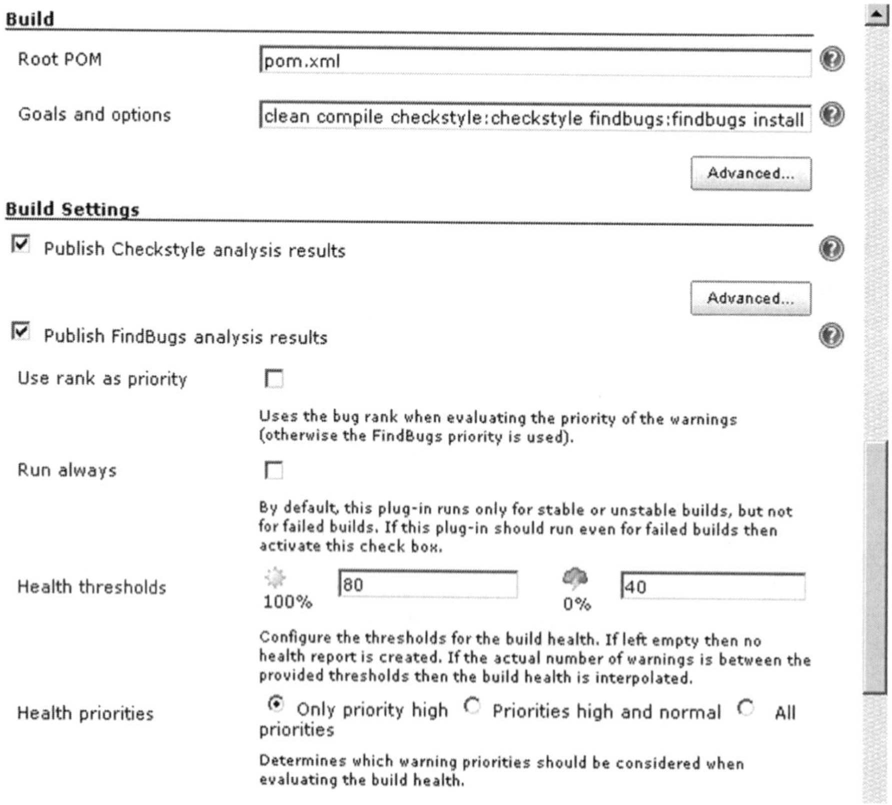

Figure 12.14 FindBugs configuration

As usual, you can go back to the Jenkins dashboard and manually execute the build. Once the build is complete, you can go to the last successful build page (via the link in the Last Success column) and click the FindBugs Warnings link in the left-hand menu to get to the pages that shows the report. Figure 12.15 shows a report that should be similar to what you'll get for the java7developer project.

As you can see, the Java7developer codebase has some valid warnings. Book authors certainly aren't always perfect programmers! You can dive into each of the warnings to get an explanation as to why the violation has occurred, and if you're so inclined, you can correct it for the next build cycle.

FindBugs will find the vast majority of common Java gotchas and coding mistakes. As your development team learns from these mistakes, the reports will show a decreasing number of warnings. Not only have you improved the quality of your code, but you've also improved your own coding!

That completes the section on Jenkins, Maven, and code metrics. The tooling in this area is quite mature now (with Scala and Groovy still requiring more support), and it's very easy to get up and running. If you're a CI fiend and want to explore the full power of Jenkins, we highly recommend John's Smart's constantly updated *Jenkins: The Definitive Guide* (O'Reilly). You may have noticed that we're still missing

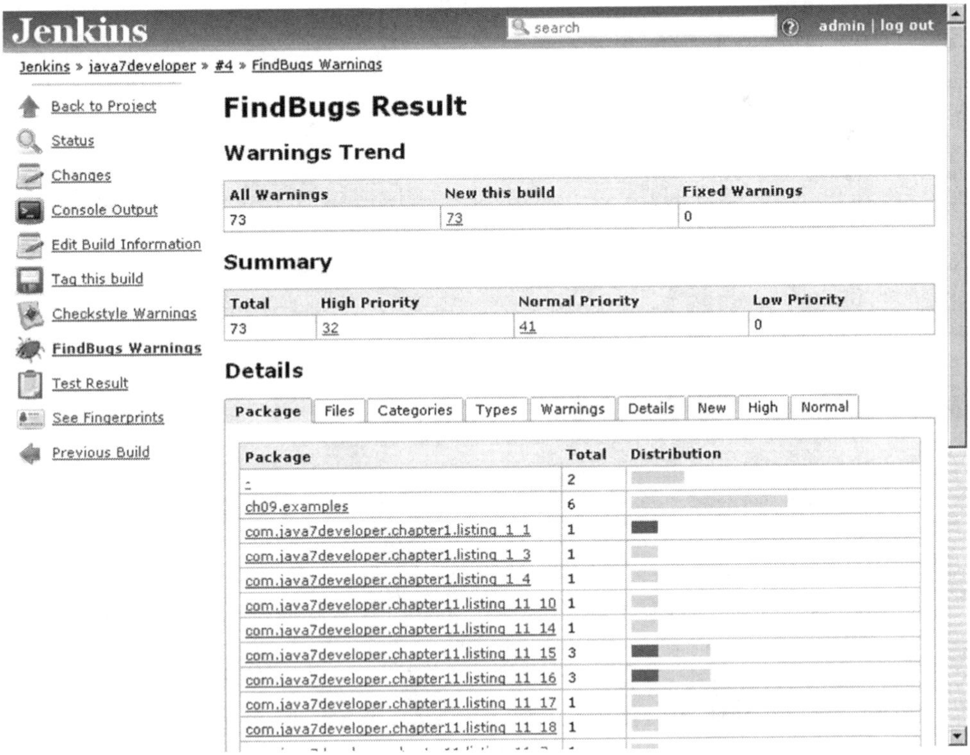

Figure 12.15   FindBugs report

one piece of the puzzle with regards to polyglot programming on the JVM and build and CI—we haven't dealt with Clojure projects. Fortunately, the Clojure community has produced several build tools that are geared toward pure-Clojure projects and are in common use. One of the most popular is Leiningen, which is a build tool that's written in Clojure itself.

12.6   Leiningen

As you've already seen, a build tool needs to provide several capabilities to be as useful as possible to the developer. These are the key ones:

- Dependency management
- Compilation
- Test automation
- Packaging for deployment

Leiningen takes the position that it's better to divide up these aspects. It reuses existing Java technology to provide each of the capabilities, but it does so in a way that isn't dependent on a single package for all of them.

This sounds potentially complicated and a bit scary, but in practice the complexity is hidden from you as a developer. In fact, Leiningen can be used even by developers who don't have experience with the underlying Java tools. We'll begin by installing Leiningen via a very simple bootstrapping process. Then we'll discuss Leiningen's components and overall architecture, and we'll finally try it with a Hello World project.

We'll show you how to start a new project, add a dependency, and work with that dependency inside the Clojure REPL that Leiningen provides. This naturally leads to a discussion of how to do TDD in Clojure using Leiningen. We'll conclude the chapter by looking at how you can package your code for deployment as an application or library for others to use.

Let's see how we can get started with Leiningen.

12.6.1   Getting started with Leiningen

Leiningen provides a very simple way to get started. For Unix-like systems (including Linux and Mac OS X), start by grabbing the `lein` script. This can be found on GitHub (from https://github.com/ search for Leiningen, or use your preferred search engine).

Once the lein script is on your PATH and is executable, it can simply be run. The first time lein is run, it will detect which dependencies need to be installed (and which are already present). This will even install other needed components that aren't part of core Leiningen. As a result, the first run could be slightly slower than subsequent runs as dependencies are installed.

In the next section, we'll explain the architecture of Leiningen and the Java technologies that it relies upon to provide its core functionality.

> ### Installing Leiningen on Windows
>
> One of the annoying things about Windows from an old Unix hacker's viewpoint is the lack of standard, simple tools that command-line lovers rely upon. For example, a vanilla Windows install lacks a `curl` or `wget` utility for pulling down files via HTTP (which Leiningen needs to pull down jars from Maven repositories). The solution is to use a Leiningen Windows install—a zip file containing the `lein.bat` batch file and a prebuilt wget.exe that need to be placed into a directory on your Windows PATH for lein `self-install` to work properly.

12.6.2 Leiningen's architecture

As we discussed, Leiningen wraps up some mainstream Java technologies and simplifies them to provide its capabilities. The main components that are wrapped are Maven (version 2), Ant, and `javac`.

In Figure 12.16, you can see that Maven is used to provide dependency resolution and management, while `javac` and Ant are used for the actual build, running tests, and other aspects of the build process.

Leiningen's approach allows the power user to reach through the abstraction that it provides to access the full power of the underlying tools used at each stage. But the basic syntax and usage is very simple and doesn't require any previous experience with the underlying tools.

Let's look at a simple example to see how the syntax of a project.clj file works and the basic commands that are used in the Leiningen project lifecycle.

12.6.3 Example—Hello Lein

With lein on your path, let's start a new project using it. The way to do this is by using the lein new command:

```
ariel:projects boxcat$ lein new hello-lein
Created new project in: /Users/boxcat/projects/hello-lein
ariel:projects boxcat$ cd hello-lein/
ariel:hello-lein boxcat$ ls
README  project.clj  src  test
```

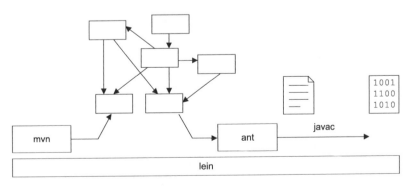

Figure 12.16 Leiningen and its components

This command creates a project called hello-lein. There's a project directory that contains a simple README description file, a project.clj file (which we'll talk more about in just a minute), and parallel src and test directories.

If you import the project that Leiningen has just set up into Eclipse (for example, with the CounterClockwise plugin installed), the project layout will look like it does in figure 12.17.

This project structure mirrors the straightforward layout of Java projects—there are parallel test and src structures with a core.clj file in each one (for tests

Figure 12.17   A newly created Leiningen project

and top-level code, respectively). The other important file is the project.clj, which is used by Leiningen to control the build and hold metadata.

Let's take a look at the skeletal file that's generated by `lein new`.

```
(defproject hello-lein "1.0.0-SNAPSHOT"
  :description "FIXME: write description"
  :dependencies [[org.clojure/clojure "1.2.1"]])
```

Parsing this Clojure form is relatively straightforward—there's a macro called `(defproject)` that makes new values that represent Leiningen projects. This macro needs to be told what the project is called—`hello-lein` in this case. You also need to tell the macro what version of the project this is—`1.0.0-SNAPSHOT` by default (a Maven version number as discussed in section 12.3.1)—and then provide a map of metadata that describes the project.

Out of the box, lein provides two pieces of metadata: a description string and a vector of dependencies, which is a handy place to start adding new dependencies. Let's add a new dependency—the `clj-time` library. This provides a Clojure interface to a useful Java date and time library (Joda-Time, but you don't need to know the Java library to make sense of this example). After adding the new dependency, your project.clj file will look like this:

```
(defproject hello-lein "1.0.0-SNAPSHOT"
  :description "FIXME: write description"
  :dependencies [[org.clojure/clojure "1.2.1"]
                 [clj-time "0.3.0"]])
```

The second element of the vector describing the new dependency is the version of the library to use. This is the version that will be retrieved from a repository if Leiningen can't find a copy in its local dependencies repository.

By default, Leiningen uses a repository at http://clojars.org/ to retrieve missing libraries. As Leiningen uses Maven under the hood, this is essentially just a Maven repository. Clojars provides a search tool, which is useful if you know the libraries you need but don't know the version you want.

With this new dependency in place, you need to update the local build environment. This is done with the command `lein deps`.

```
ariel:hello-lein boxcat$ lein deps
Downloading: clj-time/clj-time/0.3.0/clj-time-0.3.0.pom from central
Downloading: clj-time/clj-time/0.3.0/clj-time-0.3.0.pom from clojure
Downloading: clj-time/clj-time/0.3.0/clj-time-0.3.0.pom from clojars
Transferring 2K from clojars
Downloading: joda-time/joda-time/1.6/joda-time-1.6.pom from clojure
Downloading: joda-time/joda-time/1.6/joda-time-1.6.pom from clojars
Transferring 5K from clojars
Downloading: clj-time/clj-time/0.3.0/clj-time-0.3.0.jar from central
Downloading: clj-time/clj-time/0.3.0/clj-time-0.3.0.jar from clojure
Downloading: clj-time/clj-time/0.3.0/clj-time-0.3.0.jar from clojars
Transferring 7K from clojars
Downloading: joda-time/joda-time/1.6/joda-time-1.6.jar from clojure
Downloading: joda-time/joda-time/1.6/joda-time-1.6.jar from clojars
Transferring 522K from clojars
Copying 4 files to /Users/boxcat/projects/hello-lein/lib
ariel:hello-lein boxcat$
```

Leiningen has used Maven to pull down the Clojure interface, but also the underlying Joda-Time JAR. Let's make use of it in some code and demonstrate how to use Leiningen as a REPL for development in the presence of dependencies.

You need to modify your main source file, src/hello_lein/core.clj, like this:

```
(ns hello-lein.core)

(use '[clj-time.core :only (date-time)])

(defn isodate-to-millis-since-epoch [x]
  (.getMillis (apply date-time
   (map #(Integer/parseInt %) (.split x "-")))))
```

This provides you with a Clojure function that converts an ISO standard date (in the form YYYY-MM-DD) to the number of milliseconds since the Unix epoch.

Let's test it out, REPL-style, using Leiningen. First you need to add an additional line to project.clj, so that it looks like this:

```
(defproject hello-lein "1.0.0-SNAPSHOT"
  :description "FIXME: write description"
  :dependencies [[org.clojure/clojure "1.2.1"]
                 [clj-time "0.3.0"]]
  :repl-init hello-lein.core)
```

With this line in place, you can bring up a REPL that has the dependencies fully available, and which has brought into scope the functions from the namespace `hello-lein.core`:

```
ariel:hello-lein boxcat$ lein repl
REPL started; server listening on localhost:10886.

hello-lein.core=> (isodate-to-millis-since-epoch "1970-01-02")
86400000
hello-lein.core=>
```

This is the correct answer for the number of milliseconds in a day, and it demonstrates the core principle of this way of working with the REPL in a real project. Let's expand a bit on this, and look at a very powerful way of working in a test-oriented way with the Leiningen REPL.

12.6.4 *REPL-oriented TDD with Leiningen*

At the heart of any good TDD methodology should be a simple, basic loop that you can use to develop new functionality. With Clojure and Leiningen, the basic cycle can be something like this:

1 Add any needed new dependencies (and rerun `lein deps`).
2 Start the REPL (`lein repl`).
3 Draft a new function and bring it into scope inside the REPL.
4 Test the function within the REPL.
5 Iterate steps 3 and 4 until the function behaves correctly.
6 Add the final version of the function to the appropriate .clj file.
7 Add the test cases you ran to the test suite .clj files.
8 Restart the REPL and repeat from 3 (or 1 if you now need new dependencies).

This style of development is test-driven, but rather than having to answer the question of whether the code or tests are written first, with REPL-style TDD both proceed at the same time.

The reason for the restart of the REPL at step 8 when adding a newly crafted function to the source base is to ensure that the new function will compile cleanly. Sometimes when creating a new function, minor changes are made to other functions or to the environment to support it. It's sometimes easy to forget these changes when moving the function to the permanent source base. Restarting the REPL helps catch those forgotten changes early.

This process is simple and clear, but one question that we haven't addressed, either here or in chapter 11 on TDD, is how to write tests in Clojure. Fortunately, this is very simple. Let's have a look at the template that `lein new` provides you with when you create a new project:

```
(ns hello-lein.test.core
  (:use [hello-lein.core])
  (:use [clojure.test]))

(deftest replace-me ;; FIXME: write
  (is false "No tests have been written."))
```

To run tests, you use the `lein test` command. Let's run it against this autogenerated case to see what will happen (although you can probably guess).

```
ariel:hello-lein boxcat$ lein test
Testing hello-lein.test.core
FAIL in (replace-me) (core.clj:6)
No tests have been written.
```

```
expected: false
  actual: false
Ran 1 tests containing 1 assertions.
1 failures, 0 errors.
```

As you can see, the supplied case is a failure, and it nags you to write some test cases. Let's do just that, by writing a core.clj file in the test folder:

```
(ns hello-lein.test.core
  (:use [hello-lein.core])
  (:use [clojure.test]))

(deftest one-day
  (is true
    (= 86400000 (isodate-to-millis-since-epoch "1970-01-02"))))
```

The anatomy of the test is very simple—you use the `(deftest)` macro, give your test a name (`one-day`), and provide a form that has a very similar form to an assert clause.

The structure of Clojure code means that the `(is)` form can be read very naturally—almost like a DSL. This test can be read aloud as, "Is it true that 86400000 is equal to the number of milliseconds since the epoch on 1970-01-02?" Let's see this test case in action:

```
ariel:hello-lein boxcat$ lein test
Testing hello-lein.test.core
Ran 1 tests containing 1 assertions.
0 failures, 0 errors.
```

The key package here is `clojure.test`, and it provides a number of other useful forms for building up test cases where more complex environments or test fixtures need to be used. There's full coverage of TDD in Clojure in *Clojure in Action* by Amit Rathore (Manning, 2011) if you want to know more.

With your REPL-oriented TDD process in place, you can now build a sizable application in Clojure and work with it. But the time will come when you produce something that you want to share with others. Fortunately, Leiningen has a number of commands that promote easy packaging and deployment.

12.6.5 *Packaging and deploying with Leiningen*

Leiningen provides two main ways to distribute your code to others. These are essentially with and without dependencies. The corresponding commands are `lein jar` and `lein uberjar` respectively.

Let's see `lein jar` in action:

```
ariel:hello-lein boxcat$ lein jar
Copying 4 files to /Users/boxcat/projects/hello-lein/lib
Created /Users/boxcat/projects/hello-lein/hello-lein-1.0.0-SNAPSHOT.jar
```

And here's what the resulting JAR file contains:

```
ariel:hello-lein boxcat$ jar tvf hello-lein-1.0.0-SNAPSHOT.jar
    72 Sat Jul 16 13:38:00 BST 2011 META-INF/MANIFEST.MF
  1424 Sat Jul 16 13:38:00 BST 2011 META-INF/maven/hello-lein/hello-lein/
    pom.xml
```

```
    105 Sat Jul 16 13:38:00 BST 2011
META-INF/maven/hello-lein/hello-lein/pom.properties
    196 Fri Jul 15 21:52:12 BST 2011 project.clj
    238 Fri Jul 15 21:40:06 BST 2011 hello_lein/core.clj
ariel:hello-lein boxcat$
```

One obvious facet of this process is that Leiningen's basic commands lead to distribution of Clojure source files, rather than compiled .class files. This is traditional for Lisp code, as the macro and read-time components of the system would be hampered by having to deal with compiled code.

Now, let's see what happens when you use `lein uberjar`. This should produce a JAR that contains not only your code, but also your dependencies.

```
ariel:hello-lein boxcat$ lein uberjar
Cleaning up.
Copying 4 files to /Users/boxcat/projects/hello-lein/lib
Copying 4 files to /Users/boxcat/projects/hello-lein/lib
Created /Users/boxcat/projects/hello-lein/hello-lein-1.0.0-SNAPSHOT.jar
Including hello-lein-1.0.0-SNAPSHOT.jar
Including clj-time-0.3.0.jar
Including clojure-1.2.1.jar
Including clojure-contrib-1.2.0.jar
Including joda-time-1.6.jar
Created /Users/boxcat/projects/hello-lein/
➥ hello-lein-1.0.0-SNAPSHOT-standalone.jar
```

As you can see, this produces a JAR that contains not only your code, but also all your dependencies, and their dependencies. This is known as the transitive closure of your dependency graph. It means that you're completely packaged for stand-alone running.

Of course, this also means the result of `lein uberjar` will be a lot larger than the result of `lein jar` because you have all those dependencies to package. Even for the simple example we've been working with here, this difference is quite stark:

```
ariel:hello-lein boxcat$ ls -lh h*.jar
-rw-r--r--  1 boxcat  staff   4.1M 16 Jul 13:46
hello-lein-1.0.0-SNAPSHOT-standalone.jar
-rw-r--r--  1 boxcat  staff   1.7K 16 Jul 13:46
hello-lein-1.0.0-SNAPSHOT.jar
```

One useful way to think about `lein jar` and `lein uberjar` is this: You'll want to use `lein jar` if you're building a library (that builds on top of other libraries) and that others may want to use in their applications, or build on top of. If you're building a Clojure application for end use rather than extension (by the typical user), you'll want to use `lein uberjar`.

You've seen how to use Leiningen to start, manage, build, and deploy Clojure projects. Leiningen has many other useful commands built in and a powerful plugin system that allows for heavy customization. To see more of what Leiningen can do for you, just call it without a command, as `lein`.

We'll meet Leiningen again in the next chapter when we build a Clojure web application.

12.7 Summary

Having a fast, repeatable, and simple build should be the hallmark of any project that the well-grounded Java developer is involved with. If you can't build your software quickly and consistently, a great deal of time and money are being wasted, including your own!

Understanding the basic build lifecycle of compile-test-package is key to having a good build process. After all, you can't test the code if it hasn't compiled yet!

Maven takes the concept of the build lifecycle and expands it into a project lifecycle that's used consistently across all Maven projects. This convention over configuration approach is very helpful for large software teams, but some projects may need a little more flexibility.

Maven also tackles the issue of dependency management, a difficult task in the world of open source and Java, as the average project has its fair share of third-party libraries.

By hooking your build process into a CI environment, you gain the benefits of incredibly fast feedback and the ability to merge changes quickly without fear.

Jenkins is the popular CI server that can not only build almost any type of project, but also provides rich reporting support via its extensive plugin system. Over time, a team can have Jenkins execute a rich set of builds, from the fast unit testing build to an overreaching system integration build.

Leiningen is a very natural choice for Clojure projects. It brings together a very tight loop TDD and REPL approach with a very clean tool for build and deployment.

Next up, we'll cover rapid web development, a topic that most well-grounded Java developers have struggled with since the first Java-based web frameworks appeared.

Rapid web development

Rapid web development matters. A lot. A huge number of websites and applications driven by web technology dominate commercial and social activities across the globe. Businesses (especially startups) live and die by their capability to get a new product or feature rapidly into a competitive market. End users now expect near-instant turnaround of new features and rapid fixes for any bugs they discover. The modern user is less patient than ever before.

Unfortunately a vast majority of Java-based web frameworks aren't good at supporting rapid web development, and organizations have turned to technologies such as PHP and Rails to stay competitive.

So where does this leave you as a well-grounded Java developer? With the recent advancement of dynamic layer languages on the JVM, you now have some fantastic rapid web development options. There are now frameworks, such as Grails (Groovy)

> **Java EE 6—a step closer to rapid web development with Java?**
> Java Enterprise Edition (Java EE) 6 has come a long way since the days of J2EE (and
> its much maligned early JSP, Servlet, and EJB APIs). Despite the improvements in
> Java EE 6 (with much improved JSP, Servlet, and EJB APIs) it still suffers from static
> typing and compilation issues from being based on Java.

and Compojure (Clojure) that can provide you with the rapid web development capabilities that you need. This means you don't have to throw away the power and flexibility of the JVM, and you no longer have to spend hours of overtime to try to compete with technologies such as PHP and Rails.

This chapter will start by explaining why the Java-based web frameworks aren't ideal for rapid web development. Following that, you'll learn about the wide range of criteria that a great web framework should meet. Through some quantitative research and the work of Matt Raible, you'll see how you can rank the various JVM web frameworks based upon a list of 20 criteria.

One of the leading rapid web development frameworks, in terms of fulfilling many of the criteria, is Grails. We'll take you through this Groovy-based web framework, which is heavily influenced by the extremely popular Rails framework.

As an alternative to Grails, we'll also cover Compojure, a Clojure-based web framework that allows for very concise web programming and fast development.

Let's kick off by looking at why web frameworks based on Java aren't necessarily the perfect choice for modern web projects.

13.1 The problem with Java-based web frameworks

As you'll, we discussed the polyglot programming pyramid and the three layers of programming in chapter 7. It's repeated here as figure 13.1.

Java sits firmly in the stable layer, and so do all of its web frameworks. As expected for a popular and mature language, Java has a variety of web frameworks, such as these:

- Spring MVC
- GWT
- Struts 2
- Wicket
- Tapestry
- JSF (and other related "Faces" libraries)
- Vaadin
- Play
- Plain old JSP/Servlet

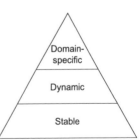

Figure 13.1   The polyglot
programming pyramid

Java has no de facto leader in this space, and this partly stems from Java simply not being an ideal language for rapid web development. The former leader of the Struts 2 project, a popular Java-based web framework, had this to say on the subject:

> I've gone over to the dark side :-) and much prefer to develop in Rails – for the conciseness mentioned above, but also because I don't ever have to do a "build" or "deploy" step during my development cycle any more. But you guys and gals need to be reminded that *this* is the kind of thing you are competing against if you expect to attract Rails developers ... or to avoid even more "previously Java web developer" defectors like me :-).
>
> —Craig McClanahan, Oct. 23, 2007
> (http://markmail.org/thread/qfb5sekad33eobh2)

This section will cover why Java isn't a good choice for rapid web development. Let's start by exploring why a compiled language slows you down when developing web applications.

13.1.1 Why Java compilation is bad for rapid web development

Java is a compiled language, and as alluded to previously, this means that every time you make a code change to a web application, you have to go through all of these steps:

- Recompile the Java code.
- Stop your web server.
- Redeploy the changes to your web server.
- Start your web server.

As you can imagine, this wastes a tremendous amount of time! Especially when you're making lots of small code changes, such as altering the destinations in a controller or making small changes to the view.

> **NOTE** The line between what is an application server and what is a web server is starting to get very blurred. This is due to the advent of JEE 6 (allowing you to run EJBs in a web container) and the fact that most application servers are highly modular. When we refer to a "web server," we mean any server that has a Servlet container.

If you're a seasoned web developer, you'll know that there are some techniques you can use to try to solve this problem. Most of these approaches rely on some sort of ability to apply code changes without stopping and starting the web server, which is also known as *hot deployment*. Hot deployment can come in the form of replacing all of the resources (such as an entire WAR file) or just a select few (such as a single JSP page). Unfortunately, hot deployment has never been 100 percent reliable (due to classloading limitations and container bugs), and the web server often still has to perform expensive recompilation of code.

Generally speaking, Java-based web frameworks don't reliably allow you to have a fast turnaround time for your changes. But that isn't the only concern with Java-based

> ## Hot deployment with JRebel and LiveRebel
>
> If you must use a Java-based web framework, we highly recommend products called JRebel and LiveRebel (http://www.zeroturnaround.com/jrebel/). JRebel sits between your IDE and your web server, and when you make source code changes locally, they're automatically applied to your running web server through some genuinely impressive JVM trickery (LiveRebel is used for production deploys). It's basically hot deployment done right, and these tools are seen as de facto industry standards for solving the hot deployment problem.

web frameworks. Another factor that slows down rapid web development is the flexibility of the language, and this is where static typing can be a drawback.

13.1.2 Why static typing is bad for rapid web development

In the early stages of developing a new product or feature, it's often wise to keep an open-ended design (with regards to typing) of the user presentation layer. It's all too easy for a user to demand that a numeric value have decimal precision, or for a list of books to become a list of books and toys instead. Having a statically typed language can be a great hindrance here. If you have to change a list of Book objects into a list of BookOrToy[1] objects, you'd have to change your static types throughout your codebase.

Although it's true that you can always use the base type as the type of objects in container classes (for example, Java's Object class), this is certainly not seen as a best practice—this is effectively reverting to pregenerics Java.

As a result, choosing a web framework that's based on a language in the dynamic layer is certainly a valid option to investigate.

> **NOTE** Scala is, of course, a statically typed language. But due to its advanced type inference, it can sidestep a lot of the problems associated with Java's approach to static typing. This means Scala can be, and is, used as a viable web layer language.

Before you go leaping into the deep end and choosing a dynamic language for your web development, let's take a step back and look at the bigger picture. Let's consider what criteria should be supported by a good rapid web development framework.

13.2 Criteria in selecting a web framework

There are a number of powerful Java-based web frameworks to choose from, as you'd expect, given the number of years Java has been the top programming language in the world. More recently there has been a rise in web frameworks based on other JVM languages, such as Groovy, Scala, and Clojure. Unfortunately, there has not been a clear leader in this space for many years, and it's up to you to decide which framework to choose.

---

[1] Spidey senses tingling! If you have a domain class with the words Or or And in it, then you're likely breaking the SOLID principles as discussed in chapter 11.

You should expect a great deal of help from your web framework, and you must evaluate the available frameworks on a number of criteria. The more criteria that a web framework supports, the more likely you are to be able to rapidly develop web applications.

Matt Raible has come up with a list of 20 criteria for web frameworks.[2] Table 13.1 briefly explains these criteria.

Table 13.1   The 20 criteria

Criteria	Examples
Developer productivity	Can you build a CRUD page in 1 day or 5 days?
Developer perception	Is it fun to use?
Learning curve	Are you productive after 1 week or 1 month of learning?
Project health	Is the project in dire straits?
Developer availability	Are there developers on the market who have the expertise?
Job trends	Will you be able to hire developers in the future?
Templating	Can you follow the DRY (Don't Repeat Yourself) principle?
Components	Are there things such as date pickers out of the box?
Ajax	Does it support asynchronous JavaScript calls from the client?
Plugins or add-ons	Can you bolt on functionality like Facebook integration?
Scalability	Does its default controller deal with 500+ concurrent users?
Testing support	Can you test drive the development?
I18n and I10n	Does it support other languages and locales out of the box?
Validation	Can you easily validate user input and provide rapid feedback?
Multilanguage support	Can you use, say, both Java and Groovy?
Quality of documentation/tutorials	Are common use cases and questions documented?
Books published	Have industry experts used it and shared their war stories?
REST support (client and server)	Does it support using the HTTP protocol as it was designed?
Mobile support	Is it easy to support Android, iOS, and other mobile devices?
Degree of risk	"Storing recipes" application or "nuclear power station controller"?

As you can see, that's quite a large list, and you'll need to decide which criteria hold more weight in making your decision. Luckily, Matt has recently done some brave[3] research in this area, and although the results are hotly debated, a clear picture does start to emerge. Figure 13.2 shows how the various frameworks score (out of a possible

---

[2] Matt Raible, "Comparing JVM Web Frameworks" (March 2011), presentation. http://raibledesigns.com/rd/page/publications.

[3] As you can imagine, people are somewhat *passionate* about their favorite web framework!

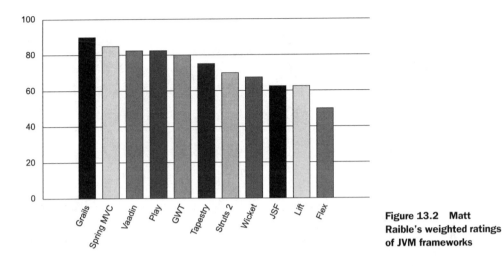

Figure 13.2 Matt Raible's weighted ratings of JVM frameworks

100) when given a high weighting on the criteria that we see as being the most important for rapid web development. Those criteria are developer productivity, testing support, and quality of documentation.

Your needs are possibly going to be different, and you can easily run your own analysis by altering Matt's weightings at http://bit.ly/jvm-frameworks-matrix and producing a graph.

> **TIP** We highly recommend that you prototype some functionality in the top two or three frameworks that meet your weighted criteria, before settling down with one particular framework.

Now that you know what criteria to evaluate on, and you have access to Matt's handy tool, you can make an informed decision on choosing a rapid web development framework. For us, the Grails framework came out on top when using our weighted criteria analysis (Compojure doesn't score in the top, but it's very new, and we expect it to rapidly rise up the leader board in the near future).

Let's take a look at the winner, Grails!

13.3 Getting started with Grails

Grails is a Groovy-based rapid web application framework that utilizes several third-party libraries to implement its functionality, including Spring, Hibernate, JUnit, a Tomcat server, and more. It's a full-stack web framework, providing solutions for all 20 criteria that we listed in section 13.2. Another important point is that Grails borrows heavily from the Rails concept of *convention over configuration*. If you write your code according to the conventions, the framework will perform a lot of boilerplate work for you.

In this section, we'll cover building your first quick-start application. While building the quick-start application, you'll see plenty of evidence as to why Grails puts the

> ### Don't like Groovy? Try Spring Roo
>
> Spring Roo (www.springsource.org/roo) is a rapid development web framework that's based on the same principles as Grails but uses Java as its core language and exposes more of the Spring DI framework to the developer. We don't feel that it's as mature as Grails, but if you really dislike Groovy, this could be a viable alternative for you.

"rapid" into rapid web development. We'll also give you pointers to important Grails technologies that you'll want to explore further, in order to build serious production-ready applications.

If you aren't familiar with Groovy, it may be prudent to review chapter 8 where we covered the Groovy language. Once you're happy with that, you'll want to get Grails downloaded and installed. Head on over to appendix C for the full instructions.

Once you've got Grails installed, it's time to kick-start your first Grails project!

13.4   *Grails quick-start project*

This section will take you through a Grails quick-start project, highlighting parts where Grails really shines as a rapid web framework. You'll touch on the following steps as you go through this section:

- Domain object creation
- Test-driven development
- Domain object persistence
- Test data creation
- Controllers
- GSP views
- Scaffolding and automatic UI creation
- Rapid development turnaround

In particular, we're going to get you to work on a basic building block (`PlayerCharacter`) for supporting a role-playing game.[4] By the end of this section, you'll have created a simple domain object (`PlayerCharacter`) that

- Has some running tests
- Has prepopulated test data
- Can be persisted to a database
- Has a basic UI that enables CRUD operations

The first important time-saver that Grails gives you is its ability to automatically create a quick-start project structure for you. By running the `grails create-app <my-project>` command, you get an instantly built project! All you need is to make sure you have an

---

[4]   Think Dungeons and Dragons or Lord of the Rings :).

active internet connection, because it will download the standard Grails dependencies (such as Spring, Hibernate, JUnit, the Tomcat server, and more).

Grails uses a technology called Apache Ivy for managing and downloading dependencies. It's a very similar concept to how Maven (which you met in chapter 12) downloads and manages dependencies. The following command will create an application called pcgen_grails, creating for you a project structure that's optimized for Grails conventions.

```
grails create-app pcgen_grails
```

Once the dependencies have been downloaded and other automated installation steps have completed, you should have a project structure that looks similar to figure 13.3.

Now that you have a project structure, you can get started with producing some running code! The first step is to create your domain classes.

13.4.1 Domain object creation

Grails treats domain objects as the central part of your application, thus encouraging you to think along a domain-driven design (DDD) approach.[5] You create domain objects by executing the grails create-domain-class command.

In the following example, you're creating a PlayerCharacter object that represents a character in a role-playing game:

```
cd pcgen_grails
grails create-domain-class com.java7developer.chapter13.PlayerCharacter
```

```
pcgen_grails
  application.properties      ---> basic application info/versioning
  + grails-app
    + conf                    ---> location of configuration artifacts
      + hibernate             ---> optional hibernate configuration
      + spring                ---> optional spring configuration
    + controllers             ---> location of controller artifacts
    + domain                  ---> location of domain classes
    + i18n                    ---> location of message bundles for i18n
    + services                ---> location of services
    + taglib                  ---> location of tag libraries
    + util                    ---> location of special utility classes
    + views                   ---> location of views
      + layouts               ---> location of layouts
  + lib
  + scripts                   ---> scripts
  + src
    + groovy                  ---> optional; location for Groovy source files
                                   (of types other than those in grails-app/*)
    + java                    ---> optional; location for Java source files
  + test                      ---> generated test classes
  + web-app
    + WEB-INF
```

Figure 13.3 Grails project layout

---

[5] For more on DDD (coined by Eric Evans), see the Domain-Driven Design Community website (http://domaindrivendesign.org/).

Grails automatically creates the following for you:

- A PlayerCharacter.groovy source file that represents your domain object (under grails-app/domain/com/java7developer/chapter13)
- A PlayerCharacterTests.groovy source file for developing your unit tests (under test/unit/com/java7developer/chapter13)

Already you can see that Grails encourages you to write your unit tests!

You're going to flesh out the `PlayerCharacter` object by defining some attributes, such as strength, dexterity, and charisma. With these attributes, you can start to imagine how the character will interact in your imaginary world.[6] But having just read chapter 11, you'll of course want to write a test first!

13.4.2 *Test-driven development*

Let's flesh out `PlayerCharacter` by following the TDD methodology by writing a failing test and then making that test pass by implementing `PlayerCharacter`.

We're going to make use of another rapid web development feature that Grails has: support for automatically validating domain objects. The `validate()` method can be automatically called on any domain object in Grails in order to ensure that it's a valid object. The following code listing will test that the three statistics of `strength`, `dexterity`, and `charisma` are all numeric values from 3 to 18.

Listing 13.1   Unit tests for `PlayerCharacter`

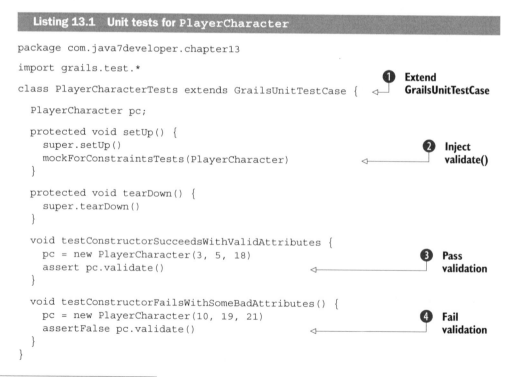

```
package com.java7developer.chapter13

import grails.test.*

class PlayerCharacterTests extends GrailsUnitTestCase {          ❶ Extend
                                                                    GrailsUnitTestCase
  PlayerCharacter pc;

  protected void setUp() {
    super.setUp()
    mockForConstraintsTests(PlayerCharacter)                      ❷ Inject
  }                                                                  validate()

  protected void tearDown() {
    super.tearDown()
  }

  void testConstructorSucceedsWithValidAttributes {
    pc = new PlayerCharacter(3, 5, 18)                            ❸ Pass
    assert pc.validate()                                             validation
  }

  void testConstructorFailsWithSomeBadAttributes() {
    pc = new PlayerCharacter(10, 19, 21)                          ❹ Fail
    assertFalse pc.validate()                                        validation
  }
}
```

---

[6]   Will Gweneth be good at arm wrestling, juggling, or disarming opponents with a smile?

Grails unit tests should always extend from `GrailsUnitTestCase` ❶. As is standard with any JUnit-based test, you have `setUp()` and `tearDown()` methods. But in order to use the Grails built-in `validate()` method during the unit test phase, you have to pull it in via the `mockForConstraintsTest` method ❷. This is because Grails treats `validate()` as an integration test concern and typically only makes it available then. You want faster feedback, so you can bring it into the unit test phase. Next, you can call `validate()` to check whether or not the domain object is valid ❸, ❹.

You can now run the tests by executing the following on the command line:

```
grails test-app
```

This command runs both unit and integration tests (though we only have unit tests so far), and you'll see via the console output that the tests have failed.

In order to get the full details as to why the tests failed, you need to look in the target/test-reports/plain folder. For the example application that you're working on, look for a file called TEST-unit-unit-com.java7developer.chapter13.PlayerCharacterTests.txt. This file will tell you that the tests failed due to a lack of a matching constructor when trying to create a new `PlayerCharacter`. This makes perfect sense, as you haven't yet fleshed out the `PlayerCharacter` domain object!

You can now build up the `PlayerCharacter` class, repeatedly running the tests until you get them passing. You'll add the three attributes of `strength`, `dexterity`, and `charisma` as you'd expect. But for specifying the minimum (3) and maximum (18) constraints on those attributes, you need to use special `constraint` syntax. That way you can utilize the helpful default `validate()` method that Grails provides.

> ### Constraints in Grails
> Constraints are implemented by the underlying Spring validator API. They allow you to specify validation requirements for the properties of your domain classes. There is a long list of constraints produced by Grails (we used `min` and `max` in listing 13.2), and you can write your own. See http://grails.org/doc/latest/guide/validation.html for further details.

The following code listing contains a version of the `PlayerCharacter` class that provides the minimum set of attributes and constraints to pass the tests.

Listing 13.2 `PlayerCharacter` class

```
package com.java7developer.chapter13

class PlayerCharacter {

    Integer strength
    Integer dexterity
    Integer charisma

    PlayerCharacter() {}
```
 ❶ **Typed variables are persisted**

```
PlayerCharacter(Integer str, Integer dex, Integer cha) {
    strength = str
    dexterity = dex
    charisma = cha
}
static constraints = {
    strength(min:3, max:18)
    dexterity(min:3, max:18)
    charisma(min:3, max:18)
}
}
```

❷ **Constructor to pass test**

❸ **Constraints for validation**

The `PlayerCharacter` class is quite simple. You have three basic attributes that will automatically be persisted in a `PlayerCharacter` table ❶. You provide a constructor that takes the three attributes as arguments ❷. The special `static` block for `constraints` allows you specify the `min` and `max` values ❸ that the `validate()` method can check against.

With the `PlayerCharacter` class fleshed out, you should now have happily passing tests (run `grails test-app` again to make sure). If you're following true TDD, at this stage you'd look at refactoring `PlayerCharacter` and the tests to make the code that little bit cleaner.

Grails also ensures that the domain objects can be persisted to a datastore.

13.4.3 *Domain object persistence*

Persistence support is automatically taken care of because Grails treats any class variable that has a specific type as a field that should be persisted to the database. Grails automatically maps the domain object to a table of the same name. In the case of the `Player-Character` domain object, all three attributes (`strength`, `dexterity`, and `charisma`) are of type `Integer` and will therefore be mapped to the `PlayerCharacter` table. By default, Grails uses Hibernate under the hood and provides a HSQLDB in-memory database (you'll remember this database from chapter 11, when we used a test double known as a *fake*), but you can override that default with your own datasource.

The file grails-app/conf/DataSource.groovy contains the datasource configuration. Here you can specify datasource settings for each environment. Remember, Grails already provides a default HSQLDB implementation in the pcgen_grails project, so in order to run the application, you don't need to change anything! But listing 13.3 shows you how you could change your configuration to use an alternative database.

For example, you could have MySQL for your production database but leave the development and test environments to be HSQLDB. The syntax is fairly standard Java Database Connectivity (JDBC) configuration that you'll be familiar with from your Java development.

Listing 13.3 Possible datasource for `pcgen_grails`

```
dataSource {}

environments {
    development { dataSource {} }
```

```
test { dataSource {} }

production {
    dataSource {
        dbCreate = "update"
        driverClassName = "com.mysql.jdbc.Driver"
        url = "jdbc:mysql://localhost/my_app"
        username = "root"
        password = ""
    }
}
}
```

Production datasource

Database driver

JDBC connection URL

The developers behind Grails have also thought of the annoyance of having to create lots of manual test data, and they provide a mechanism to prepopulate your database whenever your app starts.

13.4.4 Test data creation

Creating test data is typically done via the Grails `BootStrap` class, which you can find at grails-app/conf/BootStrap.groovy. Whenever the Grails app is started or the Servlet container starts, the `init` method is run. This is synonymous with the startup servlet that most Java-based web frameworks use.

NOTE   The `Bootstrap` class lets you initialize whatever else you like, but we're focusing on test data for now.

The following code listing generates two `PlayerCharacter` domain objects during this initialization phase and saves them to the database.

Listing 13.4   Bootstrapping test data for `pcgen_grails`

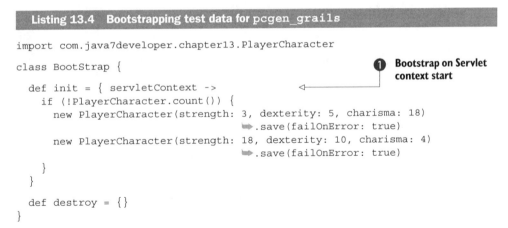

```
import com.java7developer.chapter13.PlayerCharacter

class BootStrap {

  def init = { servletContext ->
    if (!PlayerCharacter.count()) {
      new PlayerCharacter(strength: 3, dexterity: 5, charisma: 18)
                          .save(failOnError: true)
      new PlayerCharacter(strength: 18, dexterity: 10, charisma: 4)
                          .save(failOnError: true)
    }
  }

  def destroy = {}
}
```

❶ Bootstrap on Servlet context start

The `init` code is executed every time code is deployed to the Servlet container (so on application start and whenever Grails autodeploys) ❶. To make sure you don't override any existing data, you can perform a simple `count()` of existing `PlayerCharacter` instances. If you've determined there are no instances, you can create some. An important feature here is that you can ensure that the `save` will fail if an exception is thrown or if the construction of the object fails validation. You can perform teardown logic, if you're so inclined, in the destroy method.

Now that you have a basic domain object with persistence support, you can move on to the next stage, visualizing your domain objects in a web page. For that, you need to build what Grails calls a *controller*, which should be a familiar term from the MVC design pattern.

13.4.5   *Controllers*

Grails follows the MVC design pattern and uses controllers to handle web requests from the client, typically a web browser. The Grails convention is to have a controller for each domain object.

To create a controller for your PlayerCharacter domain object simply execute this command:

```
grails create-controller com.java7developer.chapter13.PlayerCharacter
```

It's important to specify the fully qualified class name of the domain object, including its package name.

Once the command has completed, you'll find that you have the following files:

- A PlayerCharacterController.groovy source file that represents your controller for the PlayerCharacter domain object (under grails-app/controller/com/java7developer/chapter13).
- A PlayerCharacterControllerTests.groovy source file for developing your controller unit tests (under test/unit/com/java7developer/chapter13).
- A grails-app/view/playerCharacter folder (you'll use this later).

The controllers support RESTful URLs and action mapping in a simple manner. Let's say you wanted to map the RESTful URL http://localhost:8080/pcgen_grails/playerCharacter/list to return a list of PlayerCharacter objects. Grail's convention over configuration approach allows you to map that URL in the PlayerCharacter-Controller class with a minimum amount of source code. The URL is constructed from these elements:

- The server (http://localhost:8080/)
- The base project (pcgen_grails/)
- A derived potion of the controller name (playerCharacter/)
- The action block variable declared in the controller (list)

To see this in code, replace the existing PlayerCharacterController.groovy source code with the code in the following listing.

Listing 13.5   PlayerCharacterController

```
package com.java7developer.chapter13

class PlayerCharacterController {
  List playerCharacters
```

```
  def list = {
    playerCharacters = PlayerCharacter.list()
  }
}
```

① Return a list of **PlayerCharacters**

By using the Grails conventions, the `playerCharacters` attribute will be used in the view referenced by the RESTful URL **①**.

But if you had the Grails app up and running and then went to http://localhost:8080/pcgen_grails/playerCharacter/list, it would fail, because you haven't yet created a JSP or GSP view. Let's resolve that now.

13.4.6 *GSP/JSP views*

You can create either GSP or JSP views with Grails. In this section, you'll create a simple GSP page to list the `PlayerCharacter` objects. (Designers, web developers, and HTML/CSS gurus, look away now!)

The GSP page for the following code listing resides at grails-app/view/player-Character/list.gsp.

Listing 13.6 `PlayerCharacter` listing GSP page

```
<html>
  <body>
    <h1>PC's</h1>
    <table>
      <thead>
        <tr>
          <td>Strength</td>
          <td>Dexterity</td>
          <td>Charisma</td>
        </tr>
      </thead>
      <tbody>
      <% playerCharacters.each({ pc -> %>
        <tr>
          <td><%="${pc?.strength}"%></td>
          <td><%="${pc?.dexterity}"%></td>
          <td><%="${pc?.charisma}"%></td>
        </tr>
        <%})%>
      </thead>
    </table>
  </body>
</html>
```

① Start loop

② Output attribute

③ Close off loop

The HTML is very simple. The key area is how you use Groovy scriptlets. You'll notice the familiar Groovy functional literal syntax from chapter 8, which simplifies iterating over a collection **①**. You then reference the character attributes (note the safe null dereference operator use, also from chapter 8) **②**, and you close off the functional literal **③**.

Now that you've prepared a domain object, its controller, and its view, you can run your Grails application for the first time! Simply execute the following on the command line:

```
grails run-app
```

Grails automatically starts up a Tomcat instance on http://localhost:8080 and deploys the pcgen_grails application to it.

> **WARNING**   Many developers already have the popular Tomcat server installed for their Java work. If you intend on having more than one Tomcat instance up and running, you'll need to change the port numbers so that only one instance is listening on port 8080.

If you open your favorite web browser and go to http://localhost:8080/pcgen_grails/, you'll see the `PlayerCharacterController` listed, as shown in figure 13.4.

Click on the com.java7developer.chapter13.PlayerCharacterController link and you'll be taken to a screen that shows a list of `PlayerCharacter` domain objects.

Although this GSP page is pretty quick to whip up, wouldn't it be nice if the framework could do this for you? With Grail's scaffolding feature, you can rapidly prototype the CRUD pages for your domain.

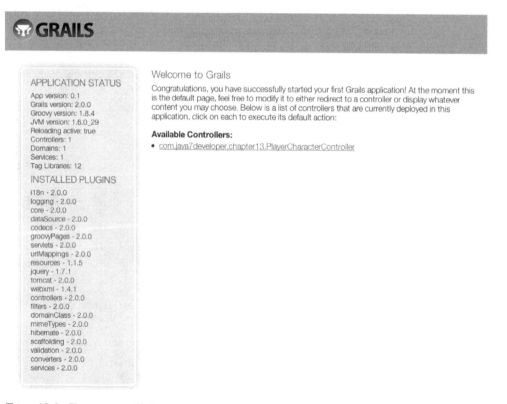

Figure 13.4   The pcgen_grails home page

13.4.7 *Scaffolding and automatic UI creation*

Grails can use its *scaffolding* feature to automatically create a UI that allows you to perform CRUD operations on your domain object.

To utilize the scaffolding feature, replace the existing code in the PlayerCharacterController.groovy source file with the following:

> **Listing 13.7 `PlayerCharacterController` with scaffolding**

```
package com.java7developer.chapter13

class PlayerCharacterController {
  def scaffold = PlayerCharacter                    ❶ Scaffolding for
}                                                      PlayerCharacter
```

The `PlayerCharacterController` class is very simple. By using the convention of assigning the name of the domain object to the `scaffold` variable ❶, Grails can then instantly build the default UI for you.

You'll also need to temporarily rename your list.gsp to list_original.gsp so that it doesn't get in the way of what the scaffolding wants to produce. Once you've done that, refresh the http://localhost:8080/pcgen_grails/playerCharacter/list page and you'll see the automatically generated list of `PlayerCharacter` domain objects, as in figure 13.5.

From this page you can also create, update, and delete more `PlayerCharacter` objects as you like. Make sure you add a couple of `PlayerCharacter` domain objects, then move on to the following section about the fast turnaround of changes.

13.4.8 *Rapid turnaround development*

There's something a little special about the Grails `run-app` command that helps put the "rapid" into rapid web development. By running your application using the `grails run-app` command, Grails can keep a link between your source code and the running server. Although this isn't recommended for production installations (as there are performance issues), it's highly recommended for development and test purposes.

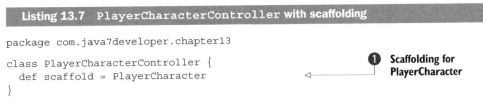

Figure 13.5 List of `PlayerCharacter` instances

TIP For production, you'd typically use `grails war` to create a WAR file, which you can then deploy via your standard deployment process.

If you change some source code in your Grails application, that change will automatically be applied to your running server.[7] Let's try this by altering the `PlayerCharacter` domain object. Add a `name` variable to the PlayerCharacter.groovy file and save it.

```
String name = 'Gweneth the Merciless'
```

You can now reload the http://localhost:8080/pcgen_grails/playerCharacter/list page and you'll see that the `name` attribute has been added as a column for `Player-Character` objects. Notice how you didn't have to stop Tomcat? Or recompile code? Or perform any other actions? This near instant turnaround time is a major factor in making Grails a leading rapid web development framework.

That finishes our quick-fire introduction, giving you a taste for the rapid web development that you can get with Grails. There is, of course, a wide range of ways you can customize the default behavior that you'll also want to explore. Let's look at some of those now.

13.5 *Further Grails exploration*

Sadly, we can't cover the entirety of the Grails framework in this chapter, as that would require a book in its own right! In this short section, we'll cover the extra areas that you, as a new Grails developer, will want to explore:

- Logging
- GORM—Grails object-relational mapping
- Grails plugins

Additionally, you can look at the http://www.grails.org website, which covers these topics with basic tutorials. We can also highly recommend *Grails in Action* by Glen Smith and Peter Ledbrook (Manning, 2009) for a full treatment of the Grails framework.

Let's begin by looking at logging for Grails.

13.5.1 *Logging*

Logging is provided by log4j under the hood, and it can be configured in the grails-app/conf/Config.groovy file.

You might want to show WARN messages for the code in the chapter13 package, for example, yet only show ERROR messages for the `PlayerCharacter` domain class. To do so, you can prefix the following snippet to the existing log4j configuration section in the Config.groovy file:

```
log4j = {
    ...
    warn    'com.java7developer.chapter13'
    error   'com.java7developer.chapter13.PlayerCharacter',
```

---

[7] For most types of source code, and assuming your change doesn't cause an error.

```
        'org.codehaus.groovy.grails.web.servlet', // controllers
    ...
}
```

The logging configuration can be just as flexible as the log4j.xml configuration that you're used to when using log4j for Java.

Next up, we'll look at GORM, the object-relational mapping technology for Grails.

13.5.2 *GORM—object-relational mapping*

GORM is implemented by Spring/Hibernate under the hood, a familiar technology mix for Java developers. It has a wide range of capabilities, but at its heart it works much like Java's JPA.

To quickly test out some of this persistence behavior, open a Grails console by executing the following on the command line:

```
grails console
```

Remember the Groovy console from chapter 8? This is a very similar environment that's aware of your Grails application.

First, let's save a `PlayerCharacter` domain object:

```
import com.java7developer.chapter13.PlayerCharacter
new PlayerCharacter(strength:18, dexterity:15, charisma:15).save()
```

Now that the `PlayerCharacter` is stored you can retrieve it in a number of ways. The simplest way is to get the full writable instance back via the implicit id property that Grails adds to your domain class. Replace the previous code in the console with the following snippet and execute it.

```
import com.java7developer.chapter13.PlayerCharacter
def pc = PlayerCharacter.get(1)
assert 18 == pc.strength
```

In order to update an object, alter some properties and call `save()` again. Once more, clear your console and then run the following snippet.

```
import com.java7developer.chapter13.PlayerCharacter
def pc = PlayerCharacter.get(1)
pc.strength = 5
pc.save()
pc = PlayerCharacter.get(1)
assert 5 == pc.strength
```

To delete an instance, use the `delete()` method. Again, clear your console and run the following snippet to delete the `PlayerCharacter`.

```
import com.java7developer.chapter13.PlayerCharacter
def pc = PlayerCharacter.get(1)
pc.delete()
```

GORM has the full rich capabilities of specifying many-to-one and many-to-many relationships, as well as other familiar Hibernate/JPA support.

Let's now look at the time-saving concept borrowed from the Rails world, that of plugins.

13.5.3 Grails plugins

A powerful aid to rapid web development is that Grails has a large repository of plugins to perform common work for you. Some of the more popular plugins are:

- Cloud Foundry Integration (for deploying Grails apps to the cloud)
- Quartz (for scheduling)
- Mail (for dealing with email)
- Twitter, Facebook (for social integration)

To see what plugins are available, execute the following on the command line:

```
grails list-plugins
```

You can then execute `grails plugin-info [name]` to find out more information about an existing plugin; just replace `[name]` with the name of the plugin you want to find out more about. Alternatively, you can visit http://grails.org/plugins/ for in-depth information about the plugins and their ecosystem.

To install one of these plugins, run `grails install-plugin [name]`, replacing `[name]` with the name of the plugin you want to install. For example, you can install the Joda-Time plugin for better date and time support.

```
grails install-plugin joda-time
```

By installing the Joda-Time plugin, you can now alter the `PlayerCharacter` domain object and add a `LocalDate` attribute. Add the following `import` statements to the domain class.

```
import org.joda.time.*
import org.joda.time.contrib.hibernate.*
```

Now add the following attribute to the `PlayerCharacter` domain class.

```
LocalDate timestamp = new LocalDate()
```

Why is this different from referencing an API in a JAR file? Because the Joda-Time plugin ensures that its types are compatible with the Grails *convention over configuration* philosophy. This means that Joda-Time's types are mapped to database types, and mapping and scaffolding is fully supported. If you now go back to the http://localhost:8080/pcgen_grails/playerCharacter/list page, you'll see the dates listed.

Grails developers can build an amazing amount of functionality in a very short space of time due to this type of plugin support.

That ends our initial look at Grails, but that's not the end of the rapid web development story in this chapter. The next section deals with Compojure, which is a rapid web development library for Clojure. It enables the developer who is familiar with Clojure to build small- to medium-scale web apps very quickly in clean Clojure code.

13.6 *Getting started with Compojure*

One of the most pernicious ideas in web development is that every website needs to be engineered as if it were Google Search. Overengineering can be as much of an issue as underengineering for web apps.

The pragmatic and well-grounded developer considers the context that a web application exists in and doesn't try to add any complexity beyond what is needed. Careful analysis of the nonfunctional requirements of any application is a key prerequisite to avoiding building the wrong thing.

Compojure is an example of a web framework that doesn't try to conquer the world. It's a great choice for such applications as web dashboards, operations monitoring, and many other simple tasks where massive scalability and other nonfunctionals are less important than simplicity and speed of development. From this description, it's easy to guess that Compojure sits in the domain-specific and dynamic layers of the polyglot programming pyramid.

In this section, we'll build a simple Hello World application, then discuss Compojure's simple rules for wiring up a web application. Then we'll introduce a useful Clojure HTML library (Hiccup) before using all of these strands to build a sample application.

As you can see in figure 13.6, Compojure builds upon a framework called Ring, which is a Clojure binding to the Jetty web container. But in order to make use of Compojure/Ring you don't need an in-depth knowledge of Jetty.

Let's get started with a simple Hello World application that uses Compojure.

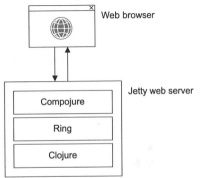

Figure 13.6 Compojure and Ring

13.6.1 *Hello World with Compojure*

Getting started with a new Compojure project is very easy, as Compojure naturally fits into the workflow of the Leiningen build tool that you met in the last chapter. If you haven't got Leiningen installed and read the section on it in chapter 12, you should do that now because the following discussion assumes that you're familiar with it.

To start the project, execute the usual Leiningen command:

```
lein new hello-compojure
```

As noted before, in the section on Leiningen, you can easily specify the dependencies for a project in the project.clj file. The following listing shows how to do this for your simple Hello World example.

Listing 13.8   Simple Compojure project.clj

```
(defproject hello-compojure "1.0.0-SNAPSHOT"
  :description "FIXME: write description"
  :dependencies [[org.clojure/clojure "1.2.1"]
                 [compojure "0.6.2"]]
  :dev-dependencies [[lein-ring "0.4.0"]]
  :ring {:handler hello-compojure.core/app})
```

As you can see, the (defproject) macro looks a lot like the basic case you saw in chapter 12. There are two additional bits of metadata:

- :dev-dependencies enables useful lein commands at development time. You'll see an example of this later when we discuss lein ring server.
- :ring brings in the hook needed for the Ring library. This takes a map of Ring-specific metadata.

In this case, there's a :handler property passed to Ring. This looks like it's expecting a symbol called app from the namespace hello-compojure.core. Let's look at the specification of this bit of wiring in core.clj to see how it fits together.

Listing 13.9   Simple core.clj file for a Compojure Hello World

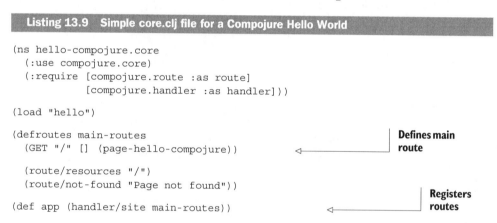

```
(ns hello-compojure.core
  (:use compojure.core)
  (:require [compojure.route :as route]
            [compojure.handler :as handler]))

(load "hello")

(defroutes main-routes
  (GET "/" [] (page-hello-compojure))          ⟵——————  Defines main
                                                         route
  (route/resources "/")
  (route/not-found "Page not found"))
                                               ⟵——————  Registers
(def app (handler/site main-routes))                     routes
```

This pattern, of keeping core.clj for the wiring and other information, is quite a useful convention. It's a simple matter to load a separate file containing the functions that are called when URLs are requested (the *page functions*). This is really just a convention to promote readability and a simple separation of concerns.

Compojure uses a set of rules, called *routes*, to determine how to handle an incoming HTTP request. These are provided by the Ring framework, which Compojure depends upon, and they're both simple and useful. You can probably guess that the GET "/" rule in listing 13.9 tells the web server how to handle GET requests for the root URL. We'll have more to say about routes in the next subsection.

To complete the code for this example, you need a file called hello.clj in the src/hello_compojure directory. In this file you need to define your solitary page function (page-hello-compojure) as shown here:

```
(ns hello-compojure.core)

(defn page-hello-compojure [] "<h1>Hello Compojure</h1>")
```

The page function is a regular Clojure function, and it returns a string that will be used as the contents of the HTML <body> tag in the document that's returned to the user.

Let's get this example up and running. As you might expect, in Compojure this is quite a simple operation. First, ensure that you have all the dependencies installed:

```
ariel:hello-compojure boxcat$ lein deps
Downloading: org/clojure/clojure/1.2.1/clojure-1.2.1.pom from central
Downloading: org/clojure/clojure/1.2.1/clojure-1.2.1.jar from central
Copying 9 files to /Users/boxcat/projects/hello-compojure/lib
Copying 17 files to /Users/boxcat/projects/hello-compojure/lib/dev
```

So far, so good. Now you need to bring it up, using one of the useful features from Ring that Compojure builds upon—the ring server method.

```
ariel:hello-compojure boxcat$ lein ring server
2011-04-11 18:02:48.596:INFO::Logging to STDERR via org.mortbay.log.StdErrLog
2011-04-11 18:02:48.615:INFO::jetty-6.1.26
2011-04-11 18:02:48.743:INFO::Started SocketConnector@0.0.0.0:3000
Started server on port 3000
```

This starts up a simple Ring/Jetty webserver (by default on port 3000) that can be used as a way to do rapid-feedback development. By default, the server will reload any modified files as you change them.

> **WARNING** Be aware that the development server reload is done at the file level. This can mean that a running server can have its state flushed (or worse, partially flushed) by the reload of a page. If you suspect that this has occurred and is causing problems, you should shut down the server and restart. Ring/Jetty is a very quick server to start, so this should not impact your development time too much.

If you navigate to port 3000 of your development machine (or http://127.0.0.1:3000 for a local machine) in your favorite browser, you should see the "Hello Compojure" text.

13.6.2 Ring and routes

Let's take a more in-depth look at how the routes are configured for a Compojure application. The specification of the routes should have reminded you of a domain-specific language:

```
(GET "/" [] (page-hello-compojure))
```

These routing rules should be read as rules that attempt to match against incoming requests. They break up in a very simple way:

```
(<HTTP method> <URL> <params> <action>)
```

- *HTTP method*—This is usually GET or POST, but Compojure supports PUT, DELETE, and HEAD as well. This must match against the incoming request if this rule is to match.

- *URL*—The URL to which the request was addressed. This must match against the incoming request if this rule is to match.
- *params*—An expression covering how parameters should be handled. We'll have more on this subject shortly.
- *action*—The expression to return (usually expressed as a function call with the arguments to pass in) if this rule matches.

The rules are matched from top to bottom until a match is found. The first rule to match causes the action to execute, and the value of the expression is used as the contents of a body tag in a return document.

Compojure gives a lot of flexibility in specifying rules. For example, it's very simple to create a rule that can extract a function parameter from part of the URL. Let's modify the routes for the Hello World shown in listing 13.5:

```
(defroutes main-routes
  (GET "/" [] (page-hello-compojure))
  (GET ["/hello/:fname", :fname #"[a-zA-Z]+" ]
  [fname] (page-hello-with-name fname))

  (route/resources "/")
  (route/not-found "Page not found"))
```

This new rule will only match if a browser targets a URL that consists of /hello/ <name>. The name must be made up of a single sequence of letters (which can be uppercase or lowercase or a mixture)—this constraint is provided by the Clojure regular expression #"[a-zA-Z]+".

If the rule matches, Compojure will call (page-hello-with-name) with the matched name as a parameter. The function is defined very simply:

```
(defn page-hello-with-name [fname]
  (str "<h1>Hello from Compojure " fname "</h1>"))
```

Although it's possible to write inline HTML for very simple applications, it quickly becomes a pain. Fortunately, there's a straightforward module called Hiccup that provides useful functionality to web apps that need to output HTML. We'll take a look at it in the next subsection.

13.6.3 *Hiccup*

To get Hiccup hooked up with your hello-compojure application, you need to do three things:

- Add in the dependency to project.clj; for example, [hiccup "0.3.4"]
- Rerun lein deps
- Restart the web container

So far so good. Let's now look at how you can use Hiccup to write nicer HTML from within Clojure.

One key form that Hiccup provides is the (html) form. This allows HTML to be written very directly. Here's how you might rewrite (page-hello-with-name) to use Hiccup:

```
(defn page-hello-html-name [fname]
  (html [:h1 "Hello from Compojure " fname]
        [:div [:p "Paragraph text"]]))
```

The nested format of HTML tags now reads much more like Clojure code itself, so it seems to sit much more naturally within the code. The (html) form takes one or more vectors (the tags) as arguments, and allows tags to be nested as deeply as required.

Next, we'll introduce you to a slightly larger example application—a simple site for voting on your favorite otters.

13.7   *A sample Compojure project—"Am I an Otter or Not?"*

The internet never seems to get tired of two things—online polls and pictures of cute animals. You've been hired by a startup that intends to make money from the ad revenue obtained by combining these two trends—allowing people to vote on pictures of otters. Let's face it, stupider ideas for startups have been tried.

We'll get started by considering the basic pages and functionality that the otter voting site needs:

- The site's home page should present the user with a choice of two otters.
- The user should be able to vote for their preferred otter out of the two presented.
- A separate page should allow users to upload new pictures of otters.
- A dashboard page should display the current votes for each otter.

In figure 13.7 you can see how the pages and HTTP requests that make up the application are arranged.

One other equally important aspect is the nonfunctional requirements that are considered out of scope for this application:

- No attempt is made to control access to the site.
- There are no safeguards about the files being uploaded as new otter images. They will be displayed as images on the pages, but neither the content nor the safety of the uploaded objects is checked. We trust our users not to upload anything unsuitable.
- The site is nonpersistent. If the web container crashes, all votes are lost. But the app will scan the disk at startup to prepopulate the store of otter images.

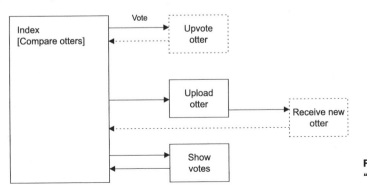

Figure 13.7   Page flow for "Am I an Otter?"

There's a version of this project hosted on github.com, which you may find easier to work with. We will include and cover the important files in this chapter, though.

13.7.1 Setting up "Am I an Otter"

To start this Compojure project, you need to define the basic project, its dependencies, some routes, and some page functions. Let's start by looking at the project.clj file.

Listing 13.10   Am I an Otter project.clj

```
(defproject am-i-an-otter "1.0.0-SNAPSHOT"
  :description "Am I an Otter or Not?"
  :dependencies [[org.clojure/clojure "1.2.0"]
                 [org.clojure/clojure-contrib "1.2.0"]
                 [compojure "0.6.2"]
                 [hiccup "0.3.4"]
                 [log4j "1.2.15" :exclusions  [javax.mail/mail
                                               javax.jms/jms
                                               com.sun.jdmk/jmxtools
                                               com.sun.jmx/jmxri]]
                 [org.slf4j/slf4j-api "1.5.6"]
                 [org.slf4j/slf4j-log4j12 "1.5.6"]]
  :dev-dependencies [[lein-ring "0.4.0"]]
  :ring {:handler am-i-an-otter.core/app})
```

There should be no real surprises in this project.clj file. You've seen everything except the log4j libraries in earlier examples.

Let's move on to the wiring and routing logic in the core.clj file.

Listing 13.11   Routes—core.clj

```
(ns am-i-an-otter.core
  (:use compojure.core)
  (:require [compojure.route :as route]
            [compojure.handler :as handler]
            [ring.middleware.multipart-params :as mp]))

(load "imports")                                              Import
(load "otters-db")                                            functions
(load "otters")

(defroutes main-routes                          ◁————————┘  Main
  (GET "/" [] (page-compare-otters))                          routes
  (GET ["/upvote/:id", :id #"[0-9]+" ] [id] (page-upvote-otter id))
  (GET "/upload" [] (page-start-upload-otter))
  (GET "/votes" [] (page-otter-votes))

  (mp/wrap-multipart-params                     ◁————————┐  File upload
    (POST "/add_otter" req (str (upload-otter req)        handler
⮑
  (page-start-upload-otter))))

  (route/resources "/")
  (route/not-found "Page not found"))

(def app
  (handler/site main-routes))
```

The file upload handler introduces a new way of handling parameters. We'll have more to say about this in the next subsection, but for now, read it as "we're passing the whole HTTP request to the page function for handling."

The core.clj file provides wiring and lets you see clearly which page functions are related to which URLs. As you can see, all of the page functions start with "page"—this is just a handy naming convention.

The next listing shows the page functions for the application.

> **Listing 13.12   Page functions for "Am I an Otter?"**

```
(ns am-i-an-otter.core
  (:use compojure.core)
  (:use hiccup.core))

(defn page-compare-otters []                              ◄──────── Compare
  (let [otter1 (random-otter), otter2 (random-otter)]               otters page
    (.info (get-logger) (str "Otter1 = " otter1 " ; Otter2 = "
  otter2 " ; " otter-pics))
    (html [:h1 "Otters say 'Hello Compojure!'"]
          [:p [:a {:href (str "/upvote/" otter1)}
               [:img {:src (str "/img/"
  (get otter-pics otter1))} ]]]
          [:p [:a {:href (str "/upvote/" otter2)}
               [:img {:src (str "/img/"
  (get otter-pics otter2))} ]]]
          [:p "Click " [:a {:href "/votes"} "here"]
              " to see the votes for each otter"]
          [:p "Click " [:a {:href "/upload"} "here"]
              " to upload a brand new otter"])))
(defn page-upvote-otter [id]                              ◄──────── Handle
  (let [my-id id]                                                  voting
    (upvote-otter id)
    (str (html [:h1 "Upvoted otter id=" my-id]) (page-compare-otters))))

(defn page-start-upload-otter []        ◄──────── Select otter for upload page
  (html [:h1 "Upload a new otter"]
        [:p [:form {:action "/add_otter" :method "POST"       Set up
  :enctype "multipart/form-data"}                ◄──────────   form
            [:input {:name "file" :type "file" :size "20"}]
            [:input {:name "submit" :type "submit" :value "submit"}]]]
        [:p "Or click " [:a {:href "/"} "here" ] " to vote on some otters"]))

(defn page-otter-votes []               ◄────────
  (let []                                                   Show
    (.debug (get-logger) (str "Otters: " @otter-votes-r))  votes
    (html [:h1 "Otter Votes" ]
          [:div#votes.otter-votes
            (for [x (keys @otter-votes-r)]
              [:p [:img {:src (str "/img/" (get otter-pics x))} ]
  (get @otter-votes-r x)])])))
```

In the listing there are two other useful Hiccup features. The first is being able to loop through a group of elements—in this case, the otters that have been uploaded. This lets Hiccup act very much like a simple templating language—with the embedded (for) form in this snippet:

```
[:div#votes.otter-votes
  (for [x (keys @otter-votes-r)]
    [:p [:img {:src (str "/img/" (get otter-pics x))} ]
➡ (get @otter-votes-r x)])]
```

The other useful feature is the :div#votes.otter-votes syntax. This is a quick way to specify the id and class attributes of a particular tag. It becomes the HTML tag <div class="otter-votes" id="votes">. This enables the developer to separate out the attributes most likely to be used by CSS, without obscuring too much of the HTML structure.

In general, the CSS and other code (for example, JavaScript source files) will be served out of a static content directory. By default, this would be under the resources/public directory of the Compojure project.

HTTP method choice

In our example otter-voting application, we've included an architectural flaw. We specified the routing rule for the upvoting page as a GET rule. This is incorrect.

An application should never use a GET request to change state on the server side (such as the vote count of your favorite otter). That's because web browsers are allowed to retry GET requests if the server seems unresponsive (for example, if it was paused for garbage collection when the request came in). This retry behavior could result in duplicate votes for the same otter being received, even though the user only clicked once. For an ecommerce application, the results could be disastrous!

Remember this rule: No meaningful server state should be changed by an incoming GET request.

We've looked at the wiring up of the app and its routes, and the page functions. Let's continue our discussion of the app by looking at some of the backend functions that you need to make the otter voting happen.

13.7.2 Core functions in "Am I an Otter"

When we discussed the core functionality for the application, we mentioned that the app should scan the image directory to locate any existing otter images that are already present on disk. This listing shows the code that scans the directories and performs this prepopulation.

Listing 13.13   Directory scanning functions

```
(def otter-img-dir "resources/public/img/")
(def otter-img-dir-fq
  (str (.getAbsolutePath (File. ".")) "/" otter-img-dir))
```

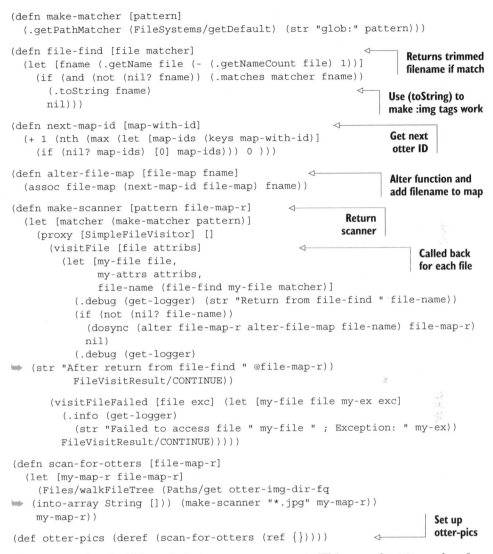

```clojure
(defn make-matcher [pattern]
  (.getPathMatcher (FileSystems/getDefault) (str "glob:" pattern)))

(defn file-find [file matcher]                                    ◁————  Returns trimmed
  (let [fname (.getName file (- (.getNameCount file) 1))]                filename if match
    (if (and (not (nil? fname)) (.matches matcher fname))
      (.toString fname)                                           ◁————  Use (toString) to
      nil)))                                                             make :img tags work

(defn next-map-id [map-with-id]                                   ◁————  Get next
  (+ 1 (nth (max (let [map-ids (keys map-with-id)]                       otter ID
    (if (nil? map-ids) [0] map-ids))) 0 )))

(defn alter-file-map [file-map fname]                             ◁————  Alter function and
  (assoc file-map (next-map-id file-map) fname))                        add filename to map

(defn make-scanner [pattern file-map-r]                           ◁————  Return
  (let [matcher (make-matcher pattern)]                                  scanner
    (proxy [SimpleFileVisitor] []
      (visitFile [file attribs]                                   ◁————  Called back
        (let [my-file file,                                              for each file
              my-attrs attribs,
              file-name (file-find my-file matcher)]
          (.debug (get-logger) (str "Return from file-find " file-name))
          (if (not (nil? file-name))
            (dosync (alter file-map-r alter-file-map file-name) file-map-r)
            nil)
          (.debug (get-logger)
➥           (str "After return from file-find " @file-map-r))
          FileVisitResult/CONTINUE))

      (visitFileFailed [file exc] (let [my-file file my-ex exc]
        (.info (get-logger)
          (str "Failed to access file " my-file " ; Exception: " my-ex))
        FileVisitResult/CONTINUE)))))

(defn scan-for-otters [file-map-r]
  (let [my-map-r file-map-r]
    (Files/walkFileTree (Paths/get otter-img-dir-fq
➥     (into-array String [])) (make-scanner "*.jpg" my-map-r))
    my-map-r))
                                                                         Set up
(def otter-pics (deref (scan-for-otters (ref {}))))              ◁————   otter-pics
```

The entry point for this code is (scan-for-otters). This uses the Files class from Java 7 to walk the filesystem starting at otter-img-dir-fq, and returns a ref to a map. This code uses the simple convention that a symbol name that ends with -r is a ref to a structure of interest.

The code that walks over the files is a Clojure proxy of the SimpleFileVisitor class (from the package java.nio.file), which you saw in chapter 2. You provide customized implementations of two methods—(visitFile) and (visitFileFailed)—which is sufficient for this case.

The other interesting functions are those that implement the voting functionality. These are detailed in the following listing.

Listing 13.14   Otter voting functions

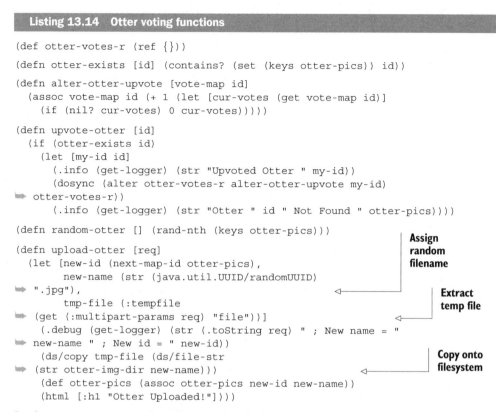

```
(def otter-votes-r (ref {}))

(defn otter-exists [id] (contains? (set (keys otter-pics)) id))

(defn alter-otter-upvote [vote-map id]
  (assoc vote-map id (+ 1 (let [cur-votes (get vote-map id)]
    (if (nil? cur-votes) 0 cur-votes)))))

(defn upvote-otter [id]
  (if (otter-exists id)
    (let [my-id id]
      (.info (get-logger) (str "Upvoted Otter " my-id))
      (dosync (alter otter-votes-r alter-otter-upvote my-id)
  otter-votes-r))
      (.info (get-logger) (str "Otter " id " Not Found " otter-pics))))

(defn random-otter [] (rand-nth (keys otter-pics)))

(defn upload-otter [req]
  (let [new-id (next-map-id otter-pics),
        new-name (str (java.util.UUID/randomUUID)
  ".jpg"),
        tmp-file (:tempfile
  (get (:multipart-params req) "file"))]
    (.debug (get-logger) (str (.toString req) " ; New name = "
  new-name " ; New id = " new-id))
    (ds/copy tmp-file (ds/file-str
  (str otter-img-dir new-name)))
    (def otter-pics (assoc otter-pics new-id new-name))
    (html [:h1 "Otter Uploaded!"])))
```

Assign random filename

Extract temp file

Copy onto filesystem

In the (upload-otter) function, you're dealing with the full HTTP request map. This contains a lot of useful information that can be of use to the web developer—some of this may already be familiar to you:

```
{:remote-addr "127.0.0.1",
 :scheme :http,
 :query-params {},
 :session {},
 :form-params {},
 :multipart-params {"submit" "submit", "file" {:filename "otter_kids.jpg",
     :size 122017, :content-type "image/jpeg", :tempfile #<File /var/tmp/
     upload_646a7df3_12f5f51ff33__8000_00000000.tmp>}},
 :request-method :post,
 :query-string nil,
 :route-params {},
 :content-type "multipart/form-data; boundary=----
     WebKitFormBoundaryvKKZehApamWrVFt0",
 :cookies {},
 :uri "/add_otter",
 :server-name "127.0.0.1",
 :params {:file {:filename "otter_kids.jpg", :size 122017, :content-type
     "image/jpeg", :tempfile #<File /var/tmp/
     upload_646a7df3_12f5f51ff33__8000_00000000.tmp>}, :submit "submit"},
 :headers {"user-agent" "Mozilla/5.0 (Macintosh; U; Intel Mac OS X 10_6_6;
     en-US) AppleWebKit/534.16 (KHTML, like Gecko) Chrome/10.0.648.205
```

```
     Safari/534.16", "origin" "http://127.0.0.1:3000", "accept-charset" "ISO-
     8859-1,utf-8;q=0.7,*;q=0.3", "accept" "application/xml,application/
     xhtml+xml,text/html;q=0.9,text/plain;q=0.8,image/png,*/*;q=0.5", "host"
     "127.0.0.1:3000", "referer" "http://127.0.0.1:3000/upload", "content-
     type" "multipart/form-data; boundary=----
     WebKitFormBoundaryvKKZehApamWrVFt0", "cache-control" "max-age=0",
     "accept-encoding" "gzip,deflate,sdch", "content-length" "122304",
     "accept-language" "en-US,en;q=0.8", "connection" "keep-alive"},
  :content-length 122304,
  :server-port 3000,
  :character-encoding nil,
  :body #<Input org.mortbay.jetty.HttpParser$Input@206bc833>}
```

From this req map, you can see that the container has already uploaded the content of the incoming file into a temp file in /var/tmp. You can access the File object that corresponds to it via (:tempfile (get (:multipart-params req) "file")). Then it's a simple use of the (copy) function from clojure.contrib.duck-streams to save it to the filesystem.

The otter-voting application is small, but complete. Within the constraints of the functional and nonfunctional requirements that we stated at the start of this section, it performs as we intended it. This concludes our tour of Compojure and some of the related libraries.

13.8   Summary

Rapid web development is something that all well-grounded Java developers should be capable of. But with a poorly chosen language or framework, you can quickly fall behind non-Java/JVM technologies such as Rails and PHP. In particular, Java isn't always a great choice for web development due to its static and compiled nature. Conversely, with the right language or framework, building new features quickly without sacrificing quality puts you at the top of the web development food chain, able to react quickly to the needs of your users.

As a well-grounded Java developer, you don't want to throw away the power and flexibility of the JVM. Luckily, with the advancement of languages and their web frameworks on the JVM, you don't have to! Dynamic layer frameworks, such as Grails and Compojure, provide you with the rapid web development capabilities that you need.

In particular, Grails allows you to build a full end-to-end (UI to database) prototype very quickly and then allows you to flesh out parts of that stack with a powerful view technology (GSP), persistence technology (GORM), and a host of useful plugins.

Compojure is a natural fit for projects that are already written in Clojure. It's also very suitable for adding small web components, such as dashboards and operations consoles, to projects that may be written in Java or another language. Clean code and speed of development are Compojure's main strengths.

This brings us to the end of the chapters in which we walk through examples of polyglot programming on the JVM. In the final chapter, we'll draw all the threads together, and look beyond what you've learned so far. There are exciting challenges that are outside our current experience, but we now have the tools to tackle them.

Staying well-grounded

14

This chapter covers

- What Java 8 holds for you as a developer
- The future of polyglot programming
- Where concurrency is heading next
- New JVM-level features

To stay ahead of the curve, the well-grounded Java developer should always be aware of what's coming around the corner. In this final chapter, we'll discuss several topics that we feel point the way toward the future of the Java language and the platform.

As we don't have a TARDIS or crystal ball, this chapter focuses on language features and platform changes that we know are already under way. That means that this is inevitably a point-in-time view, which is a polite way of saying that it's partially a work of (science) fiction.

Our discussion represents a possible future, at the time when we were writing this book. How things will turn out remains to be seen. It will doubtless differ in some important ways from what we present here, and getting there should be an interesting ride. It usually is.

Let's get under way by taking a look at our first topic, which is a quick tour of the likely major features of Java 8.

14.1   What to expect in Java 8

In autumn 2010, the Executive Committee for Java SE met and decided to proceed with Plan B. This was the decision to release a Java 7 version as soon as possible, and defer some major features to Java 8. This conclusion came after extensive consultation and polling of the community as to which option would be preferred.

Some of the features that had been originally in Java 7 were pushed out to Java 8, and some others were reduced in scope so that they effectively laid the groundwork for features still to come. In this section, we'll give a brief overview of some of the highlights that we expect for Java 8, including the features that were deferred. At this stage, nothing is set in stone, and especially not language syntax. All code examples are preliminary and may well look very different in the version of Java 8 that ships. Welcome to the bleeding edge!

14.1.1   Lambdas (a.k.a. closures)

A good example of Java 7 features that will be built upon in Java 8 is `MethodHandles` and `invokedynamic`. They're useful features in their own right (in Java 7, `invokedynamic` is of most use to language and framework implementers).

In Java 8, these features will be built upon to introduce lambda expressions in the Java language. You can think of lambdas as being similar to the function literals that in all of the alternative languages we looked at, and they can be used to solve the same sorts of problems that we highlighted in previous chapters.

In terms of the Java 8 language syntax, there is still work to be done to decide what a lambda will look like in code. But the basic features have been determined, so let's take a look at the basic Java 8 syntax.

> **Listing 14.1   Schwartzian transform in Java with lambdas**

```
public List<T> schwarz(List<T> x, Mapper<T, V> f) {
  return x.map(w -> new Pair<T,V>(w, f.map(w)))
        .sorted((l,r) -> l.hashed.compareTo(r.hashed))
        .map(l -> l.orig).into(new ArrayList<T>());
}
```

The method called `schwartz()` should look familiar—it's an implementation of the Schwartzian transform in section 10.3, where you saw it done in Clojure. Listing 14.1 shows the basic syntax features of lambdas in Java 8.

- There's a list of parameters to the lambda upfront.
- The braces denote the block that comprises the lambda body.
- The arrow (`->`) separates the parameter list from the body of the lambda.
- The types of parameters in the argument list are inferred.

In chapter 9, you learned about Scala's function literals, which are written in a very similar way, so this syntax shouldn't be too surprising. In listing 14.1 the lambdas are very short—just a single line each. In practice, lambdas can be multiline and even have large bodies. A preliminary analysis of some sizable codebases that are suitable for retrofitting with lambdas indicates that most lambda code bodies will be 1–5 lines in length.

In listing 14.1, we've also introduced another new feature. The variable x is of type List<T>. As part of the code, we call a method map() on x. The map() method takes a lambda as its argument. But hold on! The List interface doesn't have a map() method, and in Java 7 and before there aren't any lambdas.

Let's take a closer look at how this problem can be resolved.

EXTENSION AND DEFAULT METHODS

The essential problem we have is this: how can we add methods to existing interfaces to "lambda-ify" them without breaking backward compatibility?

The answer comes from a new feature of Java—extension methods. These work by providing a default method that can be used if an implementation of the interface doesn't provide a version of the extension method.

These default method implementations must be defined inside the interface itself.

As examples, List is paired with AbstractList, Map with AbstractMap, and Queue with AbstractQueue. These classes are ideal places to keep the default implementation of any new extension methods for their respective interfaces. The built-in Java collections classes are a primary use case for both extension methods and lambda-fication, but this model seems suitable for use in end-user code as well.

> ## How Java could implement extension methods
> Extension methods will be handled at class load time. When a new implementation of an interface with extension methods is loaded, the classloader checks to see if it has defined its own implementations of the extension methods. If not, the class-loader locates the default method and inserts a bridge method into the bytecode of the newly loaded class. The bridge method will call the default implementation using invokedynamic.

Extension methods provide a major new capability to evolve interfaces after their initial publication, without breaking backward compatibility. This allows you to breathe new life into old APIs with the addition of lambdas. But what do lambdas look like to the JVM? Are they objects? If so, what type are they?

SAM CONVERSION

Lambdas provide a compact way to declare a small amount of code inline and pass it around as though it were data. This means that a lambda is an object, as we explained when you met lambdas and function literals in the non-Java languages in part 3 of this book. Specifically, you can think of a lambda as a subclass of Object that has no parameters (so no state) and just one method.

A useful way of thinking about this is in terms of the single abstract method (SAM). The concept of the SAM comes from looking around at the various Java APIs that exist and noticing a common theme. A lot of APIs have interfaces that specify just a single method. `Runnable`, `Comparable`, `Callable`, and listeners such as `ActionListener` all specify just one method and are thus examples of a SAM type.

As you start to work with lambdas, you can think of them as a bit of syntactic sugar—a shorter way of writing an anonymous implementation of a given interface. Over time, you can start to bring more functional techniques to bear, perhaps even importing your favorite tricks from Scala or Clojure into your Java code. Learning functional programming is often quite a gradual process—learning to use mapping, sorting, and filtering techniques on collections as a first step, and building outward from there.

Now let's move on to the next big topic: the modularization program, which has been carried out under the auspices of Project Jigsaw.

14.1.2 Modularization (a.k.a. Jigsaw)

There's no doubt that dealing with the Java classpath is sometimes not ideal. There are well-known problems associated with the ecosystem that has built up around JAR files and the classpath:

- The JRE itself is massive.
- JAR files promote monolithic deployment models.
- Too much cruft and rarely needed classes still have to be loaded.
- Startup is slow.
- Classpaths are fragile beasts and are tightly coupled to the filesystem of the machine.
- The classpath is basically a flat namespace.
- JARs aren't inherently versioned.
- There are complex interdependencies, even among classes that aren't logically related.

To solve these issues, a new module system is needed. But there are architectural questions that need to be addressed. The most important of these is illustrated in figure 14.1.

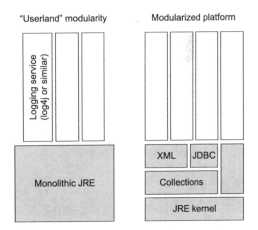

Figure 14.1 Module system architecture choices

Should we bootstrap the VM and then use a "userland" module system (such as OSGi), or try to move to a completely modular platform?

The latter option would involve booting a minimal, module-aware VM as a "kernel," then adding only those modules that are needed for the specific application being started. This would require root-and-branch changes to the VM and many of the existing classes in the JRE, but it potentially offers much greater gains:

- JVM applications could rival shell and scripting languages for startup time.
- Application deployments could become significantly less complicated.
- Java's footprint for special-purpose installs could be greatly reduced (with positive implications for disk, memory, and security). If you don't need CORBA or RMI, you wouldn't need to have it installed!
- Java installs could be upgraded in a much more flexible manner. If a critical bug was found in the Collections, only that module would need to be upgraded.

At the time of writing, it seems that Project Jigsaw will choose the second route. There is still a long way to go before Project Jigsaw is released and ready for prime time. These are some of the most important questions that are still being discussed:

- What is the correct unit of platform or application distribution?
- Do we need a new construct that is distinct from both package and JAR?

The consequences of this design decision are hugely important—Java is *everywhere*, and the modularity design needs to scale up and down that space. It also needs to make sense across OS platforms.

The Java platform needs to be able to deploy modular apps on Linux, Solaris, Windows, Mac OS X, BSD Unix, and AIX at the very least. Some of these platforms have package managers that Java modules will need to integrate with (such as Debian's apt, Red Hat's rpm, and Solaris packages). Others, such as Windows, don't have a package management system that's readily usable by Java.

The design has other constraints as well. There are already some well-established projects in this space—dependency management systems such as Maven and Ivy, as well as the OSGi initiative. The new modularity system should integrate with the incumbents if at all possible, and provide a painless upgrade path in the event that full integration and compatibility proves to be impossible.

Whatever lies ahead, the release of Java 8 should bring with it a revolution in the way that Java applications are delivered and deployed.

Let's move on and take a look at some of the features that JDK 8 should bring to the other citizens of the JVM, including the languages that we've studied in earlier chapters.

14.2   *Polyglot programming*

As you've seen in numerous other chapters, starting with chapter 5, the JVM is a fantastic foundation on which to base a language runtime. The OpenJDK project, which you met in chapter 1, became the reference implementation for Java over the course of the Java 7 release lifecycle. One very interesting offshoot of this was the development of the JVM as a language-agnostic and truly polyglot virtual machine.

In particular, with the release of Java 7, the privileged position of the Java language on the VM is removed. All languages are now considered equal citizens on the platform. This has led to a strong interest in adding features to the VM that may be of high importance to alternative languages, and only of marginal interest to Java itself.

Much of this work was carried out in a subproject called the Da Vinci Machine, or `mlvm` (for multilanguage VM). Features were incubated in this project and moved into the main source tree. The example that you saw in chapter 5 (section 5.5) is `invoke-dynamic`, but there are a number of other features that would be very useful for non-Java languages. There are also issues to solve.

Let's meet the first of these language features—a means for different languages to communicate seamlessly with each other when running within the same JVM.

14.2.1 *Language interoperability and metaobject protocols*

Language equality is a major step toward a terrific environment for polyglot programming, but some thorny issues remain. Chief among these is the simple fact that different languages have different type systems. Ruby's strings are mutable, whereas Java's are immutable. Scala regards everything as an object—even entities that would be primitives in Java.

Dealing with these differences, and providing better ways for different languages to communicate and interoperate within the same JVM, is a currently unsolved problem, and one that there is active interest in resolving soon.

Imagine a web application that you might work on in the future. This could combine a core of Java code with the web part of the application being written in Compojure (that is, Clojure) and that makes use of a JSON processing library written in pure JavaScript. Now suppose that you want to test this using some of the cool TDD features provided by ScalaTest.

This leads to a situation in which JavaScript, Clojure, Scala, and Java could all be calling each other directly. This need for interoperability and a standard way for JVM languages to call each other's objects is one that will grow over time. The general consensus in the community is that a Metaobject Protocol (MOP) is required, so that all of this can be made to work in a standard way. A MOP can be thought of as a way of describing within code how a particular language implements object orientation and related concerns.

To achieve this goal, we need to think about ways in which objects from one language could be made useful in another. One simple approach would be to cast to a type that was native to the foreign language (or even create a new "shadow" object in the foreign runtime). This is a simple approach, but has serious problems:

- Every language must have a common "master" interface (or superclass) that is implemented by all types within that language implementation (such as `IRubyObject` for JRuby).
- If used, the shadow objects lead to a lot of allocation and poor performance.

Instead, we can consider building a service to act as the entry point to the foreign runtime. This service would provide an interface that can allow one runtime to do standard operations on objects of the foreign runtime, such as

- Create a new object in the foreign runtime and return a reference to it
- Access (get or set) a property of a foreign object

- Call a method on a foreign object, and get the result back
- Cast a foreign object to a different, relevant type
- Access additional capabilities of a foreign object, which may have different semantics than a method call for some languages

In such a system, the foreign method or property can be accessed via a call to the "navigator" of the foreign runtime. The caller would need to provide a way to identify the method being accessed—someMethod. This would typically be a string, but it may also be a MethodHandle under some circumstances.

```
navigator.callMethod(someObject, someMethod, param1, param2, ...);
```

For this approach to work effectively, the Navigator interface would have to be the same for all cooperating language runtimes. Behind the scenes, the actual linkages between languages would likely be built using invokedynamic.

Let's move on to look at how the multilanguage JVM would look with Java 8's modularity subsystem in the mix as well.

14.2.2 *Multilanguage modularity*

With the advent of Jigsaw and modularization of the platform, it's not just Java that would benefit from (and need to participate in) modularity. Other languages would be able to get in on the act as well.

We can imagine that the navigator interfaces and helper classes would be likely to form one module, and the runtime support for individual non-Java languages would be provided by one or more modules. In figure 14.2, you can see how this system of modules could look.

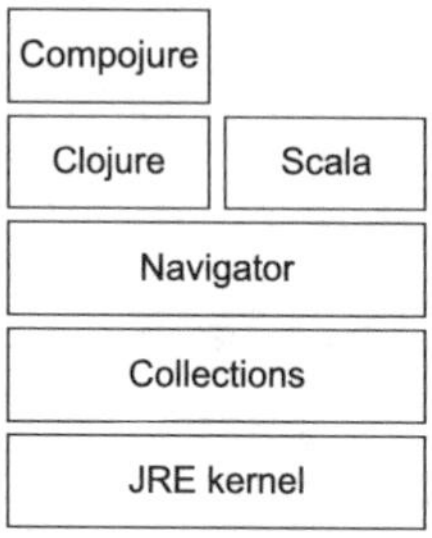

As you can see, we can build well-contained polyglot applications using the modules system. The Clojure module provides the basic Clojure platform, and the Compojure module brings in the components required to run the webapp stack, including specific versions of JARs that may be present in different versions elsewhere in the running process. Scala and its XML stack are present, and the Navigator module is also present for language interoperability between Scala and Clojure.

Figure 14.2 Modules implementing a multilanguage solution

In the next section, we'll discuss another programming trend that has been driven by the explosion of non-Java languages onto the platform—concurrency.

14.3 *Future concurrency trends*

Twenty-first century computer hardware isn't necessarily very well served by twentieth century languages. This is an observation that has been implicit in a lot of our discussion so far. In chapter 6 (section 6.3.1) when we discussed Moore's Law of increasing transistor counts, there was one very important consequence that we discussed only briefly. This is the interplay between Moore's Law, performance, and concurrency, and it's our first topic.

14.3.1 *The many-core world*

While transistor counts have increased exponentially in line with predictions, memory access times have not improved by the same amount. In the 1990s and early years of the 2000s, this led chip designers to use a larger amount of the available transistors to work around the relative slowness of main memory.

As we discussed in chapter 6, this was to ensure that a steady stream of data was available for processing cores to work upon. But this is a fundamentally losing battle: the gains from using transistors to work around the speed of main memory become more and more marginal. This is because the tricks used (such as instruction-level parallelism and speculative execution) have now exhausted the easy gains and have become more and more speculative.

In recent years, attention has shifted to using the transistors to provide multiple processing cores per chip. Now almost all laptop or desktop machines have at least 2 cores, and 4 or 8 are quite common. In higher spec server equipment, you can find 6 or 8 cores per chip, and up to 32 (or more) cores per machine. The many-core world is here, and to take full advantage of it, you need programs that are written in a less serial style. Those programs need language and runtime support.

14.3.2 *Runtime-managed concurrency*

We've already looked at the beginnings of a possible future of concurrent programming. In Scala and Clojure we discussed perspectives on concurrency that didn't look a lot like Java's `Thread` and lock model—the actor model from Scala and the software transactional memory approach from Clojure.

Scala's actor model allows for messages to be sent between executing blobs of code that are potentially running on totally different cores (and there are even extensions that allow actors to be remote). This means that code written in a completely actor-centric way can potentially scale out to a many-core machine relatively simply.

Clojure has agents to fill much of the same evolutionary niche as Scala actors, but it also has shared data (refs) that can only be modified from within a memory transaction—the software transactional memory mechanism.

In both of these cases, you can see the germ of a new concept—the management of concurrency by the runtime, rather than explicitly by the developer. While the JVM provides thread scheduling as part of the low-level services it provides, it doesn't provide higher-level constructs for managing concurrent programs.

This shortcoming is visible in the Java language, which essentially makes the JVM's low-level model available to the Java programmer.

With the large body of code that's in the wild, it will be very difficult to produce an entirely new mechanism for Java, enforce it, and have it interoperate seamlessly with

Don't be too hard on Java's concurrency

When Java was released in 1996, it was one of the first major languages to have concurrency considerations baked in from the start. With the benefit of 15 years of widespread industrial practice as hindsight, we can see that the model of mutable data, state shared by default, and exclusion enforced by collaborating locks has problems. But the engineers who released Java 1.0 had no such benefit. In many ways, Java's initial attempts at concurrency support allowed us to get to this point.

existing code. This is why a lot of attention is being paid to non-Java languages on the JVM for new concurrency directions. They have two important features:

- They're based on the JMM as a low-level model.
- They have a "clean slate" language runtime that can provide different abstractions (and enforce more) than the Java language can.

It isn't impossible that additional concurrency support could appear at the VM level (as discussed in the next section), but for now the major direction of innovation seems to be new languages on top of the JMM's solid foundation, rather than low-level changes to the basic threading model.

There definitely are areas of the JVM that may see changes in JDK 8 and beyond. Some of these possible changes follow on from the `invokedynamic` work in Java 7, and they form the next topic of our discussion.

14.4   New directions in the JVM

In chapter 1 we introduced the VMSpec—the JVM Specification. This is a document that spells out exactly how a VM must behave to be considered an implementation of the JVM standard. When new behavior is introduced (such as `invokedynamic` with Java 7) all implementations must upgrade to include the new capabilities.

In this section, we'll talk about possibilities for changes that are being discussed and prototyped. This work is being carried out within the OpenJDK project, which is also the basis of the reference implementation for Java and the starting point for Oracle's JDK. As well as possible spec changes, we'll also cover significant changes to the OpenJDK/Oracle JDK codebase.

14.4.1   VM convergence

After Oracle bought Sun Microsystems, it was in possession of two very strong virtual machines for Java: the HotSpot VM (inherited from Sun) and JRockit (which had come from the earlier acquisition of BEA).

It was quickly decided that trying to maintain both VMs would be a waste of resources, so Oracle decided merge the two. The HotSpot VM was chosen as the base VM, with JRockit features being carefully ported over to it in future releases of Java.

> ## What's in a name?
> There is no official name for the merged VM, although VM enthusiasts and the Java community at large have dubbed it "HotRockit." This is certainly a catchy title, but it remains to be seen whether Oracle's marketing department agrees!

So why is this important to you, the developer? The existing VM that you likely use today (the HotSpot VM) will over time gain a host of new features including (but not limited to) the following:

- *Elimination of PermGen*—Will prevent a large category of classloader-related crashes.
- *Enhancement JMX Agent support*—Will give you more insight into aspects of a running VM.
- *New approach to JIT compilation*—Brings in new optimizations from the JRockit codebase
- *Mission Control*—Provides advanced tooling to help with tuning and profiling of production apps. Some of these tools will be for-pay additional components to the JVM, not part of the free download.

> ## Eliminating PermGen
> As you learned in section 6.5.2, metadata about your classes currently gets held in a special memory space in the VM (PermGen). This can quickly fill up, especially in non-Java languages and frameworks that create a lot of classes at runtime. PermGen space isn't reclaimed, and running out will crash your VM. Work is under way to make metadata live in native memory instead, making the dreaded "java.lang.OutOfMemory-Error: PermGen space" message a thing of the past.

There are plenty of other small improvements all aimed at making the VM smaller, faster, and more flexible. Given the approximately 1000 person-years of effort that's already gone into HotSpot, we can only see a bright future for the combined VM as many more years of JRockit effort comes in to join it.

In addition to the VM merge, there are plenty of new features also being worked on. One of these is the possible addition of a concurrency feature known as *coroutines*.

14.4.2 Coroutines

Multithreading is the form of concurrency most widely understood by Java and JVM language programmers. It relies on the JVM's thread scheduling services to start and stop threads on the physical processing cores, and threads have no way to control this scheduling. For this reason, multithreading is called "preemptive multitasking" because the scheduler is able to preempt the running threads and force them to surrender control of the CPU.

The idea behind coroutines is to allow execution units to partially control how they're scheduled. Specifically, a coroutine will run like an ordinary thread until it hits a command to "yield." This causes the coroutine to suspend itself and allow another coroutine to run in its place. When the original coroutine is given another chance to run, it will carry on from the next statement after the yield, rather than from the beginning of the method.

As this approach to multithreading relies on the cooperation of the currently live coroutines to yield occasionally to allow other coroutines, this form of multiprocessing is called "cooperative multitasking."

The exact design of how coroutines could work is still very much under discussion, and there's no commitment to definitely include them. One possible model is to have coroutines created and scheduled within the scope of a single shared thread (or possibly a threadpool similar to those in `java.util.concurrent`). This design is illustrated in figure 14.3.

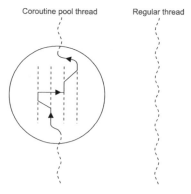

Figure 14.3 A possible coroutine model

The threads that are executing coroutines can be preempted by any other thread in the system, but the JVM thread scheduler can't force a yield on a coroutine. This means that, at the price of having to trust all the other coroutines within your execution pool, a coroutine can control when it's context-switched.

This control means that switches between coroutines can be synchronized better. Multithreaded code has to build complex, fragile locking strategies to protect data, because a context switch can happen at any time. This is the problem of concurrent type safety we discussed in section 4.1. By contrast, a coroutine needs to ensure only that its data is consistent at yield points, because it knows it can't be preempted at other times.

This trade-off of additional guarantees in exchange for having to trust others is a useful complement to threading for some programming problems. Some non-Java languages have support for coroutines (or a closely related concept called *fibers*)—notably Ruby and newer versions of JavaScript. The addition of coroutines at the VM level (but not necessarily to the Java language) would be a great help to those languages that could make use of them.

As our final example of possible VM changes, let's consider a proposed VM feature called "tuples," which could have a great impact in the performance-sensitive computing space.

14.4.3 *Tuples*

In the JVM today, all data items are either primitives or references (which can either be to objects or arrays). The only way to create a more complicated type is define it in a class and pass around references to objects that are instances of the new type. This is a simple and fairly elegant model that has served Java well.

But there are a couple of drawbacks to this model that appear when trying to build high-performance systems. In particular, in applications such as games and financial software it's quite common to run up against the limitations of this simple model. One of the ways that we could address these issues is with a concept called a tuple.

Tuples (sometimes called *value objects*) are a language construct that bridges the gap between primitives and classes. Like classes, they allow for the definition of custom complex types that can contain primitives, references, and other tuples. Like primitives, their whole value is used when passing them to and from methods and storing them in arrays and other objects. Think of them as an equivalent to structs in C (or .NET), if you're familiar with those environments.

Let's look at an example—an existing Java API.

```
public class MyInputStream {
  public void write(byte[], int off, int len);
}
```

This allows a user to write a specified amount of data into a specific point in the array, which is useful. But it's not particularly well-designed. In an ideal OO world, the offset and length would be encapsulated inside of the array, and neither the user nor the implementer of the method would need to track the additional information separately.

In fact, with the introduction of NIO came the concept of a `ByteBuffer` that encapsulates this information. Unfortunately, it doesn't come for free—creating a new slice from a `ByteBuffer` requires the allocation of a new object, which puts pressure on the garbage collection subsystem. While most garbage collectors are pretty good at collecting short-lived objects, in a latency-sensitive environment that's dealing with very high throughput rates, this allocation can add up and result in unacceptable pauses in the application.

Let's imagine what could happen if we were able to define a `Slice` as a value object (i.e., tuple) type that held the reference to the array, an offset, and a length. In the following listing, we'll use a new `tuple` keyword to indicate this new concept.

Listing 14.2   Array slice as a tuple

```
public tuple Slice {
  private int offset;
  private int length;
  private byte[] array;

  public byte get(int i) {
    return array[offset + i];
  }
}
```

The slice construction combines many of the advantages of both primitive and reference types:

- Slice values could be copied into and out of methods just as efficiently as passing the array reference and int values manually.
- Slice tuples would be cleaned up by exiting methods (because they're like value types).
- The handling of the offset and length would be cleanly encapsulated by the tuple.

There are numerous examples of types common in everyday programming that would benefit from the use of tuples, such as rational numbers with a numerator and denominator, complex numbers with a real and imaginary value, or a user principal reference with an ID and a realm identifier (for you MMORPG fans out there!).

The other area that tuples bring a performance benefit to is in the handling of arrays. Arrays currently hold homogeneous collections of data values—either primitives or references. The existence of tuples would give us more control over the layout of memory when using arrays.

Let's consider an example—a simple hash table that uses a primitive long as a key.

```
public class MyHashTable {
  private Entry[] entries;
}
public class Entry {
  private long key;
  private Object value;
}
```

In the current incarnation of the JVM, the entries array has to hold references to instances of Entry. Every time the caller looks up a key in the table, the relevant Entry must be dereferenced before its key can be compared to the value passed in.

When implemented using a tuple, it would be possible to lay out the Entry type inline in the array, thereby removing the cost of dereferencing to reach the key. Figure 14.4 shows the current case, and the improvement available using tuples.

The key to the performance benefit of tuples is also clearer when we consider arrays of tuples. As you saw in chapter 6, the performance of most application code is

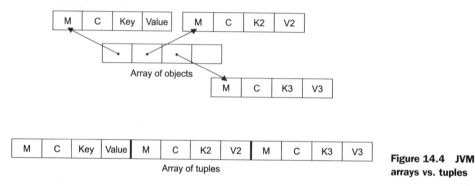

Figure 14.4   JVM arrays vs. tuples

dominated by L1 cache misses. In figure 14.4 you can see that code that scans through the hash table would be more efficient if it used tuples. It would be able to read key values without incurring additional cache fetches. This the essence of the performance benefit of tuples—they allow the programmer to employ better spatial locality when laying out data in memory.

This marks the end of our discussion of the possible new features of Java and JDK 8. How many of them will come to pass is something we'll only find out as the release nears. If you're interested in the evolution of the features, you can join the OpenJDK project and the Java Community Process and take part in the active development of these features. Look up these projects and how to join them if you're not already familiar with them.

14.5 *Summary*

Hot on the heels of Java 7, you'll soon have Java 8—full of the sorts of productivity improvements that you'll need in order to write code for modern hardware, from the smallest of embedded devices to the largest of mainframes.

The myth of a single language being able to solve all programming problems has been well and truly punctured. In order to build effective solutions, such as a highly concurrent trading system, you'll need to learn new languages that can interoperate with core Java code.

Concurrency will continue to be a hot topic as multicore hardware and OSs increasingly offer highly parallel architectures to code on. In order to solve large data, complex computational, or speedy applications, this is an area you'll want to keep on top of.

The Java VM is quite rightly seen as the best of the virtual machines out there today. The well-grounded Java developer will want to keep an eye on further advances because they'll likely open up new fields, such as high performance computing.

As you can see, there's an awful lot going on! We think that the Java ecosystem is undergoing a massive resurgence and that over the next few years the well-grounded Java developer will truly shine.

appendix A
Java7developer—
source code installation

We all love working with the actual code when reading through a new technical book. It helps you gain a proper working understanding of the material, which you can't get from reading a code example.

You can download the source code for this book from www.manning.com/evans/ or www.java7developer.com/. We'll refer to the location that you put the code in as $BOOK_CODE.

The project that holds all of the source code for this book is called *java7developer*. It's a mix of Java, Groovy, Scala, and Clojure source code, along with their supporting libraries and resources. It isn't your typical Java-only source code project, and you'll need to follow the instructions in this appendix in order to run the build (that is, compile the code and run the tests). We'll use the Maven 3 build tool to execute various build lifecycle goals, such as example `compile` and `test`.

Let's look at how the source code is laid out for the java7developer project.

A.1   Java7developer source code structure

The java7developer project structure follows the Maven conventions discussed in chapter 12 and is therefore laid out in the following manner:

```
java7developer
|-- lib
|-- pom.xml
|-- sample_posix_build.properties
|-- sample_windows_build.properties
`-- src
    |-- main
    |   '-- groovy
    |       `-- com
```

```
|                 `-- java7developer
|                         `-- chapter8
|         `-- java
|             `-- com
|                 `-- java7developer
|                         `-- chapter1
|                             `-- ...
|                             `-- ...
|         `-- resources
|         `-- scala
|             `-- com
|                 `-- java7developer
|                         `-- chapter9
`-- test
      `-- java
          `-- com
              `-- java7developer
                      `-- chapter1
                          `-- ...
                          `-- ...
          `-- scala
              `-- com
                  `-- java7developer
                          `-- chapter9
`-- target
```

As part of its conventions, Maven splits your main code from your test code. It also has a special resources directory for any other files that need to be included as part of the build (for example, log4.xml for logging, Hibernate configuration files, and other similar resources). The pom.xml file is the build script for Maven; it's discussed in detail in appendix E.

The Scala and Groovy source code follows the same structure as the Java source code in the java folder, except that their root folders are called scala and groovy respectively. Java, Scala, and Groovy code can happily sit side by side in a Maven project. The Clojure source code needs to be handled a little differently. Clojure is handled via an interactive environment most of the time (and uses a different build tool called Leiningen), so we've just provided a directory called clojure which houses the source code as snippets that can be copied into a Clojure REPL.

The target directory doesn't get created until a Maven build is run. All classes, artifacts, reports, and other files that the build produces will appear under this directory.

The lib directory holds some libraries, just in case your Maven installation can't access the internet to download what it needs.

Take a look around the project structure to familiarize yourself with where the source code lies for the various chapters. Once you're happy with where the source code lives, it's time to install and configure Maven 3.

A.2 *Downloading and installing Maven*

You can download Maven from http://maven.apache.org/download.html. For the examples in chapter 12, we used Maven 3.0.3. Download the apache-maven-3.0.3-bin.tar.gz file if you're a running a *nix OS or apache-maven-3.0.3-bin.zip file if you're a Windows user. Once the file is downloaded, simply untar/gunzip or unzip the contents into a directory of your choosing.

> **WARNING**   As in many Java/JVM-related software installations, it pays to not install Maven into a directory with spaces in its name, because you might get PATH and CLASSPATH errors. For example, if you're using a MS Windows operating system, don't install Maven into a directory that looks like *C:\Program Files\Maven*.

After downloading and unzipping, the next step is to set the M2_HOME environment variable. For *nix-based operating systems, you'll need to add something like this:

```
M2_HOME=/opt/apache-maven-3.0.3
```

For Windows-based operating systems, you'll add something like this:

```
M2_HOME=C:\apache-maven-3.0.3
```

You may be wondering, "Why M2_HOME and not M3_HOME? This is Maven 3, right?" The reason for this is that the team behind Maven really wanted to ensure backward compatibility with the widely used Maven 2.

Maven needs the Java JDK to run. Any version greater than 1.5 is fine (of course, by this stage, you already have JDK 1.7 installed). You'll also need to make sure that your JAVA_HOME environment variable is set—this has probably already been set if you have Java installed. You'll also need to be able to execute Maven-related commands from anywhere in your command line, so you should set the M2_HOME/bin directory to be in your PATH. For *nix-based operating systems, you'll need to add something like this:

```
PATH=$PATH:$M2_HOME/bin
```

For Windows-based operating systems, you'll add something like this:

```
PATH=%PATH%;%M2_HOME%\bin
```

You can now execute Maven (mvn) with its -version parameter to make sure the basic install has worked.

```
mvn -version
```

You should see output from Maven that looks similar to the following snippet:

```
Apache Maven 3.0.3 (r1075438; 2011-02-28 17:31:09+0000)
Maven home: C:\apache-maven-3.0.3
Java version: 1.7.0, vendor: Oracle Corporation
Java home: C:\Java\jdk1.7.0\jre
Default locale: en_GB, platform encoding: Cp1252
OS name: "windows xp", version: "5.1", arch: "x86", family: "windows"
```

As you can see, Maven churns out a bunch of useful configuration information so that you know that it and its dependency on your platform are all OK.

TIP   Maven is supported by the major IDEs (Eclipse, IntelliJ, and NetBeans), so once you're comfortable with using Maven on the command line you can swap to using the IDE-integrated version instead.

Now that you've got Maven installed, it's time to look at where the user settings are located. In order to trigger the creation of the user settings directory, you'll need to ensure that a Maven plugin is downloaded and installed. The simplest one to execute is the Help plugin.

```
mvn help:system
```

This downloads, installs, and runs the Help plugin, giving you some extra information over and above `mvn -version`. It also ensures that the .m2 directory is created. Knowing where the user settings are located is important, as there are a couple of instances where you may need to edit your user settings; for example, to allow Maven to work behind a proxy server. In your home directory (which we'll refer to as $HOME), you'll see the directories and files listed in table A.1.

Table A.1   Maven user directories and files[1]

Theme	Explanation
$HOME/.m2	A hidden directory that contains user configuration for Maven.
$HOME/.m2/settings.xml	A file containing user-specific configuration. Here you can specify proxy bypasses, add private repositories, and include other information to customize the behavior of your installation of Maven.
$HOME/.m2/repository/	Your local Maven repository. When Maven downloads a plugin or a dependency from Maven Central (or another remote Maven repository), it stores a copy of the dependency in your local repository. The same is true when you install your own dependencies with the `install` goal. This way, Maven can use the local copy instead of downloading a new copy each time.

Note again the use of the backward compatibility with Maven 2 via the .m2 directory (as opposed to the .m3 directory you'd expect).

Now that you have Maven installed and you know the location of the user configuration, you can get started on running the java7developer build.

A.3   *Running the java7developer build*

In this section, you'll start by going through a couple of one-off steps in order to prepare the build.[2] This includes manually installing a library as well as renaming a properties file and editing it to point to your local Java 7 installation.

---

[1]   Courtesy of Sonatype, in its *Maven: the Complete Reference* online manual, www.sonatype.com/Request/Book/Maven-The-Complete-Reference.

[2]   Despite recent improvements in the Maven build tool and its polyglot programming support, there are still a couple of gaps.

You'll then go through the most common Maven build lifecycle goals (`clean`, `compile`, and `test`). The first build lifecycle goal (`clean`) is used to clean up any left-over artifacts from a previous build.

Maven calls its build scripts Project Object Model (POM) files. These POM files are in XML, and each Maven project or module will have an accompanying pom.xml file. There is alternative language support coming for POM files, which should give you much more flexibility should you require it (much like the Gradle build tool).

In order to execute builds with Maven, you ask it to run one or several goals that represent specific tasks (such as compiling your code, running tests, and more). Goals are all tied into the default build lifecycle, so if you ask Maven to run some tests (for example, `mvn test`), it'll compile both the main source code and the source code for the tests before trying to run those tests. In short, it forces you to adhere to a correct build lifecycle.

Let's begin with the one-off task to get it out of the way.

A.3.1   *One-off build preparation*

To run the build successfully, you need to first rename and edit a properties file. If you have not already done so in section 12.2, then in the $BOOK_CODE directory, copy over the sample_<os>_build.properties file (for your OS) to build.properties, and edit the value of the `jdk.javac.fullpath` property to point to your local install of Java 7. This ensures that the correct JDK gets picked up and used by Maven when building the Java code.

Now that you've gotten that step out of the way, you can run the `clean` goal that you should always execute as part of your build.

A.3.2   *Clean*

The Maven `clean` goal simply deletes the target directory. To see this in action, change to the $BOOK_CODE directory and execute the Maven `clean` goal.

```
cd $BOOK_CODE
mvn clean
```

At this point, you'll see your console filling up with output from Maven stating that it's downloading various plugins and third-party libraries. Maven needs these plugins and libraries to run goals, and by default it downloads them from Maven Central—the primary online repository for these artifacts. The `java7developer` project is also configured with one other repository so that the asm-4.0.jar file is downloaded.

> **NOTE**   Maven will occasionally perform this task for other goals, so don't be alarmed if you see it "downloading the internet" when you execute other goals. It will only perform those downloads once.

Apart from the "Downloading..." information, you should also see a statement similar to the following in your console:

```
[INFO] ------------------------------------------------------------------------
[INFO] BUILD SUCCESS
[INFO] ------------------------------------------------------------------------
```

```
[INFO] Total time: 1.703s
[INFO] Finished at: Fri Jun 24 13:51:58 BST 2011
[INFO] Final Memory: 6M/16M
[INFO] ------------------------------------------------------------------
```

If the `clean` goal fails, it's likely that your proxy server is blocking access to Maven Central, where the plugins and third-party libraries are held. To resolve this issue, simply edit the $HOME/.m2/settings.xml file and add the following, filling out the values for the various elements.

```
<proxies>
  <proxy>
    <active>true</active>
    <protocol></protocol>
    <username></username>
    <password></password>
    <host></host>
    <port></port>
  </proxy>
</proxies>
```

Rerun the goal, and you should see the BUILD SUCCESS message as expected.

> **TIP** Unlike the other Maven build lifecycle goals you'll be using, `clean` isn't automatically called. If you want the previous build artifacts cleaned up, you always need to include the `clean` goal.

Now that you've removed any leftover remnants from the previous build, the next build lifecycle goal you typically want to execute is to `compile` your code.

A.3.3   *Compile*

The Maven `compile` goal uses the compiler plugin configuration in the pom.xml file to compile the source code under src/main/java, src/main/scala, and src/main/groovy. This effectively means executing the Java, Scala, and Groovy compilers (`javac`, `scalac`, and `groovyc`) with the `compile`-scoped dependencies added to the CLASSPATH. Maven will also process the resources under src/main/resources, ensuring that they're part of the CLASSPATH for compilation.

The resulting compiled classes end up under the target/classes directory. To see this in action, execute the following Maven goal:

```
mvn compile
```

The compile goal should execute pretty quickly, and in your console you'll have something similar to the following output.

```
...
[INFO] [compiler:compile {execution: default-compile}]
[INFO] Compiling 119 source files to
     C:\Projects\workspace3.6\code\trunk\target\classes
[INFO] [scala:compile {execution: default}]
[INFO] Checking for multiple versions of scala
[INFO] includes = [**/*.scala,**/*.java,]
```

```
[INFO] excludes = []
[INFO] C:\Projects\workspace3.6\code\trunk\src\main\java:-1: info: compiling
[INFO] C:\Projects\workspace3.6\code\trunk\target\generated-sources\groovy-
       stubs\main:-1: info: compiling
[INFO] C:\Projects\workspace3.6\code\trunk\src\main\groovy:-1: info:
       compiling
[INFO] C:\Projects\workspace3.6\code\trunk\src\main\scala:-1: info: compiling
[INFO] Compiling 143 source files to
       C:\Projects\workspace3.6\code\trunk\target\classes at 1312716331031
[INFO] prepare-compile in 0 s
[INFO] compile in 12 s
[INFO] [groovy:compile {execution: default}]
[INFO] Compiled 26 Groovy classes
[INFO] ------------------------------------------------------------------
[INFO] BUILD SUCCESSFUL
[INFO] ------------------------------------------------------------------
[INFO] Total time: 43 seconds
[INFO] Finished at: Sun Aug 07 12:25:44 BST 2011
[INFO] Final Memory: 33M/79M
[INFO] ------------------------------------------------------------------
```

At this stage, your test classes under src/test/java, src/test/scala, and src/test/groovy haven't been compiled. Although there is a specific test-compile goal for this, the most typical approach is to ask Maven to run the test goal.

A.3.4 *Test*

The test goal is where you really see Maven's build lifecycle in action. By asking Maven to run the tests, it knows it needs to execute all of the earlier build lifecycle goals in order to run the test goal successfully (including compile, test-compile, and a host of others).

Maven will run the tests via the Surefire plugin, using the test provider (in this case JUnit) that you've supplied as one of the test-scoped dependencies in the pom.xml file. Maven not only runs the tests, but produces report files that can be analyzed later to investigate failing tests and to gather test metrics.

To see this in action, execute the following Maven goals:

```
mvn clean test
```

Once Maven has completed compiling the tests and running them, you should see it report something similar to the following output.

```
...
Running com.java7developer.chapter11.listing_11_3.TicketRevenueTest
Tests run: 5, Failures: 0, Errors: 0, Skipped: 0, Time elapsed: 0 sec
Running com.java7developer.chapter11.listing_11_4.TicketRevenueTest
Tests run: 5, Failures: 0, Errors: 0, Skipped: 0, Time elapsed: 0 sec
Running com.java7developer.chapter11.listing_11_5.TicketTest
Tests run: 1, Failures: 0, Errors: 0, Skipped: 0, Time elapsed: 0.015 sec

Results :

Tests run: 20, Failures: 0, Errors: 0, Skipped: 0
```

```
[INFO] -------------------------------------------------------------
[INFO] BUILD SUCCESSFUL
[INFO] -------------------------------------------------------------
[INFO] Total time: 16 seconds
[INFO] Finished at: Wed Jul 06 13:50:07 BST 2011
[INFO] Final Memory: 24M/58M
[INFO] -------------------------------------------------------------
```

The results of the tests are stored at target/surefire-reports. You can take a look at the text files there now and see that the tests passed successfully.

A.4   *Summary*

By running the source code samples as you read the chapters, you'll gain a deeper understanding of the material presented in this book. If you're feeling adventurous, you can alter our code or even add new code and compile and test it in the same way.

Build tools like Maven 3 are surprisingly complex under the hood. If you want to gain an in-depth understanding of this subject, read chapter 12, which discusses build and continuous integration.

appendix B
Glob pattern
syntax and examples

Glob patterns are used by the Java 7 NIO.2 libraries for applying filters when iterating over directories and other similar tasks, as seen in chapter 2.

B.1 Glob pattern syntax

Glob patterns are simpler than regular expressions and follow the basic rules shown in table B.1.

Table B.1 Glob pattern syntax

Syntax	Description
*	Matches zero or more characters.
**	Matches zero or more characters across directories.
?	Matches exactly one character.
{}	Delimits a collection of subpatterns to match with an implicit OR for each pattern; e.g. matches pattern A or B or C etc.
[]	Matches a single set of characters, or if a hyphen (-) character is used, matches a range of characters.
\	Escape character; used if you want to match a special character such as *, ?, or \.

Further information on glob pattern syntax can be found in the Java Tutorial hosted online by Oracle (http://docs.oracle.com/javase/tutorial/essential/io/fileOps.html#glob) and in the Javadoc for the FileSystem class.

B.2   Glob pattern examples

Some basic examples on using glob patterns, sometimes known as globbing, are shown in table B.2.

Table B.2   Glob pattern examples

Syntax	Description
`*.java`	Matches all strings that end in .java, such as Listing_2_1.java.
`??`	Matches any two characters, such as ab or x1.
`[0-9]`	Matches any digit from 0 to 9.
`{groovy, scala}.*`	Matches any string starting with groovy. or scala., such as scala.txt or groovy.pdf.
`[]a-z, A-Z`	Matches an uppercase or lowercase western alphabet character.
`\\`	Matches the \ character.
`/usr/home/**`	Matches all strings starting with /usr/home/, such as usr/home/karianna or /usr/home/karianna/docs.

Further examples on glob pattern matches can be found in the Java Tutorial hosted online by Oracle and in the Javadoc for the `FileSystem` class.

> **WARNING**   The Java 7 specification defines its own glob semantics (rather than adopting an existing standard one). This leads to a few potential gotchas, particularly on Unix. For example, doing the equivalent of `rm *` in Java 7 will remove files whose names begin with a dot (`.`), whereas the Unix `rm/glob` will not.

appendix C
Installing alternative
JVM languages

This appendix covers the download and installation instructions for the three JVM languages (Groovy, Scala, and Clojure) as well as the Groovy-based web framework (Grails) covered in chapters 8, 9, 10, and 13 respectively.

C.1 Groovy

Groovy is fairly simple to install, but if you're unfamiliar with setting environment variables or you're new to your particular operating system, you should find this guide helpful.

C.1.1 Downloading Groovy

First of all, go to http://groovy.codehaus.org/Download and download the latest stable version of Groovy. We used Groovy 1.8.6 for the examples, so we recommend downloading the groovy-binary-1.8.6.zip file. Then unzip the contents of the zip file you downloaded into a directory of your choosing.

> **WARNING** As in many Java/JVM-related software installations, it pays to not install Groovy into a directory with spaces in the path, because you might get PATH and CLASSPATH errors. For example, if you're using an MS Windows operating system, don't install Groovy into directory that looks like C:\Program Files\Groovy\.

There aren't many steps to go. Next you need to set environment variables.

C.1.2 Installing Groovy

After downloading and unzipping, you'll need to set three environment variables to be able to run Groovy effectively. We'll look at both the POSIX-based operating systems (Linux, Unix, and Mac OS X) as well as Microsoft Windows.

POSIX-BASED OSS (LINUX, UNIX, MAC OS X)

Where you set environment variables on a POSIX-based OS usually depends on what user shell you're running when you open a terminal window. Table C.1 covers the common names and locations of your user shell configuration file on the various POSIX operating system shells.

Table C.1 **Common locations of user shell configuration files**

Shell	File location
bash	~/.bashrc and/or ~/.profile
Korn (ksh)	~/.kshrc and/or ~/.profile
sh	~/.profile
Mac OS X	~/.bashrc and/or ~./.profile and/or ~./bash_profile

You'll want to open your user shell configuration file with your favorite editor and add three environment variables: GROOVY_HOME, JAVA_HOME, and PATH.

First you need to set the GROOVY_HOME environment variable. Add the following line and replace <installation directory> with the location where you unzipped the contents of the Groovy binary file.

```
GROOVY_HOME=<installation directory>
```

In the following example, we unzipped the Groovy binary file to /opt/groovy-1.8.6:

```
GROOVY_HOME=/opt/groovy-1.8.6
```

Next, Groovy needs the Java JDK to run. Any version greater than 1.5 is fine (though, by this stage you likely have JDK 1.7 installed). You'll also need to make sure that your JAVA_HOME environment variable is set. This has probably already been set if you have Java installed, but if it hasn't, you can add the following line:

```
JAVA_HOME=<path to where Java is installed>
```

In the following example, we set JAVA_HOME to /opt/java/java-1.7.0:

```
JAVA_HOME=/opt/java/java-1.7.0
```

Finally, you'll need to be able to execute Groovy-related commands from anywhere in your command line, so you should set the GROOVY_HOME/bin directory to be in your PATH:

```
PATH=$PATH:$GROOVY_HOME/bin
```

Save your user shell configuration file, and when you next start a new shell, the three environment variables will be set. You can now execute groovy with its -version parameter on the command line to make sure the basic install has worked:

```
groovy -version
Groovy Version: 1.8.6 JVM: 1.7.0
```

That completes the POSIX-based section on installing Groovy. You can now go back to chapter 8 to compile and run Groovy code!

MS WINDOWS

In MS Windows, the best place to set the environment variables is via the GUI provided when you manage your computer. Follow these steps:

1 Right-click My Computer, then click Properties.
2 Click the Advanced tab.
3 Click Environment Variables.
4 Click New to add a new variable name and value.

Now you need to set the GROOVY_HOME environment variable. Add the following line and replace <installation directory> with the location where you unzipped the contents of the Groovy binary file.

```
GROOVY_HOME=<installation directory>
```

In the following example, we unzipped the contents of the Groovy binary file to C:\languages\groovy-1.8.6:

```
GROOVY_HOME=C:\languages\groovy-1.8.6
```

Groovy also needs the Java JDK to run, and any version greater than 1.5 is fine (though, by this stage you likely have JDK 1.7 installed). You'll also need to make sure that your JAVA_HOME environment variable is set. This has probably already been set if you have Java installed, but if it hasn't, you can add the following line:

```
JAVA_HOME=<path to where Java is installed>
```

In the following example, we set JAVA_HOME to C:\Java\jdk-1.7.0:

```
JAVA_HOME=C:\Java\jdk-1.7.0
```

You'll also need to be able to execute Groovy-related commands from anywhere in your command line, so you should set the GROOVY_HOME/bin directory to be in your PATH:

```
PATH=%PATH%;%GROOVY_HOME%\bin
```

Click OK until you've exited the management screens for My Computer. When you next start a new command line, the three environment variables will be set. You can now execute groovy with its -version parameter on the command line to make sure the basic install has worked:

```
groovy -version
Groovy Version: 1.8.6 JVM: 1.7.0
```

That completes the MS Windows section on installing Groovy. You can now go back to chapter 8 to compile and run Groovy code!

C.2   *Scala*

The Scala environment can be downloaded from www.scala-lang.org/downloads. The current version at the time of writing is 2.9.1, but there may have been newer versions released by the time you read this. Scala does tend to introduce language changes with each new revision of the language, so if you find that some of the examples don't work with your (newer) Scala install, check the version of the language carefully and make sure you have a 2.9.1 install for the purposes of this book.

Windows users will want to download the .zip version of the archive; users of Unix-based OSs (including Mac and Linux users) will want the .tgz version. Unpack the archive, and put it where you choose on your machine's filesystem. As with the Groovy installation, you should avoid locating it in a directory that has a space in its name.

There are a number of ways that you can set up the Scala installation on your machine. The simplest is probably to set up an environment variable called SCALA_HOME that points to the directory where you installed Scala. Then follow the instructions for your OS in section C.1.2 (on installing Groovy), but replace GROOVY_HOME with SCALA_HOME throughout.

After you've finished configuring your environment, you can type scala at a command prompt, and the Scala interactive session should open. If it doesn't, that means that your environment isn't properly configured, and you should retrace your steps to ensure that you've set SCALA_HOME and your PATH correctly.

You should now be able to run the Scala listings and interactive code snippets in chapter 9.

C.3   *Clojure*

To download Clojure, go to http://clojure.org/ and get the zip file containing the latest stable version. In our examples, we'll be using Clojure 1.2, so if you're using a later version, be aware that there might be some slight differences.

Unzip the file you downloaded and change into the directory that's been created. Provided that you have JAVA_HOME set and java on your PATH, you should now be able to run a basic REPL as shown in chapter 10, like this:

```
java -cp clojure.jar clojure.main
```

Clojure is a little different from the previous two new languages in this appendix—all you really need to make use of the language is the clojure.jar file. There isn't any need to set up an environment variable as you did for Groovy and Scala.

While you're learning Clojure, it's probably easiest to work with a REPL. When the time comes to think about using Clojure for a production deployment, a proper build tool, like Leiningen (which you'll meet in chapter 12), will be used to manage not only the deployment of apps, but also the install of Clojure itself (by downloading the JAR from a remote Maven repository).

This basic install of Clojure has some limitations, but thankfully there are a number of very good integrations of Clojure with a number of IDEs. If you're a user of the

Eclipse IDE, we heartily recommend the Counterclockwise plugin for the Eclipse IDE, which is very functional and easy to set up.

Having a slightly richer development experience can be very useful, as developing large amounts of code in the simple REPL can be a bit distracting. But for many applications (and especially while you're learning), the basic REPL will suffice.

C.4 Grails

Grails is fairly simple to install, but if you're unfamiliar with setting environment variables or if you're new to your OS, you should find this guide helpful. Full installation instructions can be found at www.grails.org/installation.

C.4.1 Downloading Grails

First, go to www.grails.org and download the latest stable version of Grails. For this book, we used version 2.0.1. Once you've downloaded the zip file, unzip the contents into a directory of your choosing.

> **WARNING**   Like with many Java/JVM-related software installations, it pays to not install Grails into a directory with spaces in the path, because you might get PATH and CLASSPATH errors. For example, if you're using an MS Windows OS, don't install Grails into a directory that looks like C:\Program Files\Grails\.

Next you need to set environment variables.

C.4.2 Installing Grails

After downloading and unzipping Grails, you'll need to set three environment variables in order to be able to run Grails effectively. This section will cover the POSIX-based operating systems (Linux, Unix, and Mac OS X) as well as Microsoft Windows.

POSIX-BASED OSs (LINUX, UNIX, MAC OS X)

Where you set environment variables on a POSIX-based OS usually depends on what user shell you're running when you open up a terminal window. Table C.2 covers the common names and locations of your user shell configuration file on the various POSIX operating system shells.

Table C.2   Common locations of user shell configuration files

Shell	File location
bash	~/.bashrc and/or ~/.profile
Korn (ksh)	~/.kshrc and/or ~/.profile
sh	~/.profile
Mac OS X	~/.bashrc and/or ~./.profile and/or ~./bash_profile

You'll want to open your user shell configuration file with your favorite editor and add three environment variables: GRAILS_HOME, JAVA_HOME, and PATH.

First, you need to set the GRAILS_HOME environment variable. Add the following line, replacing <installation directory> with the location where you unzipped the contents of the Grails zip file:

```
GRAILS_HOME=<installation directory>
```

In the following example we unzipped the contents to /opt/grails-2.0.1:

```
GRAILS_HOME=/opt/grails-2.0.1
```

Grails also needs the Java JDK to run. Any version greater than 1.5 is fine (though, by this stage you likely already have JDK 1.7 installed). You'll also need to make sure that your JAVA_HOME environment variable is set. This has probably already been set if you have Java installed, but if it hasn't, you can add the following line:

```
JAVA_HOME=<path to where Java is installed>
```

In the following example, we set JAVA_HOME to /opt/java/java-1.7.0:

```
JAVA_HOME=/opt/java/java-1.7.0
```

You'll need to be able to execute Grails-related commands from anywhere in your command line, so you should set the GRAILS_HOME/bin directory to be in your PATH, as follows:

```
PATH=$PATH:$GRAILS_HOME/bin
```

Save your user shell configuration file, and when you next start a new shell, the three environment variables will be set. You can now execute grails with its -version parameter to make sure the basic install has worked:

```
grails -version
Grails version: 2.0.1
```

That completes the POSIX-based section on installing Grails. You can now go back to chapter 13 to start your first Grails project!

MS WINDOWS

In MS Windows, the best place to set the environment variables is via the GUI provided when you manage your computer. To do so, follow these steps:

1 Right-click My Computer, then click Properties.
2 Click the Advanced tab.
3 Click Environment Variables.
4 Click New to add a new variable name and value.

Now you need to set the GRAILS_HOME environment variable. Add the following line, replacing <installation directory> with the location where you unzipped the contents of the Grails zip file.

```
GRAILS_HOME=<installation directory>
```

In the following example, we unzipped the Grails file to C:\languages\grails-2.0.1:

```
GRAILS_HOME=C:\languages\grails-2.0.1
```

Grails also needs the Java JDK to run, and any version greater than 1.5 is fine (though, by this stage you likely have JDK 1.7 installed). You'll also need to make sure that your JAVA_HOME environment variable is set. This has probably already been set if you have Java installed, but if it hasn't, you can add the following line:

```
JAVA_HOME=<path to where Java is installed>
```

In the following example, we set JAVA_HOME to C:\Java\jdk-1.7.0:

```
JAVA_HOME=C:\Java\jdk-1.7.0
```

You'll need to be able to execute Grails-related commands from anywhere in your command line, so you should also set the GRAILS_HOME\bin directory to be in your PATH:

```
PATH=%PATH%;%GRAILS_HOME%\bin
```

Click OK until you've exited the management screens for My Computer. When you next start a new command line, the three environment variables will be set. You can now execute grails with its -version parameter on the command line to make sure the basic install has worked:

```
grails -version
```

```
Grails version: 2.0.1
```

That completes the MS Windows section on installing Grails. You can now go back to chapter 13 to start your first Grails project!

appendix D
Downloading
and installing Jenkins

This appendix covers the download and installation of Jenkins, which is required for chapter 12. Downloading and installing Jenkins is simple. If you do run into any trouble, you can probably find some help in the wiki at https://wiki.jenkins-ci.org/display/JENKINS/Meet+Jenkins.

D.1 Downloading Jenkins

You can download Jenkins from http://mirrors.jenkins-ci.org/. For the examples in chapter 12, we used Jenkins 1.424.

The common, OS-independent way to install Jenkins is to use the `jenkins.war` package. But if you're not familiar with running your own web server, such as Apache Tomcat or Jetty, you can download the standalone package for your OS.

> **TIP** The Jenkins team puts out new releases with impressive frequency, which can be disconcerting for teams who like a little more stability in their CI server. The Jenkins team has addressed this concern, and they now offer a Long Term Support (LTS) version of Jenkins.

Next up, you need to follow some simple installation steps.

D.2 Installing Jenkins

After downloading either the WAR file or the standalone package for your OS, you need to install Jenkins. Jenkins needs the Java JDK to run, and any version greater than 1.5 is fine (though, by this stage, you likely already have JDK 1.7 installed). We'll cover the WAR installation first, followed by the standalone package installation.

D.2.1   *Running the WAR file*

You can install Jenkins very quickly by executing the Jenkins WAR file directly on the command line:

```
java -jar jenkins.war
```

This installation method should probably only be used for a quick trial of Jenkins as it is harder to configure other web server–related variables that a smoothly running installation might need.

D.2.2   *Installing the WAR file*

For a more permanent installation, deploy the WAR file to your favorite Java-based web server. For the purposes of the java7developer project, we simply copied the `jenkins` `.war` file into the `webapps` directory of a running Apache Tomcat 7.0.16 server.

If you're unfamiliar with WAR files and Java-based web servers, you can always go for the standalone package installation.

D.2.3   *Installing the standalone package*

The standalone package is also simple to install. For Windows-based OSs, unzip the `jenkins-<version>.zip` file and run the `exe` or `msi` installer. For the various Linux distributions, you'll need to run the appropriate `yum` or `rpm` package manager. For Mac OS X, you run the `pkg` file.

In all cases, you can select the default options that the installer offers, or, if you wish, you can customize installation paths and other settings.

By default, Jenkins stores its configuration and jobs under the home directory of the user (which we'll refer to as $USER) in a `.jenkins` directory. If you need to edit any configuration outside of the UI, you can do so there.

D.2.4   *Running Jenkins for the first time*

You'll know that you've installed Jenkins correctly by going to its dashboard (typically located at http://localhost:8080/ or http://localhost:8080/jenkins) with your favorite web browser. You should see a screen similar to figure D.1.

Now that you have Jenkins installed, you can get started on creating a Jenkins job. Head back to the Jenkins section in chapter 12!

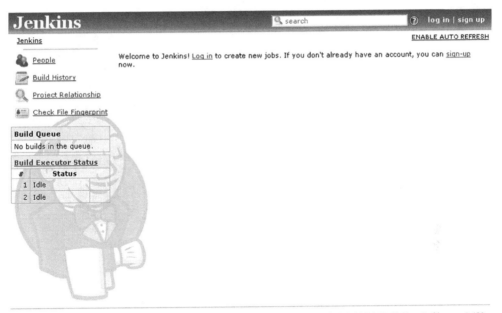

Figure D.1 Jenkins dashboard

appendix E
Java7developer—
the Maven POM

This appendix covers sections of the pom.xml file that builds the java7developer project discussed in chapter 12. This appendix expands on the contents of the important parts of the pom.xml file, so you can understand the full build. Basic project information (section 12.1) and profiles (listing 12.4) are covered adequately in chapter 12, so we'll look at these two sections of the POM here:

- The build configuration
- The dependencies

We'll begin with the longest section, the build configuration.

E.1 *Build configuration*

The build section contains the plugins and their configuration, which you need in order to execute the Maven build lifecycle goals. For many projects, this section is quite small, because the default plugins at their default settings are usually adequate. But for the java7developer project, the `<build>` section contains several plugins that override some of the defaults. We do this so that the java7developer project can

- Build the Java 7 code
- Build the Scala and Groovy code
- Run Java, Scala, and Groovy tests
- Provide Checkstyle and FindBugs code metric reports

If you need to configure further aspects of your build, you can check out the full list of plugins at http://maven.apache.org/plugins/index.html.

The following code listing shows the build configuration for the `java7-developer` project.

Listing E.1   POM—build information

```xml
<build>
  <plugins>

    <plugin>
      <groupId>org.apache.maven.plugins</groupId>
      <artifactId>maven-compiler-plugin</artifactId>
      <version>2.3.2</version>
      <configuration>
        <source>1.7</source>
        <target>1.7</target>
        <showDeprecation>true</showDeprecation>
        <showWarnings>true</showWarnings>
        <fork>true</fork>
        <executable>${jdk.javac.fullpath}</executable>
      </configuration>
    </plugin>

    <plugin>
      <groupId>org.scala-tools</groupId>
      <artifactId>maven-scala-plugin</artifactId>
      <version>2.14.1</version>
      <executions>
        <execution>
          <goals>
            <goal>compile</goal>
            <goal>testCompile</goal>
          </goals>
        </execution>
      </executions>
      <configuration>
        <scalaVersion>2.9.0</scalaVersion>
      </configuration>
    </plugin>

    <plugin>
      <groupId>org.codehaus.gmaven</groupId>
      <artifactId>gmaven-plugin</artifactId>
      <version>1.3</version>
      <dependencies>
        <dependency>
          <groupId>org.codehaus.gmaven.runtime</groupId>
          <artifactId>gmaven-runtime-1.7</artifactId>
          <version>1.3</version>
        </dependency>
      </dependencies>
      <executions>
        <execution>
          <configuration>
            <providerSelection>1.7</providerSelection>
          </configuration>
          <goals>
            <goal>generateStubs</goal>
            <goal>compile</goal>
            <goal>generateTestStubs</goal>
```

① **Specify plugin to use**

② **Compile Java 7 code**

③ **Set compiler options**

④ **Set path to javac**

⑤ **Force Scala compilation**

```
          <goal>testCompile</goal>
        </goals>
      </execution>
    </executions>
  </plugin>

  <plugin>
    <groupId>org.codehaus.mojo</groupId>
    <artifactId>properties-maven-plugin</artifactId>
    <version>1.0-alpha-2</version>
    <executions>
      <execution>
        <phase>initialize</phase>
        <goals>
          <goal>read-project-properties</goal>
        </goals>
        <configuration>
          <files>
            <file>${basedir}/build.properties</file>
          </files>
        </configuration>
      </execution>
    </executions>
  </plugin>
</plugins>

<plugin>
  <groupId>org.apache.maven.plugins</groupId>
  <artifactId>maven-surefire-plugin</artifactId>
  <version>2.9</version>
  <configuration>
    <excludes>
    <exclude>
    com/java7developer/chapter11/listing_11_2
    /TicketRevenueTest.java
      </exclude>
      <exclude>
    com/java7developer/chapter11/listing_11_7
    /TicketTest.java
      </exclude>
      ...
    </excludes>
  </configuration>
</plugin>

<plugin>
  <groupId>org.apache.maven.plugins</groupId>
  <artifactId>maven-checkstyle-plugin</artifactId>
  <version>2.6</version>
  <configuration>
    <includeTestSourceDirectory>
      true
    </includeTestSourceDirectory>
  </configuration>
</plugin>
```

⑥ Exclude tests

Run Checkstyle on tests

```
<plugin>
  <groupId>org.codehaus.mojo</groupId>
  <artifactId>findbugs-maven-plugin</artifactId>
  <version>2.3.2</version>
  <configuration>
    <findbugsXmlOutput>true</findbugsXmlOutput>
    <findbugsXmlWithMessages>
      true
    </findbugsXmlWithMessages>
    <xmlOutput>true</xmlOutput>
  </configuration>
</plugin>

</build>
```

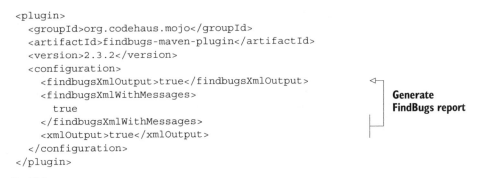

Generate FindBugs report

You need to specify that you're using the Compiler plugin (at a particular version) **1** because you want to change the default behavior of compiling Java 1.5 code to Java 1.7 **2**.

And because you've already broken from convention, you might as well add a few other useful compiler warning options **3**. You can also specify where your Java 7 installation is **4**. Simply copy over the sample_build.properties file for your OS to build.properties and edit the value of the `jdk.javac.fullpath` property in order for the location of javac to be picked up.

In order to get the Scala plugin working, you need to ensure that it gets executed when you run the `compile` and `testCompile` goals **5**.[1] The Surefire plugin allows you to configure the tests. In the configuration for this project, you're excluding several tests **6** that deliberately fail (you'll remember these two tests from chapter 11 on TDD).

Now that we've covered the build section, let's move on to the other vital part of the POM, the dependency management.

E.2 Dependency management

The list of dependencies for most Java projects can be quite long, and the `java7developer` project is no different. Maven helps you manage those dependencies—it has a vast store of third-party libraries in the Maven Central Repository. Crucially, those third-party libraries have their own pom.xml files that declare their respective dependencies, allowing Maven to figure out and download any further libraries you require.

There are two main scopes (`compile` and `test`) that you'll initially use.[2] These pretty much correspond to putting the JAR files on your `CLASSPATH` for compiling your code and then running your tests.

The following listing shows the `<dependencies>` section for the java7developer project.

---

[1] We expect future versions of this plugin to hook into the goals automatically.
[2] J2EE/JEE projects also typically have some dependencies declared with a `runtime` scope.

Listing E.2   POM—dependencies

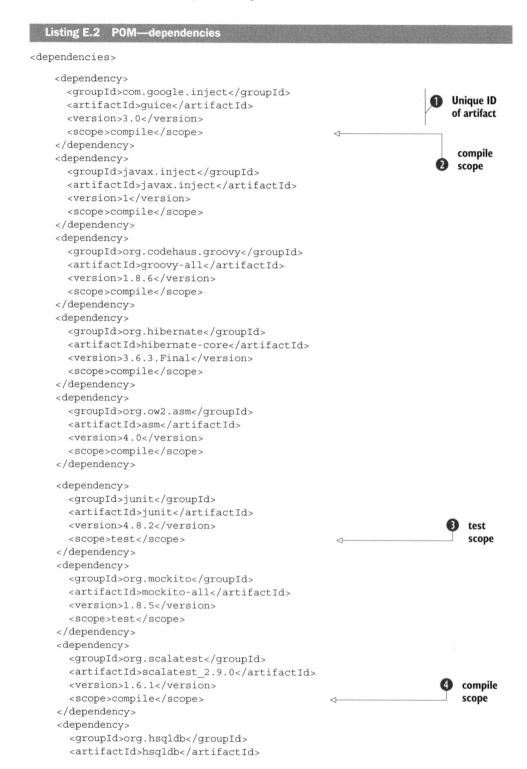

```
<dependencies>

    <dependency>
      <groupId>com.google.inject</groupId>
      <artifactId>guice</artifactId>
      <version>3.0</version>
      <scope>compile</scope>
    </dependency>
    <dependency>
      <groupId>javax.inject</groupId>
      <artifactId>javax.inject</artifactId>
      <version>1</version>
      <scope>compile</scope>
    </dependency>
    <dependency>
      <groupId>org.codehaus.groovy</groupId>
      <artifactId>groovy-all</artifactId>
      <version>1.8.6</version>
      <scope>compile</scope>
    </dependency>
    <dependency>
      <groupId>org.hibernate</groupId>
      <artifactId>hibernate-core</artifactId>
      <version>3.6.3.Final</version>
      <scope>compile</scope>
    </dependency>
    <dependency>
      <groupId>org.ow2.asm</groupId>
      <artifactId>asm</artifactId>
      <version>4.0</version>
      <scope>compile</scope>
    </dependency>

    <dependency>
      <groupId>junit</groupId>
      <artifactId>junit</artifactId>
      <version>4.8.2</version>
      <scope>test</scope>
    </dependency>
    <dependency>
      <groupId>org.mockito</groupId>
      <artifactId>mockito-all</artifactId>
      <version>1.8.5</version>
      <scope>test</scope>
    </dependency>
    <dependency>
      <groupId>org.scalatest</groupId>
      <artifactId>scalatest_2.9.0</artifactId>
      <version>1.6.1</version>
      <scope>compile</scope>
    </dependency>
    <dependency>
      <groupId>org.hsqldb</groupId>
      <artifactId>hsqldb</artifactId>
```

① Unique ID of artifact

② compile scope

③ test scope

④ compile scope

```
      <version>2.2.4</version>
      <scope>test</scope>
   </dependency>
   <dependency>
      <groupId>javassist</groupId>
      <artifactId>javassist</artifactId>
      <version>3.12.1.GA</version>
      <scope>test</scope>
   </dependency>
</dependencies>
```

In order for Maven to find the artifact that you're referencing, it needs the correct `<groupId>`, `<artifactId>`, and `<version>` ❶. As we alluded to earlier, setting the `<scope>` to `compile` ❷ will add those JARs to the CLASSPATH for compiling the code. Setting the `<scope>` to `test` ❸ will ensure that those JARs are added to the CLASSPATH when Maven compiles and runs the tests. The scalatest library is the odd one out—it should be at the `test` scope, but it requires a `compile` scope ❹ to work.[3]

The Maven pom.xml file isn't quite as compact as we'd like, but we're performing a three-language build (Java, Groovy, and Scala) with some reporting thrown in as well. We expect to see polyglot language Maven build scripts become more concise as tooling support improves in this area.

---

[3] We expect this to be resolved in future versions of the plugin.

index

Spring in Action, Third Edition
by Craig Walls

ISBN: 978-1-935182-35-1
424 pages
$49.99
June 2011

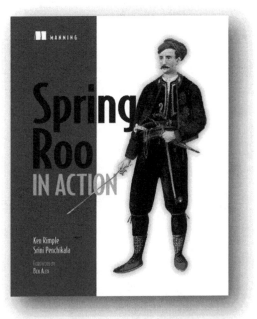

Spring Roo in Action
by Ken Rimple and Srini Penchikala

ISBN: 978-1-935182-96-2
408 pages
$49.99
April 2012

For ordering information go to www.manning.com

MORE TITLES FROM MANNING

Spring Integration in Action
by Mark Fisher, Jonas Partner,
    Marius Bogoevici, Iwein Fuld

ISBN: 978-1-935182-43-6
400 pages
$49.99
July 2012

DSLs in Action
by Debasish Ghosh

ISBN: 978-1-935182-45-0
376 pages
$44.99
December 2010

For ordering information go to www.manning.com

Scala in Depth
by Joshua D. Suereth

ISBN: 978-1-935182-70-2
304 pages
$49.99
May 2012

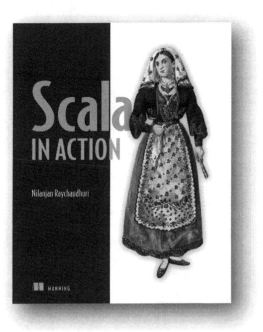

Scala in Action
by Nilanjan Raychaudhuri

ISBN: 978-1-935182-75-7
525 pages
$44.99
September 2012